# Financial Astrology

## How to Forecast Business and the Stock Market

LCdr. David Williams

*The Ultimate Test of All Formulae Must Lie in Prediction—Dr. D Justin Schove*

*Prediction must inevitably fail unless we have lighted on the true cause of the phenomena; Success is therefore a guarantee of the truth of the theory.—Professor G. H. Darwin*

Copyright by American Federation of Astrologers, Inc. 1982, 1984, 2004

All rights reserved.

No part of this book may be reproduced or transmitted in any form or by any means, electronic or mechanical, including photocopying or recording, or by any information storage and retrieval system, without written permission from the author and publisher. Requests and inquiries may be mailed to: the American Federation of Astrologers, Inc., 6535 S. Rural Road, Tempe, AZ 85283.

First Printing: 1982

Revised Printing: 1984

Fourth Printing: 2004

ISBN: 0-86690-045-4

Library of Congress Catalog Card Number: 82-73126

Published by:
American Federation of Astrologers, Inc.
6535 S. Rural Road
Tempe, Arizona 85283

Printed in the United States of America

# Dedication

This book is gratefully dedicated to the memory of
Ernest A. Grant (1873-1968),
one of the founders of the
American Federation of Astrologers
and for many years its first executive secretary.

# Acknowledgements

The author wishes to thank the following for:

a) invaluable aid in making available long out-of-print material:
The libraries of The Consolidated Edison Company of New York, Inc.;
The New York Public Library; The Library of Congress, Washington DC.;
and The British Museum, London.

b) Edward and Julia Wagner, editors of Dell *Horoscope* magazine,
for their aid and encouragement in making available the results
of the author's search to the astrological public through their magazine.

c) Edward R Dewey, for many years Executive Director, Foundation
for the Study of Cycles, for his encouragement to write
for *Cycles* and *The Journal of Cycle Research*.

d) The editors of *Cycles, The Journal of Cycle Research,* and *Horoscope*,
as well as The Foundation for the Study of Cyclesm for permission to quote from
published articles by the author and others that have appeared in those magazines.

e) M. C. Horsey & Co. for permission to reproduce certain price charts,
which have been updated by the author.

f) Bob and Sara Cooper, and staff members Sharon Camer, Frances Merriman,
Barbara Scott, and Richard and Jimmie Benjamin for their painstaking
care in preparing the hand-written manuscript for publication.

# Preface

This book contains the results of more than a half century of research by the author into the causes of the business and stock market cycles.

Progress reports in the form of unpublished lectures, beginning in 1947, were followed by the simultaneous publication in April 1959 of two books:

a) *Astro-Economics,* published by Llewellyn Publications, Ltd., for the astrological and general reader.

b) *Business Cycle Forecasting,* published by *The Journal of Cycle Research,* for the business and scientifically oriented reader.

Since both books dealt solely with the business cycle, it became necessary to apply the principles expounded in them to the stock market, as public awareness of the effects of planetary influences on mass investor psychology grew. This was accomplished through the author's annual business and stock market forecasts published in Dell *Horoscope* magazine since 1964, which have had an average accuracy of 80 percent. The unparalleled speculation in gold and silver during the past few years had made it necessary to add information on those commodities.

This book is therefore divided into two sections, viz:

Part I which deals with the business cycle.

Part II, which deals with the stock market, stocks and precious metals

To aid the general reader who may be unfamiliar with some of the technical terms used, an extensive glossary has been provided.

A word of caution is necessary. This book will not make you rich overnight, nor will it signal the end of the world, as the popular "prophets of doom" would have you believe. But it will show you how to keep ahead of double digit INFLATION in the years to come.

# Contents

| | |
|---|---:|
| Preface | v |
| Introduction | xv |

**Part I, Business Cycle Forecasting**

| | |
|---|---:|
| Chapter 1, Conventional Business Cycles | 3 |
|     Introduction | 3 |
|     Business Cycle History | 5 |
|     19th Century Business Cycle Theories | 6 |
|     20th Century Business Cycle Theories | 7 |
| Chapter 2, the Sunspot Theory of Business Cycles | 11 |
|     Introduction | 11 |
|     Summary of Sunspot Theory of Business Cycles | 20 |
| Chapter 3, The Planetary Cause of Sunspots | 23 |
|     Introduction | 23 |
|     Sunspot Theory | 24 |
|     Sunspot-Planetary Correlations | 27 |
| Chapter 4, Terrestrial Effects of Solar Activity | 39 |
|     On Agriculture and Climatology | 39 |
|     Terrestrial Effects of Solar Activity in Science | 42 |
|     Effects of Solar Activity on Telegraph, Submarine and Telephone Lines | 43 |
|     Effects of Solar Activity on Radio Transmission | 46 |
|     Effects of Solar Activity on Electric Power Systems | 50 |
|         On Overhead Transmission Lines | 50 |
|         On High Voltage Underground Cable | 53 |
|     Effects of Solar Activity in Other Fields of Technology | 59 |
|     Effects of Solar Activity on Health | 60 |
| Chapter 5, Planetary Theories of the Business Cycle | 63 |
|     Benner's Price Cycles | 63 |
|     Moore's 8-year Venus Cycle | 65 |
|     McWhirter's North Node Business Cycle | 67 |
|     The 56-year Pattern in American Business Activity | 70 |
|         First Period: 1761-1816 | 71 |
|         Second Period: 1817-1872 | 74 |
|         Third Period: 1873-1928 | 79 |
|         Fourth Period: 1929-1984 | 79 |

| | |
|---|---:|
| Chapter 6, The Theory of Unknown Causes | 89 |
|     Harmonic Analysis | 89 |
|     Empirical Curve Fitting | 90 |
| Chapter 7, Conclusion of Part I | 97 |

## Part II, Stock Market Forecasting

| | |
|---|---:|
| Chapter 8, The Art of Prediction | 103 |
|     Introduction | 103 |
|     Prediction Through Dream Interpretation | 104 |
|     Prognostication from Omens | 107 |
|     Prognostication from Astrology | 108 |
| Chapter 9, The Rationale of Prediction | 113 |
| Chapter 10, Rhythmic Stock Market Cycles | 121 |
|     Introduction | 121 |
|     The 9.2-year Stock Market Cycle | 122 |
|     The 38 to 41 Month Cycle in Stock Prices | 123 |
|     Combination of Cycles in Stock Market Prices | 124 |
|     The Decennial Pattern in Stock Prices | 126 |
|     Cycles—Real and Synthetic | 128 |
| Chapter 11, Planetary Cycles in the Stock Market | 131 |
|     Introduction | 131 |
|     The Planetary Cause of the 9.225-year Stock Market Cycle | 135 |
|     Moore's 8-year Venus Cycle | 137 |
|     The 11-year Sunspot Cycle | 138 |
|     The Planetary Cause of the 4-4½ Year Cycle in Market Lows | 138 |
|     Stock Prices and Planets in the Tenth House | 141 |
| Chapter 12, Stock Market Forecasting Systems | 147 |
|     Introduction | 147 |
|     The Dow Theory | 147 |
|     Chartist Medications for Major Market Turning Points | 150 |
|     The McWhirter Theory | 153 |
|     The Williams Solar Ingress Method | 158 |
|     The Williams Running Total Aspect Method | 162 |
|     Conclusion | 162 |
| Chapter 13, Personal Investing | 169 |
|     Introduction | 169 |
|     Who Should Invest or Speculate | 170 |
|     Which Stock Should Be Bought | 170 |
|     Corporation Horoscope Analysis | 172 |
|     Fairchild Camera & Instrument Corp. | 173 |
|     Consolidated Edison Co. of N.Y. | 178 |

| | |
|---|---|
| Asarco (Formerly Amer. Smelt. and Refining Co.) | 181 |
| Homestake Mining Company | 187 |
| Conclusion | 191 |
| Chapter 14, Epilogue | 193 |
| Review of Parts I and | 193 |
| Buying on Margin | 193 |
| Short-selling | 193 |
| Stock Options (Puts and Calls) | 194 |
| Interest Rates | 194 |
| Interest Rate Futures | 195 |
| Kondratieff Wave Misconceptions | 196 |
| History of Silver Prices | 199 |
| History of Gold Prices | 202 |
| Conclusion | 209 |

## Appendices

| | |
|---|---|
| 1. Zurich Relative Sunspot Numbers | 211 |
| 2. Systematic Period Reconnaisances of Sunspot Numbers 1700-1965 | 215 |
| 3. Data for Wood's Planet Sunspot Correlations | 217 |
| 4. Crawford 9-year Cycle Vs. Cleveland Trust Company Index | 220 |
| 5. Hutner Composite Cycle Vs. Cleveland Trust Company Index | 221 |
| 6. The 30 Stocks Used in the Dow-jones Industrial Average | 222 |
| Glossary | 223 |
| Bibliography | 232 |
| Index | 239 |

# Illustrations

| | |
|---|---|
| Fig. 1a Jevons Chart of English and Wheat Cycles 1731-1769 | 13 |
| Fig. 1b Jevons Chart of English Business and Wheat Cycles 1770-1808 | 13 |
| Fig. 1c Jevons Chart of English Business and Wheat Cycles 1809-1846 | 14 |
| Fig. 1d Jevons Chart of English Business and Wheat Cycles 1847-1883 | 14 |
| Fig. 2 Garcia-Mata/Shaffner Sunspot vs. Business Cycles | 18 |
| Fig. 3 Sunspot Numbers and Business Cycles 1760-1980 | 19 |
| Fig. 4 Sunspot Cycle vs. Jupiter Cycle | 26 |
| Fig. 5 Resultant of 11.86- and 9.93-year Cycles vs. Sunspot Cycles | 28 |
| Fig. 6 Clayton's Sunspot Curve | 33 |
| Fig. 7 Bollinger's Planet-Sunspot Correlations | 33 |
| Fig. 8 Dewey's Sunspot Cycles | 36 |
| Fig. 9 Wood's Planet-Sunspot Correlations | 37 |
| Fig. 10a Planetary Pattern During August 28, 1859 Magnetic Storm | 44 |
| Fig. 10b Planetary Pattern During Predicted Magnetic Storm of August 28, 1959 | 45 |
| Fig. 11 Planetary Pattern During Great Magnetic Storm of March 24, 1940 | 48 |
| Fig. 12 Planetary Pattern During Great Magnetic Storm of November 12, 1960 | 49 |
| Fig. 13 U.S. Wars and Depressions vs. Sunspots | 54 |
| Fig. 14 Planetary Pattern August 17, 1959 Con-Edison Power Blackout | 55 |
| Fig. 15 Planetary Pattern on July 21, 1977 (Near Blackout at Con-Edison) | 56 |
| Fig. 16 Planetary Pattern on July 13, 1977 (Con-Edison Blackout) | 57 |
| Fig. 17 Planetary Pattern on September 26, 1977 (Near Blackout of Con-Edison) | 58 |
| Fig. 18 Commodity Price, Business and Sunspot Cycles | 64 |
| Fig. 19a Samuel Benner's Business Cycle Chart | 65 |
| Fig. 19b Wall St. Journal Chart "The Forecast of an Earlier Generation" | 65 |
| Fig. 20 Moore's 8-Year Venus Cycle vs. Business and Sunspot Cycles | 66 |
| Fig. 21 McWhirter's North Node Business Cycle | 68 |
| Fig. 22 Moon's 18.6-Year Nodal vs. Business and Sunspot Cycles | 69 |
| Fig. 23 Funk's Cycles of Prosperity and Depression | 70 |
| Fig. 24a 56-Year Pattern of Business vs. Planetary Cycles 1761-1816 | 72 |
| Fig. 24b 56-Year Pattern of Business vs. Planetary Cycles 1817-1872 | 76 |
| Fig. 24c 56-Year Pattern of Business vs. Planetary Cycles 1873-1928 | 80 |
| Fig. 24d 56-Year Pattern of Business vs. Planetary Cycles 1929-1984 | 84 |
| Fig. 25 Prof. King's Sine Curve vs. Houghton-Annalist Index of Business Activity | 91 |
| Fig. 26 The Crawford 9-year Cycle of Business Activity | 92 |

| | |
|---|---|
| Fig. 27 Hutner's Cycles of Optimism and Pessimism vs. American Business Activity | 94 |
| Fig. 28 Typical Stock and Commodity Chart Patterns | 109 |
| Fig. 29 Effect of Moving Average of Different Lengths Upon an Ideal 9-Year Rhythm | 122 |
| Fig. 30 Dewey's 9.2-year Cycles in Stock Prices 1830-1966 | 123 |
| Fig. 31 Coe's Coordinated 3⅓- and 9-Year Cycles vs. DJI Average | 125 |
| Fig. 32 Smoothed Detrended Stock Prices vs. the 9.225 and 10.36 Year Cycles Combined | 126 |
| Fig. 33 Dewey's 11-Cycle Combination vs. the S & P 500 Stock Index | 127 |
| Fig. 34 The Decennial Pattern in Stock Prices | 129 |
| Fig. 35 The Market 1789-1980 | 133 |
| Fig. 36 DJI vs. Value Line Industrial Averages | 134 |
| Fig. 37 DJI Average vs. Indicator Digest Average and Market Logic Index | 135 |
| Fig. 38 Indications of 1981 DJI Market Top | 141 |
| Fig. 39 Percentage Rise in Stock Prices 30 Days Prior to Tenth House Aspects | 142 |
| Fig. 40 Our Solar System in the Milky Way Galaxy | 145 |
| Fig. 41 Three Cycles and Their Combinations | 148 |
| Fig. 42 End of 1966 Bull Market | 149 |
| Fig. 43 Dow Theory Sell Signal July 2, 1981 | 150 |
| Fig. 44 Daily Range of 1981 DJI Average vs. Zurich Sunspot Numbers | 151 |
| Fig. 45 End of 1981 Bull Market | 152 |
| Fig. 46 Forecasts a Downturn in the Stock Market | 154 |
| Fig. 47 Forecasts an Upturn in the Stock Market | 155 |
| Fig. 48 Movements of DJI Average During March and May 1938 | 156 |
| Fig. 49 McWhirter Theory Forecast for June 1981 | 157 |
| Fig. 50 Aspects Made by Transiting Planets on June 17, 1981 to Natal Positions of N.Y.S.E. Chart of May 17, 1792 | 159 |
| Fig. 51 Winter Solstice December 22, 1966 Forecasts Rising Prices | 162 |
| Fig. 52 Summer Solstice June 21, 1969 Forecasts Declining Prices | 163 |
| Fig. 53 1980 Williams Forecast vs. Stock Market Averages | 166 |
| Fig. 54 1981 Williams Forecast vs. Stock Market Averages | 167 |
| Fig. 55 Natal Chart of Author | 171 |
| Fig. 56 Natal Chart of Fairchild Camera & Instrument Co. | 174 |
| Fig. 57 Fairchild Camera & Instrument Co. | 176 |
| Fig. 58 Natal Chart of Consolidated Edison Co. of N.Y. | 179 |
| Fig. 59 Transits to Edison Natal Chart on November 9, 1965 Blackout | 180 |
| Fig. 60 Consolidated Edison Co. Prices | 182 |
| Fig. 61 Natal Chart of Asarco | 184 |
| Fig. 62 Asarco Prices | 184 |
| Fig. 63 Natal Chart of Homestake Mining Company | 188 |
| Fig. 64 Homestake Mining Company Prices | 188 |
| Fig. 65 The Average Annual Yield on Consols 1729-1978 | 195 |

| | |
|---|---:|
| Fig. 66 U.S. Wholesale Prices vs. Idealized Kondratieff Wave | 197 |
| Fig. 67 Wholesale Prices-All Commodities-Yearly Average-1926 = 100 | 198 |
| Fig. 68 Silver Prices 1850-1980 | 200 |
| Fig. 69 Daily Cash Silver Prices 1979-1981 | 203 |
| Fig. 70 Gold Prices in England 1343-1980 | 205 |
| Fig. 71. 200 Years of American Gold Prices 1781-1981 | 206 |
| Fig. 72 Daily Cash Gold Prices 1979-1981 | 208 |

# Tables

| | |
|---|---|
| Table 1. Tidal Force of Planets (Meldahl) | 31 |
| Table 2. Tidal Force of Planets (Stetson) | 32 |
| Table 3. Planetary Periods vs. Sunspots | 35 |
| Table 4. Heliocentric Longitude of Planets during 1859 and 1959 Storms | 44 |
| Table 5. Key to Planetary Symbols | 50 |
| Table 6. U.S. Wars and Depressions vs. Sunspots | 53 |
| Table 7. High and Low Points in 18.6-Year Nodal Cycle | 69 |
| Table 8. Jupiter-Saturn Aspects vs. Business Cycle—First 56-Year Period | 74 |
| Table 9. Jupiter-Uranus Aspects vs. Business Cycle—First 56-Year Period | 75 |
| Table 10. Jupiter-Saturn Aspects vs. Business Cycle—Second 56-Year Period | 77 |
| Table 11. Jupiter-Uranus Aspects vs. Business Cycle—Second 56-Year Period | 78 |
| Table 12. Jupiter-Saturn Aspects vs. Business Cycle—Third 56-Year Period | 81 |
| Table 13. Jupiter-Uranus Aspects vs. Business Cycle—Third 56-Year Period | 82 |
| Table 14. Jupiter-Saturn Aspects vs. Business Cycle—Fourth 56-Year Period | 85 |
| Table 15. Jupiter-Uranus Aspects vs. Business Cycle—Fourth 56-Year Period | 86 |
| Table 16. Saturn-Uranus Aspects vs. Business Cycle—1761-1980 | 87 |
| Table 17. Summary of 3 Planetary Cycles | 88 |
| Table 18. Accuracy of Planetary Aspects at Business Cycle Turning Points | 88 |
| Table 19. The 9.3-year North Node Cycles Stock Market Lows and Highs | 136 |
| Table 20. Moore's 8-year Venus Cycle vs. Stock Market Highs and Lows | 137 |
| Table 21. Sunspot vs. Stock Market Highs and Lows | 138 |
| Table 22. Beans "7 Come 11" Rhythm and Mars-Jupiter Oppositions | 139 |
| Table 23. 4-year Cycle in Market Lows from 1949 to 1978 | 139 |
| Table 24. Other Stock Market Lows Between 1878 and 1978 | 140 |
| Table 25. Market Lows vs. Mars-Jupiter Aspects Prior to 1878 | 140 |
| Table 26. Daily Stock Prices 1897-1961 | 143 |
| Table 27. Uranus in Gemini | 145 |
| Table 28. Conjunctions and Oppositions to 266° Longitude | 146 |
| Table 29. Summation of Aspects to N.Y.S.E. Horoscope on June 17, 1981 | 157 |
| Table 30. Conversion of Signs into Longitude | 159 |
| Table 31. Polarity of Conjunctions | 160 |
| Table 32. Record of Quarterly Stock Market Forecasts vs. DJI Averages | 161 |
| Table 33. Record of Quarterly Stock Market Forecasts vs. Unweighted Averages | 164 |
| Table 34. January 1980 Running Total Aspects | 164 |

| | |
|---|---|
| Table 35. Record of Running Total Aspects vs. Unweighted Averages | 165 |
| Table 36. Williams Forecast for 1982 | 165 |
| Table 37. Major Aspects Between Transiting and Fairchild Natal Planets July 1958 Low | 174 |
| Table 38. Major Aspects Between Transiting and Fairchild Natal Planets June 1960 High | 175 |
| Table 39. Major Aspects Between Transiting and Fairchild Natal Planets June 1964 Low | 175 |
| Table 40. Major Aspects Between Transiting and Fairchild Natal Planets February 1966 High | 175 |
| Table 41. Major Aspects Between Transiting and Fairchild Natal Planets August 1970 Low | 176 |
| Table 42. Major Aspects Between Transiting and Fairchild Natal Planets October 1973 High | 176 |
| Table 43. Major Aspects Between Transiting and Fairchild Natal Planets December 1974 Low | 177 |
| Table 44. Major Aspects Between Transiting and Natal Edison Planets December 1941 Low | 183 |
| Table 45. Major Aspects Between Transiting and Natal Edison Planets Jan. 1965 High | 183 |
| Table 46. Major Aspects Between Transiting and Natal Edison Planets December 1974 Low | 183 |
| Table 47. Major Aspects Between Transiting and Asarco Natal Planets July 1962 Low | 185 |
| Table 48. Major Aspects Between Transiting and Asarco Natal Planets December 1968 High | 185 |
| Table 49. Major Aspects Between Transiting & Asarco Natal Planets December 1978 Low | 186 |
| Table 50. Major Aspects Between Transiting and Asarco Natal Planets February 1980 High | 186 |
| Table 51. Major Aspects Between Transiting Homestake Natal Planets November 1971 Low | 189 |
| Table 52. Major Aspects Between Transiting Homestake Natal Planets August 1974 High | 189 |
| Table 53. Major Aspects Between Transiting Homestake Natal Planets August 1976 Low | 190 |
| Table 54. Major Aspects Between Transiting and Homestake Natal Planets October 1980 High | 190 |
| Table 55. The 22.11-Year Cycle of Tops in U.S. Gold Prices | 209 |
| Table 56. Correlation Between Peaks in Gold Prices and Peaks in Sunspots | 209 |

# Introduction

Many times during my long business career I have been asked: "How did a hard-boiled purchasing agent like you ever get interested in such an occult subject as astrology?" Well, it's a long and fascinating story that began more than half a century ago in January 1927, when I transferred from the Engineering Department to the Purchasing Department of the New York Edison Company (now known as Con-Edison). A purchasing agent's job is to "buy the right product, at the right time and at the right price." To help him do this successfully the purchasing agent refers to historic price records of the particular commodity in which he is interested. A glance at commodity price charts would tell even a tyro that prices are seldom stable, that they rise and fall throughout the day, week, month or year. But what makes prices rise and fall? That led me to an exhaustive study of the dismal science of economics.

Early in my studies I found two important clues in Volume I of *Financial Forecasting* by Dr. Warren F. Hickernell, Director, Bureau of Business Conditions, Alexander Hamilton Institute, New York. Thus began a long and wide-ranging research project over the next 30 years, which culminated in two books published simultaneously in April 1959, viz: *Business Cycle Forecasting,* published by *The Journal of Cycle Research,* and *Astro-Economics,* published by Llewellyn Publications, Ltd.

The first clue was a reference to the theory advanced in December 1867, in a paper read before the Manchester (England) Statistical Society by John Mills, an English businessman, who believed that business cycles were essentially credit cycles determined by the rate of interest and business confidence, and that the *mental mood of businessmen tends to run in cycles.* The *mental mood theory* of Mills received strong support in 1938 from Dr. Frederick R. Macaulay, an eminent American economist who wrote in *The Movements of Interest Rates, Bank Yields and Stock Prices in the United States since 1856,* as follows:

"The very essence of economics is that it is a study of human behavior, of the life of man, and basically of the *mental* life of man. It takes cognizance of facts in the external world, not for their own sakes, but only because of their relations to the mind of man. It is a study of some of the *causes and effects* of those conscious or unconscious decisions that men inevitably make in their rational or instinctive struggle 'to earn a living' and to satisfy at least some of their desires by adjusting the external world to themselves and—perhaps—thereby securing happiness and well-being."

Ninety years after the English businessman John Mills propounded his *mental mood* theory, an American businessman, Charles G. Mortimer, President, General Foods Corporation, was quoted in the June 12, 1958 *New York World-Telegram and Sun* as follows: "I do not think it is an exaggeration to say that recessions begin and end in the *minds of men.* Nervousness in the front office about business prospects can be quickly translated into lower carloadings." The Mills and other conventional business cycles are discussed in Chapter 1.

The second clue that I found in Dr. Hickernell's book was his reference to "The Sunspot Theory of the Business Cycle," which was first propounded in 1801 by the famous English astronomer, Sir William Herschel, and then in 1875, by the eminent English economist, Professor William Stanley Jevons. The trail led to a study of musty volumes in the library of the New York Edison Company, The New York Public Library, The Library of Congress in Washington and the British Museum in London. The results of this research are given in Chapter 2. But what causes sunspots? The answer is given in Chapter 3, "The Planetary Cause of Sunspots."

Why are sunspots and other solar disturbances important to man? On January 24, 1952, I had the pleasure of meeting John H. Nelson, then Radio Propagation Analyst, R.C.A. Communications, Inc., who had just presented an epoch-making paper before the American Institute of Electrical Engineers, entitled "Sunspots and Planetary Effects on Short Wave Radio," in which he elaborated on his earlier paper published in the March 1951 *RCA Review*, entitled "Shortwave Radio Propagation Correlation and Planetary Positions."

Although Nelson knew nothing about astrology, his findings validated some of the basic teachings of that ancient art, viz: planets in the same degree of longitude (0° or conjunction), 90° apart (square), or 180° apart (opposition) were accompanied by unfavorable long-distance radio transmission, while planets 60° apart (sextile) or 120° apart (trine) were associated with favorable radio transmission conditions. Then Nelson correctly predicted in advance the severe magnetic storm of August 17, 1959, which blacked out radio transmission over the North Atlantic, triggered a power blackout in the Central Park area of Con-Edison in New York, and precipitated the disastrous earthquake in Yellowstone National Park. This made such a profound impression on me that I began to use Nelson's angular planetary patterns to predict in advance the severe magnetic storm that occurred two weeks later and which resulted in failures of Con-Edison underground high-voltage cables at three times the normal rate. These examples and others are more fully described in Chapter 4, "Terrestrial Effects of Solar Activity."

Since Professor Jevons had hinted in his 1875 paper, "that the configurations of the planets may prove to be the remote causes of the greatest commercial disasters," research was directed in that direction and the results were recorded in Chapter 5, "Planetary Theories of the Business Cycle." My findings, which were published during the next 20 years, originally aroused much skepticism, but now are generally accepted by forward looking students of the business cycle.

Unknown to Professor Jevons in England, a retired iron and steel manufacturer from Cincinnati, Ohio published in 1875 a remarkable but little known book, *Benner's Prophecies of Future Ups and Downs in Prices*, which Edward R. Dewey, Executive Director, Foundation for the Study of Cycles considered to be "the most notable forecast of prices in existence." These forecasts were continued annually thereafter until Benner's death in 1904. Benner attributed the cause of these price changes to the influence of the planets Jupiter, Saturn, Uranus and Neptune. Details are given in Chapter 5.

Chapter 6 covers several business cycle theories that come under the heading of "The Theory of Unknown Cause" or "Empirical Curve Fitting." In this chapter we see how different economists try to fit the business cycle into periodic curves of 3½, 9, 3.35, 9.93, 11-14 years duration or some combination of the last three by Simeon Hutner, which has been labeled "Hutner's Cycles of Optimism and Pessimism."

During the depression of the early 1930s, a middle-western wire and cable manufacturer came into my office in New York one day and showed me a fascinating chart in spiral form made in 1932 by a "technocrat," J. M. Funk of Ottawa, Illinois, labeled "The Cycles of Prosperity and Depression." Upon examination, the chart showed a very definite 56-year pattern in American business activity. I redrew the chart into a more easily visualized form and it became the basis of a lecture I gave on April 16, 1947 at the Henry George School of Social Science in New York.

After having been convinced of the reasonableness of John Nelson's planetary patterns, I added to the foregoing chart the aspects made by Jupiter, Saturn and Uranus among themselves during the period 1761-1958, and found that the ups and downs of these planetary cycles showed a correlation of 68 percent with the movements of the business cycle during that period. From this chart, I was able to predict in advance the business recessions of 1949-1950 and 1969-1970. The chart further indicates a serious depression in 1985, and details are given in Chapter 5.

Part II on Stock Market Prediction was added because of the increasing participation of the general public in stock ownership, which has climbed from about 7 million in 1929 to 29 million in 1980, according to an article in *The Wall Street Journal* of May 13, 1981.

Part II begins with Chapter 8, "The Art of Prediction." Most people who have read the Bible are familiar with the classic examples of prediction through dream interpretation, viz: a) Joseph's interpretation of Pharaoh's dream that 7 years of famine would follow 7 years of plenty, and b) Daniel's interpretation of Nebuchadnezzar's dream of the four kingdoms. But few people seem to know that there were two other methods of predicting the future that were in use for thousands of years in ancient times, viz: a) predicting the future from the patterns seen in the entrails of newly slain animals, and b) predicting the future from the patterns formed by the planets. All three methods are thoroughly reviewed in Chapter 9.

Because the ownership of stock in a corporation is an expression of the owner's belief that the value of the stock will increase with time, Chapters 10, 11 and 12 give several methods of stock market forecasting, as well as the author's technique for determining the general direction of the stock market. The reader may thus determine for himself when would be a favorable time to buy and when to sell.

But, since one cannot buy the "averages," although some large institutional investors do pattern their portfolios after the Standard & Poor's Index of 500 stocks, it is necessary to buy a particular stock. Chapter 13 shows the reader what to look for in studying corporation charts.

However, it is commonplace on Wall Street that many investors pick the wrong stock. This question is frequently asked: "Why don't my stocks go up when everything else is going up?" Chapter 13 tells the reader how to pick a stock with which he will be comfortable and eventually successful.

Finally, in Chapter 14, the reader is introduced to some of the more useful technical methods to aid him in timing his buying and selling activities.

The reader is cautioned that no technique can be 100 percent accurate. He should not expect that the techniques expounded herein will make him a millionaire overnight, despite the flamboyant claims of the authors of some best-selling books. For example, one Wall Street professional wrote a book entitled *How I Helped More Than 10,000 Investors to Profit in Stocks.* Unfortunately, when he changed his advice, his readers became so critical that the poor man committed suicide! A second man who was a professional dancer got in trouble with the IRS after writing a book telling how he made a million dollars on Wall Street. A third man wrote a book about how he made a million dollars in commodities, but he fails to tell his readers why he lost it.

To hedge against the depreciation of the currency, it has been a practice that has grown hoary with age, to put something aside in the form of gold or silver, either in coins or bullion bars. Chapter 14 includes a study of the price fluctuations in these precious metals.

In conclusion, the reader is reminded that the ups and downs of the business cycle, the stock market, gold, silver, real estate, etc. are caused by men. And since the actions of men are the result of their thinking, be it positive or negative, the cure must lie in a change of thought. Economics and psychology go hand in hand—hence the need for studying economic psychology. The oldest technique for this study has been indicated by Dr. Carl G. Jung of Zurich, Switzerland, one of the world's greatest psychologists, who stated: "Astrology represents the summation of all the psychological Knowledge of Antiquity." Therefore, do not let the "tyranny of words" becloud your use of one of the best tools for keeping your head above water in the troublesome times that lie ahead.

An extensive bibliography of all the sources referenced has been added, as well as a glossary of terms which may be unfamiliar to the non-technical reader, and a complete index.

## About the Author

David Williams was born September 20, 1897, in Leeds, England. His natal chart shows the Sun in Virgo, the Moon in Cancer, and Leo rising. He came to the United States at age seven.

Educated as an electrical engineer, he served the Consolidated Edison Company of New York for 43 years, first in the Engineering Department and then in the Purchasing Department. He retired in February 1963.

His military activities included service as a private in the Mexican Border Campaign in 1916, and in World War I in 1918. He served as a Lieutenant Commander in the U. S. Navy during World War II, where he procured engineering equipment for the Navy while stationed in Washington, and then served as executive officer and later as supply officer in command of the Naval Supply Depot in Milne Bay, New Guinea.

Commander Williams lectured and wrote extensively on astrology, business and stock market cycles, comparative religion and mass psychology, and wrote *Simplified Astronomy for Astrologers, Astro-Economics*, and *Business Cycle Forecasting*.

He was a life member of the American Institute of Electrical and Electronic Engineers and a member of The New York Academy of Sciences, and served as a director of The Foundation for the Study of Cycles, president of the Astrologers Guild of America, and president of the American Federation of Astrologers.

# Part I
# Business Cycle Forecasting

# Chapter 1

# Conventional Business Cycles

*The end and aim of all science is the prediction and control of phenomena—Professor Jacques Loeb*

## Introduction: Why Study Business Cycles?

The importance of business cycles has been well expressed by the late Brigadier-General Leonard P. Ayres of the Cleveland Trust Company as follows: "Business cycles are as old as the industrial era. Their prosperities have created thousands of fortunes and their depressions have made millions of workers hungry and desperate. They have overturned governments, fomented revolutions, and caused wars. They are our most serious political problem."

Ayres goes a step further. In "The Nature and Status of Business Research," printed in the March 1922 *Journal of the American Statistical Association*, he concludes: "The job of the business statistician is to look into the future. He is employed to furnish those in positions of top control in the firm with a fact-basic for their thinking and acting. If he can do this successfully, he becomes one of the most valuable men in the organization."

What is the business cycle? Burns and Mitchell, in *Measuring Business Cycles* (1947), state that the National Bureau of Economic Research gives the following definition: "Business cycles are a type of fluctuation found in the aggregate economic activity of nations that organize their work mainly in business enterprises; a cycle consists of expansions occurring at about the same time in many economic activities, followed by similarly general recessions, contractions, and revivals which merge into the expansion phase of the next cycle; this sequence of changes is recurrent but not periodic; in duration, business cycles vary from more than one year to ten or twelve years."

A slightly contrary view is taken by Professors Warren and Pearson of Cornell, who state in *Prices* (1933): "There is no such thing as a definite business cycle. There are a large number of cycles of different lengths for wheat, hogs, sheep, poultry, cattle, cotton, and automobile production, for building construction, and for prices of pig iron, stocks, bonds, etc. The algebraic sum of all these cycles properly weighted makes the business cycle. Therefore, no two cycles are alike. The way to forecast future business cycles is to estimate each of the elements of the business cycle and to combine them according to their relative importance."

A somewhat similar view is expressed by Professor W. C. Mitchell in *Business Cycles and Their Causes* (1950), in which he says, "Business history repeats itself, but always with a difference. A thoroughly adequate theory of business cycles, applicable to all cycles, is consequently unattainable. Every business cycle, strictly speaking, is a unique series of events and has a unique explanation, because it is the outgrowth of a preceding series of events likewise unique."

One of the obstacles to developing a method of successfully forecasting the ups and downs of the business cycle is the defeatist attitude that surrounds the subject. Thus, Thomas W. Lamont of J. P. Morgan & Co. is quoted as saying, "The forecasts of the wisest economists or businessmen are, at best, mere guesses." In similar vein, Dr. Arthur F. Burns, former Chairman of the President's Council of Economic Advisers, and considered to be the world's foremost authority on business cycles once observed: "The gift of prophecy has never loomed large in the endowment of economists, whether lay or professional." On another occasion he said, "Economists have not yet evolved, if they ever will, a technique for making dependable forecasts."

Dr. Leo Barnes, Chief Economist, Prentice-Hall, Inc. sums up the situation in *Handbook for Business Forecasting* (1949) as follows: "Economic experts of the National Bureau of Economic Research have been studying business cycles for more than two decades. They have emerged with the discouraging conclusions that no two cycles are exactly alike, and that there is no automatic, inevitable periodicity on the basis of which a business analyst can spot the high and low of the current business cycle."

Stuart Chase, in *Power of Words* (1953), reviews the sorry record of economic forecasters and comes to this conclusion: "Economics has with some reason been called the dismal science. A major difficulty is that economics is so completely interwoven with human behavior that reliable theory cannot be formulated unless the economist takes both psychology and anthropology into account. Most economists have stubbornly held to pre-scientific assumptions about human behavior."

Bernard M. Baruch is quoted in *Forbes* September 15, 1958 as follows: "Colleges don't teach economics properly. Unfortunately, we learn little from the experience of the past. An economist must know, besides his subject, ethics, logic, philosophy, the humanities and sociology; in fact, everything that is part of how we live and react to one another."

At least one economist has begun to see the light, for Dr. George Katonah, Professor of Economics and Psychology, University of Michigan, wrote in the October 1954 *Scientific American*: "As yet we know far too little about the origin of mass attitudes, their spread among people and the effects of different attitudes on action. But what we do know is that economic psychology may usefully supplement the theoretical and statistical approach of traditional economics. It contributes to the understanding and prediction of economic fluctuations, and thereby promises to provide policy makers with better tools which they may use to combat the recurrence of periodic depressions and inflations."

A more optimistic note is sounded by Dr. David F. Jordan in Business *Forecasting* (1923) who summarizes: "Men in business are constantly obliged to consider the future. In fact, their prosperity is dependent chiefly upon their ability successfully to foresee economic developments. The future is by no means indeterminable. By careful analysis of concurrent events, and with due regard to the experience of former years, economic forecasting is now being successfully accomplished in many lines."

The Law of Causality forms the basis of all intelligent forecasting. This Law is stated by

Arne Fisher in *The Mathematical Theory of Probabilities* as follows: "Everything that happens, and everything that exists, necessarily happens or exists as the consequence of a previous state of things." Jordan further states: "Since everything that happens necessarily occurs as the consequence of a previous state of things, the predetermination of economic developments is predicated upon adequate knowledge of existing conditions."

Successful predictions of business conditions have been made in the past. Perhaps the most dramatic ever recorded is the biblical account of Joseph's interpretation of Pharaoh's dream to the effect that 7 fat years would be followed by 7 lean years. Pharaoh profited by Joseph's prophetic advice to store surplus food during the 7 years of plenty so that there was ample food available during the succeeding 7 famine years.

Joseph's successful prediction was based on his peculiar gift of dream interpretation. But successful prediction can also be based on knowledge. Thus, Aristotle, the father of Greek science, relates that Thales of Miletus (636-546 B.C.), the first of the Greek astronomers, amassed a small fortune by putting his astronomical knowledge to practical use. One winter he foresaw that there would be an abundant olive crop the following summer. So he quietly hired all the olive oil presses in Miletus and Chios at a very low rental. Then at harvest time, when all the growers wanted presses for their abundant crops, he rented the presses out at a much higher price, thus proving that scientific prediction could be very profitable.

In 1801, Sir William Herschel, the famous English astronomer who discovered the planet Uranus, correctly predicted a good crop year in England concurrent with a period of abundant sunspots. Peter Cooper (1791-1883), the eminent American philanthropist, added considerably to his fortune by applying his belief in the decennial pattern of American business activity, buying the choicest Wall Street securities at low prices during panic periods. In more modern times the eminent English economist, Lord Keynes, became a millionaire through the successful use of arbitrage operations in the financial markets.

## Business Cycle History

A brief review of the history of economic thought is essential to a proper understanding of the subject. The origin of the theory of business cycles may be traced to a treatise published in French in 1819 by the Swiss historian, J. C. L. de Sismondi (1773-1842), who was among the first historians to appreciate the influence of economic factors on political and cultural developments. He called attention to the importance of the study of commercial crises, and advanced some of the theories concerning them which have been incorporated in modern explanations of these events.

In 1838, Dr. Hyde Clarke, an English statistician, wrote a paper on the laws of periodical or cyclical action in Herapath's *Railway Magazine*. He mentioned 10, 13, and 14 year periods in speculation, but when he sought to explain the cycle as due to physical causes, he was unable to find any astronomical periods or meteorological theories with which to connect it. In the *Railway Register* for 1847, Dr. Clarke wrote another paper, "Physical Economy—A Preliminary Inquiry Into the Physical Laws Governing the Periods of Famines and Panics." He pointed out that the panic conditions existing in 1847 had also occurred in 1837, 1827, 1817, 1806 and 1796. He also divided the 54-year period between the famine of the French Revolution and the then current famine in England into five intervals of 10 or 11 years, giving the following famine years: 1793, 1804, 1815, 1826, 1837, 1847. Dr. Clarke may thus be considered to be the discover of the so-called *11-year cycle*.

In February 1848, J. T. Danson read a paper before the Statistical Society of London, attempting to trace a connection between the decennial periodic changes in the condition of the people and the variations occurring in the same period in the prices of the most necessary articles of food. William Langton, in "Transactions of the Manchester Statistical Society for 1857," stated: "These disturbances are the accompaniment of another wave, which appears to have a decennial period and in the generation of which moral causes have no doubt an important share."

In 1860, Clement Juglar, the eminent French economist showed that trade fluctuations were cyclical in nature, and that periods of prosperity, crisis, and liquidation followed each other in the same order. He believed the cycle to be self-perpetuating and gave the length as approximately *9 years*; hence this cycle is sometimes called the *"Juglar Cycle."*

In 1923, Joseph Kitchin, an American economist, discovered the 3½ year or 40-42 month cycle, which thereafter became known as the *"Kitchin Cycle."* In 1926, Russian economist N. D. Kondratieff discovered a 47-60 year cycle which has become known as the *"Kondratieff Wave."*

Since business cycles are peculiar to the industrial nations and the Industrial Revolution began in England, it is not surprising that the first attempts at a scientific explanation of the nature of business cycles and the periodic return of crises should be undertaken by English economists.

## 19th Century Business Cycle Theories

In 1863, Professor W. Stanley Jevons of Manchester, England discussed the nature of commercial fluctuations in a paper, "A Serious Fall in the Value of Gold." In it, while showing a clear understanding of the financial interpretation of business cycles, Jevons tentatively broached the theory of a "crop cycle."

However, the first attempt at a complete theory of the business cycle was made by John Mills, an English businessman, in a paper, "On Credit Cycles and the Origin of Commercial Panics," presented at a meeting of .the Manchester Statistical Society in December 1867. While using some of Jevons's ideas on credit, gold, and interest rates, Mills originated the theory that the *mental mood* of businessmen tends to run in cycles. According to Mills, business cycles are essentially cycles of credit.

Dr. Warren F. Hickernell summarizes the Mills theory in *Financial and Business Forecasting* (1928) as follows: "Mills bases his credit cycle theory upon two main elements; *first*, the tendency of human nature to exaggerate prospects for prosperity when prices rise and to underestimate business opportunities when trade is depressed. The *second* factor is the rate of interest, which causes wide-awake and intelligent men to extend operations when capital is abundant and to curtail operations when credit is distended relative to metallic banking reserves. Intelligent men furnish the initial impulse toward expansion when business is depressed, and they are followed by the ignorant. Later, the intelligent contract operations when inflation appears, but the ignorant expand excessively until checked by a crisis. In a state of panic, the ignorant curtail abnormally. Their activities cause violent and extreme fluctuations, whereas the policy of the intelligent tends to check extreme tendencies and minimize fluctuations."

In view of the fact that business tends to move toward normal conditions through the activity of intelligent men and tends to move toward, extremes through the actions of the ignorant, Mills concludes that *"the most effective remedy for commercial panics is to increase the average intelligence and elevate the average moral tone."*

Clement Juglar's theory of economic cycles is very similar to John Mills's *credit* cycle, but Juglar believed them to be self-perpetuating. Thus, prosperity, with high prices, engenders overspeculation and leads to a crisis. Liquidation removes the unfavorable factors in the business situation and paves the way for revival.

The "mental-mood" theory of Mills received strong support from Dr. Warren M. Persons, Professor of Economics, Harvard University, who stated in *Forecasting Business Cycles* (1931): "The world of affairs in which we live is not a mechanistic world; it is a bewildering world of multiplicities, complexities, interactions, repercussions and the vagaries of human wants, fears and hopes. It is a world in which, at times, facts and logic become subordinated to human emotions. At such times individuals, who by themselves are rational, join with other rational individuals to form an unreasoning mob. The business world then suffers from an epidemic of optimism, with hope, recklessness and indolence as its leading symptoms, or from an epidemic of pessimism with fear, timidity and inertia as its leading features. It is also a world of wars, droughts, floods, earthquakes and monetary changes. In such a world there can be neither a 'sure-fire' system nor a reliable 'trick' method of forecasting business cycles."

Others favoring the Mills theory were the economist Dr. Frederick R. Macaulay and the businessman Charles Mortimer, whose views are given in the previous chapter, as well as; Dr. David F. Jordan, who, in 1923, stated: "Alternate periods of prosperity and depression are money phenomena. Panics are psychological phenomena and no country can ever be panic-proof until the minds of men substantially change."

## 20th Century Business Cycle Theories

Modern research has indicated a tendency of the rhythmical movements of business to conform to the principles of harmonic motion—that is that the swings are like those of the pendulum, or like the waves in the ocean. Hence, modern economists classify business cycle theories into three groups, i.e., 1) free oscillations, 2) forced oscillations and 3) erratic shock. Harold Hotelling explains the first two as follows:

"The theory *of free oscillations* depends only upon the internal structure of the system. In this category may be placed the credit cycles of Juglar and Mills. Another is the 'Corn-Hog Cycle,' during which the high price of hogs and the low price of corn lead to overproduction in the first instance and under production in the second. This in turn reverses the price structure and cyclical fluctuations ensue. The causes of variations are here apparent, and for this reason any observed correlations derive more significance than those which may have appeared in an attempt to test the theory of forced oscillations.

"The theory of *forced oscillations* depends upon forces external to the system itself, forces whose origins are non-economic."

One of these is the so-called Sunspot Theory of which Jevons was the most prominent advocate. Another is the 8 year Venus cycle of H. L. Moore. Commenting on such theories, Hotelling observes: "The trouble with all such theories is the tenuousness, in the light of physics, of the long chain of causation which they are forced to postulate. Even if a statistical test should yield a very high correlation, the odds thus established in favor of such an hypothesis would have to be heavily discounted on account of its strong a priori improbability."

The theory of *erratic shock* is credited by Ragnar Frisch to Knut Wicksell, who was the first to explicitly formulate the theory that the source of energy which maintains the economic cycle is erratic shocks. According to Wicksell, the economic system is being pushed along irregularly and jerkily by new innovations and exploitations which may cause more or less regular cyclical movements.

Since the theory of *forced oscillations* is the earliest in which attempts have been made to predict the future of business, a more detailed study will be made of the various predictive elements that have been used in the past.

There are three main theories relative to forced oscillations. One of these theories attributes the rhythmic ups and downs of business and other human affairs to the influence of sunspots, which are discussed in Chapter 2. A second theory attributes these regularities to planets, acting either directly or indirectly through the Sun, such as Moore's 8-year Venus cycle and the author's theory, which are discussed in Chapter 5. A third approach is purely empirical and contents itself with merely recording the regularities observable, without-as-yet attempting to postulate any theory of cause. It might be called the *Theory of Unknown Causes* and will be covered in Chapter 7.

The theory most widely used by modern economists is known as *The Historic Analogy Theory*. Thus, Professor A. B. Adams, from a study of all the business cycles since 1720, concludes in his book, *Analysis of Business Cycles* (1936): "All statistical forecasts are predicated upon the theory that business history will repeat itself, either as to fluctuations in the general trend of business, or as to correlations in the fluctuations of certain time series. *All forecasting agencies have used assumptions of historical repetition of cyclical movements, as well as assumptions of fixed sequences of time series, to aid them in making forecasts*. It is evident that the great weakness of the empirical or historical method of forecasting is the fact that business history does not repeat itself with sufficient regularity and similarity to make this method of forecasting reasonably dependable. Sound knowledge of the history of cyclical fluctuations is a necessary prerequisite to intelligent forecasting of the future trend of business. A thorough study of past cycles can be gained only through an analytical study of the economic happenings and conditions which attended each cycle."

Furthermore, Smith and Duncan, in *Elementary Statistics and Applications* (1944), state: "Business economists attempt many kinds of forecasts. *One of the most important objects of economic forecasting is to predict general business conditions; that is to say, the cyclical position of general business*. Statistically, general business is properly measured by some index of business activity. One of the methods used in forecasts of general business conditions is known as that of 'historical analogy'. It is based on the assumption that in cyclical fluctuations history tends to repeat itself. In its cruder forms, this consists merely in forecasting the course of general business, subsequent to some disturbance, from the course of general business that followed a similar disturbance in the past. For example, the forecaster might undertake to predict the course of general business following the crisis of 1939 from the course of business following the crisis of 1873."

Similarly, Professor S. J. Maisel of the University of California states in *Fluctuations, Growth & Forecasting* (1957): "Successful forecasting is intricate. Forecasts deal in probabilities. Most *forecasters make use of historical and statistical patterns. It is almost impossible to work without them*. The procedures assume that there are certain uniformities in the economy which can be discovered by an analysis of past experience. By means of statistics, observation, or theory, it is discovered that a certain situation A in the past has always been followed by another situation B. Assuming that this results from a relationship in the economy which will not change, it can be predicted that the next time A occurs, B will ensue."

Nevertheless, most economists take the position of Professor E. C. Bratt, who states in *Business Cycles and Forecasting* (1940): "Emotional response within the forces creating the self-generating oscillation may obey psychological laws, but if so, these laws are as yet too obscure to be of any value for the purpose of explanation. The emotional response must, therefore, be accepted as a chance result for the present. Every business cycle has been unique in that the combination of forces is never the same. If the cause of business cycle variation were always precisely known, forecasting would become simple."

Another sceptic was Stuart Chase, who, in *Power of Words* (1953), observed that "One revealing collection of prophecies as to the course of the American economy between 1900 and 1929 made by serious students of economics showed nearly every prophet to be either seriously or totally wrong, the majority was firmly convinced that prosperity would continue long beyond 1929. The post-World War II depression so confidently predicted by practically everybody never arrived. The facts have consistently belied the predictions of the economists. Most economists cannot even foretell the general direction of the economy. The perennial argument is raging as to whether the economy is headed for more inflation, for a recession, or for an old-fashioned depression." (This was just as true in the current recession as it was in the 1953 recession.)

The most recent critic of economists for their failure to correctly forecast the future trend of American business was the distinguished American economist Dr. John Kenneth Galbraith of Harvard University, who stated in his book *Money* (1975): "In the decade from the mid '60s to the mid '70s, economic policy was to be extensively guided by prediction that was *deeply subordinated to hope*. . . . Behind the benign facade of the New Economics in these years were serious flaws. The first was reliance on prediction and foresight—on taking action before need. Foresight is an imperfect thing—all prevision in economics is imperfect. And, even more serious, the economist in high office is under a strong personal and political compulsion to predict wrongly. That is partly because of the temptation to predict what is wanted, and it is better, not worse, economic performance that is always wanted."

(Note: Most of the material in this chapter is based on a lecture given by the author at the January 6, 1959 meeting of The New York Chapter of the Foundation for the Study of Cycles, of which he was then Vice President. It was subsequently published in the April 1959 issue of the *Journal of Cycle Research*.)

## Chapter 2

# The Sunspot Theory of Business Cycles

*Believe nothing without examination. But where reason and evidence will warrant the conclusion, believe everything and let prejudice be unknown. Search for truth on all occasions and espouse it in opposition to the World.—Andrew Jackson Davis*

## Introduction

One of the most successful economic forecasts of the 19th Century was made not by an economist but by astronomer Sir William Herschel (1738-1822), who became famous as the discoverer of the planet Uranus in 1781. In a paper read before the Royal Society of London on April 16, 1801, Herschel called attention to an apparent relationship between sunspot activity and the price of wheat. From his studies of six periods between 1650 and 1800, Herschel concluded that in periods with little or no sunspots, wheat was scarce and hence prices were high; conversely, in periods of abundant sunspots, crops were abundant and prices low.

Although his facts were too few and sketchy to justify a positive assertion, Herschel correctly predicted that the next period of abundant sunspots would be accompanied by abundant crops. The Mean Relative Sunspot Numbers increased from a low of 4.1 during 1798 to a high of 47.5 during 1804. Agricultural production increased enormously from the low reached during the wet summer of 1799, but prices continued to rise until 1801, when over-production caused a decline until the renewal of the Napoleonic Wars in 1803. The year 1809 produced a harvest almost as poor as that of 1799, and it was followed by almost equally poor harvests the following three years. No sunspots were counted in 1810, and prices continued to rise to a peak in 1813.

At this point, a word about sunspots is in order. Sunspots are vast, whirling storms on the sun's surface, similar to terrestrial cyclones or tornadoes, evidenced by dark spots, and accompanied by large, irregular, bright areas called faculae, light and dark markings called flocculi, and vast eruptions of gases rising from the chromosphere to heights as great as 1,000,000 miles called prominences.

This periodicity of sunspots was first noted by Samuel Heinrich Schwabe of Dessau, Germany, who in 1844 published the results of his observations between 1826 and 1843 inclusive, provisionally estimating the sunspot cycle to be about 10 years. Professor Rudolph Wolf of Zurich, Switzerland published in 1852 an analysis of all the recorded observation of spots from 1610 to 1850 and estimated therefrom that the average length of the cycle was 11.11 years. However, the interval has been as short as 9.0 years and as long as 13.6 years.

Dr. D. Justin Schove, in the June 1955 *Journal of Geophysical Research*, calculates the mean cycle as 11.11 years, with a range of 8 years minimum and 16 years maximum. So far in the present century the mean has been 10 years. Schove makes this significant statement: "The ultimate test of all theories and formulae must lie in prediction. Prediction of future sunspot numbers and cycles is important, but harmonic analysis has proved unsuccessful, and there is little agreement among scientists as to a suitable basis for forecasting."

It is now apparent why Dr. Clarke was unable to find an astronomical period to fit his 10-year cycle of 1838, and his 11-year cycle of 1847, since Schwabe's estimate of the length of the sunspot cycle as 10 years wasn't published until 1844, and Wolf's estimate of 11.11 years wasn't published until 1852. Evidently Dr. Clarke was way ahead of his time.

The next exponent of the Sunspot Theory was the noted English economist William Stanley Jevons (1835-82), who felt that financial fluctuations might depend upon changes in the production of food. He labored for 12 years to establish a fundamental physical law of commercial fluctuations, which culminated in a paper, "The Solar Period and the Price of Corn," read before the Bristol meeting of the British Association in 1875.

In this paper Jevons stated: "It is true that Mr. John Mills, in his very excellent papers upon Credit Cycles in the Transactions of the Manchester Statistical Society (1867-8) has shown that these periodic collapses are really mental in their nature, depending upon variations of despondency, hopefulness, excitement, disappointment, and panic. But it seems to me very probable that these moods of the commercial mind, while constituting the principal part of the phenomena, may be controlled by outward events, especially the condition of the harvests."

But what affects the harvests? Jevons answered: "It has lately been proved, beyond all reasonable doubt, that there is a periodic variation in the Sun's condition, which was first discovered in the alternate increase and decrease of area of the sunspots, but which is also marked by the occurrence of auroras, magnetic storms, cyclones, and other meteorological disturbances. Little doubt is now entertained moreover, that the rainfall and other atmospheric phenomena of any locality are more or less influenced by the same changes in the Sun's condition, though we do not yet know either the exact nature of these solar variations nor the way in which they would act upon the weather of any particular country.

"Now if weather depends in any degree upon the solar period, it follows that the harvest and the price of grain will depend more or less upon the solar period, and will go through periodic fluctuations in periods of time equal to those of the sunspots."

Jevons used tables for wheat, barley, oats, beans, peas, vetches, and rye derived from Professor James E. Thorold Rogers's monumental *History of Agriculture and Prices in England from 1259 to 1793*, published in 1866. Expressing prices in grains of silver in order to eliminate fluctuations due to currency changes during the 140 years under review, Jevons obtained an 11.11-year cycle which was the supposed average length of the principal sunspot cycle. The price of wheat has been used as an index of farm products for moee than 1,000 years in England. The price of 3 percent Consols (British perpetual government bonds) is used as an index of interest rates.

Professor Jevons then made the following prophetic statements: "Assuming that variations of commercial credit and enterprise are essentially mental in their nature, must there not be external events to excite hopefulness at one time or disappointment and despondency at another? It may be that the commercial classes of the English nation, as at present constituted, form a body, suited by mental and other conditions, to go through a complete oscillation in a period nearly corresponding to that of the sunspots. In such conditions, a comparatively slight variation of the prices of food, repeated in a similar manner, at corresponding points of the oscillation, would suffice to produce violent effects.

"If, then, the English money market is naturally fitted to swing or roll in periods of ten or eleven years, comparatively slight variations in the goodness of harvests repeated at like intervals would suffice to produce those alternations of depression, activity, excitement, and collapse which undoubtedly recur in well-marked suc-

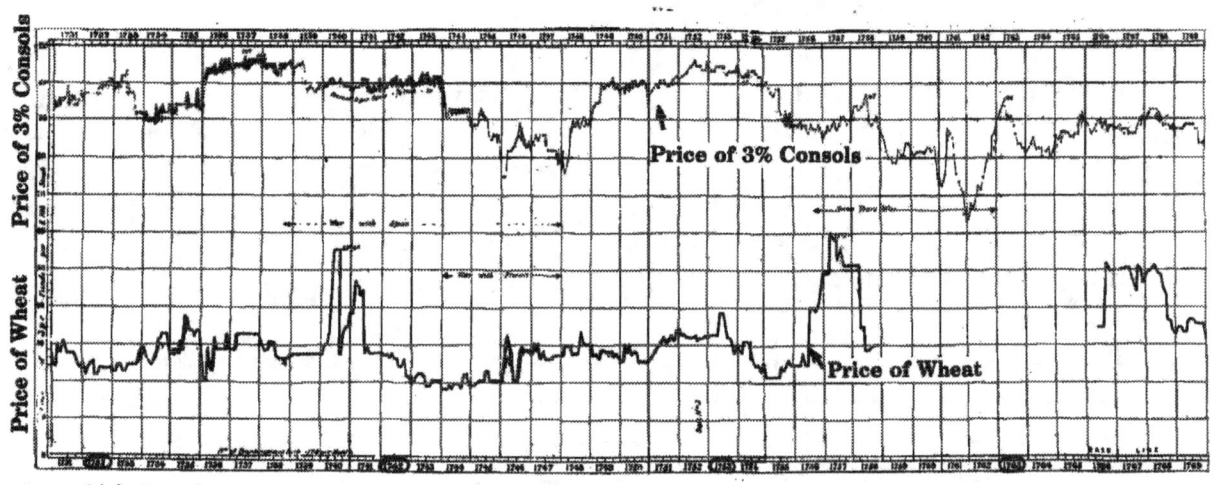

*Figure 1a. Jevons Chart of English Business and Wheat Cycles 1731-1769.*

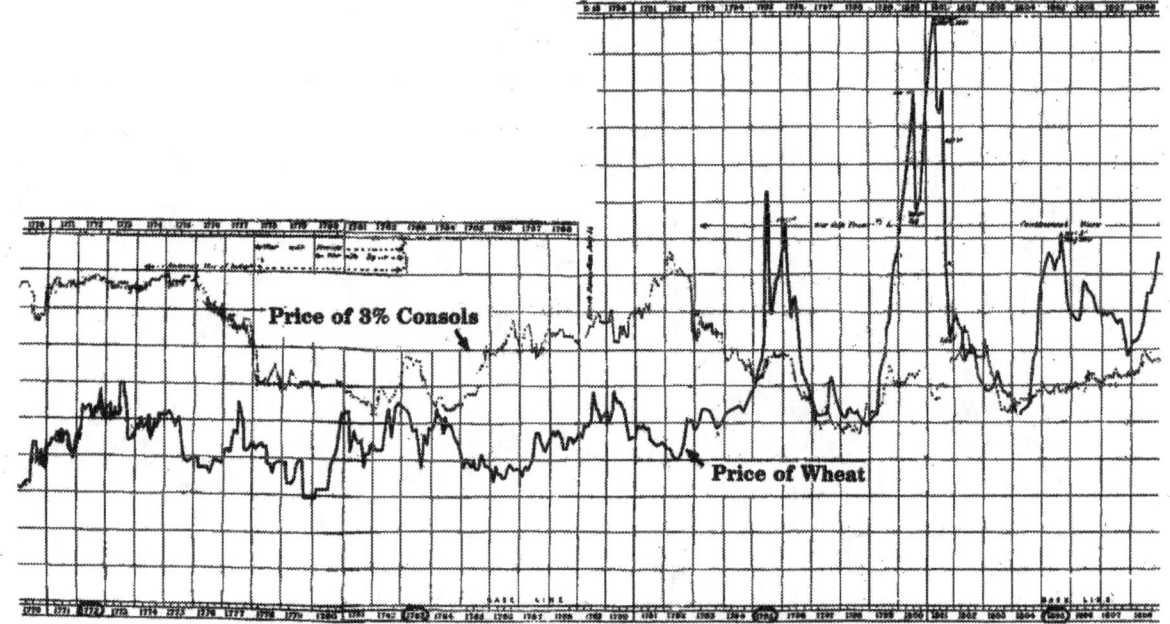

*Figure 1b. Jevons Chart of English Business and Wheat Cycles 1770-1808.*

cession. I am aware that speculations of this kind may seem somewhat farfetched and finely-wrought, but financial collapses have recurred with such approach to regularity in the last fifty years, that either this or some other explanation is needed.

"It is curious to reflect that *if these speculations should prove to have any validity, we get back to something which might be mistaken for the astrology of the Middle Ages.* Professor Balfour Stewart has shown much reason for believing that the sunspot period is connected with the configuration of the planets. [I have since read Professor Stewart's memoirs on the subject and am inclined to think that the relation of the planets and solar variations is of a more remote nature than he believes.]

"Now, if the planets govern the Sun, and the

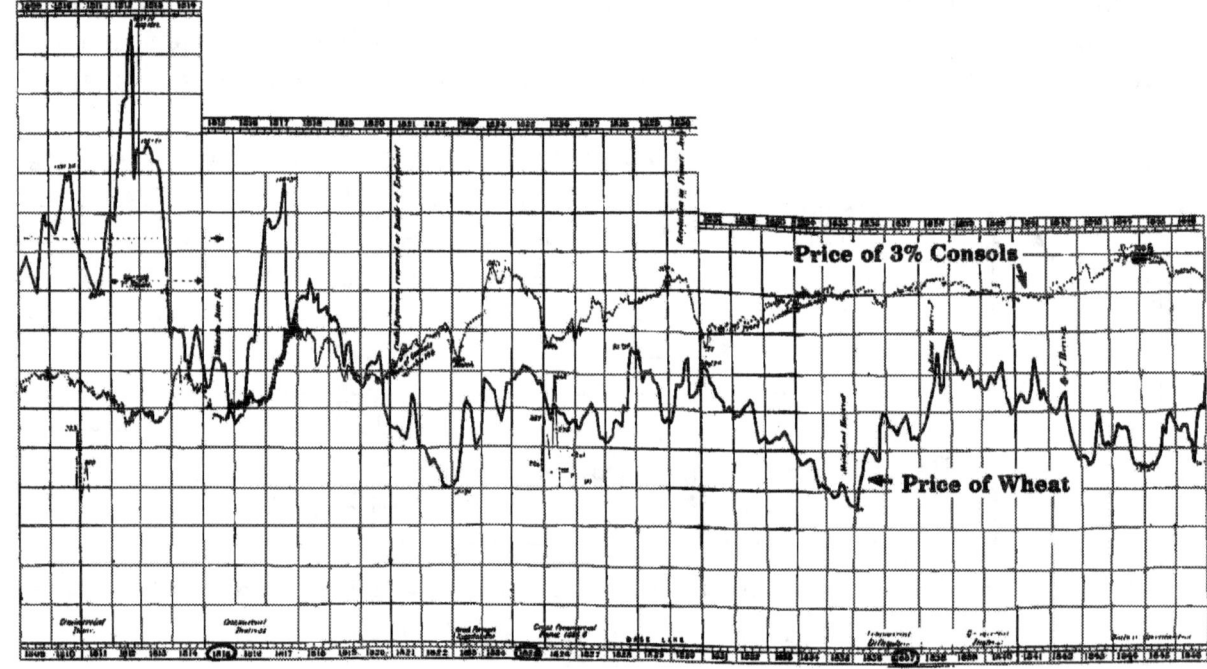

*Figure 1c. Jevons Chart of English Business and Wheat Cycles 1809-1846.*

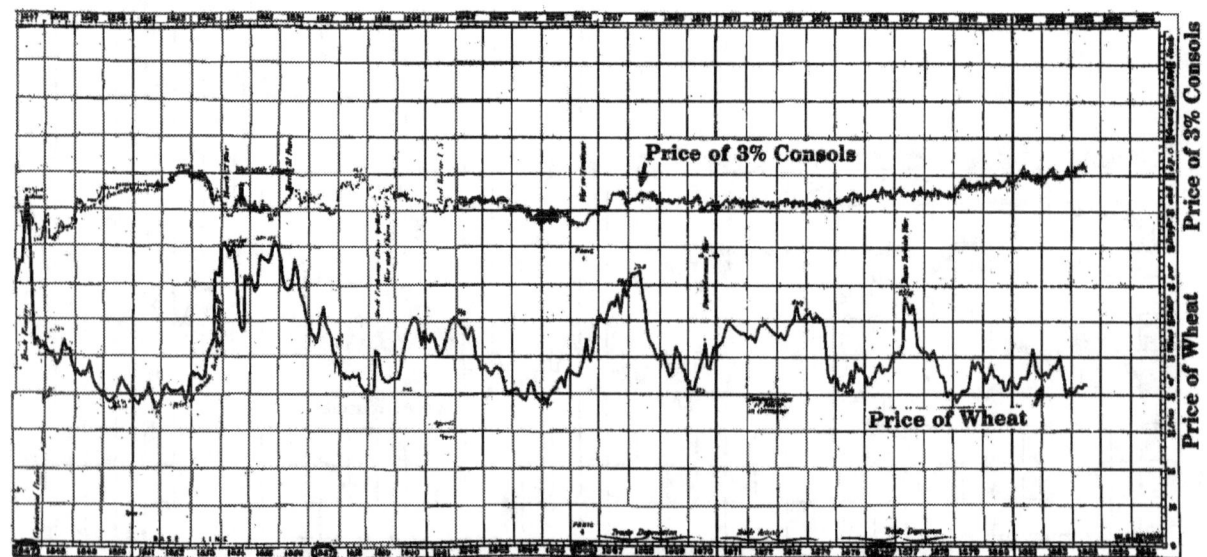

*Figure 1d. Jevons Chart of English Business and Wheat Cycles 1847-1883.*

Sun governs the vintages and harvests, and thus the prices of food and raw materials, and the state of the money market, it follows that *the configuration of the planets may prove to be the remote causes of the greatest commercial disasters.*

"It is a curious fact, not sufficiently known, that the electric telegraph was a favorite dream of the physicists and romanticists of the sixteenth and seventeenth centuries. It would be equally curious if the *pseudo-science of astrology* should, in like manner, foreshadow the triumphs which precise and methodical investigations may yet disclose, as to the obscure periodic causes affecting our welfare when we are least aware of it." He concluded: "I do not venture to assert positively that the average fluctuations as given in the preceding tables are solely due to variations in solar power. They seem to show that the subject deserves further investigation, which I hope to give to it when I have leisure."

At the Dublin meeting of the British Association held on August 19, 1878, Jevons read a paper, "The Periodicity of Commercial Crises and its Physical Explanation," in which he states: "Three years ago, at the Bristol Meeting of the British Association, I read a paper giving the supposed results of a new attempt to prove the relation suspected by Herschel. Subsequent inquiry convinced me that my figures would not support the conclusion I derived from them, and I withdrew the paper from publication. I have since made several attempts to discover a regular periodicity in the price of corn in Europe, but without success. [What frankness!] Nevertheless, I have long felt convinced that a well-marked decennial periodicity can be traced in the activity of trade and the recurrence of commercial crises."

Jevons then lists the following years when English trade reached a maximum of activity:

1701, 1711, 1721, 1732, 1742, 1753, 1763, 1772, 1783, 1795, 1805, 1815, 1825, 1837, 1847, 1857, 1866. See Figures 1a and 1d, where the panic years are encircled. Of them, he says, "These years, whether marked by the bursting of a commercial panic or not, are, as nearly as I can judge, corresponding years, and the intervals vary only from nine to twelve years. There being in all an interval of one hundred and sixty-five years, broken into sixteen periods, the average length of the period is about 10.3 years."

By eliminating the years 1701 and 1711, which he considers as not well-established, Jevons gets a period of 10.43 years, which compares with the mean duration of the sunspot period at that time of 10.45 years. Jevons concludes: "Judging this close coincidence of results according to the theory of probabilities, it becomes highly probable that two periodic phenomena, varying so nearly in the same mean period, are connected as cause and effect." However, this conclusion was not, at that time, susceptible of scientific proof.

In "Commercial Crisis and Sunspots," printed in *Nature* November 14, 1878, Jevons repeats most of the material contained in his British Association paper. He goes on to state: "All kinds of distinct reasons can be given why trade should be now inflated and again depressed and collapsed. But, so long as these causes are various and disconnected, nothing emerges to explain the remarkable appearance of regularity and periodicity which characterizes these events. I can entertain no doubt whatever that the principal commercial crises do fall into a series having the average period of about 10.466 years. Moreover, the almost perfect coincidence of this period with Broun's estimate of the sunspot period (10.45 years) is by itself strong evidence that the phenomena are causally connected. *The exact nature of the connection cannot at present be established.*"

In 1959, the author was informed by a fellow member of The Foundation for the Study of Cycles, Dr. Carlos Garcia-Mata, that he had been told by H. S. Jevons that his father William Stanley Jevons had been compelled to withdraw his 1875 paper on the "Sunspot Theory" and subsequently died of a broken heart because of the adverse criticism he had received from his fellow economists. What had evidently aroused the ire of the latter were the underlined unorthodox phrases the elder Jevons used in his 1875 paper.

A great forward step was taken by the younger Jevons (H. Stanley Jevons), who wrote a paper entitled "The Sun's Heat and Trade Activity," published in the August 1909 *Contemporary Review*, which he summarized as follows: "The heat emitted by the Sun undoubtedly varies, increasing and decreasing in such a way that the interval from one maximum of warmth to the next is, on the average 3½ years. Every third fluctuation is emphasized, so that there is a major variation occupying about 11 years, which harmonizes exactly with the variations of sunspots.

"It is not, as used to be supposed, the 11-year or sunspot period which is the important factor in determining the cycle of trade and the occurrence of commercial crises. Probably the sunspot period does have some effect; but it is the 3½ year, or 'solar prominence' period with which we are primarily concerned in accounting for trade fluctuations.

"This short, or 3½ year variation in the Sun's heat has a very marked effect upon terrestrial weather. Meteorologists have shown, indeed, that the average barometric pressure in places all over the earth varies in this period of 3½ years, and this fluctuation of pressure is only the result of changes of temperature and moistness of the air, occurring in the same period. In other words, the Sun, by his changes, gives us alternately a hot dry climate and a comparatively cold and wet climate. The hot, dry years—those probably in which the earth's surface has received the most heat from the Sun, have been of recent times: 1889, 1882-1883, 1896-1897, 1900, 1903-1904, 1907; whilst the coldest and dampest years, falling between them, have been:

1891, 1895, 1896-1899, 1902, 1905, 1909.

"It is supposed that the Sun emits a stream of electrons, which is greatest at sunspot maximum. The effect on our atmosphere of an increased bombardment of electrons would be to increase condensation of water vapor, thus causing more cloudy weather, increasing the rainfalls, and lowering the temperature.

"The evidence which I have collected on the subject brings me to the conclusion that my father (William Stanley Jevons), with his usual remarkable power of intuition, was perfectly correct in connecting the occurrence of commercial fluctuations and crises with changes in the sun's heat, but that the facts are much more complicated than he apparently supposed. I wish, however, to emphasize my conviction that if I have succeeded in making any advance upon his statement of the theory, it is only by means of the progress of astronomical and meteorological investigation and the publication of detailed crop statistics, which were not available in his time."

In the January 1923 *Review of Economic Statistics*, the American economist Joseph Kitchin, confirmed the findings of the younger Jevons. He found a cycle averaging 3⅓ years, or 40 months, based on careful measurements of certain indexes during the years 1890-1922 in both Great Britain and the United States. This cycle was thereafter called the *"Kitchin Cycle."* He also found that major cycles are merely aggregates, usually of two, less commonly of three, minor cycles, and that the limits of these major cycles are marked by a high maximum of the indexes, and sometimes a panic. The *average* of these major cycles he stated was *eight years*, and the most usual interval seven or ten years. These major cycles have been called *"Juglar Cycles,"* as previously noted.

In a paper, "The Causes of Fluctuations of Industrial Activity and the Price Level," read before the Royal Statistical Society, May 16, 1933, the younger Jevons took another forward step, for he said: "This tendency of business—commercial, industrial and financial—to severe fluctuations is partly due to the psychological states which current economic conditions create in groups of business men, and also partly due to the reactions which arise from the financial and credit customs and organization of the country. The 3½ year cycle is sufficiently powerful, however, to force the swing of trade and industry to adapt itself to its period, so that the boom, or maximum, of the trade cycle proper must coincide with a maximum of the minor cycle."

Most economists, however, tended to belittle the "Sunspot Theory" until Dr. Carlos Garcia-Mata and Dr. Felix I. Shaffner reported in the *Quarterly Journal of Economics,* November 1934, the results of a careful and impartial investigation into the relation between solar activity and business cycles. They found a startlingly high degree of correlation between the 11-year cycle of solar activity and that of total production, exclusive of agriculture, for the period from 1875 to 1930. Exceptions were found only during the depressions of 1903-1904 and 1913-1914, which were due to the enormous quantity of volcanic dust blown into the atmosphere during the volcanic eruptions of Mount Pelee in 1902-1903 and Mount Katmai in 1912-1913.

Garcia-Mata and Shaffner used the areas of sunspots and solar faculae compiled by the Greenwich Observatory of the Royal Astronomical Society as their index of solar activity, and Dr. Warren M. Persons's indices of crop, mineral and manufacturing production in the United States for periods ranging from 1875 to 1930. The curves in Figure 2 show that regardless of whether raw or smoothed data are used, there is excellent correlation between the index of solar activity and the index of manufacturing, as well as the index of total production, exclusive of crops, but very poor correlation with the crop index.

The Garcia-Mata and Shaffner studies confirmed the Herschel-Jevons theory, although the former used sunspot and faculae areas, whereas the latter used sunspot numbers as measures of solar activity. The poor correlation of the Garcia-Mata/Shaffner data for crops is undoubtedly due to the declining importance of agriculture in the U.S. economy. The value of agricultural production at the time of their studies was only 10 percent of total annual production, whereas in the days of Herschel and Jevons, some 40 percent of the population of England were engaged in agriculture.

Where Jevons was unable to advance a theory for the causal relationship he had found, Garcia-Mata and Shaffner advanced the following two theories:

1) Mass psychology is influenced by waves of optimism or pessimism caused by variations in the amount of ultraviolet rays emitted by the Sun, which variations are determined by variations in sunspot and solar faculae.

2) Changes in solar activity cause changes in the electromagnetic field of the earth which affects the electrical field of humans. Dr. E. D. Adrian of Yale University, in 1929, and E. G. Weaver and C. W. Bray, in 1930, discovered through experimentation with nerve tissue the existence of electrical currents in the human body. Changes in the electrical field of humans may result in biological changes affecting the individual's state of optimism or pessimism.

Garcia-Mata and Shaffner, however, state that, "we have been unable to determine whether the best correlation is with the curve of the total amount of the solar disturbances with a lag of several years, or with the cycle formed by the yearly increase or decrease in disturbances in the solar surface (spots, faculae, etc.), or with the existence or absence of spots pointing directly to the earth in the solar central zone, or through some other feature of the solar cycle."

In 1940, Dr. Garcia-Mata discovered a marked degree of correlation between the 40-month oscillations in business and variations in *terrestrial magnetism*. The fluctuations in these two variables closely resembled the oscillations in the total area of dark flocculi in the central zone of the sun.

It will be noted that Figure 3, which compares the Silberling-Ayres General Business Index with the Zurich Sunspot Numbers for the years 1750-1958 does not support the idea of a close correlation over the *entire* period. While a direct correlation does seem to persist for several decades at a time, as, for example, during the period of the Jevons and Garcia-Mata studies, (1875-1930), it is inverse at other periods, viz: World War II and Korean War. (The General Business Index is a composite of that prepared by M. J. Silberling in *Dynamics of Business* for the period of 1750-1940, to which has been added the Ayres Index of the Cleveland Trust Company. The Sunspot Index is derived from the Mean Relative Sunspot Numbers of the Zurich Observatory in Switzerland.)

The Sunspot Theory of the Business Cycle has not been generally accepted by economists as a group. Thus, Paul A. Samuelson, Professor of Economics, Massachusetts Institute of Technology writes in his book, *Economics*, as follows: "The business cycle is a pulse common to almost all sectors of economic life and to all capitalistic countries. Movements in national income, unemployment, production, prices, and profits are not so regular and predictable as the orbits of the planets or the oscillations of a pendulum, and there is no magical method of forecasting the turns of business activity.

"Unfortunately, the field of economics has not the classic simplicity of physics or mathematics. In economics, it is not quite so easy to demonstrate that sunspot theories of the business cycle are all moonshine, especially if their proponents are willing to spend a lifetime manipulating statistics until they produce agreement. This sad fact is important, not because we find it difficult to disprove the sunspot theory—no one really cares much today about sunspot theories—but rather because our cockiness about what we think are better and truer theories must always be subject to liberal reservations in view of the complexity of economic observations and data which make it difficult to disprove a bad theory or verify a good one."

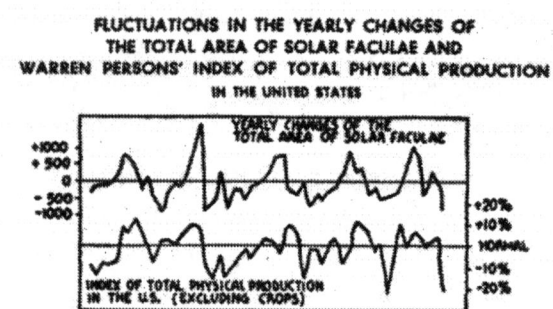

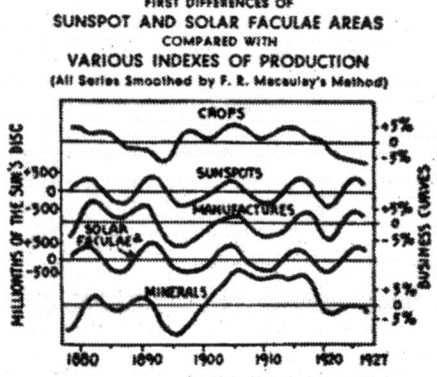

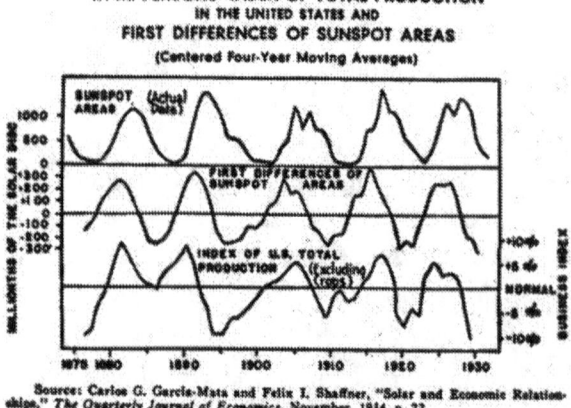

*Figure 2. Garcia-Mata/Shaffner Sunspot vs. Business Cycles.*

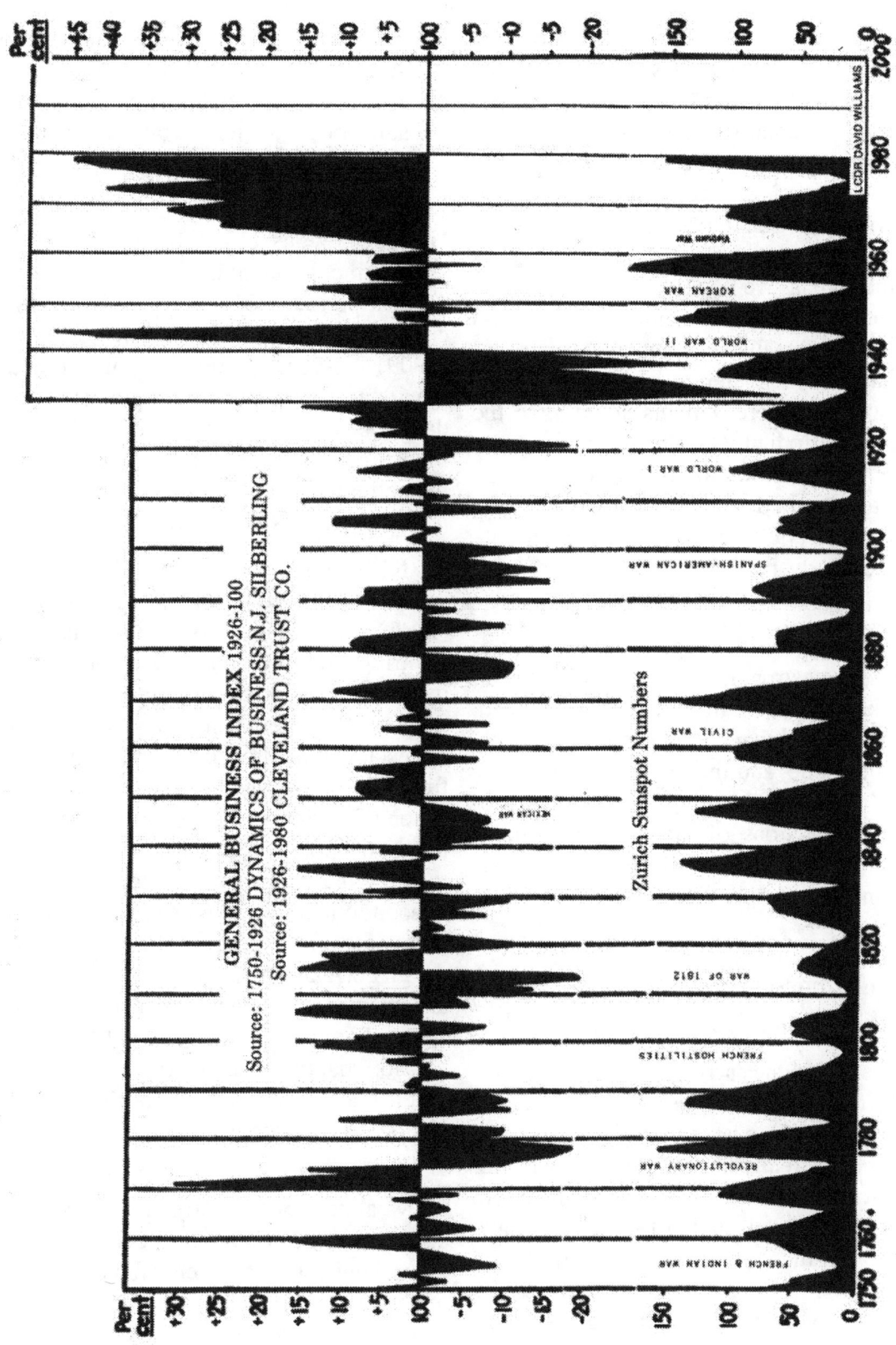

*Figure 3. Sunspot Numbers and Business Cycles 1750-1980.*

H. T. Davis, in *The Analysis of Economic Time Series,* disagrees with Professor Samuelson, for he says that the Herschel/Jevons/Garcia-Mata Shaffner theory of explaining crises and depressions in terms of solar variations is a possibility "which has never been completely discredited because of a persistent correlation." He then goes on to state: "The interest for economics in sunspots seems, however, to lie in another direction. In these data, we have a phenomenon, expressed as a time series, for which no a priori explanation is universally accepted by the astronomers. That the phenomenon is periodic is unquestionable, but there remains doubt as to the nature of the periodicity. Hence, the data on sunspots provide an almost perfect example upon which to test methods of periodogram analysis, which might be applicable to the more variable and less regularly periodic phenomena of economics.

"Historically, the investigation of time series began with the astronomers, and it will be well for us to keep this fact in mind as we proceed. Their problem and that of the economists is essentially the same, and the methods which they have employed in untangling the complex motions and interactions of the heavenly bodies contain much that is illuminating in an analysis of the complicated behavior of economic time series."

## Summary of the Sunspot Theory of Business Cycles

The history of the early attempts to link sunspot activity and the business cycle in a cause and effect relationship has been handicapped by the lack of sufficiently accurate data to affirmatively prove the reality of such a connection. Thus, Sir William Herschel in 1801 did not have the benefit of the data on the sunspot cycle, which was first made available to the world by Heinrich Schwabe in 1844. Although Carrington in 1863 had the benefit of considerable data on sunspot activity, he was handicapped by a lack of sufficient economic data.

While the elder Jevons in 1875 was perhaps the first of the great English economists to apply the statistical method to economics, he erred in his attempts to correlate the presumed length of the sunspot cycle and the business cycle.

The Garcia-Mata/Shaffner studies of 1934, which so powerfully confirmed the earlier Herschel/Jevons (1801-1875) efforts to correlate business and sunspot cycles in terms of an 11-year periodicity, and the 1940 studies of Garcia-Mata, which confirmed the younger Jevons (1909) 3½-year periodicity, may revolutionize our ideas concerning the origin of the ups and downs of business. This is particularly so since investigations in other fields of science reinforce the belief that the timing of business oscillations is the result of well-defined natural forces.

Referring to the Sunspot Theory, H. T. Davis, in *The Analysis of Economic Time Series* (1941), concludes: "It is obvious that if business is influenced by conditions external to its own institutions, a correlation must first be observed between the external and the internal cycles. But the establishment of such correlations is not sufficient to prove such influences without the addition of a priori evidence to show the causal nature of the postulated relationship. The argument to show that empirical relationships discovered in economic time series are essentially problems in inverse probability is valid here. Even though a high correlation may be observed between historical crises and the maxima and minina of sunspots, this is totally insufficient to prove scientifically that the observed relationship is real and that it may be relied upon for the forecasting of business depressions.

"Those who now favor the theory, realizing the weakness of the correlation argument, have attempted to establish a direct relationship between sunspots and psychic factors such as optimism and pessimism. If it could be demonstrated, for example, that a highly ionized atmosphere exerted a direct influence upon the human spirit, then there might be a valid basis for accepting the thesis that sunspot activity may lead to group optimisms or group pessimisms with their ancillary reactions upon the business cycle.

"The greatest stumbling block to the acceptance of the theory has been the lack of evidence to indicate the kind of mechanism which would convert solar variation into economic variation. The best clue is now found in the ultraviolet curve, but one must freely admit that the data are meager and that the chain of causation, through the effects upon human psychology is tenuous indeed.

"The theory, however, is suggestive enough to warrant further study. It is to be hoped that we may have in time more adequate data regarding first, the variation of ultraviolet in the Sun throughout a wider range of frequencies, and second, a more thorough understanding of the effect that this may have upon human behavior.

"The actual construction of a new science is a long and difficult task since the interrelationships between the observed phenomena must be discovered by the process of experimentation on the one hand and intuition on the other. The difficulties in constructing a social science are even greater than the difficulties encountered in constructing a physical science since in the former the relationships are seldom functionally exact and must be explored through the medium of correlations instead of complete functional relationships."

What causes Sunspots? The answer to this question will be found in the next chapter.

## Chapter 3

# The Planetary Cause of Sunspots

## Introduction

What are sunspots and what causes them? In the latter part of the 19th Century, the astronomical world was bitterly divided as to the cause of sunspots. Professor C. A. Young of Princeton University summarized the opposing views in *The Sun* (1882) as follows, "There is no question of solar physics more interesting or important than that which concerns the cause of this periodicity (of sunspots), but a satisfactory solution remains to be found. It has been supposed by astronomers of very great authority that the influence of the planets in some way produces it. Jupiter, Venus, and Mercury have been especially suspected of complicity in the matter, the first on account of his enormous mass, the others on account of their proximity.

"Even more important than the problem of the cause of sunspot periodicity is the question whether this periodicity produces any noticeable effects upon the earth, and, if so, what? In regard to this question the astronomical world is divided into two almost hostile camps, so decided is the difference of opinion, and so sharp the discussion. One party holds that the state of the Sun's surface is a determining factor in our terrestrial meteorology, making itself felt in our temperature, barometric pressure, rainfall, cyclones, crops, and even our financial condition, and that, therefore, the most careful watch should be kept upon the Sun for economic as well as scientific reasons. The other party contends that there is, and can be, no sensible influence upon the earth produced by such slight variations in the solar light and heat, though, of course they all admit the connection between sunspots and the condition of the earth's magnetic elements. It seems pretty clear that we are not in a position yet to decide the question either way; it will take a much longer period of observation, and observations conducted with special reference to the subject of inquiry, to settle it. At any rate, from the data now in our possession, men of great ability and laborious industry draw opposite conclusions."

Although Young believed that the facts at that time did not seem to warrant the conclusion that sunspots were connected with various terrestrial phenomena, he was fair enough to state that "The latest, and one of the most interesting, of the essays in this general direction, is that of Professor Jevons, who seeks to show a relation between sunspots and commercial crises. The idea is by no means absurd, as some have declared—it is a mere question of fact. If sunspots have really any sensible effect upon terrestrial meteorology, upon temperature, storms, and rainfall, they must thus indirectly affect the crops, and so disturb financial relations; in such a delicate organization as that of the world's commerce, it needs but a featherweight, rightly applied, to alter the course of trade and credit, and produce a 'boom' (if we may be forgiven the use of so convenient a word) or a crash."

## Sunspot Theory

The Sun is the most important member of our solar system since it contains 99.9 percent of the mass of the system, and thus regulates the movements of the other bodies. From the Sun we obtain our light, heat, and energy, and on its life-giving rays depends all human activity. It acts on us through the atmospheric shell surrounding the Earth, which is being bombarded by electronic influences varying in intensity with cyclonic disturbances on the Sun's surface evidenced by dark spots called sunspots, large, irregular, bright areas called faculae, light and dark markings called flocculi, and vast eruptions of gases rising from the chromosphere to heights as great as 1,000,000 miles, called prominences.

According to Dr. D. Justin Schove of Bakenham, England, sunspots have been observed as far back as 649 B.C. But the earliest continuous records of sunspot observations are contained in the great *Chinese Encyclopedia* of 1322 A.D., which lists 45 sunspots between 301 A.D. and 1206 A.D. Nineteen additional sunspots were observed by the Chinese up to 1370 A.D. An Inca observer, Huyana-Capec, made sunspot observations between 1495 A.D. and 1525 A.D. However, the first scientific study of sunspots began in 1610 A.D. with the telescopic observations of Galileo and his contemporaries, Fabricius, Harriot, and Scheiner. Reliable counts of sunspot numbers have been kept continuously since 1749 A.D. The Danish astronomer Horrebow discovered from observations between 1761 and 1769 that sunspots varied with time.

The periodicity of sunspots was first noted by an amateur astronomer, Samuel Heinrich Schwabe of Dessau Germany, who in 1844 published the results of his observations between 1826 and 1843 inclusive, provisionally estimating the sunspot cycle to be about 10 years long. Rudolph Wolf of Zurich, Switzerland published in 1852 an analysis of all the recorded observations of sunspots which could be collected from 1610 to 1850 and estimated therefrom that the cycle averaged 11.11 years in length, with periods as short as 9.0 years and as long as 13.6 years. Wolf's value was confirmed a century later by Schove, who in 1955, published the results of his studies of the years 649 B.C. to 2000 A.D., which showed an average length of 11.11 years, with the interval between peaks as short as 8 years and as long as 16 years. In 1958, Edward R. Dewey, Executive Director, Foundation for the Study of Cycles, estimated the average length of the cycle to be 11.094 years for the period 300 B.C. to A.D. 1958.

Sir John Herschel was perhaps the first astronomer to suggest that sunspots may be vast, whirling storms on the Sun, similar to terrestrial tornadoes, for he reported in 1867 that W. Rutter Dawes, in tracing the changes in sunspots from day to day between December 23, 1851 and January 17, 1852 "was led to conclude that in many instances, they have a movement of rotation about their own centers." But it was not until October 7, 1908 that photographs taken with the newly invented spectroheliograph at Mt. Wilson Observatory under the direction of Dr. George Ellery Hale revealed great vortices, whirling in opposite directions on opposite sides of the solar equator, and centering over two large sunspots. Subsequent spectroheliograms taken in hydrogen light revealed a structure around spot groups resembling the lines of force formed by a bar magnet in iron filings, or the lines of flow in a whirlpool.

The electromagnetic nature of sunspots was suggested as early as 1833 by Sir John Herschel who wrote that "A continual current of electric matter may be constantly circulating in the Sun's immediate neighborhood, or traversing the planetary spaces, and exciting, in the upper regions of its atmosphere, those phenomena of which we have yet an unequivocal manifestation in our aurora borealis." In 1867, he wrote that solar spots coincided with great disturbances in the magnetic system of the earth, and that "the coincidence of epochs of maxima and minima in the two series of phenomena amounts indeed to identity, a fact evidently of most important significance, but which neither astronomical nor magnetic science is yet sufficiently advanced to interpret."

Hence, proof of the electromagnetic nature of sunspots had to wait for three important scientific discoveries. First, Michael Faraday had noted in his *Experimental Researches* (1837) the possibility that a moving electric charge might produce a magnetic field. This effect was observed by Rowland in 1876 and again by Roentgen in 1885, and was measured quantitatively by Rowland and Hutchinson in 1889. Second, on September 13, 1845, Faraday proved that a magnetic field can rotate a beam of light passing through it from a luminous source outside of its influence. Third, in 1896, Pieter Zeeman of Leyden, Holland discovered that when a luminous vapor is placed between the pole pieces of a powerful electromagnet, the spectrum lines, instead of having their normal appearance, are split into several components.

As early as 1892, Young had noticed that certain lines were doubled in the spectra of sunspots, and Hale suspected that this doubling was a Zeeman effect due to the magnetic field of the sunspot vortex. In 1908, Hale announced observational proof that each sunspot center was a powerful magnet. Observations at Mt. Wilson Observatory of the Zeeman effect in several thousand spot groups have shown that in the majority of cases the two spots of a pair, or the clusters at opposite ends of a stream, are of opposite magnetic polarity, and that spot groups in the Northern and Southern Hemispheres are of opposite polarity. Then in 1912, when spot groups of a new cycle began to appear in high latitudes, the polarities were found to be the reverse of groups in the previous cycle. This reversal in polarity of spot groups has subsequently been corroborated by observations at the minima of 1922, 1933 and 1944. Thus, the true sunspot cycle is now considered to be twice the 11-year period, or 22-23 years.

Commenting on this brilliant discovery by Hale and his assistants, Dr. Harlan True Stetson of the Massachusetts Institute of Technology wrote in 1949, "It had long been known that the frequencies of light waves were distorted if there was a powerful magnetic field at the light source. When the Mt. Wilson observers examined and actually measured the frequency of the light coming from the centers of sunspots, it was found to be distorted in exactly the way that light waves are distorted in the laboratory when a powerful electromagnet is placed around a source of light. Thus came the startling revelation not only that sunspots were terrific hurricanes, but also that every hurricane center was in itself a powerful magnet. . . . The magnetism in some sunspots is nearly a million times as powerful as that of the earth." (The possible analogy of the solar light to that of the aurora had been pointed out as early as 1801 by Sir William Herschel.) Stetson concluded that "the close correlation of changes in the earth's magnetism with the coming and going of sunspots is one of the best established connections between sunspots and the earth that is known to science."

Now that we have reviewed what sunspots are thought to be, the next question is: What causes sunspots? There are a number of theories, but the best documented is the planetary theory.

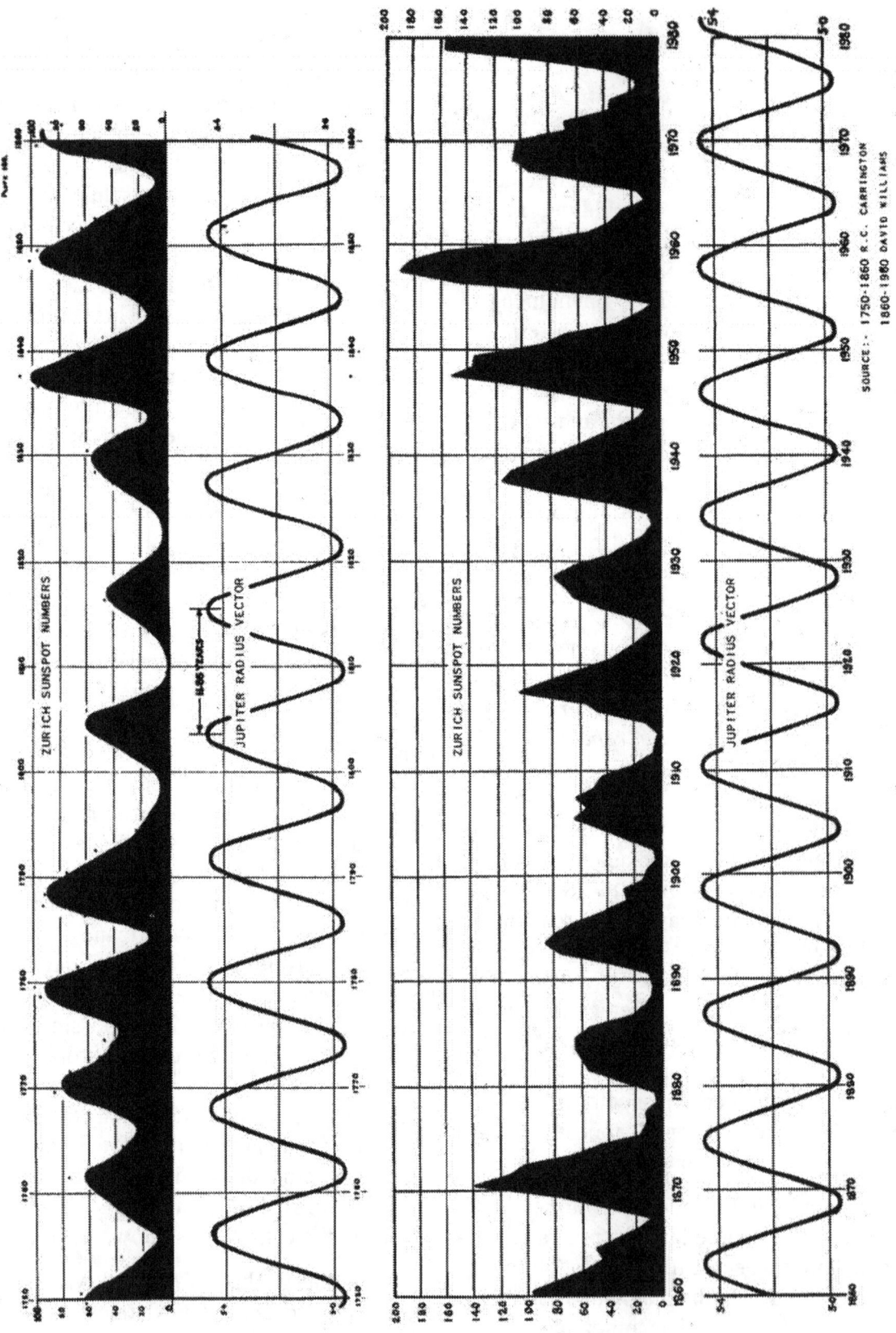

*Figure 4. Sunspot Cycle vs. Jupiter Cycle.*

## Sunspot-Planetary Correlations

During the past 50 years, the author has found in the writings of noted European and American scientists covering more than a century the following evidence in support of the theory of the planetary cause of sunspots. The earliest worker in this field was the Swiss astronomer Rudolph Wolf, who in 1859 devised a formula by which the mass, distance and angular position of the planets might be used to produce a curve agreeing in its main outlines with that of the sunspot curve.

In 1863, English astronomer R. C. Carrington (1826-75) published his *Observations of the Spots on the Sun from November 9, 1853 to March 24, 1861*, at the end of which he showed a chart (Figure 4). This chart was intended to show what, if any, correlation existed between the 11.11-year sunspot cycle, and Jupiter's orbital period of 11.86 years. (The Radius Vector of a planet is the line joining the planet and the Sun.) He thereby sought to combine the work of Herschel and Wolf. Of the chart, Carrington wrote the following account:

"I purposely contrast with the sunspot curve the variations of Jupiter's Radius Vector, as offering the only approximate agreement which I have been able to perceive. It will be seen that from the year 1770 there is a very fair general agreement between maxima of frequency and maxima of Jupiter's Radius Vector, and between minima and minima, with such an amount of loose discrepancy as to throw grave doubt on any hasty conclusion of physical connexion. In the two periods which precede that date there appears to be a total disagreement, and although the data for frequency are less certain for those years, yet the general form of the curve of Professor Wolf is probably too well established to admit of anything like reversion by the addition of other observations which have not yet come to hand. In this case, though unfavorable to our purpose, it is important to see before us an instance in which *eight consecutive cases of general but imperfect agreement* between the variations of two physical phenomena are shown to be insufficient to base any conclusions upon, at the same time that they powerfully stimulate further inquiry with the view of ascertaining whether the discrepancy may admit of future explanation."

This degree of correlation did not continue during the next 100 years for the lower half of Figure 4 shows that the peaks of the two curves become more and more displaced until in 1917 they were 180 degrees apart. Not until 1957 did the two curves again fall into synchronism.

The periodic nature of the recurrences of sunspots had suggested that the planets in some way were the cause of the atmospheric disturbances in the surface layers of the sun. Hence, some scientists believed that the gravitational, magnetic, or electrical influences of the planets revolving around the sun set up tides in the solar atmosphere, in a manner similar to the tides in the oceans of the earth set up by the Moon.

Thus, American astronomer Professor W. A. Norton of Yale College believed that both Jupiter and Venus were involved in the production of sunspots. He wrote in his book, *A Treatise on Astronomy* (1867), the following item:

*"The sun's spots are for the most part developed by, or in some way connected with, the operation of a physical agency exerted by the planets upon the photosphere.* This remarkable fact has been conclusively established by the observations of Schwabe, Carrington, Secchi, and others; and especially by the detailed discussion to which all the reliable observations upon the spots, made during the last 100 years, have been subjected by Professor Wolf of Zurich. The planets which exercise the greatest influence are Jupiter and Venus. The planetary agency is directly recognized in the origination of spots on the sun's surface brought by the rotation into favorable positions, and in the subsequent changes experienced by the spots while subject to the direct action of the planet. It is also shown by the

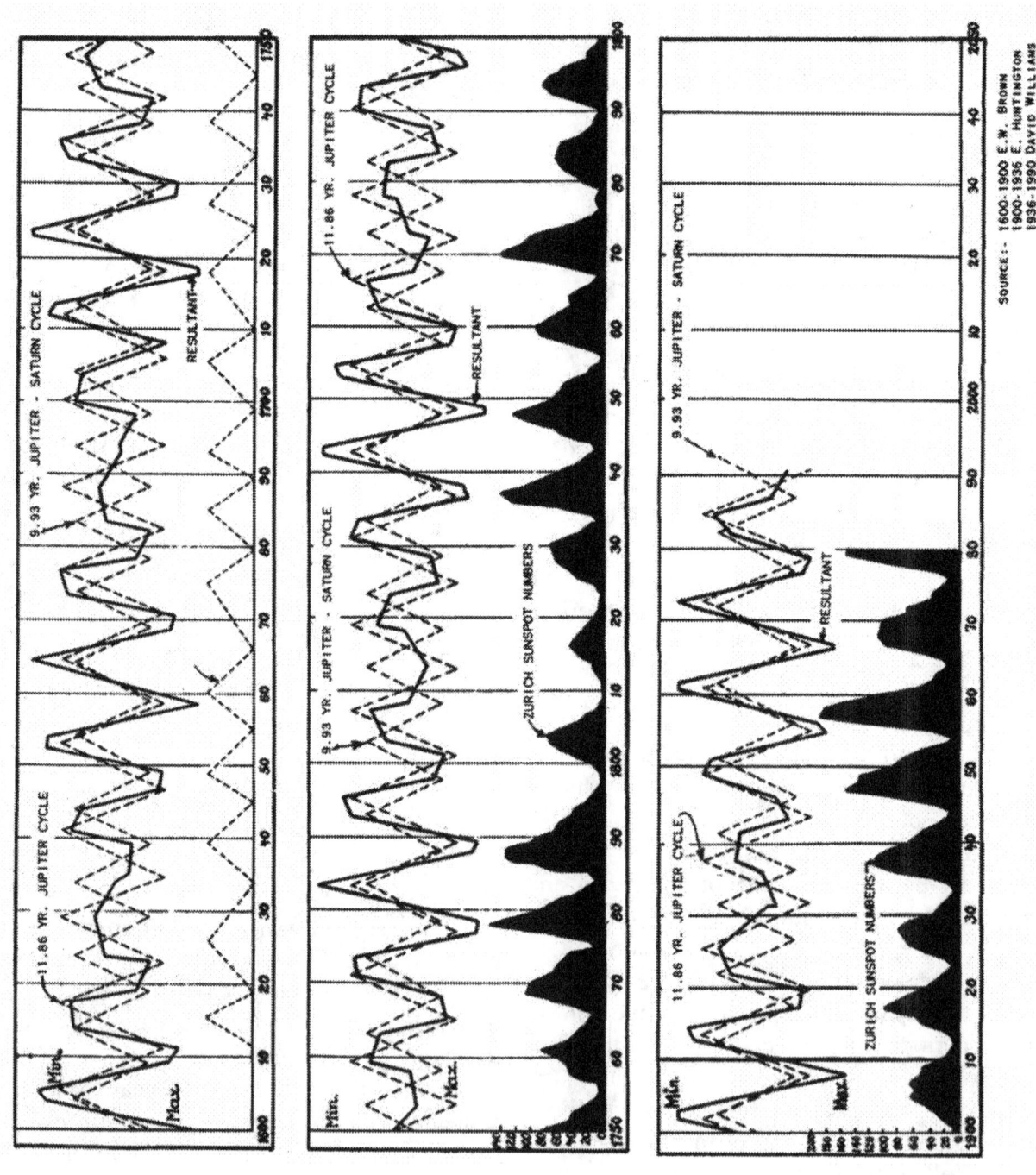

*Figure 5. Resultant of 11.86 and 9.93 Year Cycles vs. Sunspot Cycles.*

dependence of the epochs of the maximum and minimum of spots upon the positions of the planets, especially of Jupiter and Venus. *It appears from the results of observation, that the planets operate unequally in different parts of the ecliptic, and in different relative positions; and their effects are apparently modified, in certain positions, by the motion of the solar system through space.*"

Additional findings were reported in 1869-1870 by English astronomers W. de la Rue, Balfour Stewart and Loewy in *Researches on Solar Physics*. They found some influence on sunspots due to the configurations of not only Jupiter and Venus, but Venus and Mercury, Mars and Jupiter, and Mercury alone.

In 1875, the American meteorologist John H. Tice stated in his book, *The Elements of Geology*, that the planetary equinoxes were the cause of solar perturbations; that the maximum disturbance upon the earth must occur at or near Jupiter's equinox, and that the energy of the equinox of any planet was intensified when that of another occurred at or about the same time.

In 1882, Young credited Professor Loomis with the original suggestion that the conjunctions and oppositions of Jupiter and Saturn, which occurred at intervals of 9.93 years, might be the cause of sunspots, but when he found, that in some cases sunspot minima have coincided with this alignment of the two planets, while in others the alignment occurred as sunspot maxima, he dropped the matter.

However, Professor E. W. Brown of Yale was more persevering, for in 1900 he wrote a paper entitled "A Possible Explanation of the Sunspot Period," which was published in the *Monthly Notices* of the Royal Astronomical Society. Estimating the tide-raising force of Saturn to be approximately one-third that of Jupiter, Brown constructed a curve in which he had added Saturn's tide-making force to that of Jupiter when the two planets were in the same direction from the Sun (conjunction) and also when they were on opposite sides of the Sun (opposition), since there are always tides on both sides of a celestial body disturbed by gravity. He then subtracted Saturn's tide-making force from that of Jupiter when the two planets were at right angles (square) to each other.

Figure 5 shows the results of Brown's work for the period 1600-1900, its extension to 1936 by Dr. Ellsworth Huntington of Yale University, and to 1980 by this author. The middle portion of the chart, covering the period 1750-1900 shows 12 out of 14 cases (87½ percent) where the maximum disturbing force of the two planets coincided with sunspot peaks. For this period, Huntington calculated that the odds against a chance relationship were billions to one. This high degree of correlation continued during the period 1900-1980, which shows 7 out of 8 cases (87½ percent) of close relationship.

On December 25, 1900, Irish meterologist Hugh Clements wrote in *The Solution of the Sunspot Mystery* that sunspot frequency was due to the particular grouping of the planets and their tide-lifting power, which is greatest at an angle of 45 degrees, because at that angle the planet is pulling more or less at right angles to gravity and is therefore unopposed by it.

In 1902, English statistician William Digby wrote in *Natural Law in Terrestrial Phenomena*: "De la Rue found that when two powerful planets were in line, as seen from the Sun, the spotted area was much increased." Digby further stated: "If we take the grouping of the planets at a time of maximum sunspots, we find that they are usually on the same side of the sun as the earth. When they are not on one and the same side, they are placed in line exactly opposite to act in unison with another planet; or, not being in line, they are so situated on the other side of the sun as to produce their tide-raising power within an angle of 45 degrees from the earth or other powerful planet, and the spots are produced on the Sun's face next to us."

In an effort to answer the 1882 objections of

Professor Young that a) "It is very difficult to conceive in what manner the planets, so small and so remote, can possibly produce such profound and extensive disturbances on the sun, and b) no planet-lifted tides can directly account for sunspots." Digby combined the researches of de la Rue, Stewart and Loewy and those of Clements and concluded that "The planets Mercury, Venus, Mars, Earth, Jupiter and Saturn would each have at an angle of about 45 degrees considerable tide-lifting power; and the effect would be very much greater when two or more of them acted together at the maximum tide-lifting angle." Digby correctly predicted the sunspot maxima of 1905 from the positions of the aforementioned planets.

Papers on the subjects of planets and sunspots began to increase, for in 1907, English astronomer Mrs. A. S. D. Maunder showed in "An Apparent Influence of the Earth on the Numbers and Areas of Sunspots in the Cycle 1899-1901" that more sunspots were born on the side of the sun away from the earth than on the face of the sun toward the earth and that more sunspots appear to die on the face of the sun toward the earth than on the hemisphere turned away from the earth.

This was confirmed by Professor Arthur Schuster in 1911, who also found a similar relationship with respect to the planets, particularly in the case of Venus. He suggested that in a solar atmosphere in which the downward gravitational pull was nearly balanced by the outward pressure of light or by electrostatic repulsion, the pull of the planets might well raise tides of appreciable size. Schuster thus supported the Clements-Digby theory of the tide-producing power of planetary formations.

One of the most active exponents of the planetary theory of sunspot causation was American meteorologist H. H. Clayton. He was so impressed by Schuster's findings that he began his own investigation of the subject, covering Jupiter and Saturn for the period 1749-1913 and Mercury, Earth and Venus during 1856-1913. According to Huntington, Clayton in 1923 found that a double maximum of sunspots was formed for each planet during a sidereal revolution. He also found that the tide-raising power of Jupiter was two to three times that of the earth and that the observed amplitude of sunspots was more nearly the cube of three. Hence he concluded that spot production increased much more rapidly than the tidal force. Huntington therefore, suggested an electrostatic influence (vide Schuster). Huntington wrote: "The energy derived from the planets may be no more than that of pressing a button, which starts an explosion. When a little eddy is once started, the slight movement so generated may be reinforced by stresses due to the rapid cooling of the sun's outer layer or to the sun's varying rate of rotation at different latitudes."

The planetary theory received strong support evert behind the Iron Curtain, for in 1926, A. H. Tchijevsky, Professor of History, Moscow University, published a startling but little known paper, "Epidemic Catastrophes and Periodical Solar Activity" in which he showed a striking correlation between sunspot activity and the positions of Jupiter, Earth, Venus, and Mercury. He, however, stated: "One difficulty with all planetary theories for explaining the appearance of sunspots is that the tidal action of the planets is too small to be significant in causing eruptions in the solar atmosphere on gravitational grounds. If one were to suppose, however, that the planets are at different electric potentials, then there is perhaps a fresh basis for attack on the sunspot theory from the planetary viewpoint." When Tchijevsky's paper was published in the U.S.S.R., he was exiled to Siberia by Stalin, but was released when Khruschev came to power. But he died shortly thereafter in 1964.

In 1928, H. Voigt, a German investigator, constructed a chart in which the influences of Neptune, Uranus, Saturn, and Jupiter were combined to give a close resemblance to the sunspot curve from 1749 to 1942.

An important but little known contribution was that of Norwegian scientist K. G. Meldahl, who in 1932, published a provisional essay in Norwegian, and in 1938 an English translation, of "Tidal Forces in the Sun's Corona due to the Planets" of his researches during the period 1921-1938. He calculated the tidal forces of Mercury, Venus, Earth, Jupiter and Saturn to be as shown in Table 1.

**Table 1. Tidal Force of Planets (Meldahl)**

| Planet | Tidal Force |
|---|---|
| ☿ Mercury | 16.3-57.3 |
| ♀ Venus | 63.4-66.1 |
| ⊕ Earth | 28.9-31.9 |
| ♃ Jupiter | 58.9-78.7 |
| ♄ Saturn | 3.3-Approx. |
| ♂ Mars | 0.9-Approx. |

He then added the above forces vectorially to get the height of the force wave running around the equator, and produced a chart of the tidal forces for every eleventh day from 1923 to 1966. Meldahl concluded: "Variations in the Sun's corona are due to tidal action from the planets, consisting of positive and negative vertical forces, combined with tangential forces." The values shown in Table 1 are based on Sir Isaac Newton's classic Law of Gravitation, which states that the tidal force exerted by a planet upon the Sun varies directly as its mass is divided by the cube of its distance from the Sun. It therefore takes into account the effect of orbital eccentricities of the planets. He found that when Saturn, Jupiter, Earth and Venus were south of the Sun's equator, that their combined tidal force was at its peak.

In 1935, Clayton constructed a curve based on the mean periods of Saturn, Jupiter, Venus, Mercury and Earth, from which he very closely forecast the sunspot maximum of 1937. He took the mean period of pairs of these planets when they were at their maximum distance from Earth's equator, and found that the two greatest factors in sunspot production appeared to be the conjunction periods of Jupiter-Saturn and Venus-Mercury. He suggested in 1943 that the reason might be because Jupiter and Saturn are the two largest planets, while Mercury and Venus are the two nearest the Sun.

In 1936, California astronomer Fernando Sanford reported in "Influence of Planetary Configurations Upon the Frequency of Sunspots" that 1) "The sunspottedness was 76.9 percent greater when Venus and Earth were on opposite sides of the Sun than when they were on the same side; 2) there was an increase of 15 percent in sunspottedness when Mercury and Earth were on opposite sides of the Sun; 3) the mean value of the sunspot numbers when Venus and Mercury were on opposite sides of the Sun was 24.9 percent greater than when they were on the same side; 4) the observed spottedness when Venus and Mercury were at an angular separation of 90 degrees was 8.8 percent greater than when they were on the same side of the Sun."

In 1940, Professor William A. Luby, writing in *Popular Astronomy,* advanced the theory that the action of the planets was by precessional pull on the equator of an oblate Sun rather than by tidal action. After discussing the small values of tidal pulls of the planets, Professor Luby states: "However, precessional action of a planet on the Sun is enormously greater than is tidal action and its disturbance of solar equilibrium is correspondingly large." This caused Clayton to reexamine his 1923 findings and he reported in 1941 that "both for the Earth and for Venus the maximum of sunspots in a sidereal revolution is surprisingly close to that called for by Professor Luby's theory." In the case of Venus, the period studied covered the 104 years from 1837 to 1940, while in the case of Earth it was the 100 years from 1838 to 1937. Sunspot maxima occurred when the two celestial bodies were at their greatest distance from the plane of the solar equator.

In 1943, Clayton reported: "The important periods in spot formation are not the individual planets, but the conjunction of the planets when at or near their greatest distance above or below the plane the Sun's equator. The two largest factors in spot production appear to be the conjunction period of Jupiter and Saturn (vide Brown); and the conjunction period of Venus and Mercury when they are at their points of greatest departure from the plane of the Sun's equator."

In 1946, American meteorologist Maxwell O. Johnson, in *Correlation of Cycles in Weather, Solar Activity, Geomagnetic Values and Planetary Configurations,* expressed views similar to those of Tchijevsky 20 years earlier, for he stated: "In our analysis of sunspot numbers, all the main periodicities are found correlated with the synodic periods of the major planets. These striking correlations indicate that variations in solar activity, as indicated by sunspot numbers, are influenced by planetary configurations. *These planetary influences cannot be gravitational but must be magnetic or electrical in character.* If the planets are electrically charged, their tidal like forces of attraction or repulsion at the Sun might cause periodic variations in sunspots correlating with their synodic periods and furnish a better explanation than a purely magnetic theory. Periodicities in solar radiation, weather, and geomagnetic data also appear correlated with periodicities in sunsppts and planetary configurations. Gravitational forces may play a more important part in periodicities in solar radiation than they do in sunspot numbers."

Johnson found a repressing tidal-like influence on sunspots when Saturn was in opposition or conjunction with Uranus, Neptune, or Pluto. Coulomb's Law states that the force between electrostatic charges is directly proportional to the magnitude of each charge and inversely proportional to the square of their separation. Johnson assumed that Saturn-Uranus, Saturn-Neptune, and Saturn-Pluto had about equal charges; that their relative distances from the Sun are 1, 1.5, and 2, and that their maximum effect was therefore about 80, 35, and 20 in sunspot numbers.

**Table 2. Stetson's Tidal Force of Planets.**

| *Planets* | *Tidal Force* |
|---|---|
| ♀ Mercury | 1.10 |
| ♀ Venus | 2.11 |
| ⊕ Earth | 1.00 |
| ♂ Mars | 0.03 |
| ♃ Jupiter | 2.17 |
| ♄ Saturn | 0.11 |
| ♅ Uranus | 0.02 |

In 1947, American Astronomer H. T. Stetson, in *Sunspots in Action,* stated: "Kr. Birkeland made an exhaustive study of the sunspot curve and the effects of Jupiter, Earth, and Venus. In this way, he could account not only for many of the major maxima of sunspots, but also for many of the minor fluctuations." Stetson calculated the values for the tidal effect of the planets as seen in Table 2.

Stetson's values are based on Sir Isaac Newton's Law of Gravitation, which states that the tide-raising force varies directly as the mass of the planet and inversely as the cube of its distance from the Sun (vide Meldahl). He stated: "It is possible that even the slight tide-raising forces of the planets could in the course of time set up a major oscillation in the Sun's atmosphere very much the way in which synchonized footsteps of a regiment may set a steel bridge asway. The composite tidal wave at any moment would therefore depend upon the positions of the planets in respect to one another and to the Sun."

Stetson reproduced a curve (Figure 6) prepared by Clayton, which involved seven planets. Seeking out the times when a pair of planets were at their maximum distance from the Sun's equator as an epoch, Clayton utilized the mean periods of the planets in constructing a curve which had a remarkable coincidence with the curve of sunspot numbers from 1840 to 1945. The predicted curve indicated that the next sunspot peak would come in 1948; it actually came in 1947. Similarly, the low came in 1954 instead of in 1955.

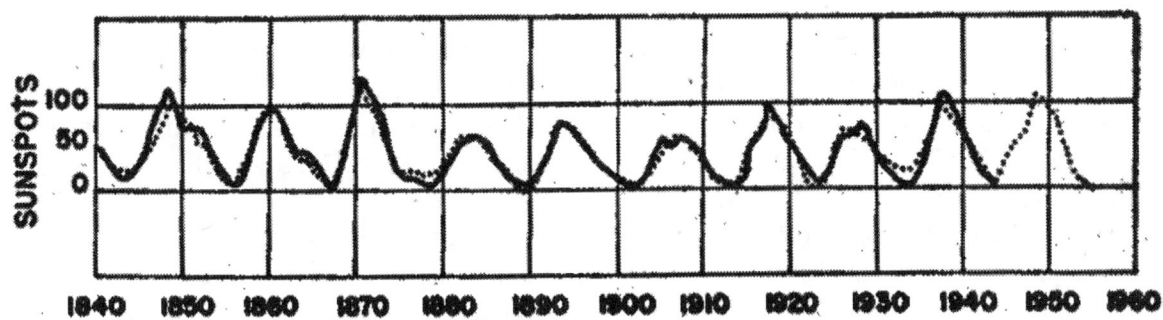

Predicted curve of sunspot numbers based on planetary positions, as depicted by H.H. Clayton. Dotted curve=predicted. Full-line curve =observed

*Figure 6. Clayton's Sunspot Curve.*

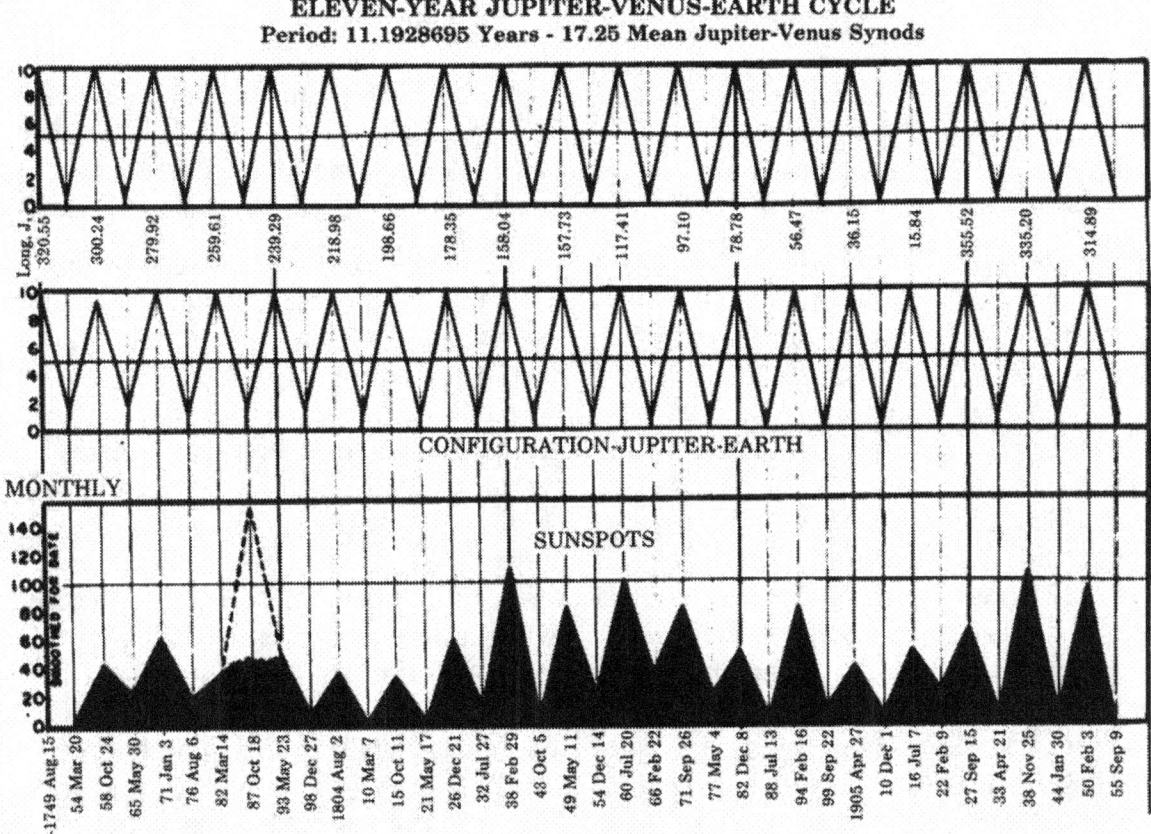

The relation between the recurrent 90° and 45° configuration patterns at 11.192694 year intervals along with smoothed monthly sunspots for phase dates during the period of record starting in 1749 are shown graphically.

A consistent relation is evident except in the cycle maximum of 1787 which may represent an error in the sunspot record.

*Figure 7. Bollinger's Planet-Sunspot Correlations.*

In 1953, Professor C. J. Bollinger of the University of Oklahoma, in *Atlas of Planetary Solar Climate,* constructed a curve (Figure 7) showing a consistent relation between the 11.19 year sunspot cycle and a similar cycle formed by the 0, 45, and 90 degree configurations of Jupiter-Venus-Earth for the period 1749-1955. (It will be recalled that in 1867, Professor Norton of Yale stated: "The planets which exercise the greatest influence are Jupiter and Venus").

Bollinger stated: "The Solar System viewed in the tradition of Copernicius, Kepler, Newton, Euler, and Laplace is a heliocentric, perpetual motion mechanism, in which it is reasonable to assume that the planets, through their gravitational attractions on the Sun, cause direct equilibrium Sun-tides analogous to the tides in the oceans and atmosphere caused by the gravitational attraction of the Moon and Sun. Planetary Sun-tide indicies, calculated according to generally accepted mechanical principles, have been found to vary up to 30 percent above and below mean values, and hence should influence the pressure and stability of the solar gasses and hence radiation and the climates of the planets.

"Eccentricity of the planetary orbits make orientation as well as degree of alignment important. Jupiter and Venus, the two planets having the strongest tide forces, 2.233 and 2.1333 respectively in a system where the tide force of Earth at mean distance equals 1.00, have recurrent alignment with the Sun at a little under four months (118.4 days average). The phases of this fundamental cycle recur about 9½ days earlier on successive years. Venus and Earth have recurrent orientation alignment at 4-year intervals. At 12-year intervals Earth and Venus have approximately recurrent orientation and alignment with Jupiter. At 83-year intervals Jupiter, Venus and Earth have almost precise recurrent orientation and alignment. At 59-year intervals, Mercury and Saturn, both with very eccentric orbits and with apse lines only 15 degrees apart, add strength to the fundamental Jupiter-Venus-Earth Sun-tide cycle."

In the October 1968 issue of *Cycles,* E. R. Dewey, Vice Chairman, The Foundation for the Study of Cycles, wrote a most important article, "A Key to Sunspot-Planetary Relationship," in which he stated: "We have discovered what seems to be the long sought key to planetary-sunspot relationships. The key is that the planets relate to the double (22.22 year) sunspot cycle instead of to the ordinary (11.11 year) sunspot cycle." (Discovered by Hale in 1912.)

Dewey stated: "A heliocentric (sun-centered) planetary conjunction occurs when, as seen from the Sun, any two planets line up with each other in the same celestial longitude—the same vertical plane. The 'period' of these conjunctions (called the synodic period) is the average time interval between successive conjunctions of the same two planets. As there are nine planets, and as each planet has conjunctions with each of the other planets, there are 36 synodic periods: Mercury and Venus, Mercury and Earth, Mercury and Mars, Mercury and Jupiter, etc., Venus and Earth, Venus and Mars, Venus and Jupiter, etc.

"Sunspots increase and decrease in waves that range from 7 to 17 years in length, but which have a period (average wave length of 11.11 years). Sunspots normally occur in pairs. Sunspots are magnetized. In one wave of the sunspot cycles, positive spots will lead in the Sun's Northern Hemisphere; negative spots will lead in the Sun's Southern Hemisphere. On the next wave, this situation is reversed: negative spots will lead in the Northern Hemisphere, positive spots will lead in the Southern Hemisphere. Thus it takes two sunspot waves or 'cycles,' as they are generally called, for the behavior to come around again to the place of beginning. The period of the double sunspot cycle is thus 22.22 years. This reversal of leading spots led C. N. Anderson in 1939 to assign negative values to the sunspot number in alternate sunspot cycles."

Figure 8, Part 1 shows the conventional 11.11 year sunspot cycle; Part 2 shows the Dou-

### Table 3. Planetary Periods vs Sunspots.

| Planets | Average Synodic Period | Indicated Sunspot Length | Difference in Unit Fractions |
|---|---|---|---|
| Uranus & Pluto | 126.95 yrs. | 123.72 yrs. | 0.055 |
| Saturn & Uranus | 45.36 yrs. | 45.47 yrs. | 0.014 |
| Jupiter & Saturn | 19.86 yrs. | 19.78 yrs. | 0.054 |
| Jupiter & Uranus | 13.81 yrs. | 13.78 yrs. | 0.041 |
| Jupiter & Pluto | 12.46 yrs. | 12.40 yrs. | 0.103 |

ble Sunspot Cycle (22.22 years) in which alternate cycles of Part 1 are reversed; Part 3 shows the Double Sunspot Cycle, less the 22.22 year cycle and with excessive values minimized, indicating a "clear, dominant, rhythmic cycle of about 18 years (exact length seemingly about 17.93 or 17.94 years)." Appendix 2 shows the results of a "Systematic Period Reconnaissance of Sunspot Numbers 1700-1965" made by Dewey. (A systematic period reconnaissance consists of fitting to the data a variety of cycles to see which cycles are strongest, on the average, and thus more likely to be the result of real cyclic forces.)

The five most important synodic periods which correspond dramatically to one or another of the 15 periods within the range of 12 to 133 years are shown in Table 3.

The correspondences are very close. They come within .055, .014, .054, .041, and .103 unit fractions respectively, of actual identity.

Could such correspondence come about by chance? Yes, but not easily.

In 1969, Dr. J. B. Blizard, Research Physisist, University of Denver, reported: "Long-range prediction of solar activity has now become possible. Proton events have been shown to be related to the positions of Mercury, Venus, Earth and Jupiter, which possibly affect the tidal force on the Sun or the rate of change of solar acceleration in an inertial frame of reference. The lack of a clear explanation at this time of how planet positions affect solar activity does not detract from the predictive value of such a method."

The latest development of the planetary theory of sunspot formation was reported in the November 10, 1972 issue of the international scientific journal *Nature*, by K. D. Wood of Aerospace Engineering Sciences, University of Colorado, Boulder, Colorado. Wood took Mercury, Venus, Earth and Jupiter to be the "tidal planets" and presented curves (Figure 9) showing a close relation between the average cycle lengths of sunspots at 11.05 years with planetary tides of 11.08 years for the period 1800-2000. The peaks of the next two sunspot cycles are forecast to occur in 1982.0 and 1993.4, with a "possible error of substantially less than one year." Appendix 3 shows tables comparing sunspot cycle peak dates with dates of peak planetary tidal fluctuation.

The January/February 1973 issue of *The Sciences*, published by the prestigious New York Academy of Sciences, carried the following remarkable statement concerning Woods:

"The astrological fuss about planetary conjunctions, oppositions, house and phases has always roused scientists' ire, but this negative thinking may have to be reviewed. A University of Colorado space scientist has just related the 11.1 year cycle of sunspot activity to the positions of planets. K. D. Wood points out in *Nature* for November 10 that Mercury, Venus, Earth and Jupiter all raise substantial tides on the sun. Calculating presumed variations in solar surface tides from known planetary positions since 1750, he compared them with

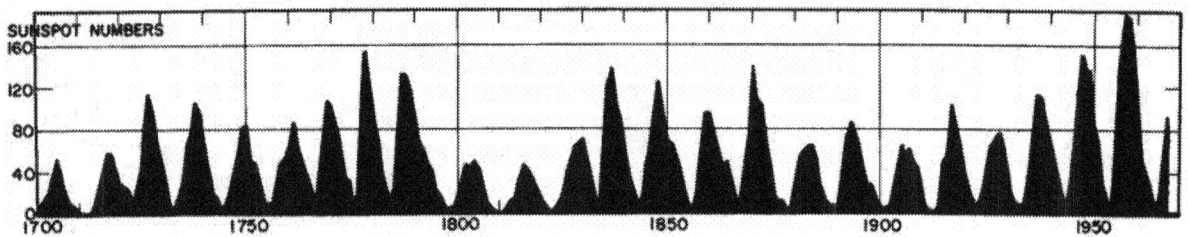

Part 1: SUNSPOT NUMBERS, BY YEARS, 1700-1967

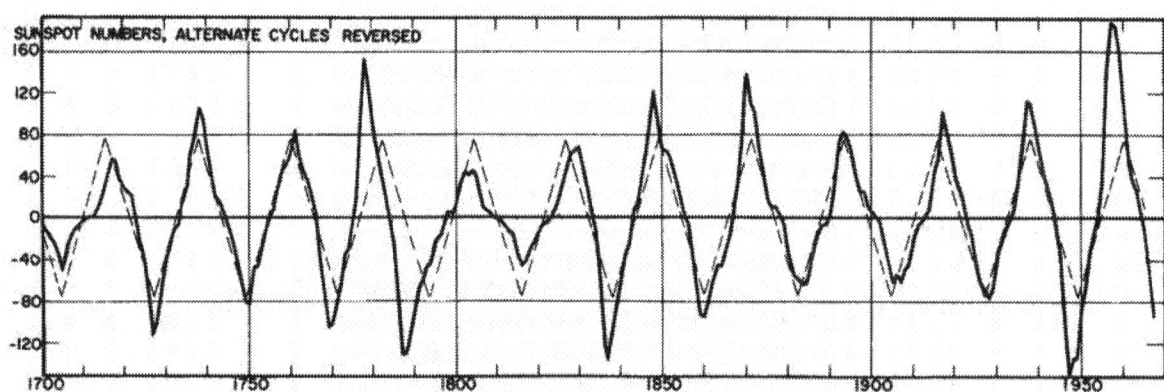

Part 2: THE DOUBLE SUNSPOT CYCLE
Sunspot Numbers, Alternate Cycles Reversed, by Years, 1700-1967, Together with the ideal 22.22-Year Cycle

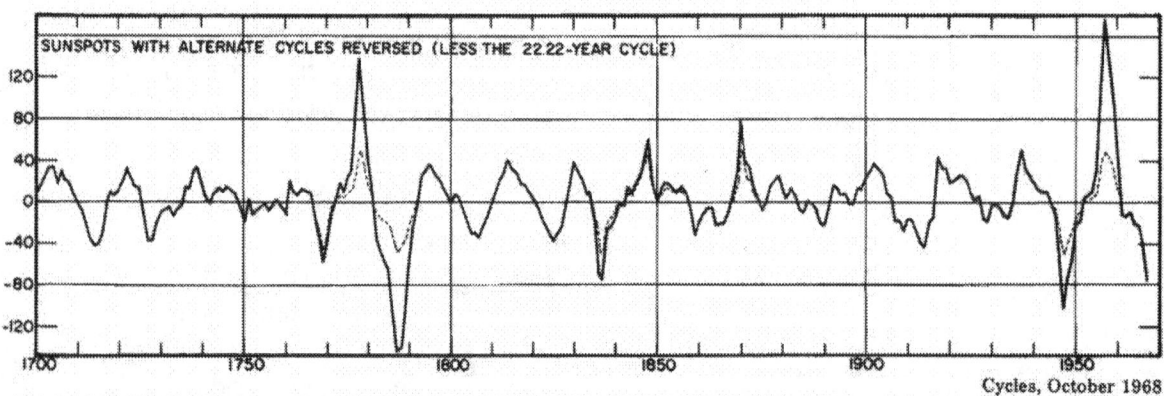

Cycles, October 1968

Part 3. THE DOUBLE SUNSPOT CYCLE LESS THE 22.22-YEAR CYCLE AND WITH EXCESSIVE VALUES MINIMIZED

*Figure 8. Dewey's Sunspot Cycles.*

Waldmeier's historical index of sunspot eruptions, finding a very close correlation between tidal ebb and flow and date of peak and quiescent sunspot activity. In a minority of cycles, sunspots lag behind the tides by several years, but this fact may indicate nontidal factors.

*"Sunspots are known to interfere with radio transmissions through the ionosphere; if they also affect other forms of Earthly behavior, astrologers would have an underpinning to their occult science."*

We shall discuss several "other forms of Earthly behavior" affected by solar activity in the following chapter.

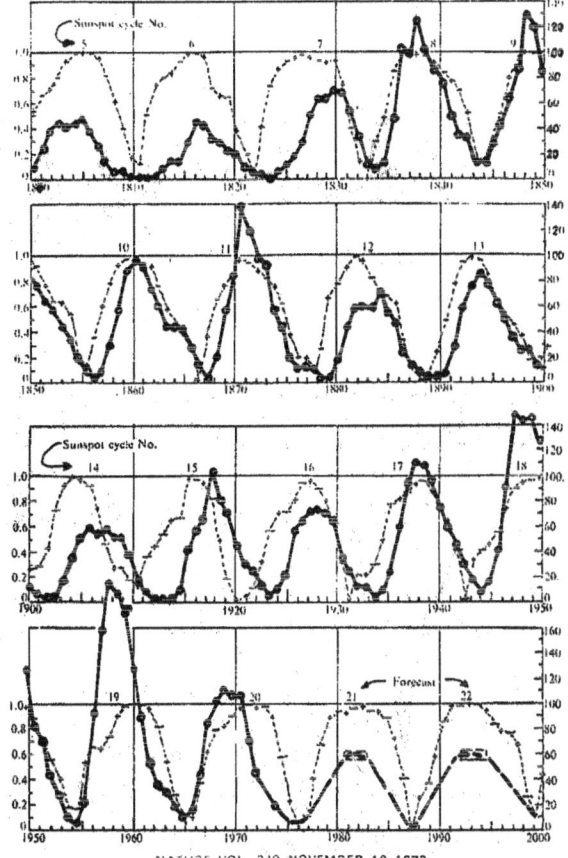

KEY:

Solid Line = Observed Sunspot Cycle
Dotted Line = Calculated Earth-Venus-Jupiter Tidal Wave
Dashed Line = Forecast for Sunspot Cycles 21 & 22

*Figure 9. Wood's Planet-Sunspot Correlations.*

## Chapter 4

# Terrestrial Effects of Solar Activity

### On Agriculture and Climatology

We have learned from Chapter 2 that in 1801 the famous English astronomer Sir William Herschel had found a correlation between sunspot activity and the size of the harvests in England during the years 1650-1800. He concluded that in periods with little or no sunspots, wheat was scarce and hence prices were high; conversely, in periods of abundant sunspots, crops were abundant and prices were low. He also found that high temperatures were associated with abundant sunspots and low temperatures with low sunspots.

Swiss astronomer Rudolph Wolf reported in 1852, from an examination of the *Chronicles of Zurich* from A.D. 1000 to 2000, that "years rich in solar spots are in general drier and more fruitful than those of an opposite character, while the latter are wetter and more stormy than the former." He also found that during years of maximum sunspots there have been an average of six to eight violent hurricanes per year, while the average number during sunspot minima was only one or two per year.

English astronomer N. R. Pogson, in 1858, stated that a relationship existed between sunspot phenomena and atmospheric conditions on the earth, as evidenced by observations made in equatorial regions. In a report to the Indian Famine Commission of 1878-79, Pogson traced an intimate connection between sunspot frequency, rainfall and grain prices in Madras, India.

In 1875, English economist William Stanley Jevons, following the trail blazed by Sir William Herschel in 1801, announced a correlation in the fluctuations in the prices of wheat, barley, oats, beans, peas, vetches, and rye with an 11.11 year sunspot cycle. But in 1878, he withdrew his former paper and proposed a 10.43 year cycle in crops as being related to a 10.45 year sunspot cycle.

In *Nature*, May 17, 1877, Professor Arthur Schuster of Owens College, England pointed out that good wine years in Germany corresponded closely with the years of minimum sunspots.

In 1878, noted English astronomer Sir Norman Lockyer also traced a relationship between sunspots and rainfall in southern India.

In 1902, E. B. Garriott, Forecaster in Chief, U. S. Government, stated: "The Sun's magnetic influence, stretching out and embracing the earth, varies the earth's magnetism and gives rise to weather changes."

In 1922, noted English economist. Sir William H. Beveridge stated that many regular, periodic movements affecting weather and crops may be accounted for through similar oscillations on the Sun, Moon, or even the planets.

American meteorologist H. H. Clayton, in *World Weather* (1923), stated: "The irregular changes known as the weather result chiefly, if not entirely, from the irregular changes in solar radiation." Clayton found that in equatorial regions a) atmospheric pressure was less at sunspot maxima than at sunspot minima, and b) temperatures were distinctly lower during sunspot maxima and higher at sunspot minima. In the Western Hemisphere, atmospheric pressure was higher at sunspot maxima than at sunspot minima, while temperatures were lower during sunspot maxima than at sunspot minima.

Professor A. E. Douglas of the University of Arizona, in *Climatic Cycles and Tree Growth* (1928), found a definite correlation between sunspots and weather from a lifetime study of tree rings. Not only has he found periods of sunspots related to periods of abundant or deficient moisture in the Southwest, which in the case of the Sequoias goes back 3,200 years, but he has found similar cycles of rainfall and drought dating back to the Egyptian pharaohs.

In *Monthly Weather Review* (April 1933), American meteorologist H. W. Clough stated that 11-, 37-, 83-, and 300-year sunspot cycles were apparent in auroral data, frequency of severe winters, frequency of Chinese earthquakes, flood and low stages of the Nile, tree growth in Arizona and California, and wheat prices in England over a period of 1,400 years. He concluded: "These consistent variations in the logs of the meteorological events and their persistency for 1,500 years afford additional proof of the reality of both solar and meteorological periods."

In that same year, Professor C. J. Fullmer of Syracuse University, in *The Latitude Shift of the Storm Track in the 11-year Solar Period* (1933), found from a study of the records extending from 1883 to 1913 that 40 percent more storms passed over the fundamental storm track of North America during sunspot maxima than at sunspot minima.

Clayton, in *Solar Relations to Weather* (1943), stated: "Weather changes are found to be closely related to changes taking place on the surface of the Sun, such as sunspots, faculae and flocculi. These are found to be related to changes in solar radiation outside our atmosphere, particularly to changes in the amount of radiant energy in the ultraviolet and blue end of the solar spectrum. If it proves correct that the sunspot period is formed by the combined action of planetary periods, and that the periods found in solar-constant changes are also related to planetary periods, then these periods can be projected indefinitely into the future, and all the terrestrial relationship in magnetic, electric, and meteorological effects can be foretold for any desired epoch." He concluded that "in general the temperature in winter in continental interiors oscillated inversely with sunspots. In summer, the relation was not so well marked, but, except in the 11-year period, it tended to oscillate with the sunspot values. The amplitude of the oscillation in sunspots was greatest with the 11-year period, but in temperature and amplitude of oscillation, was greater with an 8-year period. This fact is important because it now appears that the 11-year period in the solar constant is not so important as are the oscillations of shorter periods."

Professor Ellsworth Huntington of Yale University, in *Mainsprings of Civilization* (1945), stated: "Cyclonic storms represent the effect of the electro-magnetic field of the Sun and the solar system superposed upon the still greater effect of the Sun's heat."

M. O. Johnson, in *Correlation of Cycles in Weather, Solar Activity, Geomagnetic Values, and Planetary Configurations* (1946), stated: "There appears fairly good correlation between the synodic periods of the major planets and many of the longer term trends in weather found by different investigators."

Dr. C. G. Abbott of the Smithsonian Institution, Washington, D.C., in *The Scientific Monthly* (March 1946), stated: "It is well known that sunspots are like machine guns, in that they bombard space, including, of course, the earth, with electric ions. This bombardment is very active at times of maximum numbers of sunspots. It is also well known that electric ions, which in our atmosphere, besides reflecting radio waves around the earth so that we get programs from great distances, in addition act as centers of condensation for the water vapors of the atmosphere and so promote cloudiness, and doubtless also rain. Clouds, of course, also alter temperatures. So in this way, the 11⅓-year sunspot cycle becomes a weather cycle."

H. P. Gillette, in *Weather Cycles and their Causes* (June 1946), stated: "Weather disturbances are caused by influxes of solar electrons in five ways: 1) by generation of atmospheric currents in accordance with Faraday's principle of magnetic rotation of electric currents; 2) by the tendency of electrons to cause condensation of atmospheric moisture in accordance with Wilson's principle; 3) by increased windiness, which increases oceanic evaporation and rainfall; 4) by increased evaporation due to increased electronic charge of water; 5) by reduced influx of solar heat, due to reflection of radiant waves by atmospheric electrons, and to absorption and scattering by atmospheric moisture."

H. T. Stetson, in *Sunspots in Action* (1947), stated: "With the accumulation of increasing evidence of connections between solar activity and the earth, even conservative meteorologists are now conceding the possibility that changes in solar radiation may be ultimately connected with changes in weather patterns."

Dr. W. F. Petersen, in *Man, Weather, Sun* (1947), stated: "Changes in the atmosphere in which we exist are governed by the electronic impact on the 'ionic shells' which surround our earth; this changing electronic impact is in turn conditioned by cyclonic disturbances on the sun's surface (sunspots); these sun-storms are periodic and these periodicities, or cyclic phenomena, are possibly related to stresses associated with planetary motion and position."

S. W. Wood, in the *Illinois Engineer* of March 1949, stated that solar changes directly affect our weather and are the underlying fundamental cause of floods, droughts, and other violent meteorological phenomena, and that the gravitational or tidal pull of the planets is a primary cause in the formation of sunspots and solar prominences.

Abbot climaxed 50 years of solar research, in *Periods Related to 273 Months or 22¾ Years* (1956), wherein he listed 64 periodicities in the variation of the measurements of the solar constant of radiation conducted almost daily during the past 30 years by the Smithsonian Astrophysical Observatory. These periodicities are all, within one percent, exact submultiples of 273 months, which is close to the master sunspot cycle discovered by Dr. G. E. Hale, who in 1908 first gave observational proof of the electromagnetic nature of sunspots. In 1912, the polarities of the sunspot groups were found by Hale to be the reverse of those found in the previous cycle. Thus, the true sunspot cycle is now considered to be twice the 11.11 year period, or 22-23 years.

Abbott found that as many as 23 of the foregoing periodicities were present in periodic weather changes. By separately tabulating periods of high and low Wolf numbers of sunspots (above and below 20), dividing the year into three seasons, making allowances for secular changing conditions, and using 5-month smoothed running means of monthly records of temperature and precipitation tabulated in *World Weather Records* and subsequent U.S. Weather Bureau records, Abbot has made some remarkably accurate long-range weather forecasts.

Abbot stated in *Sixty Year Weather Forecasts* (1955): "I feel that if meteorologists could accept these proofs, governments would feel justified in supporting similar studies of temperature and precipitation at numerous stations within their borders. From such studies, maps of expected weather conditions for many years in advance could be drawn. Such maps, if found to give general conditions with reasonable approximation, would evidently be of great value for many industries. *The only fly in the ointment seems to be that tremendous disturbances of the atmosphere, such as sometimes are caused by volcanoes, and also by profuse use of powerful bombs, in war and in tests, may spoil forecasts of this ambitious type.*"

Although the relationship between sunspots and agriculture was first pointed out by Sir William Herschel as early as 1801, the Russians apparently are only beginning to catch up with the free world, for the August 20, 1966 issue of *Science News* reported that "Sunspots, known for playing havoc with radio transmissions, also affect farm prices, a Russian scientist believes. The harvest of agricultural produce, and thus farm product prices, depend on solar activity, according to V. A. Dolotov of the Central Soil Science Museum, Moscow. Studying harvest charts of a number of crops, he discovered that once in 11 years there is a drop in the harvest, resulting in a rise in the price of farm produce. According to Mr. Dolotov, this decline is connected with the 11-year cycle of maximum sunspot activity. The increased solar emissions to some degree violate the photosynthesis in plants, unfavorably influencing their development."

## Terrestrial Effects of Solar Activity in Science

Astronomers seem to be agreed that the following solar and terrestrial relationship may be considered well established:

1. There is a close parallelism between sunspot and terrestrial magnetic activity.

2. There is a correspondence between sunspots and the frequency of auroras similar to that between sunspots and terrestrial magnetic activity.

3. The amount of ultraviolet radiation from the Sun and the potential gradient of the earth vary with the sunspot cycle.

4. The earth's magnetic field is most persistently disturbed during March and September, when the Sun crosses the equator.

5. Moderate magnetic disturbances tend to recur at 27-day intervals.

6. Brilliant flares, which are frequently seen near large active spot groups of irregular magnetic polarity, occur simultaneously with sudden fade-outs in high frequency radio transmission over the daylight side of the earth.

7. Magnetic storms may occur on days without visible sunspots.

The close correlation between sunspot activity and variations in Earth's magnetism was independently established as early as 1850-1852 by John Lamont of Munich, Germany; Edward Sabine of London, England; Alfred Gautier of Geneva, Switzerland; and Rudolf Wolf of Berne, Switzerland,

Stetson in 1947 concluded from a comparison of sunspot and magnetic activity between 1850 and 1945 that "The close correlation of changes in the earth's magnetism with the coming and going of sunspots is one of the best established connections between sunspots and the earth that science knows." Nevertheless, Professor G. Abetti, in *The Sun* (1957), cautions: "This is clearly shown when ANNUAL averages are used, but becomes confused in the monthly averages and disappears in the daily." Abetti credits G. B. Donati as the first to state that auroras must be dependent on causes located in the Sun, based on the latter's study of the great aurora of February 4-5, 1872.

## Effects of Solar Activity on Telegraph, Submarine and Telephone Lines

Associated with sunspots are solar flares, complex patterns of white-hot gaseous filaments in the Sun's atmosphere that suddenly blaze up to 10 times normal brilliancy in hydrogen light. They reach their maximum intensity 5 or 10 minutes after their first appearance and then slowly decay in the next hour or 2. They may cover an area of up to 1,000 million square miles of the Sun's atmosphere. Their importance derives not only from their significance in solar physics but also from the effects which they produce on earth.

The first recorded example of a direct influence of a solar event upon man's technology occurred during one of the most remarkable and unusual magnetic storms on record—that of August 28-September 7, 1859. On September 1, 1859, the English astronomers R. C. Carrington and R. Hodgson, independently and simultaneously observed the eruption of a classic white flare above a large group of sunspots. Chapman and Bartels, in *Geomagnetism* (1940), quoted Dr. Balfour Stewart of the Kew Observatory, London, England, as follows:

"During the latter part of August and the beginning of September 1859, auroral displays of almost unprecedented magnificence were observed very widely throughout our globe, accompanied (as is invariably the case) with excessive disturbances of the magnetic needle ... At the time of the occurrence a very large spot might have been observed on the disk of our luminary.... In not a few instances *telegraphic communication* was interrupted, owing to the current produced in the wires; and in some cases this proved so powerful that it was used instead of the ordinary current, the batteries being cut off and the wires simply connected with the earth.... We have two distinct well-marked disturbances, each commencing abruptly and ending gradually ... on the evening of August 28, and on the early morning of September 2. They correspond in time to the two great auroral displays."

As late as 1955, the appearance of solar flares was considered to be unpredictable by no less an authority than Dr. M. A. Ellison, Principal Scientific Officer, Royal Observatory, Edinburgh, Scotland. But, 100 years after the first solar flare was observed in England, the author predicted in a letter to C. W. Franklin, Chief Electrical Engineer of Con-Edison, that there would be a severe magnetic storm during the weekend of August 28, 1959, which would greatly increase the number of electrical failures in the high voltage underground cable system of the Consolidated Edison Company of New York. Cable failures during that period were *three* times normal, but since they occurred over a weekend (when the load on the cables was light) the public was not inconvenienced. The heliocentric longitude of the planets during the 1859 and 1959 disturbances are shown in Figures 10a and 10b.

The negative aspects of the planets in heliocentric longitude are shown in Table 4.

Furthermore, on May 15, 1967, Rex Pay, in *Technology Week* magazine, described an electronic-computer technique for predicting solar flares from the gravitational effects of planets developed in 1963 by Dr. Richard Head, Principal Scientist, Electronic Research Center, NASA, Cambridge, Massachusetts. The article stated: "Principal influences on the rate of change of the gravitational field at the solar surface are the planets. Although their gravitational effects are many orders of magnitude less than that of the Sun itself, the time rate of change of

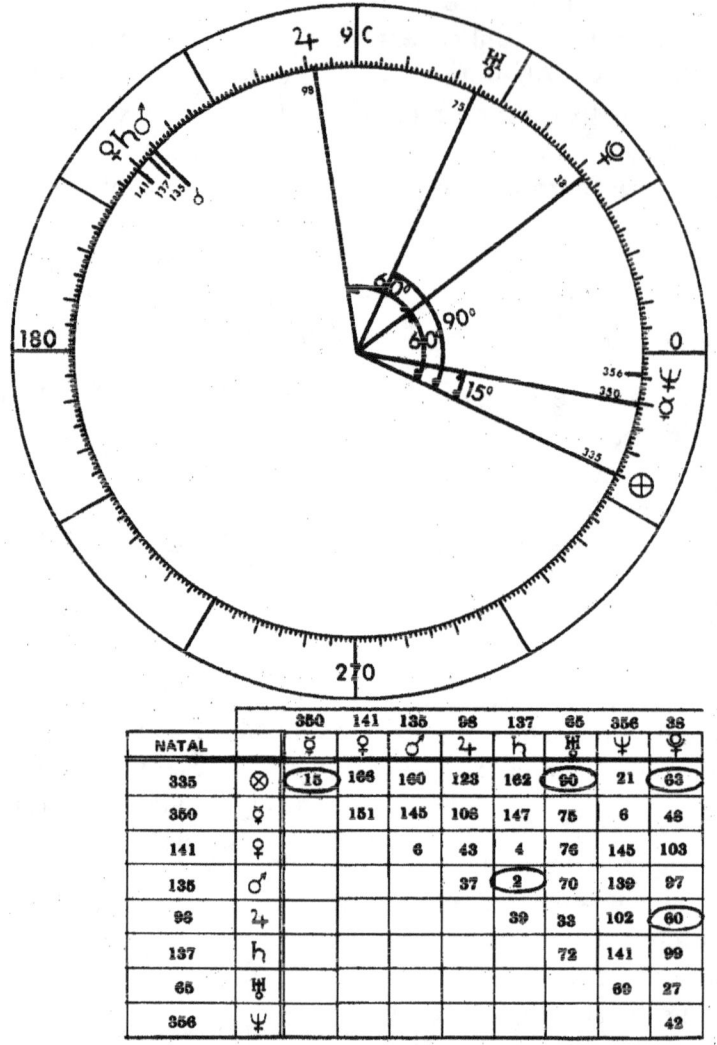

*Figure 10a. Planetary Pattern During August 28, 1859 Magnetic Storm (Heliocentric).*

### Table 4. Heliocentric Longitude of Planets During 1859 and 1959 Storms.

*Aug. 28, 1859*
Mars 0° Saturn
Earth 90° Uranus
*Earth, Jupiter,
   Pluto 60° apart
Earth 15° Mercury

*Aug. 28, 1959*
Mars 90° Saturn
Earth 180° Pluto
Jupiter 90° Earth
   and Pluto
*Earth, Saturn,
   Neptune,
   Pluto 60° apart

* J. H. Nelson in 1951 had reported that 3 or more planets 60° apart, coupled with other planets under adverse aspects were usually associated with magnetic disturbances.

the resultant planetary field vector appears to have some triggering effect on the release of solar flares. It appears, therefore, that solar flares can be predicted from the positions of the planets."

On January 16, 1968, Dr. Head showed the Society for the Investigation of Recurring Events a chart showing the resultant gravitational force vector upon the Sun due to Jupiter and Saturn for the period 1954-64. A second chart showed a curve representing the resultant due to Saturn, Jupiter, Earth, and Venus superimposed upon the Jupiter-Saturn curve. A third chart included the effect of Mercury added to

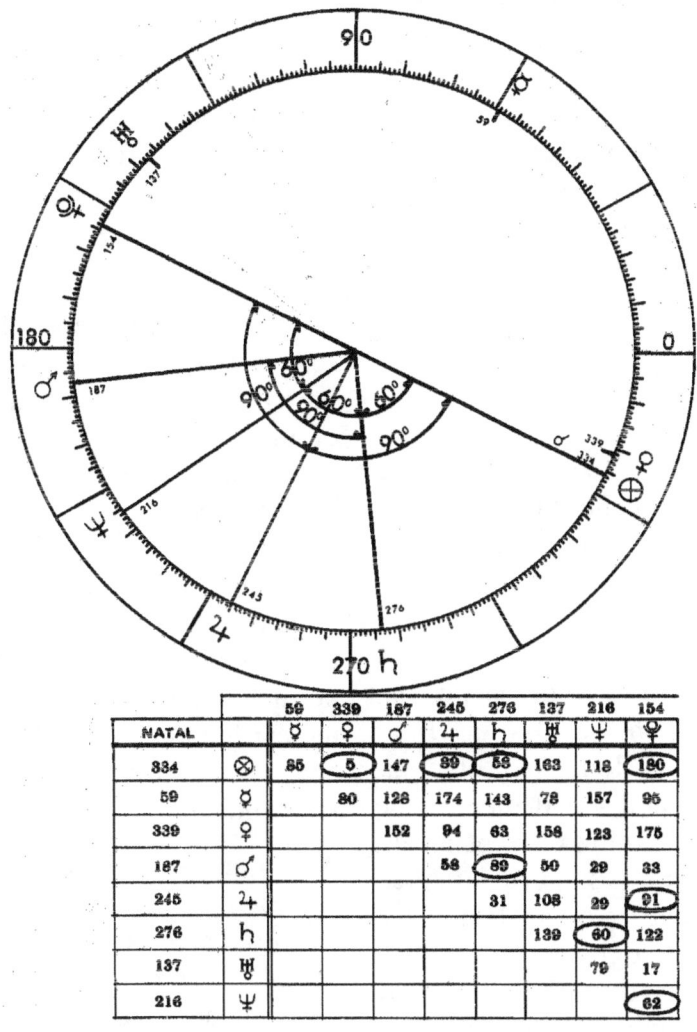

*Figure 10b. Planetary Pattern During Predicted Magnetic Storm of August 28, 1959 (Heliocentric).*

those of Saturn, Jupiter, Earth and Venus. Clearly marked near the peaks of these curves were numerous solar events, such as solar flares of varying degrees of magnitude. Dr. Head stated that he had predicted for the operations staff of Lunar Orbiter 1 the intense proton storm occurring at the end of August 1966. The prediction, made one week in advance, was only three hours away from the actual flare time and occurred exactly at the predicted Sun's latitude and only 3 degrees away from the predicted Sun's longitude. Dr. Head stated that he had subsequently made long-range predictions of solar flare occurrences through the year 1970.

With the advent of transoceanic submarine telegraph cables and transcontinental overhead telegraph lines, numerous instances of interference from magnetic storms have been recorded. To prevent burning out the instruments at the terminals of submarine telegraph cables, about 100-300 miles of the shore ends of the cables were made in the form of a twisted pair, with one conductor being bonded to the steel armor wire at its seaward end. Normally, transoceanic telegraph cables have only one conductor, but in certain instances, either or both of the shore ends were made up with one or more extra conductors to carry operating ground connections out to sea, to dissipate any currents induced in the steel wire armor by magnetic storms. This method, known as a "sea-earth" was first used on the 4,400-mile submarine cable laid in 1900 by the German Atlantic Telegraph Company from Borkum, Germany to New York City via Fayal, Azores Islands. In recent years submarine cables have been made with a non-metallic sheath instead of with wire armor, thus eliminating the problem of induced currents. To prevent interference with the operation of long distance overhead land telegraph lines, relay station, lightning arresters and similar devices have had to be installed.

The first transatlantic telephone cable was designed to withstand three times the maximum induced voltage (1,000 volts) ever recorded on the transatlantic telegraph cables during a magnetic storm. But the design voltage—3,000 volts—was almost reached during one of the greatest magnetic storms ever recorded, i.e., that of February 10, 1958. On that day the Earth moved into a gigantic cloud of solar gas 46,000,000 miles long and 4,000 miles wide, traveling at a speed of 875 miles per second, as a result of which the Earth was sprayed with electrified or ionized hydrogen atoms. Great rivers of electricity flowed through the crust of the Earth and displays of the Northern Lights or Aurora were seen in our southern states and as far south as Cuba. At 9:02 p.m., the Earth current potential between Europe and North America, as indicated by the North Atlantic Telephone cable, reached a maximum of 2650 volts. At 9:09 p.m. the current under the Atlantic reached the same potential, but in the opposite direction. At 5:00 p.m., February 11, the auroral display reached its maximum, extending 6,000 miles east to west, 250 miles north to south, and from 150 to 500 miles above the Earth.

At the time, Explorer I, the first of the U. S. earth satellites, launched only 10 days earlier, was in orbit. Its Geiger counter "choked" into silence at the high part of its path, but at the low portion of its orbit, which dipped to an elevation of 219 miles, it reported a three-fold increase in radiation when the solar cloud hit. The observations indicated that the cloud, born of a two-hour eruption on the Sun, had taken 24 hours to stream past the Earth. The effects lasted long afterwards, for on February 16, the rays were back to only 81.6 per cent of their original intensity.

## Effects of Solar Activity on Radio Transmission

The development of radio transmission since Marconi's historic experiment in 1901, provided scientists with a more sensitive means of measuring the effects of magnetic storms upon man's affairs. The first instance of radio interference was reported by Dr. C. N. Anderson of Bell Laboratories as follows: "In 1923, in connection with the systematic measuring program of transatlantic radio transmission inaugurated by the Bell System, the association of abnormal radio transmission and disturbances in the earth's magnetic field was soon discovered and is believed to be the first direct evidence of this kind."

Italian astronomer G. Abetti credits Marconi with being the first to note the interference with radio transmission on September 20 and October 24, 1927, coincident with the appearance of large sunspots and intense auroras. Telegraph lines and oceanic submarine cables were also rendered unusable on those dates.

During World War II, what was at first thought to be "jamming" of the radio channels by the Nazis, was found to be due to sunspot activity. Hence, in July 1942, Dr. D. H. Menzel and Dr. W. O. Roberts of the National Defense Research Committee began to correlate data on geomagnetic and solar activity, which formed the basis for short-term forecasts in radio propagation having an accuracy of 70 percent over a period of 15 months. This work was discontinued following the end of the war.

Then came an historic development, for, on April 19, 1946, John H. Nelson a radio technician with RCA Communications, was appointed Solar Researcher for that company and placed in charge of a telescope observatory being built on top of the RCA headquarters building in lower Manhattan, New York City. Nelson, who had learned the Morse telegraph code while a Boy Scout, and had become an amateur astronomer, building his own telescope, was assigned the task of developing a reliable method for predicting the onset of magnetic storms, which were playing havoc with long distance radio circuits.

Nelson records in his book, *The Propagation Wizard's Handbook* (1978), that by the middle of 1949, he had come to the conclusion that sunspots alone were not the answer to his problem. So he began to study the works of such well-known authorities on sunspots and planets as Huntington, Clayton and Sanford. He then correlated past magnetic storms with planetary positions for the same day, and recorded the results of five years of intensive research in a paper, "Short Wave Radio Propagation Correlation with Planetary Positions," which was published in the March 1951 *RCA Review*. He then followed this up with a paper, "Planetary Position Effects on Shortwave Signal Qualities," which was delivered at the January 1952 meeting of the American Institute of Electrical Engineers and printed in the May 1952 issue of *Electrical Engineering*.

It was at this AIEE meeting that the author met Nelson for the first time and began a friendship that was to endure for the next 30 years. Nelson at the outset only used the positions of the planets up to Saturn. But after meeting Jack Clark, a radio frequency engineer for Press Wireless, Inc., he learned that the three most distant planets—Uranus, Neptune and Pluto—were essential in the development of a reliable method of predicting magnetic storms. While the gravitational effects of these distant planets upon the Sun, was infinitesimal, their influence in the formation of magnetic storms was so great, that Nelson came to the conclusion that "we were dealing with some force in the solar system that was unknown to science."

Although Nelson knew absolutely nothing about astrology, he found that conjunctions, squares and oppositions between planets caused disturbances to shortwave radio signals. Astrologers had claimed for thousands of years that such planetary aspects were unfavorable and created stress in man and his environment. While these findings pleased the astrologers, they did not sit well with establishment astronomers. The favorable aspects were 60 degrees and 120 degrees.

Nelson records that his *Rosetta Stone*, which unlocked the secrets of the solar system to him, was the planetary positions that were operative during the great magnetic storm that began late in the day on March 23, 1940 and ended on April 23, 1940, producing the greatest blackout in shortwave radio history. These positions are shown in Figure 11. Nelson describes these positions as follows: ". . . when Venus was 90 degrees ahead of Saturn it was also 0 degrees (conjunction) with Pluto, showing us that Saturn and Pluto were also 90 degrees apart. Venus was 60 degrees behind Earth. This made a 4-planet combination with 3 hard angles and 1 harmonic tying Venus-Earth-Saturn-Pluto together in a simultaneous multiple harmonic (SMH). We also see that Mars was 90 degrees behind Neptune and 120 degrees behind Mercury, making what I refer to as a square and a trine—another SMH. This is also very effective. On the night of the 25th, Mercury made a 90 degree angle with Pluto and a 180 degree angle with Saturn."

Nelson also found the perihelion (closest approach to the Sun) position of the planets and planetary contact with the planets' nodes to be important. These nodal points are 180 degrees apart in space and represent the point in their heliocentric orbits where the planets cross the ecliptic, which is the path of the Earth around the Sun. When passing from below the ecliptic to above, it is called the Ascending or North Node, and vice versa for the Descending or South Node. The sensitivity of these points in space is probably due to the fact that on that day both the

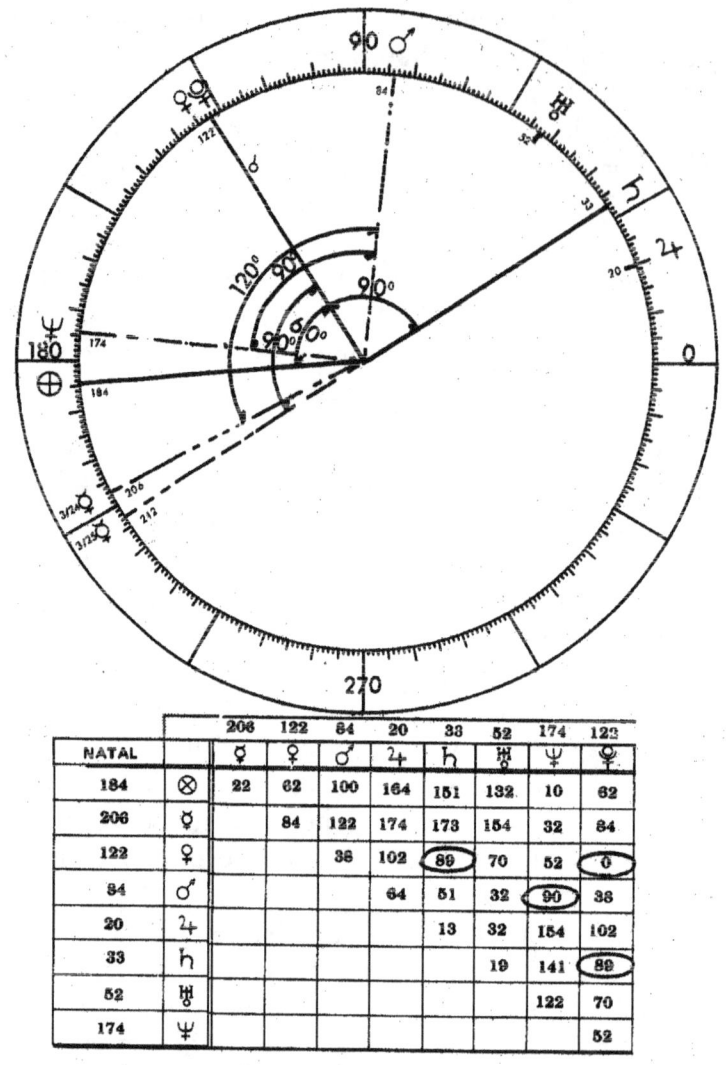

*Figure 11. Planetary Pattern During Great Magnetic Storm of March 24, 1940 (Heliocentric).*

earth and the planet have the same latitude on the Sun's surface. Thus, when the storm was regenerated on March 29, 1940, Venus was passing through perihelion and the next day Mercury passed through its South Node. Nelson stated that there were 8 hard angles and 14 major harmonics during this prolonged storm (March 23-April 3, 1940) involving all 9 planets of the solar system.

In September 1959, RCA received a request from the National Aeronautical and Space Administration (NASA) for a day-by-day forecast for November 1960. Nelson successfully predicted a year in advance the great magnetic storm of November 12, 1960. The planetary alignment is in Figure 12. The storm began suddenly at 1200 GMT (7:00 a.m. EST), almost precisely the hour that Mercury was in conjunction with Mars, while Mercury was passing through perihelion (closest to Sun). A few hours before this, Mercury was 150 degrees ahead of Jupiter and 150 degrees behind Neptune. This is a very reliable combination when a conjunction also takes place, as it did in this case. Venus was 90 degrees behind Earth and 30 degrees ahead of Saturn, making the very effective square/trine combination. This of course placed Earth 90 degrees ahead of Venus and 120 degrees ahead of Saturn—the actual square/trine. Following this,

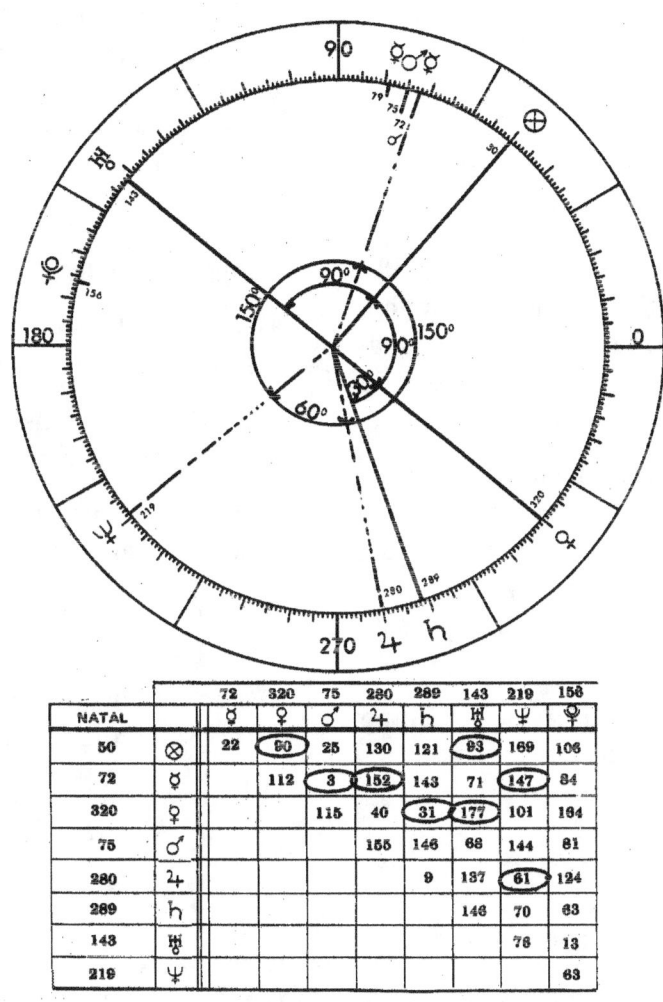

*Figure 12. Planetary Pattern During Great Magnetic Storm of November 12, 1960 (Heliocentric).*

Mercury also went into a square/trine relationship to Venus and Earth and 120 degrees ahead of Saturn, to be followed later in the day by a 60 degree angle behind Uranus and a 135 degree angle behind Neptune.

The storm continued until the 16th while Venus and Earth made hard angles to Uranus, with Venus 180 degrees from Uranus and Earth 90 degrees from Uranus. Several major solar flares preceded the storm and a very great cosmic ray shower began on the 13th and did not end until the 16th. This was one of the most severe magnetic storms since March 1940.

Although Nelson's forecasts of magnetic storms have been about 90 percent accurate during the past 15 years, he admits having failed to forecast that of August 4, 1972, which "not only affected short-wave radio signals, but also had a pronounced effect on power lines, causing voltage surges and transformer trip-outs. It also caused a change in the length of the day by changing the spin rate of the earth itself." Nelson considers this to be the most serious error in his entire forecasting career and blames it on his own carelessness.

The inharmonious aspect he had overlooked was the Venus-Earth-Saturn square arid trine arrangement that was also present in the Novem-

| | **Table 5. Key to Planetary Symbols.** | |
|---|---|---|
| ⊕ Earth | ☿ Mercury | A Aphelion (farthest from Sun) |
| ♀ Venus | ♂ Mars | P Perihelion (nearest to Sun) |
| ♃ Jupiter | ♄ Saturn | ☊ Planet's North Node |
| ♅ Uranus | ♆ Neptune | ☋ Planet's South Node |
| ♇ Pluto | ☌ Conjunction | ☍ Opposition |
| △ Trine | | |

ber 12, 1960 magnetic storm. He subsequently received a letter from Gribben and Plagemann, joint authors of *The Jupiter Effect* (1974), that the length of the day had also changed during this storm (1960).

For his historic discovery of an astoundingly accurate system of predicting magnetic storms from planetary patterns, Nelson, on October 23, 1951, was awarded a gold medal by The Foundation for the Study of Cycles (the only one in its 40-year history).

The key to the symbols used in the preceding charts is as shown in Table 5.

## Effects of Solar Activity on Electric Power Systems

### On Overhead Transmission Lines

While communication engineers have long been aware of the effects of solar disturbances, power engineers generally did not realize that magnetic storms could reach such magnitudes as to cause operating disturbances in electric power systems until the great magnetic storm of March 24, 1940 (see Figure 11 for planetary pattern). Dr. D. F. Davidson reported in the *Edison Electric Institute Bulletin* of July 1940 that on the Consolidated Edison 60-cycle system in New York, voltage dips varied from 1½ to 10 percent in different parts of the system, whereas the 25-cycle system voltage was not affected, nor was there any appreciable change in system frequency or in KW load in any part of either system. He summarized the disturbances on 10 power systems located in New England, New York, eastern Pennsylvania, southern and eastern Minnesota, Ontario and Quebec, as follows:

a) 7 cases of voltage dips ranging up to 10 percent but generally of short duration.

b) 5 cases (15 transformer banks) of transformer tripping by differential relay operation.

c) 4 cases of large increases or swings in reactive kilovolt-amperes.

d) 1 case where direct current was measured in a neutral grounding.

e) 1 case of distortion of the current wave in a neutral grounding.

f) 1 case of a few blown transformer fuses on a 2400/4150 volt radial distribution system.

L. W. Germaine reported in the same *EEI Bulletin* that the storm interrupted nearly all overseas radiotelephone circuits, service to ships at sea, and a number of long distance land telephone and other communication services, such as the telephotograph network and major network broadcasting facilities. It was believed that voltages in excess of 600 were experienced between certain stations, making it necessary to replace nearly 800 protector blocks in the state of Wisconsin alone.

The mechanism through which a solar disturbance affects large electric power systems is as follows: Changes in the earth's magnetism, probably caused by the ejection of charged particles from the disturbed portion of the Sun, cause differences in Earth potentials. Differences of Earth potential at widely separated points, where wye-connected transformers in the transmission system have their neutrals grounded, are believed to cause direct currents to flow in such a manner as to partially saturate the transformer cores. The excitation requirements of the transformers are thereby increased and the system voltage drops in an erratic pattern.

Dr. A. G. McNish of the Department of Terrestrial Magnetism, Carnegie Institution, Washington, D.C., concluded that the 1940 storm was even greater than that of April 1938, when energy was expended at the rate of two billion kilowatts for a two-hour interval. He stated that "Mathematical analysis has shown that field-changes during magnetic storms are due principally to causes above the earth's surface, presumably electric currents, and that these external effects are accompanied by effects due to the induction of currents within the earth by the primary external fields. The field changes may be divided into two classes—those which are symmetric about the earth's magnetic axis and those which are non-symmetric. The first class may be thought of as due mainly to a large ring-current about the earth, like the rings of Saturn, or to a current flowing in the outer atmosphere with intensity varying as the cosine of the geomagnetic latitude from zero at the geomagnetic poles to a maximum at the equator."

But it wasn't until 1949 that experimental proof of the existence of this overhead current system was obtained by Singer, Maple and Bowen (reported in the *Journal of Geophysical Research* Vol. 56, 1951) by means of magnetometers sent aloft in Aerobee rockets from a point in the Pacific Ocean near the equator. The results clearly established the presence of overhead currents of the order of 50,000 amperes in a layer between 93 and 105 KM above the earth.

Other ring currents as high as 1,000,000 amperes were found some 25,000 miles out in space, between 65 and 68 degrees north and south geomagnetic latitude, by the U.S. Pioneer I satellite which soared nearly 80,000 miles on October 11, 1958, and Explorer VI, which soared about 35,000 miles on August 7, 1959. Hence, C. P. Sonnet believed that fluctuating magnetism in outer space may be responsible for the earth's auroral phenomena (reported in *The New York Times*, December 30, 1959).

A ring current of 5,000,000 amperes 12,000 miles thick was reported by Sonnet, in *The New York Times*, April 29, 1960, as having been obtained from data telemetered by the U. S. Pioneer V satellite when it was about 3,000,000 miles from the Earth. This ring lies at an altitude of 40,000 to 60,000 miles, well beyond the outer Van Allen belt, and flows westward around the Earth, subtracting from the intensity of the Earth's magnetic field on its inner side and adding to it on the outer edge. Sonnet and his associates also found that the sharp start of a magnetic storm on Earth—known as a "sudden commencement"—had also been observed 3,000,000 miles out in space.

Where do the electromotive forces necessary to maintain such enormous currents originate? McNish, in the July 1940 *EEI Bulletin*, concluded: "The cause of the primary electric currents in the outer atmosphere or about the earth remains a matter of speculation." He suggested, however, that the "ring-current" was a simple manifestation of the motion of the clouds of electrified corpuscles ejected by the Sun, which upon striking the earth's upper atmosphere are focused by the earth's magnetic field, very much as electrons are focused by the magnetic field in the newly developed electron-microscope. This was based on mathematical analysis which showed that electrified particles of certain energies and masses would reach the atmosphere with greatest density in belts near the magnetic poles (auroral zones) and that others would occupy semi-stable orbits in the plane of the magnetic equator. This was experimentally demonstrated by K. Birkeland in 1896, *Archives des Sciences Physiques et Naturelles*, Geneva, Vol. 4, and seems to be confirmed by the data obtained from both Pioneer V and Explorer VI.

McNish also suggested that the auroral-zone currents, which may exceed 1,000,000 amperes, with changes exceeding 100,000 amperes per minute, resulted from the convective motion of the atmosphere in the Earth's magnetic field, by which means the currents are induced in accordance with the principles of the dynamo. This theory (the atmospheric dynamo theory) was first advanced by Professor Balfour Stewart in 1882, and was mathematically developed by Sir Arthur Schuster in 1888 and 1907, and reconfirmed by Professor Sidney Chapman in 1913, 1919 and 1936.

Because data telemetered by Pioneer V from a distance of 3,000,000 miles showed variations in magnetic activity similar to those recorded at the same time in Hawaii and Virginia, W. L. Laurence, in *The New York Times* May 15, 1960, concluded: "Pioneer V informs us that these magnetic storms are not local phenomena peculiar to our earth, but are rather due to some as yet unknown forces existing in space, possibly throughout the Milky Way Galaxy."

Dr. McNish stated in the July 1940 *EEI Bulletin* that "Judging the future by the past, great magnetic storms may be expected at the rate of one a decade. Our records go further than this. They show that, including magnetic storms of all intensities, their frequency follows the 11-year sunspot cycle, lagging behind it by about two years."

However, 20 years were to elapse before the Consolidated Edison Systems would experience a magnetic storm as severe as that of 1940. It was the magnetic storm of November 12-13, 1960 which proved to be the most severe ever to be observed up to that time by the North Atlantic Radio Warning Service of the U. S. Bureau of Standards (see Figure 12 for planetary pattern).

The system operator of the Consolidated Edison Company of New York reported that "during several hours on Sunday, November 13, 1960, there were random occurrences of uncontrolled voltage variations of considerable magnitude in the voltage of the 138KV transmission system. Similar effects were reported by the system operators of neighboring utility companies and also by the Hydro-Electric Power Commission of Ontario, Canada. It is believed that the disturbance was caused by higher than normal magnitude electric currents in the earth's surface, accompanying the present giant sunspot activity."

Since both the 1940 and 1960 storms occurred when the polarity of the sunspots was the same, i.e., north spots leading in the Northern Hemisphere of the Sun (see Figure 13), the author predicted in the July 1961 *Journal of Cycle Research*, that "electric power system disturbances might follow the 22-year sunspot cycle (alternate 11-year cycles reversed) instead of the usual 11-year cycle." This prediction was fulfilled 3 years early, during a violent thunderstorm on the hot, humid night of July 13, 1977, when a series of severe lightning strokes knocked out several 345,000 volt overhead transmission lines that were supplying 40 percent of Con-Edison's load at the time. This set in motion a series of events that 59 minutes later caused the most disastrous power blackout in the 95 year history of that company in terms of people involved (9,000,000) and claims for property damage totaling $350 million (see Figure 16 for planetary aspects). Another violent storm occurred on September 26, 1977, but this time the company was prepared and the public was not seriously inconvenienced (see Figure 17 for planetary aspects).

Figure 13 was originally prepared for a lecture given by the author before the Foundation for Metaphysical Arts and Sciences, New York City, November 15, 1950, when attention was directed to the startling fact that the United States had been engaged in a war or had been in a depression during alternate periods of low sunspot activity. These periods occur at intervals of approximately 22 years, when sunspots die out in the Southern Solar Hemisphere and reappear in the Northern Solar Hemisphere, at which time their electrical polarity changes. These periods are listed in Table 6.

### Table 6. U.S. Wars and Depressions vs. Sunspots.

| Year | Relative Sunspot # | Historical Event |
| --- | --- | --- |
| 1755 | 9.6 | French and Indian War |
| 1775 | 7.0 | American Revolutionary War |
| 1798 | 4.1 | Undeclared Naval War with France |
| 1823 | 1.8 | Depression—Monroe Doctrine (caused by threats of Holy Alliance and Russia) |
| 1843 | 10.7 | Debt Repudiation Depression |
| 1867 | 7.3 | Post-Civil War Reconstruction Depression |
| 1889 | 6.3 | Depression (Bloodless Revolution in Brazil) |
| 1913 | 1.4 | Depression caused by Second Balkan War leading To World War I |
| 1933 | 5.7 | Depression—Birth of New Deal—Rise of Hitler |
| 1954 | 4.4 | Depression—Beginning of Vietnam War |
| April 1975 | 5.1 | Recession—Index +17 in March 1975 |
| February 1976 | 4.6 | — |

## Effects on High Voltage Underground Cable

Although public utilities were aware of the fact that severe magnetic storms caused disturbances on overhead transmission lines, little or no consideration was given to the effects of such storms on underground electric cables until 3:00 p.m. EDST, August 17, 1959, when a violent storm triggered the failure of 7 out of 20 (35 percent) 13.8 KV (Kilovolt) underground cables serving the Central Park Network Area of the Consolidated Edison Company in New York City. Electric service to 500,000 people was interrupted, long-distance radio transmission was blacked out, and a disastrous earthquake in Yellowstone National Park occurred—one of the most severe in the entire history of the North American continent.

This magnetic storm had been predicted a week earlier by John Nelson of R.C.A. *The New York Times* of November 11, 1959 carried the headline, "Power Blackout Remains Mystery," and stated that "The Public Service Commission was unable to explain why 7 of the 20 cables on the Central Park Network broke down almost simultaneously. The seven-ply failure was the first of such magnitude in 30 years, according to the report." But the *New York Herald-Tribune* of August 23, 1959 had given what subsequently proved to be the correct answer when it stated that "One Con-Edison cable expert jokingly blames sunspots, but admits he is unable to convince fellow officials." That "expert" was this author.

Figure 14 shows the planetary pattern in effect on August 17, 1959. The unfavorable aspects were: Mercury 45 degrees Venus, Mercury opposition Mars, Mercury 135 degrees Uranus, Mercury square Saturn, Venus opposition Uranus, Mars square Saturn, Mars 45 degrees Uranus, and Jupiter square Pluto. The T-square formed by Saturn's square to the Mercury-Mars opposition is clearly shown. It will be observed that Mercury—the planet of communication and energy transmission—was in adverse relation to four other planets, viz, Venus, Mars, Saturn, and Uranus, while Uranus—the planet of electricity—was in adverse relation to three other planets, viz, Mercury, Venus, Mars. Cable failures that day were three times normal; the sunspot count was 158 and the K-Index of Geomagnetic Activity was 8.

The nature of the solar disturbance raging that day, as telemetered back from a distance of 35,000 miles by Explorer VI, which had been

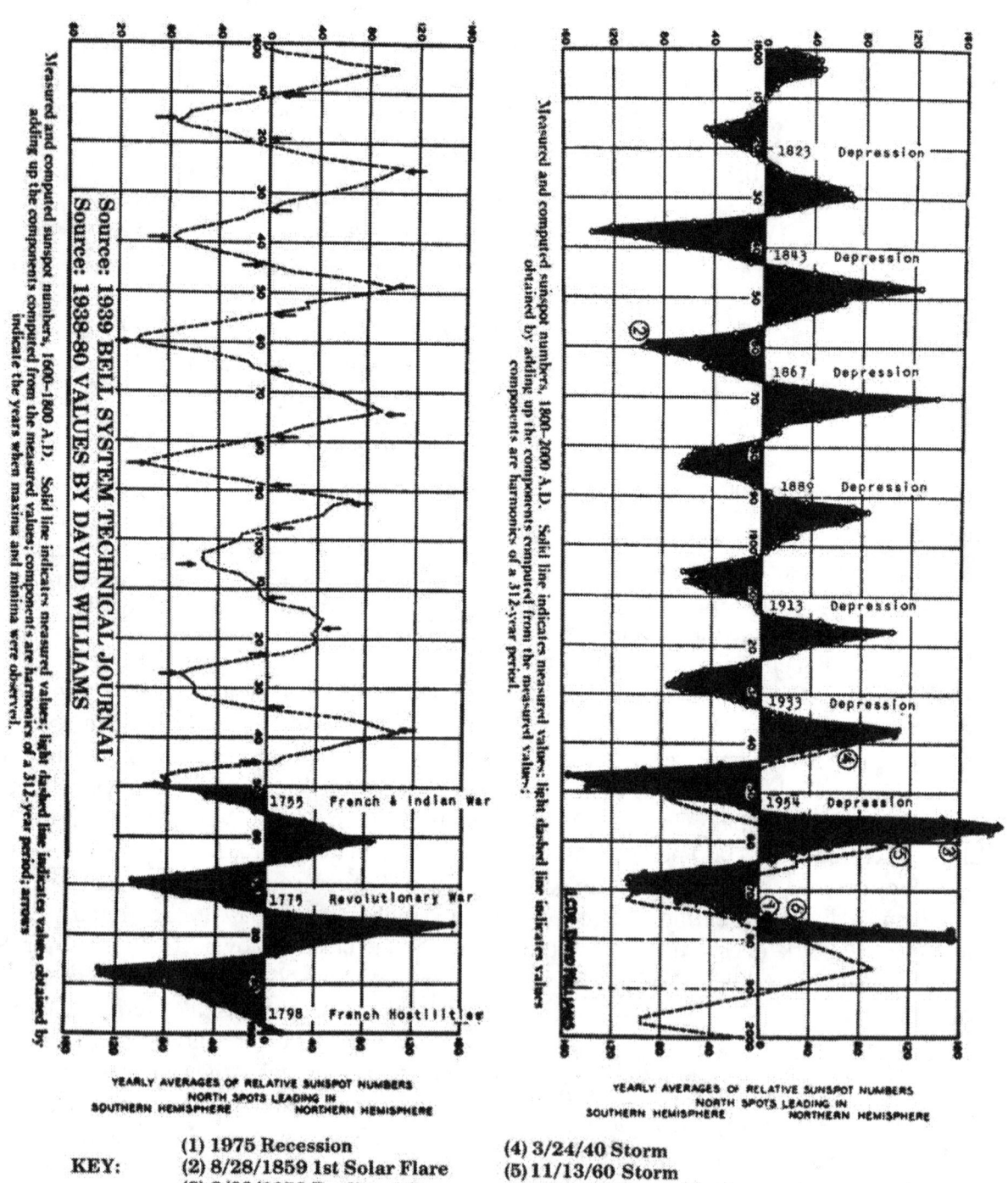

Figure 13. U.S. Wars and Depressions vs. Sunspots.

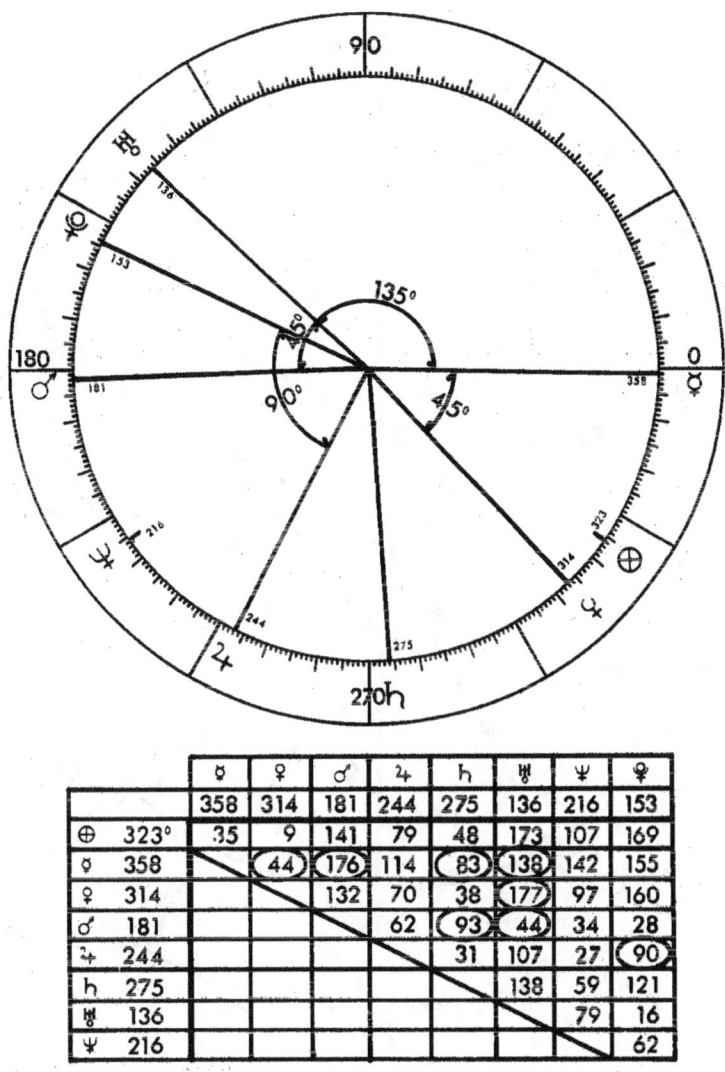

*Figure 14. Planetary Pattern August 17, 1959 Con-Edison Power Blackout (Heliocentric).*

launched from Cape Canaveral, Florida on August 7, 1959, was reported by *The New York Times* of December 30, 1959, as follows:

"It detected protons (the nuclei of hydrogen atoms) fired toward the earth at almost the speed of light—186,000 miles per second—with energies greater than 75,000,000 electron volts. It confirmed the existence of the great rings of electric currents that girdle the earth thousands of miles out in space. One of these with a strength of 1,000,000 amperes, lies 25,000 miles out in space, between 65 and 68 degrees North and South Geomagnetic Latitude. It also detected a swelling of the outer radiation belt that coincided with what is believed to have been the formation of a gigantic synchroton centered on the sun itself. The shape of the radiation belts is determined by the earth's magnetism, which keeps the trapped electrons and protons from flying off into space or crashing into the earth's atmosphere. The inner belt was within a few thousand miles of the earth's magnetic equator, while the center of the outer belt was 15,000 miles from the earth."

One writer called this storm "the most intense solar activity recorded since Galileo" in "The Sun Also Changes" in *The Sciences* of The New York Academy of Science.

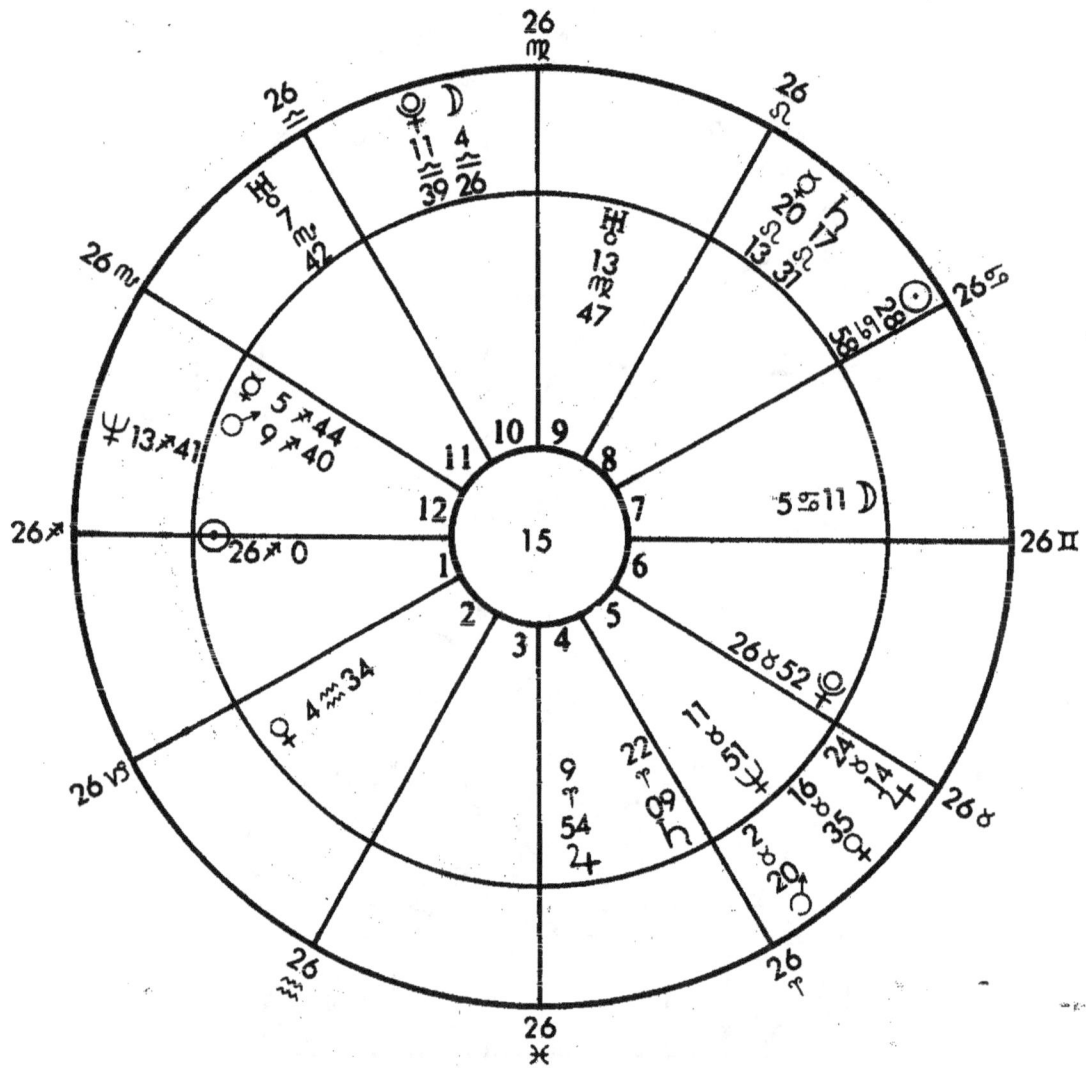

*Figure 15. Planetary Pattern on July 21, 1977 (Near Blackout at Con-Edison). Inner Circle: Solar Chart, Noon GMT, December 17, 1880, Date of Incorporation The Edison Electric Illuminating Company of New York.*

A similar blackout was narrowly averted 18 years later during a heat wave, when, at 5:07 p.m. EDST on July 21, 1977, six out of 16 (38 percent) cables failed on the Williamsburg Network that supplied service to 77,000 customers. At 4:00 p.m. the temperature had reached 104 degrees, the second highest ever recorded in the area. The electric load on the system had hit a new peak of 8266 megawatts. To prevent more cable failures and the possible collapse of the entire network, fire hydrants were turned on to pour water into transformer manholes to keep the remaining cables as cool as possible. Customers were requested to cut back on their electrical usage as much as possible. These measures enabled the network to hold out and 2 hours and 50 minutes after it failed, the sixth cable was returned to service, whereas in 1959 it took almost 13 hours to restore service.

But the saving element was the low level of geomagnetic activity, for the sunspot count was only 8 as against 158 in 1959, the K-Index of geomagnetic activity was 4 instead of 8 (out of a maximum of 10), and these were 2 positive and 2 negative planetary aspects versus 8 negative and 2 positive in 1959! (see Figure 15). The positive aspects were: 1) transiting Moon sextile

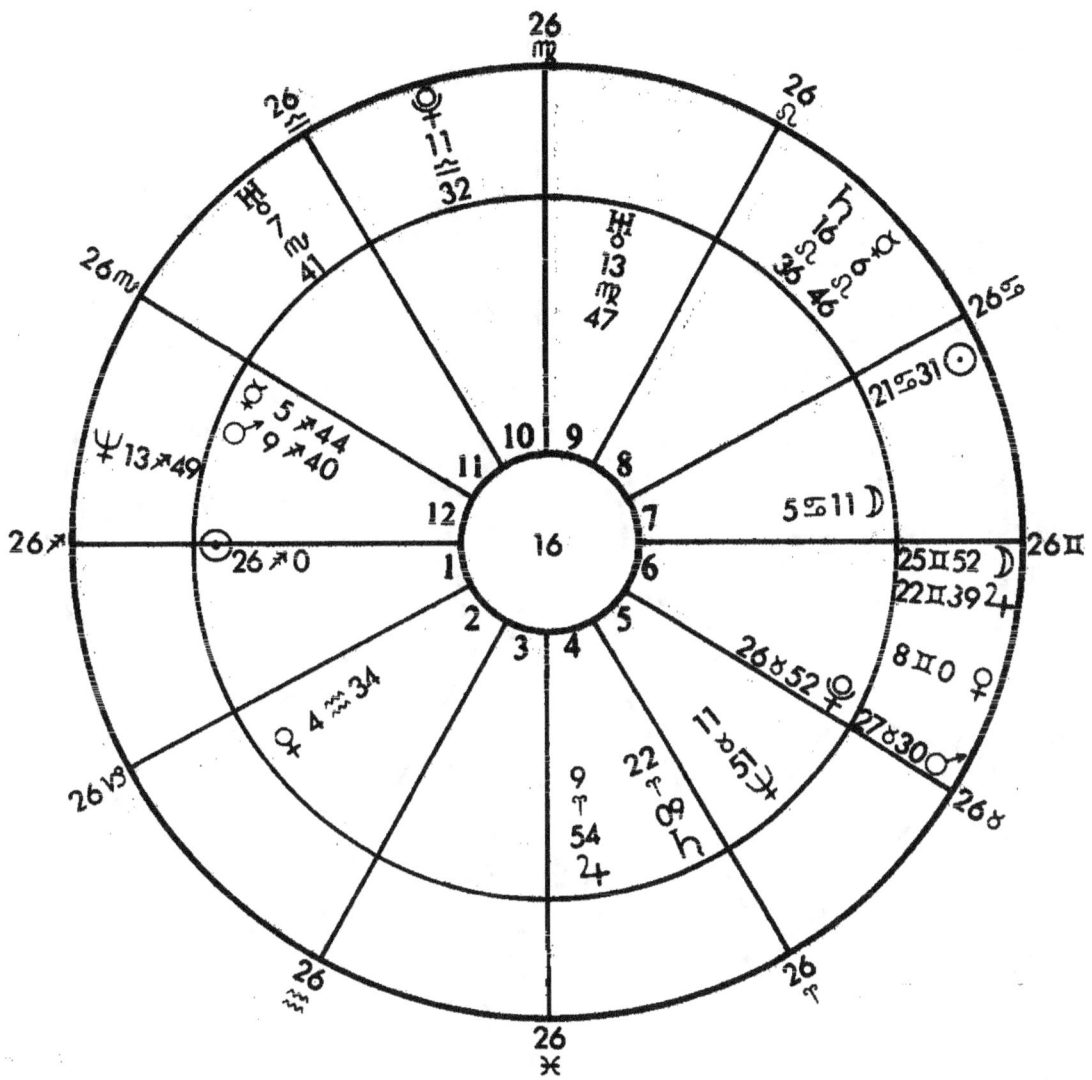

*Figure 16. Planetary Pattern on July 13, 1977 (Con-Edison Blackout). Inner Circle: Solar Chart, Noon GMT, December 17, 1880, Date of Incorporation The Edison Electric Illuminating Company of New York.*

natal Mercury and transiting Moon trine natal Venus. The negative aspects were 1) transiting Moon square natal Moon and transiting Neptune square natal Uranus.

The most disastrous blackout in Con-Edison's 95-year history in terms of people involved (9,000,000) and potential claims tor property damage ($350,000,000) occurred at 9:34 p.m. EDST on the hot, humid night of July 13, 1977. It was triggered by a series of severe lightning strokes that occurred during a violent thunderstorm that was moving across northern Westchester County, which knocked out several 345,000 volt (345KV) overhead transmission lines that were supplying 40 percent of Con-Edison's load at the time. This set in motion a series of events that 59 minutes later shut down the entire Con-Edison electrical system for the first time in history. Criminal and other elements took advantage of the darkness to engage in an orgy of looting and arson. It took the company 25 hours to restore service to its customers.

The sunspot count was 10, the K-Index of Geomagnetic Activity was 4; there were 3 positive and 1 negative aspects in the heavens at 9:34 p.m., but the transiting planets made 8 negative and only 2 positive aspects to the natal planets, per Figure 16. The negative aspects were: 1)

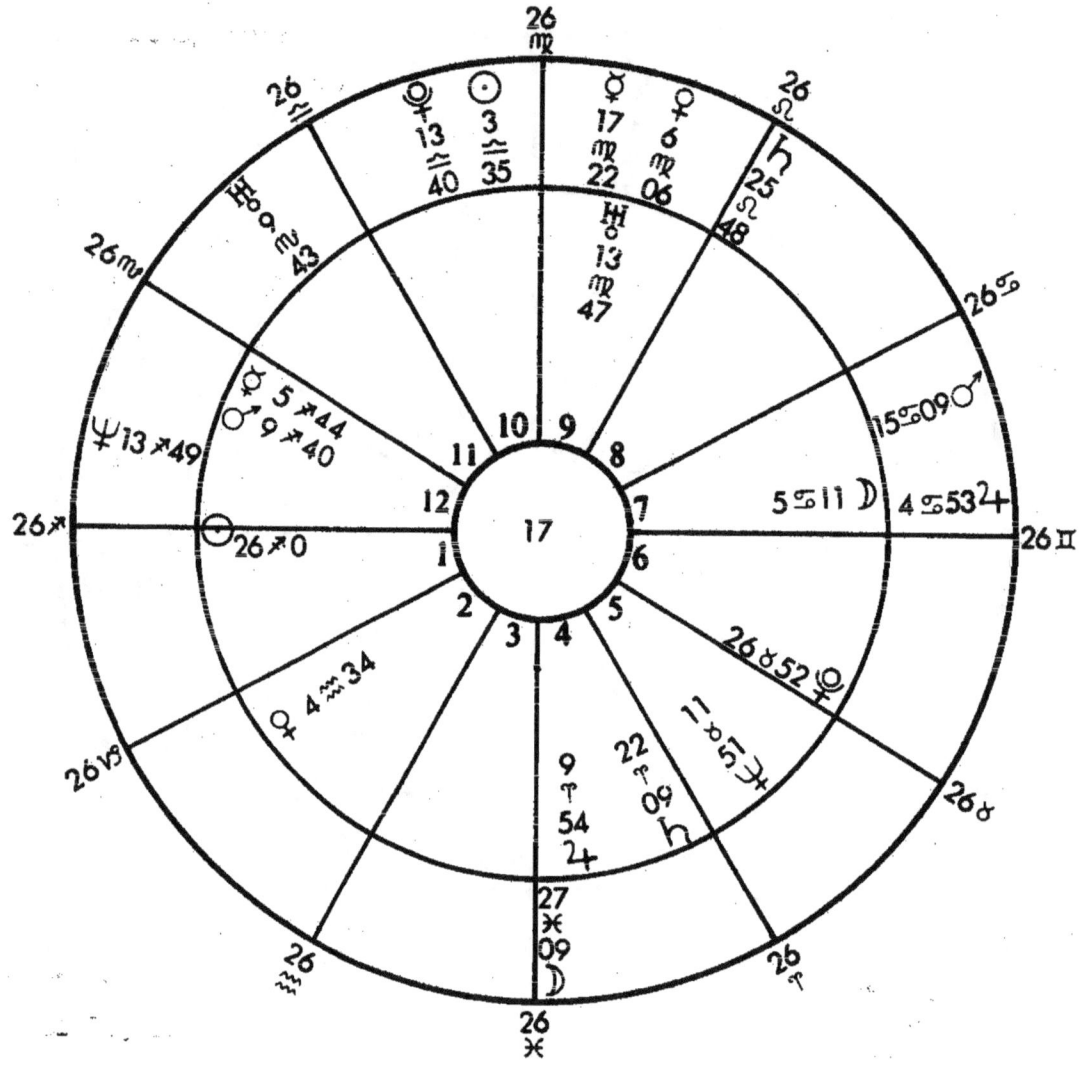

*Figure 17. Planetary Pattern on September 26, 1977 (Near Blackout of Con-Edison). Inner Circle: Solar Chart, Noon GMT, December 17, 1880, Date of Incorporation The Edison Electric Illuminating Company of New York.*

transiting Sun square natal Saturn, 2) transiting Moon opposition natal Sun, 3) transiting Venus opposition natal Mars, 4) transiting Mars conjunct natal Pluto, 5) transiting Neptune square natal Uranus, 6) transiting Pluto opposition natal Jupiter, 7) transiting Moon opposition natal Ascendant, and 8) transiting Moon square natal Midheaven. The positive aspects were: 1) transiting Mercury trine natal Mercury, and 2) transiting Jupiter sextile natal Saturn.

The history of science has shown that while man cannot prevent the occurrence of natural phenomena, he can protect himself and his environment from nature's most destructive elements. Thus, when Con-Edison's Energy Control Center in Manhattan received reports at about 2:20 p.m. on September 26, 1977, of a severe lightning storm approaching from the west and stretching in a solid line from Staten Island to Newburgh, it put into effect procedures, personnel and training adopted as a result of the July 13 blackout. Hence, when at 3:30 p.m. lightning once more knocked out 38 percent of the system load, the system operator was able to make good the deficiency and only 117,500 customers in Westchester and the Bronx were affected by manual load-shedding initiated at three Westchester substations. Full system-wide service was restored at 4:40 p.m. or 70 minutes after the trouble had started, versus 25 hours after the July 13 blackout.

At 3:30 p.m. September 26, 1977, there were 4 positive and 2 negative aspects in the heavens above New York City, the sunspot count was 49, and the K-Index of Geomagnetic Activity was 4. The transiting planets made 5 positive and 6 negative aspects to Con-Edison's natal planetary positions, per Figure 17. The positive aspects were: 1) transiting Sun trine natal Venus, 2) transiting Moon sextile natal Pluto, 3) transiting Venus sextile natal Moon, 4) transiting Jupiter conjunct natal Moon, and 5) transiting Saturn trine natal Sun.

The negative aspects were: 1) transiting Moon square natal Sun, 2) transiting Venus square natal Mercury, 3) transiting Saturn square natal Pluto, 4) transiting Neptune square natal Uranus, 5) transiting Moon square natal Ascendant, and 6) transiting Moon opposition natal Midheaven.

It should be noted that Figures 15, 16, and 17 are in geocentric longitude (Earth centered) whereas previous charts are in Heliocentric Longitude (Sun centered). The reason for this is that the magnetic disturbances on Figures 15, 16, and 17 were minor and only affected one power company, whereas major magnetic disturbances affect the entire Earth.

## Effects of Solar Activity in Other Fields of Technology

Peter M. Strang of the Whitin Machine Works, Whitinsville, Massachusetts and the Reverend Daniel Linehan, S. J., Director of the Boston College Observatory, Weston, Massachusetts reported, in the January 9, 1958 *America's Textile Reporter,* that magnetic storms cause a 200-300 percent increase in the breakage of cotton yarn. A seasonal pattern in yarn breakage was also found, the peak coming in the summer months. The explanation given is that Cotton thread is made by the cohesion of one cotton fiber to another. During a magnetic storm, an electrostatic effect is set up in the fibers which causes them to spread apart, reducing the cohesion, with resultant breakage of the thread.

There is a network of some 450,000 miles of oil and gas pipe lines in the United States. To protect long oil and gas pipe lines from the effects of voltages induced by changes in the earth's magnetic field, it had been customary to break the lines into sections by the use of insulated flange joints. Nevertheless, numerous cases of unexplained voltage surges and electric currents of large magnitude on such pipe lines puzzled corrosion engineers for many years. J. J. Meany, Jr., in the August 1960 issue of *Corrosion,* reported that from recording voltmeter readings taken across the insulating flanges of two distinct pipeline systems over 250 miles apart, data were obtained linking the voltage fluctuations with variations in the earth's magnetic field. Furthermore, such readings taken during the great solar eruption of July 15, 1959 synchronized with the disturbances that were then taking place in radio communications. (This was just 100 years after Drake's discovery of oil in Pennsylvania.) Some companies have been compelled to install spark gaps across the insulated flanges to protect them from breakdown by surges induced by lightning or during severe magnetic storms.

In 1954, two German researchers, Caroli and Richota, found that variations in the length of time of blood coagulation and variations in inorganic colloids occurred at the same time and corresponded to variations in electromagnetic wave radiation of a high frequency.

These results were confirmed by Professor Giorgio Piccardi, Director of the Institute of Physical Chemistry, University of Florence, Italy, who described, in *Wiener Medezinische Wochenschrift,* for 1956 and 1958, the effects of extraterrestrial influences that cause deviations from expected results that often occur in chemical work. He found, after seven years work and more than 105,000 experiments that variations in sunspot activity produced corresponding variations in the time required for bismuth chloride to coagulate with water into coarse particles. Similar results were obtained during the next 20 years by other experimenters in Austria, Belgium, Germany, Italy and Japan.

Piccardi also found that there were variations in average reaction ratio according to the seasons of the year. Not only did he find the reaction rates to correlate with the solar cycle, and with such transient events as magnetic storms, sudden cosmic ray bombardments and solar flares, but also with an annual cycle that peaked at the Vernal Equinox (around March 21), which he believed could only be due to effects from outside the solar system. He, therefore, formulated a "solar hypothesis," according to which chemical events on Earth correspond not only to short and long-term solar events, but also to the position of the Earth on its helicoidal path through the galaxy.

Piccardi further reasoned that if the structure and behavior of water are affected by extraterrestrial forces, then all living matter must be similarly affected. He coined the term "non-living substratum" to describe precisely what is affected; the water and colloids dispersed throughout all living matter including that of our bodies, which are at least two-thirds water. Since chemical reactions are taking place all the time inside us, keeping us alive, we are to some extent regulated by cosmic forces in our most fundamental processes. He concluded that the evidence clearly showed that living matter reacted to extra-terrestrial forces exactly like non-living matter, because what reacts is its non-living or inorganic substructure.

## Effects of Solar Activity on Health

According to Michel Gauquelin, in *The Cosmic Clocks* (1967), and others, the modem history of the cosmic influences on man began with the report of Faure, Sardov and Vallot, to the Paris Academy of Medicine on July 14, 1922. They recorded that severe magnetic disturbances were accompanied by an increased incidence of illnesses, and that the number of sudden deaths during the passage of sunspots across the Sun's central meridian, was twice as high as at any other time.

Gauquelin listed the following additional evidence:

In 1934, the German researchers G. and B. Dull reported that deaths from tuberculosis in Hamburg, Copenhagen and Zurich, were much higher on days of peak solar activity than either before or after. They also reported an increase in mental disturbances and suicides on peak days.

In 1934, A. L. Tchijevsky, a Russian professor of history reported that an historical survey of the period 550 B.C. to 1900 A.D. indicated that worldwide epidemics tended to occur during years of maximum sunspot activity.

In 1935, Dr. I. Puig of Buenos Aires noted a threefold increase in respiratory ailments on days of strong solar activity in the southern hemisphere.

In 1941 and 1951, Professor Maki Takata of Toho University in Tokyo, reported that the flocculation index of blood serum suddenly rose when a group of sunspots passed across the Sun's central meridian. The index also rose a few minutes before sunrise each day.

In 1955, Dr. O. Lingemann reported that studies in West Germany during 1948-1952 indicated that the incidence of pulmonary hemorrhage increased with solar activity.

In 1959, the French physician Dr. J. Poumailloux and the meteorologist R. Viart reported to the Paris Academy of Medicine a very high correlation between the number of cardiovascular cases and sudden increases in solar activity in 1957.

In 1960, the Soviet hematologist Nicholas Schulz reported to the USSR Academy of Sciences that increased sunspot activity was followed by an abnormal increase of some components of blood, lymphocytes, in particular, whereas certain white blood cells decreased abnormally.

In 1960, Professor N. V. Romensky, Director of the Board of Health at Sotchi on the Black Sea, reported that the number of cardiovascular incidents in the hospitals under his jurisdiction increased tenfold on May 18, 1959, following the great solar eruption of May 17, 1959.

At the 1960 International Geophysical and Meteorological convention in Ottawa, Canada, Dr. A. Giordano reported that the number of cardiovascular cases in Pavia, Italy, increased from 200 in 1964 to 450 in 1958 following the rise in solar activity.

In 1962, Professor Giorgio Piccardi, Director of the Institute for Physical Chemistry, University of Florence, Italy, reported that the speed of chemical reactions in water and blood varied with the 11-year sunspot cycle and with solar eruptions.

Furthermore, Dr. L. J. Ravitz, a psychiatrist, reported in the October 1962 Annals of the New York Academy of Sciences, additional evidence of the effects of electro-magnetic fields upon humans and showed how the cyclic nature of such forces enabled the psychiatrist to predict changes in the health of the patient. Ravitz had been a long-time student of the work of Drs. H.S. Burr and F. S. C. Northrop of the Yale School of Medicine, who found a correlation between extra-terrestrial forces and living organisms, which in 1935 formed the basis for their *Electro-Dynamic Theory of Life*. They found that the electro-magnetic fields in human beings had periodic movements paralleling those simultaneously recorded in the atmosphere, the earth, and tree potentials, such as; fortnightly, monthly, seasonal, semi-annual, annual, and sunspot cycles.

In 1963, G. Papeschi and M. Costa found that naphthalene solidified quickest at New Moon and slowest at Full Moon.

In 1963, Drs. H. Friedman, R. 0. Becker, C. H. Bachman of New York State University reported, in *Nature,* that admissions to eight large psychiatric hospitals in New York increased on days of strong magnetic disturbances. They found a definite relationship between psychiatric disturbances and some geophysical factor associated with changes in the earth's magnetic fields.

The relationship between astrology and biology was impartially reviewed in the February 25, 1965, issue of *Hospital Focus*. After referring to some of the foregoing evidence, the writer of the article posed the question, "If it is verified that human processes are affected by the magnetic interactions among celestial bodies, and if the Babylonians and Harappans knew nothing at all (SIC) about wave mechanics or the solid state, how were they able to conceive of astrology?"

The answer to the foregoing question has been given by the immortal bard William Shakespeare:

"There are more things in Heaven and Earth, Horatio, than are dreamt of in your philosophy" (from Hamlet).

## Chapter 5

# Planetary Theories of the Business Cycle

### Benner's Price Cycles

We have learned from Chapter 2 that in 1875, English economist Professor W. S. Jevons had hinted at a planetary theory of the business cycle when he stated in his paper presented at the Bristol Meeting of the British Association that "the configuration of the planets may prove to be the remote cause of the greatest commercial disasters." Though Jevons had to drop this line of inquiry because of the bitter opposition of his colleagues, an American, Samuel Benner, in that same year published a remarkable but little known book, *Benner's Prophecies of Future Ups and Downs in Prices*, which formed the basis for annual forecasts from 1875 through 1904. This book was reprinted in 1948 by The Foundation for the Study of Cycles as *Reprint No. 24*.

Benner, who was a retired iron and steel manufacturer from Cincinnati, Ohio, developed a chart of pig iron prices from 1834 to 1899, in which the lowest priced years are in a decreasing series of arithmetical progression in the order of 11, 9, 7, and repeat. The high priced years are in an increasing series of arithmetical progression in the order of 8, 9, 10, and repeat every 27 years, as shown in Part 1 of Figure 18.

Benner then found an 11-year cycle in corn and hog prices beginning in 1836, and broken up into alternate 5 and 6 year cycles, as shown in Part 2 of Figure 18. Cotton prices also were found to follow an 11-year cycle as shown in Part 3 of Figure 18. Benner then described the business cycle as composed of peaks 16, 18 and 20 years apart, and lows coinciding with the lows of the pig iron cycle, as shown in Part 4 of Figure 18. Benner stated: "It takes panics 54 years in their order to make a revolution, or to return in the same order." (It will be recalled that Dr. Clarke in 1847 divided a 54-year famine cycle into 11-year periods.) Benner combined the pig iron cycle with the business cycle, because he felt that "the iron trade is the chief and ruling industry in this country, if not in the world, and as the iron industry rises or falls in the scale of prosperity, so does the general business of the country."

Benner's theory was: "The cause producing the periodicity and length of these cycles may be

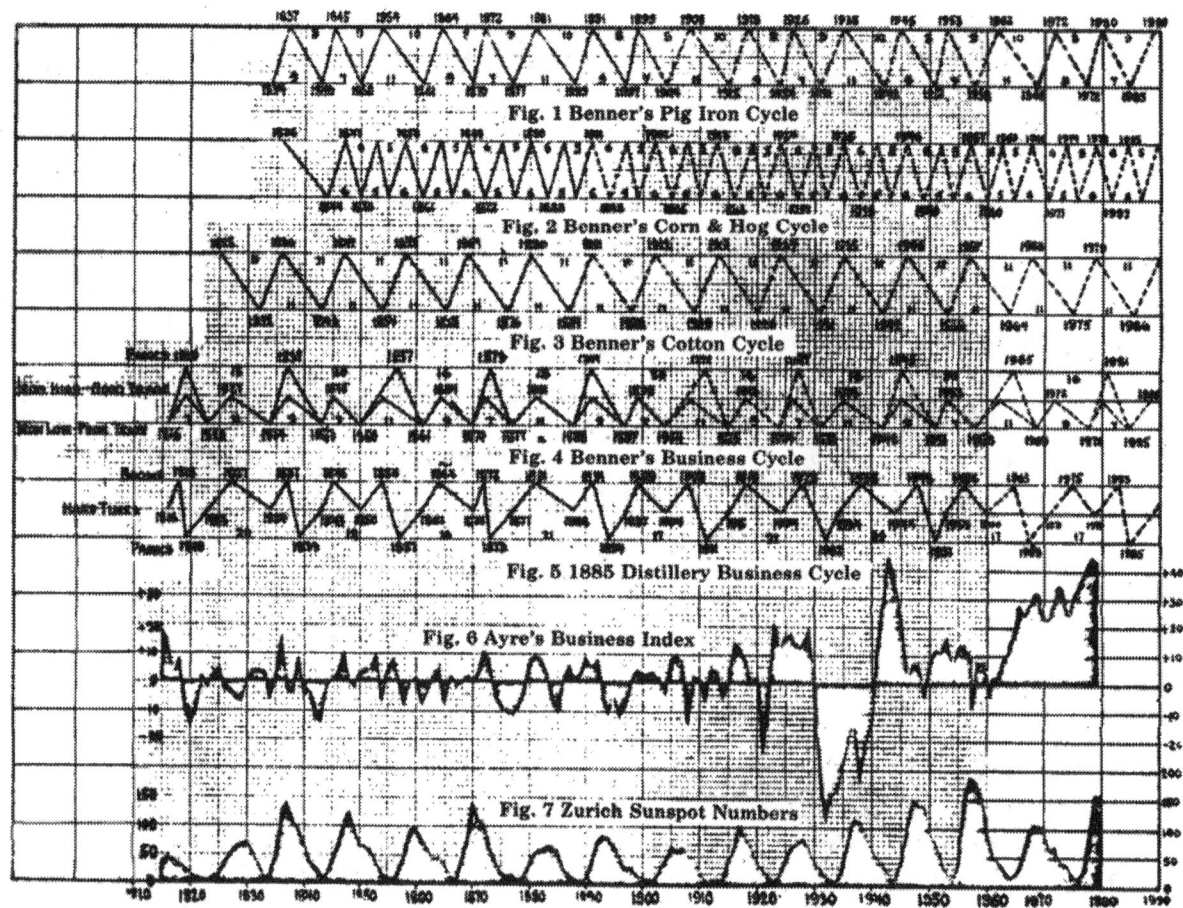

*Figure 18. Commodity Price, Business and Sunspot Cycles.*

found in our solar system." Following in Carrington's footsteps, Benner compared Jupiter's major equinox, which occurs every 11.86 years, with his 11-year cycles and found those of 1836, 1847, 1858, and 1869 to fall behind the jovial cycle. He then stated: "It may be a meteorological fact that Jupiter is the ruling element in our price cycles of natural productions, while also it may be suggested that Saturn exerts an influence regulating the cycles in manufacture and trade." He also suggested that Uranus and Neptune "may send forth an electric influence affecting Jupiter, Saturn, and, in turn, the earth."

Benner concluded: "When certain combinations are ascertained which produce one legitimate invariable manifestation from an analysis of the operations of the combined solar system, we may be enabled to discover the cause producing our price cycles, and the length of their duration. The science of *price cycles* is yet in the cradle of its infancy. Each rising science has fought and struggled with superstition and ignorance, and in all ages no effort has been spared to blast them in the bud of their being, or crush them in the cradle of their infancy."

Edward R. Dewey, Director, Foundation for the Study of Cycles, considered Benner's forecast of pig iron prices, which over a period of 60 years showed a gain-loss ratio of 45 to 1, "the most notable forecast of prices in existence." Benner's business chart has been copied and imitated by various unknown authors. Thus, one variation was reproduced by *The Wall Street Journal* in 1933 from "a chart found in an old desk in Philadelphia in 1902 that was at least forty years old." It is reproduced as Part 5 in Figure 18. This chart was also published in the October 1937 *Dun's Review* as a reproduction of a "chart found in an old distillery in 1885." Part 6 of Figure 18 shows the Cleveland Trust Company Business Index and Part 7 shows the Zurich Sunspot Cycle.

Figures 19a and 19b are enlarged versions of Parts 4 and 5 of Figure 18. *The Wall Street Journal* of February 2, 1933 reproduced Figure 19b which is very similar to the 1885 Distillery version of Benner's chart published in the 1937 *Dun's Review*. It will be noted that on Benner's chart, depressions "C" occur at 7-11-9 year intervals, or an average of 9 years, which is the Juglar cycle recognized by economists. Panics "A" occur at 16-18-20 year intervals, with every third peak coming at 54-year intervals, which would fall into Kondratieff's "Long Wave."

## Moore's 8-year Venus Cycle

In a paper, "The Origin of the Eight-Year Generating Cycle," first published in the November 1921 *Quarterly Journal of Economics* and subsequently published in book form in 1923 under the title *Generating Economic Cycles*, Professor H. L. Moore of Columbia Uni-

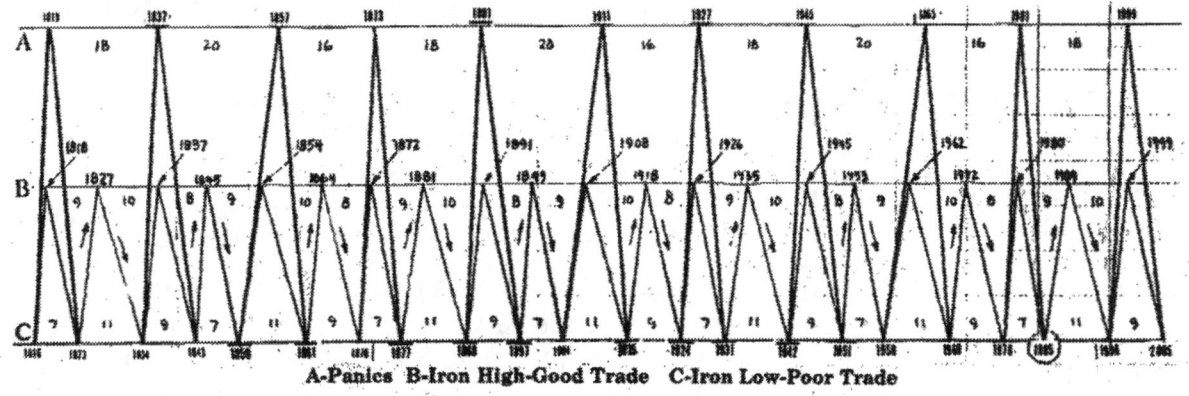

*Figure 19a. Samuel Benner's Business Cycle Chart.*

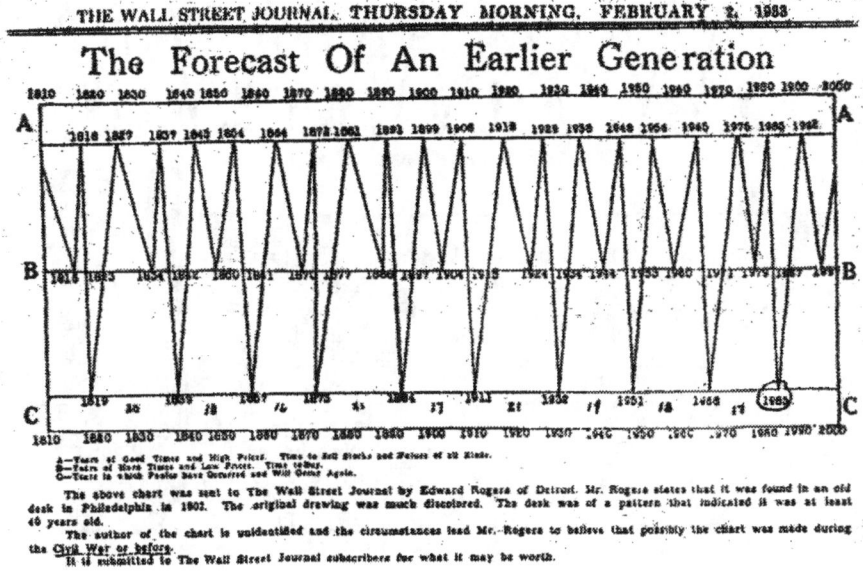

*Figure 19b. The Wall Street Journal Chart "The Forecast of an Earlier Generation."*

versity asserted that "the cause of the eight-year generating cycle is the planet Venus in its eight-yearly periodic motion with respect to the Earth and the Sun." (It may be recalled that in 1867, Professor Norton of Yale had stated that the planets which exercise the greatest influence on the formation of sunspots were Jupiter and Venus, and that in 1863 Carrington charted the Jupiter cycle, Figure 4.) Moore found closely related 8-year cycles in the following:

1. Annual rainfall in the Ohio Valley since 1842.

2. Annual rainfall in Illinois since 1874.

3. Monthly rainfall in the Dakotas since 1882.

4. Rainfall and growth of pines near Prescott, Arizona since 1866.

5. Sauerbeck's index numbers of wholesale prices since 1818.

6. Poynting's index number of wheat prices since 1761.

7. Yield per acre of crops in the Dakotas, the U.S., England and France.

8. Variations in barometric pressure.

The 8-year Venus cycle to which Professor Moore referred occurs when Earth, Venus and the Sun are in a straight line at approximately the same degree of celestial longitude, when Venus is said to be in INFERIOR conjunction. Actually, the conjunction lines of Venus and Earth regress at the rate of 2 degrees, 22 minutes (about 2 days) in each 8-year cycle. Because the orbit of Venus is inclined 3 degrees, 24 minutes to Earth's orbit, transits of Venus across the face of the Sun are rare. They can only occur about the time that Venus passes through its nodes on June 7 and December 9. The nodes are the points where the orbit of Venus intersects the Earth's orbit.

Thus, the first December transit of Venus was observed December 4, 1639 by English astronomer Jeremiah Horrocks, and the first June transit on June 5, 1761 by Russian astronomer M. V. Lomonsov. The next one occurred June 3, 1769. Venus transits occur in pairs separated by about 8 years, with an interval of more than a century between successive pairs. The last transits took place December 8, 1874, and December 6, 1882. The next transits will occur June 7,

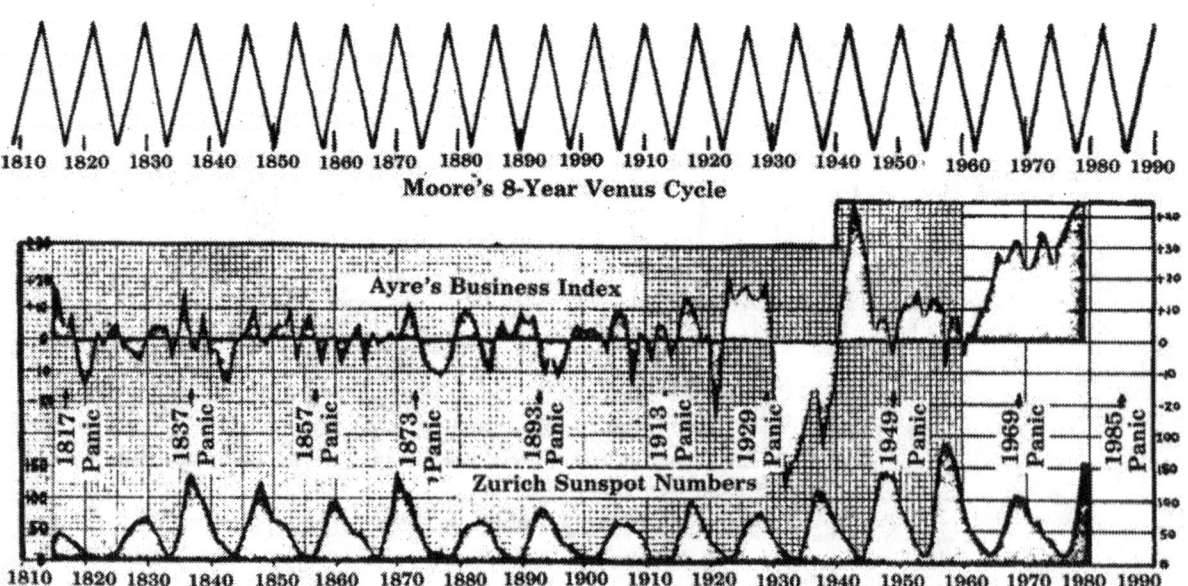

*Figure 20. Moore's 8-Year Venus Cycle vs. Business and Sunspot Cycles.*

2004 and June 5, 2012. The last Sun-Venus-Earth conjunction occurred on November 7, 1978 and the next will occur on November 5, 1986. The relationship of Moore's 8-year Venus cycle to the Business and Sunspot Cycles is shown in Figure 20.

Although Professor Moore was the first economist to use the method of harmonic analysis developed by Sir Arthur Schuster in his 1906 analysis of Wolfer's sunspot numbers, serious doubt has been cast on Moore's findings by Philip Green Wright in a review of Moore's work in the November 1921 *Quarterly Journal of Economics*. Wright states: "The work of Professor Moore shows an immense amount of painstaking research, and yet in spite of the great wealth of apparently corroborative evidence, I regret to say that I find the work unconvincing."

Wright claims that Moore's explanation of the effect of Venus conjunctions is unsatisfactory, stating: "He [Moore] explains at some length the motions of the planet relative to the Earth, and lays stress upon the peculiar climate of Venus, due to the fact that its axial rotation synchronizes with its orbital period of revolution, as having a possible effect upon terrestrial rainfall. In seeking an astronomical cause he is on the right track, but before the Venus theory can be taken seriously it is incumbent upon him to explain in much more detail the process by which either the conjunctions or the meteorological conditions of Venus can affect the Earth."

To the critics of his theory Moore answered in his book, *Generating Economic Cycles*, as follows, "We who are concerned with economic cycles—the tides in the affairs of men—may learn much from the history and theory of terrestrial tides subsequent to Kepler's suggestion that the tides are dependent upon the attraction of the Moon. Will the theory of the cosmical origin of generating cycles, like Kepler's theory of the cosmical origin of terrestrial tides, incur the scorn of eminent critics and receive an adequate development only after two hundred years?

"However ingenious may be the mathematical methods that are used to isolate periodicities, there will always be a healthy skepticism as to the reality of the cycles unless true causes are adduced. Mere empirical regularities are always suspect.

"The linking of astronomic, meteorological, agricultural, and economic causes places the whole discussion upon a rational, rather than upon an empiric basis."

Although Moore's theory has not been proven, its practical application need not wait until "warranted assertibility" has been superseded by certainty. John Dewey defines "warranted assertibility" as knowledge derived through application of the scientific method—knowledge that is highly probable to be sufficiently accurate for practical purposes.

### McWhirter's North Node Business Cycle

The first complete exposition of the planetary theory of the business cycle was given by Louise McWhirter in *McWhirter Theory of Stock Market Forecasting* (1938). Her theory was that "the major or primary trend of business volume and finance is clearly pointed out by the nineteen-year (actually 18.6 year) cycle of the North Node as it passes through the twelve signs of the zodiac."

The cycle is actually 18.6 years long and is due to the fact that the Moon's orbit is inclined 5 degrees, 8 minutes to the plane of the Earth's orbit (the ecliptic). The point where the Moon crosses the ecliptic from south to north is called the *Ascending* or *North Node,* and where the Moon crosses the ecliptic from north to south is called the *Descending or South Node*. But, the crossing points do not occur in the same place each year; they move backward or regress along the ecliptic through the 12 signs of the zodiac in a period of 18.6 years, which is known as the regression of the Moon's Nodes. McWhirter continues:

"Whenever the North Node passes through Scorpio and Libra, there is a transition period as the curve passes from normal, going from normal to high.

"The high point of business volume is reached when the North Node transits Leo. As the North Node goes through Cancer and Gemini, business volume is above normal, but slowly going to normal.

"Taurus is the transition point or normal point as the curve goes from normal to below normal in business volume.

"When the North Node enters Aquarius, the low point of business activity has been reached. As the Node transits Capricorn and Sagittarius, the normal position of the business curve is below normal going to normal.

"This is the natural position of the curve without the presence of secondary factors which can distort the curve favorably or unfavorably from one to twenty percent." (See Figure 21.)

McWhirter lists the following secondary factors which tend to raise business:

1. Jupiter conjunction the North Node.

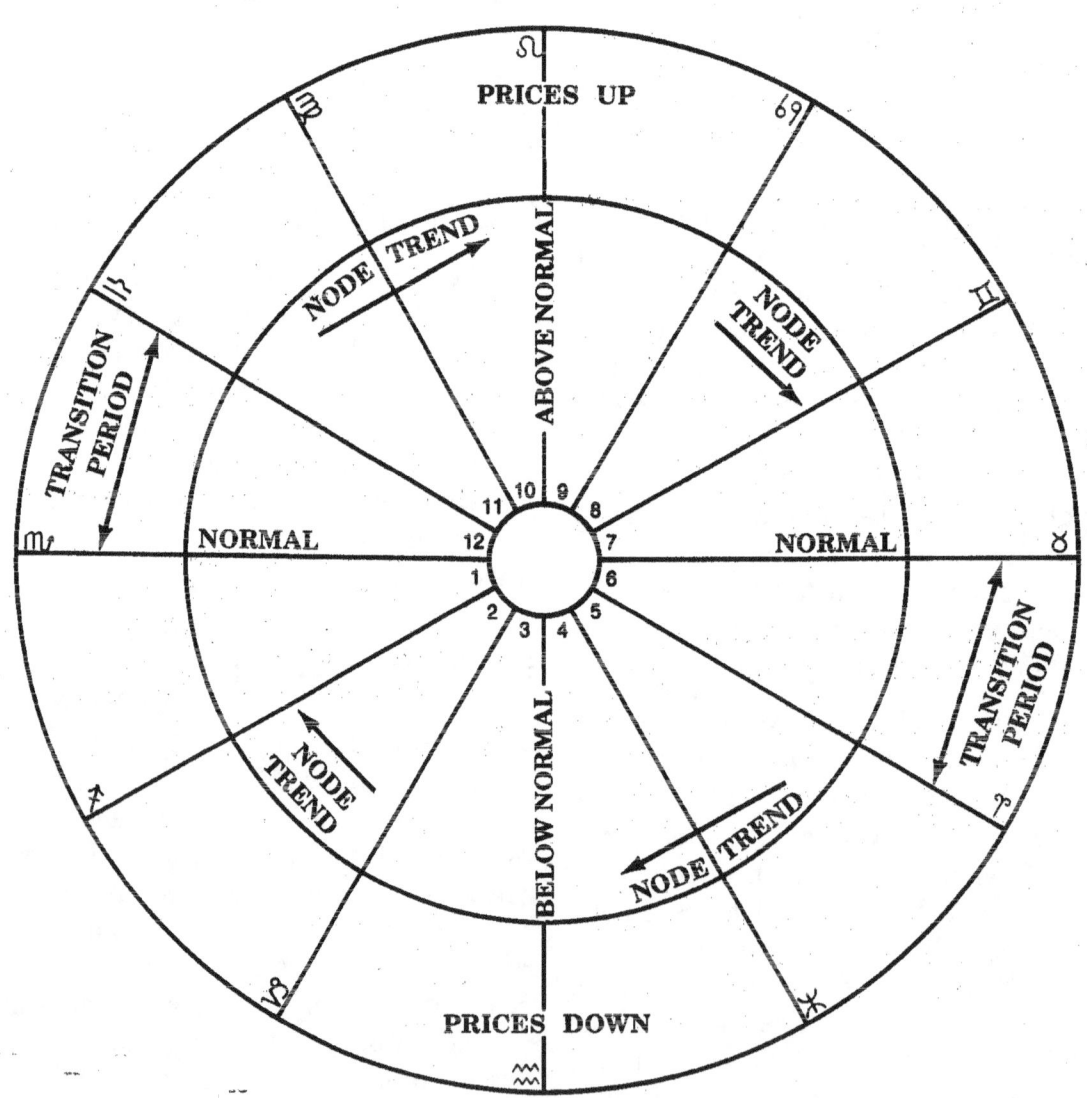

*Figure 21. McWhirter's North Node Business Cycle.*

2. Saturn trine, sextile, or semi-sextile Uranus.

3. Jupiter in Gemini or Cancer.

4. Jupiter conjunction, sextile or trine Saturn and Uranus, when in aspect to each other.

5. The North Node in Gemini.

6. Favorable aspects to Pluto.

The following secondary factors have been found to depress business:

1. Saturn conjunction, square or opposition the North Node.

2. Saturn conjunction, square, opposition, or semi-square Uranus.

3. Saturn in Gemini.

4. Uranus in Gemini.

5. Uranus square, conjunction, or opposition the North Node.

6. Unfavorable aspects to Pluto.

McWhirter concludes: "The rise and fall of prices is governed by the Law of Supply and Demand, which in turn is governed by a law in the universe, hitherto unknown or ignored, known as the Law of Action and Reaction. Periods of business prosperity and depression are not man made nor the result of chance; they come at regular intervals, the same as the seasons, and the same astronomical laws which govern nature, govern man and all man's activities. When this fact is recognized, man will work in harmony with the forces of nature and not blindly against them."

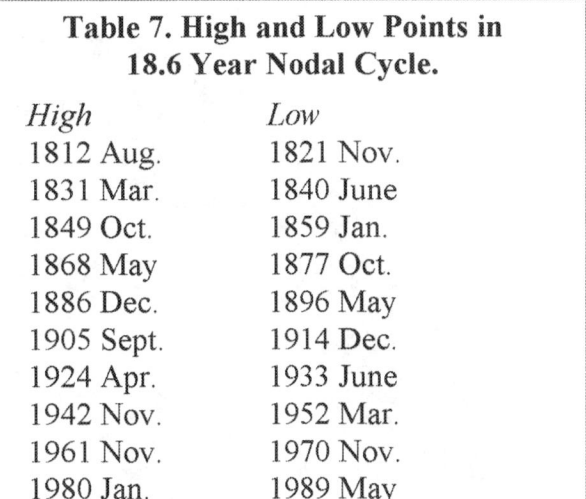

Table 7. High and Low Points in 18.6 Year Nodal Cycle.

| High | Low |
|---|---|
| 1812 Aug. | 1821 Nov. |
| 1831 Mar. | 1840 June |
| 1849 Oct. | 1859 Jan. |
| 1868 May | 1877 Oct. |
| 1886 Dec. | 1896 May |
| 1905 Sept. | 1914 Dec. |
| 1924 Apr. | 1933 June |
| 1942 Nov. | 1952 Mar. |
| 1961 Nov. | 1970 Nov. |
| 1980 Jan. | 1989 May |

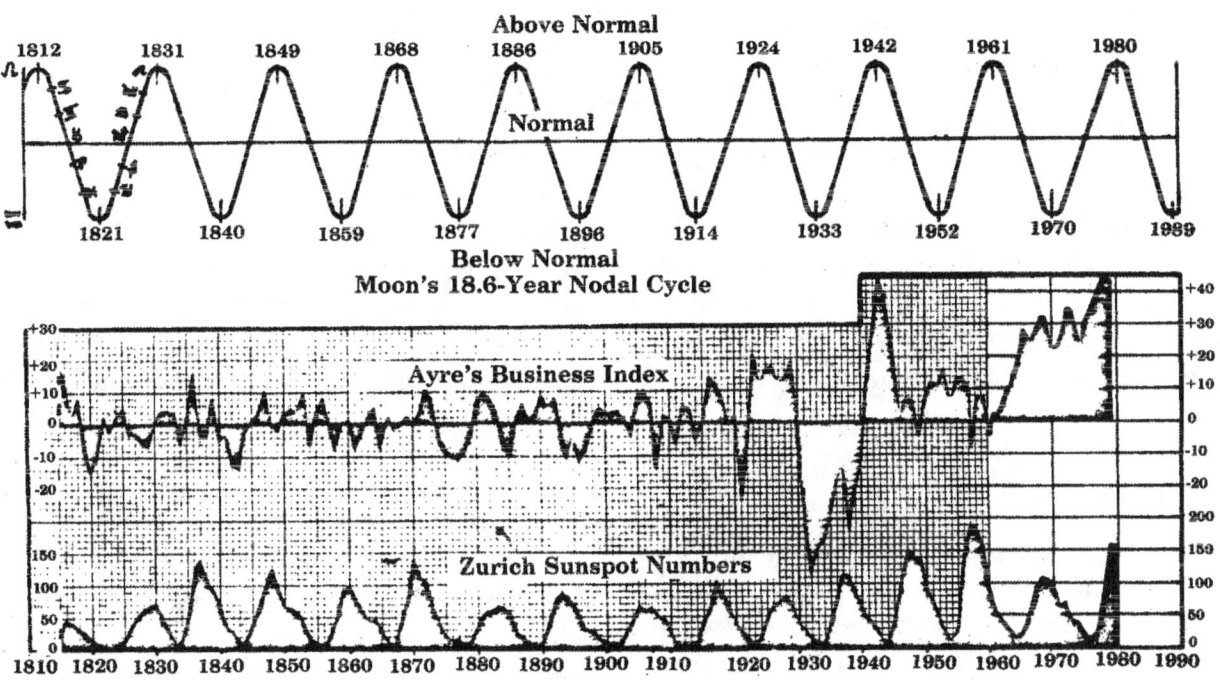

*Figure 22. Moon's 18.6-Year Nodal vs. Business and Sunspot Cycles.*

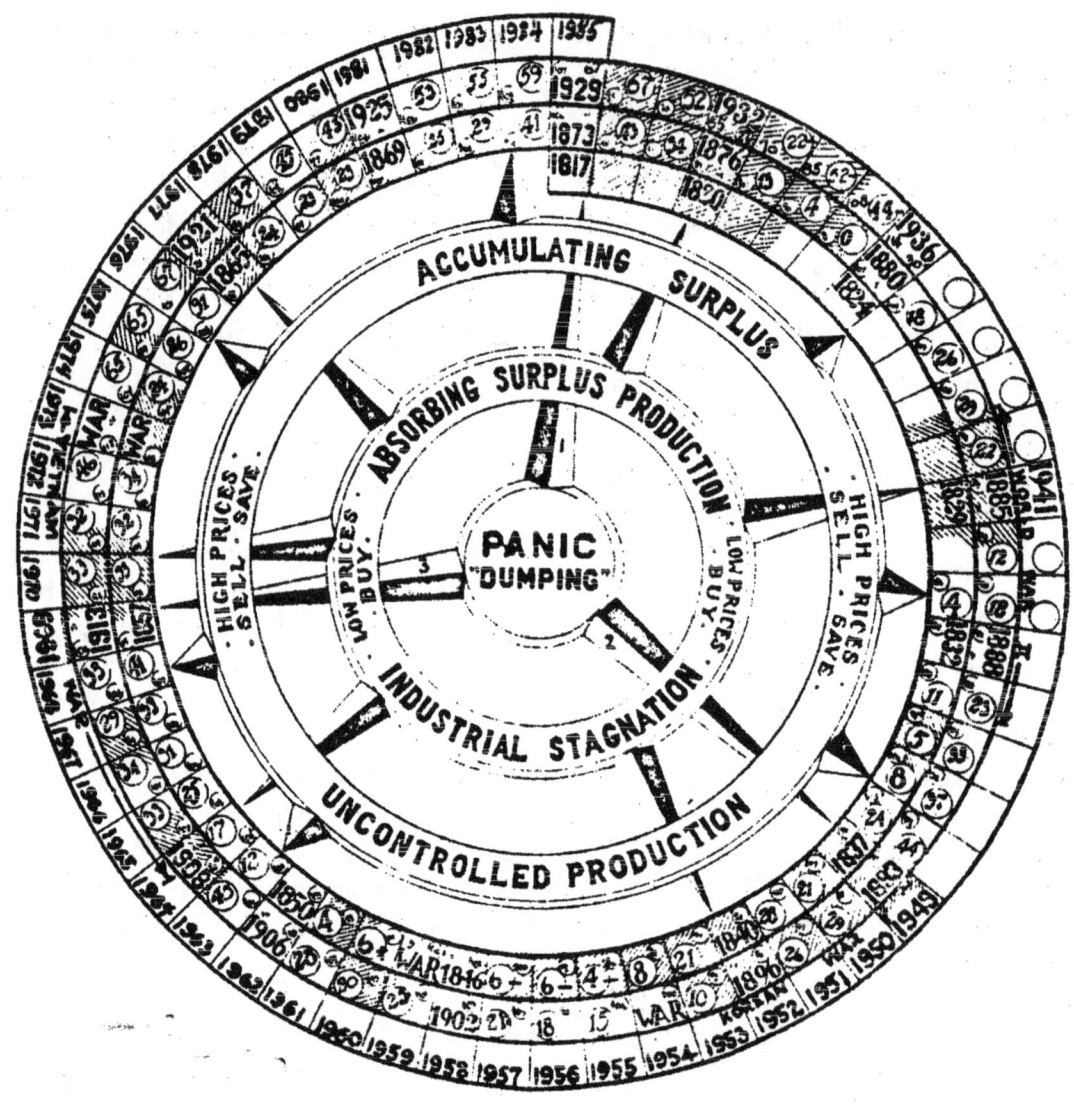

*Figure 23. Funk's Cycles of Prosperity and Depression.*

Figure 22 shows the 18.6 year nodal cycle in comparison with the *"Ayres Business Cycle"* (Cleveland Trust Co.) and the 11-year sunspot cycle. The dates of the *high* and *low* points of the 18.6 year Nodal Cycle are noted in Table 7.

### The 56-year Pattern in American Business Activity

During the mid-1930s, a cable manufacturer came into the author's office in New York and presented him with a pamphlet on *Philocracy*, written in 1932 by J. M. Funk of Ottowa, Illinois in which the latter propounded a theory of economic cycles, which he stated are "a series of events (produced by cause and effect) which recur in the same order." In a description of Figure 23, Funk stated: "A knowledge of the present and history is therefore a key to the future. Until Government Standards are based upon the recognition of exterior forces (which govern human conduct), history will repeat itself. THE CHART WILL PREDICT THE FUTURE because the human make-up includes aspiration, greed, intemperance, fickleness, etc., which traits are governed by endurance; endurance is governed by exterior forces which fluctuate in rhythm and tempo as constantly as the Sun in its journey through the heavens."

The author redrew Funk's chart in the form shown in Figure 24 a-b-c-d, which was used to illustrate a lecture delivered April 16, 1947 at the Henry George School of Social Science, New York. The results show conclusively that regardless of wars, rebellions, population changes, industrialization, technological, and monetary changes, American business has been dominated by a 56-year rhythm. In each 56-year period three major panic periods occur at 20-20-16 year intervals. While other panic periods intervene, no discernible pattern is evidenced. A brief description of each 56-year period follows.

### First Period: 1761-1816 (Figure 24a)

*Panic of 1761.* According to N. J. Silberling, late Professor of Business Research, Graduate School of Business, Stanford University, in *Dynamics of Business* (1943), "Our wars during the first half of the 18th Century were somewhat desultory; in the nature of intermittent skirmishes in the wilderness. The earliest war period shown at the beginning of the 18th Century (Queen Anne's War 1702-1713) failed to produce any pronounced price inflation, and there is no evidence of a sustained and unusual rise in business (trade) activity. King George's War (1745-1748) produced a moderate rise in the price level, but business appears to have improved after the war, rather than during the conflict, when there was evidence of a rather marked depression. The experience during the *French and Indian War (1756-1763)* is rather different; prices rose somewhat and there was a *rather pronounced business boom*, culminating at the close of the war (1760). The period of the American Revolution marks a striking instance of directly inverse movements in commodity prices and trade activity. Following a *short and violent boom in trade in 1771*, there developed a creeping paralysis of all business as the colonists organized opposition to British trade. *During the war itself,* trade conditions reached an *extremely low level of depression,* which was sufficient to deflect the intermediate trend into a pronounced trough."

While major hostilities during the French and Indian War ended with the capture of Quebec in 1759, and the surrender of Montreal in 1760, a peace treaty was not signed until February 10, 1763, when France ceded Canada and all French territory east of the Mississippi to Britain, which also obtained Florida from Spain.

*Panic of 1781.* The surrender of Cornwallis at Yorktown in 1781 marked the end of actual hostilities in the Revolutionary War, whereupon commodity prices collapsed. Farmers who had borrowed money at high prices with an inflated paper currency were unable to meet their obligations after prices dropped. Distress became widespread; land that was sold for debt brought practically nothing; everywhere the papers were filled with notices of insolvencies. In Massachusetts, the farmers' revolt against deflation was expressed in Shay's Rebellion in 1786. Although the rebellion was put down, the state recognized the injustice of the deflation and legalized a moratorium for debtors.

*Panic of 1801.* The conclusion of the first phase of the Napoleonic Wars brought to an end the Carrying Trade Prosperity the country was enjoying. Wholesale Commodity Prices declined 25 percent; domestic goods as well as imported goods and agricultural products declined in price; shipping was depressed.

The most striking feature of this first 56-year segment of American economic activity is the remarkable corroboration provided by the planetary aspects that were operative during that time, viz: the 19.86-year Jupiter-Saturn conjunctions, which occurred during the Panics of 1761, 1781, 1801. The importance attached to these conjunctions is indicated by the following writers. Moore's *Almanac* for 1762 stated: "These conjunctions have been constantly observed to stimulate the most powerful influence of any other planets; therefore their configura-

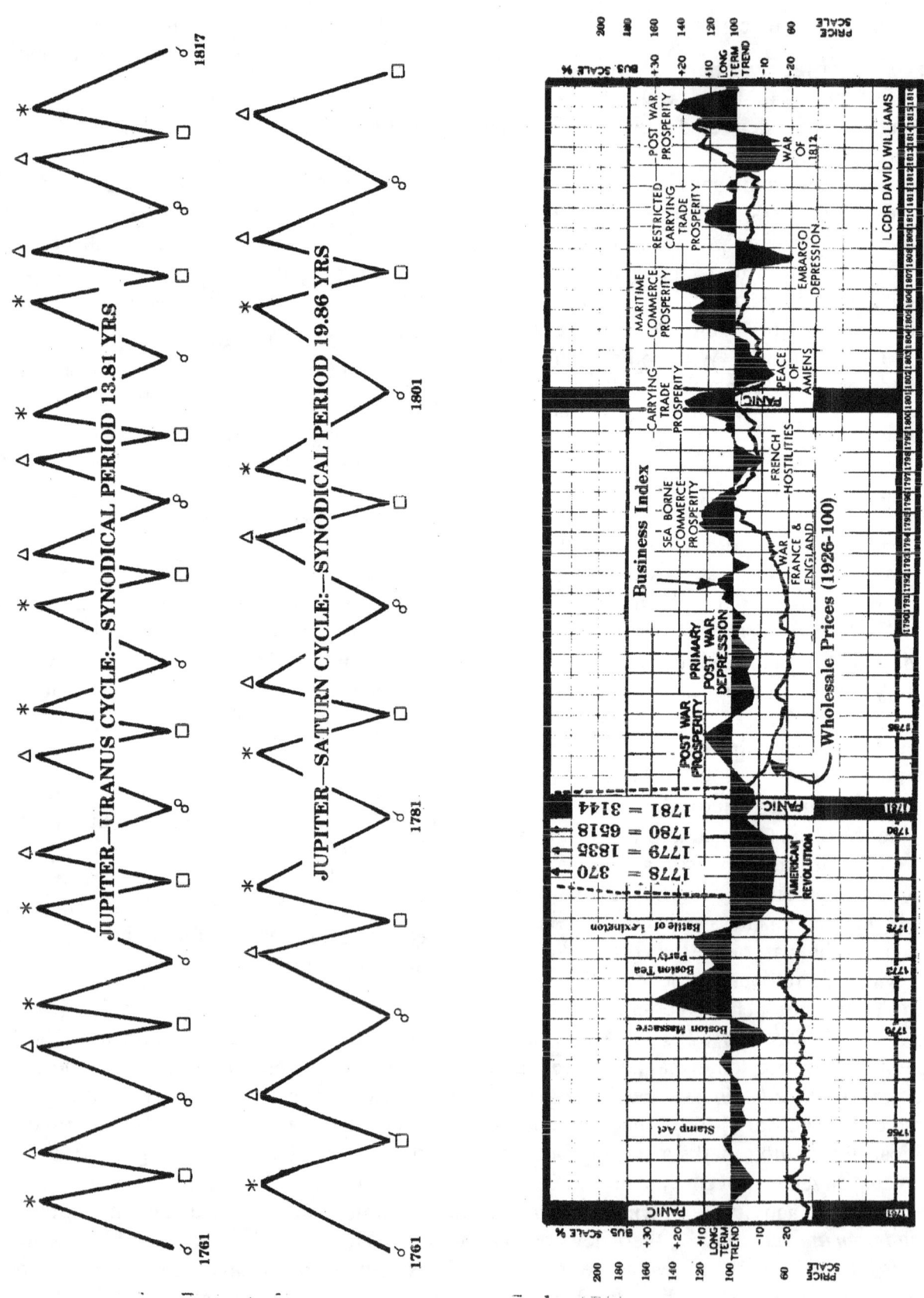

*Figure 24a. 56-Year Pattern of Business vs. Planetary Cycles 1761-1816.*

tions are properly said to dispose of times, whilst the lower planets as lesser causes do more particularly manifest the *intention* or *remission* of the influence of those greater causes."

The English astrologer Sepharial, in *A Manual of Occultism* (1926), stated: "Great importance is attached to the conjunctions of the major planets, and it may be said that no phenomenon of this kind ever happens but it is attended by great mutations and upheavals in the political, religious and physical worlds." John H. Nelson of RCA (a non-astrologer) found physical corroboration, for he stated: "Jupiter and Saturn, the largest planets in the solar system, are the most important. Due to their great size and slow motion, they can exercise the predominating influence on the Sun for prolonged periods of time and therefore establish an over-all standard of disturbed or quiet conditions."

The scientific cause of the disturbances noted at Jupiter-Saturn conjunctions eluded astronomers until recently. Although toward the end of the 19th Century astronomers had postulated the theory that the Sun emitted charged particles which frequently caused magnetic storms, it was not until 1959 and 1962 that charged particle detectors carried in space probes to the Moon and Venus provided direct evidence of such streams, called the *Solar Wind*. It was also found that the pressure exerted by the solar wind on the Earth's magnetic field forms a *Magnetic Tail*, which extends to distances beyond the Moon's orbit, or approximately 8 million miles.

In 1973, the Pioneer 10 spacecraft flew by Jupiter; in 1976 it flew by Saturn. Evidence was obtained from these flights to show that Jupiter's magnetic tail extends at least 500 million miles into outer space and that when Jupiter aligned with Saturn (Jupiter conjunct Saturn), Jupiter's magnetic tail created bizarre storms on Saturn and its nine Moons. It was also found that Saturn has a magnetic field but that *Saturn is the only planet whose magnetic field is swept by the magnetic winds of another planet—Jupiter*. This happens when Jupiter conjoins Saturn and the million-mile-an-hour solar wind blows Jupiter's magnetized particles across Saturn's path.

The Jupiter-Saturn conjunction of October 10, 1781 witnessed the complete destruction of the Continental currency which had been issued by Congress to finance the Revolutionary War. According to Warren & Pearson, in *Prices* (1933), "with subsequent emissions (of paper money), the rate of exchange for hard money at Philadelphia rose very rapidly until May 31, 1781 when a dollar of hard money exchanged for $400 to $1,000 of currency." (It took $19,390 of paper money to buy one ounce of gold!) By the Act of August 4, 1790, the Continental bills were funded at one cent on the dollar, from whence arose the expression "not worth a Continental."

The Jupiter-Saturn conjunction of April 28, 1801, not only coincided with the depression following the end of the first phase of the Napoleonic Wars, but set the stage for an enormous expansion of the territory of the United States through the Louisiana Purchase. Louisiana, which comprised all the territory between the Mississippi and the Rockies, had been a Spanish possession since 1763, when it was ceded by France following the end of the French and Indian War. But by a secret treaty on October 1, 1800, the territory was ceded by Spain back to France. Then, late in 1801, Napoleon sent an expeditionary force to suppress the Negro republic of Haiti and take possession of New Orleans and Louisiana. Late in 1802, the Spanish governor of Louisiana withdrew the right of transit at New Orleans from American traders. In March 1803, President Jefferson commissioned James Monroe to negotiate the purchase of the left bank of the Mississippi and the Gulf Coast from France. Napoleon, who was in need of money to renew the war with Britain and whose expedition to Haiti had turned into a disaster, offered the whole of Louisiana to the U.S. for 12 million dollars, and on April 30, 1803, a treaty of ces-

**Table 8. Jupiter-Saturn Aspects vs. Business Cycle, First 56-Year Period.**

| Date | Aspects | Comment |
|---|---|---|
| Apr. 1761 | 0° | DEPRESSION following end of French and Indian War |
| May 1764 | 60° | Rise in business activity |
| Apr. 1766 | 90° | Decline in business activity (Stamp Act) |
| June 1768 | 120° | Rise in business activity |
| Jan. 1772 | 180° | INCORRECT |
| June 1775 | 240° | Peak followed by decline |
| July 1776 | 270° | Decline during American Revolution |
| Mar. 1778 | 300° | INCORRECT |
| Oct. 1781 | 0° | PANIC resulting from destruction of Continental currency |
| Sept. 1784 | 60° | Post-war prosperity |
| Jan. 1786 | 90° | Primary post-war depression; Shay's Rebellion |
| Aug. 1787 | 120° | INCORRECT |
| Jan. 1791 | 180° | INCORRECT |
| June 1794 | 240° | Seaborne commerce prosperity; Index rose from 0 to +8 |
| May 1796 | 270° | Decline in seaborne commerce prosperity; Index fell from +11 to +3 |
| Nov. 1797 | 300° | INCORRECT |
| May 1801 | 0° | PANIC following end of Napoleonic War; Index fell from +19 to +4 |
| Mar. 1805 | 60° | Maritime commerce prosperity; Index rose from +11 to +17 |
| Dec. 1806 | 90° | INCORRECT |
| Apr. 1808 | 120° | INCORRECT |
| Jan. 1811 | 180° | Index fell from +8 to +1 |
| Apr. 1814 | 240° | Index rose from -16 in April to +14 in December |
| Feb. 1816 | 270° | Index fell from +21 in March to +4 in December |

sion was signed, and the size of the U.S. increased by one-third.

The next most important planetary cycle affecting the business cycle is the Jupiter-Uranus cycle. Jupiter, the largest of our planets, makes one complete revolution around the Sun in 11.86 years, while Uranus, more remote from the Sun, takes 84.02 years to complete its circuit of the Sun. The time between successive conjunctions of Jupiter with Uranus is 13.81 years, which is called their synodical period. Saturn takes 29.46 years to make one solar revolution, and its synodical period with respect to Jupiter is 19.86 years, and with respect to Uranus is 45.36 years.

The year 1761 saw a Jupiter-Saturn conjunction on April 12, a Jupiter-Uranus conjunction on May 20, a Sun-Venus-Earth conjunction (Moore's 8-year Venus Cycle) on June 5, and a Saturn-Uranus conjunction on August 28, 1761! The dates of the aspects in the Jupiter-Saturn cycle are shown in Table 8 and those for the Jupiter-Uranus cycle are shown in Table 9.

### Second Period: 1817-1872 (Figure 24b)

The planetary pattern for this 56-year period begins with the Jupiter-Uranus conjunction of January 28, 1817, which ushered in the panic that bottomed out in the *Primary Post-War Depression*, during which the Jupiter-Saturn conjunction of November 15, 1820, took place. Twenty years after the Panic of 1817 came the Panic of 1837, during which the Jupiter-Uranus opposition of April 26, 1837 occurred and the Business Index fell to 14 below normal.

*Panic of 1817.* The resumption of specie payments on February 20, 1817, (they had been suspended in August 1814) brought about by a reduction in bank loans and discounts, caused commodity prices to decline rapidly. Domestic producers complained of unemployment; importers protested that they had to sell their goods far below cost; lands and houses sold for less than half to one-fourth of their former value. There was a general scarcity of money throughout the country; little was to be had, and that at exorbitant prices. Prisons overflowed with debtors.

*Panic of 1837.* Reckless expenditures for farm land, city lots, cotton, grain, slaves, railroads, canals and public improvements culminated in the Panic of 1837. There was a scramble for liquidity; the loans and discounts of the state banks declined very rapidly. Circulation per ca-

**Table 9. Jupiter-Uranus Aspects vs. Business Cycle, First 56-Year Period.**

| Date | Aspect | Comment |
|---|---|---|
| May 1761 | 0° | DEPRESSION following end of French and Indian War |
| May 1763 | 60° | Rise in business activity |
| Aug. 1764 | 90° | INCORRECT |
| Oct. 1765 | 120° | INCORRECT |
| Apr. 1768 | 180° | INCORRECT |
| Sept. 1770 | 240° | Index rose from Boston Massacre low |
| Oct. 1771 | 270° | INCORRECT |
| Oct. 1772 | 300° | Index high though declining |
| Nov. 1774 | 0° | INCORRECT |
| Mar. 1777 | 60° | INCORRECT |
| May 1778 | 90° | Depression during American Revolution |
| Oct. 1779 | 120° | INCORRECT |
| Dec. 1781 | 180° | PANIC resulting from destruction of Continental currency |
| Apr. 1784 | 240° | Post-war prosperity |
| May 1785 | 270° | Index declining |
| June 1786 | 300° | INCORRECT |
| Nov. 1788 | 0° | Primary post-war depression |
| Apr. 1791 | 60° | Rise in Index from 0 in April to +4 in August |
| July 1792 | 90° | INCORRECT |
| Oct. 1793 | 120° | Rise in Index from -6 in May to +1 in November |
| Jan. 1796 | 180° | Index fell from +11 in January to +3 in December |
| Feb. 1798 | 240° | INCORRECT |
| Mar. 1799 | 270° | Index below normal; -4 in January to -1 in April |
| May 1800 | 300° | Carrying trade prosperity; Index +2 in May to +14 in December |
| Dec. 1802 | 0° | DEPRESSION; Peace of Amiens; Index fell from 0 in January to -15 in September |
| June 1805 | 60° | Maritime commerce prosperity; Index varied from +11 to +17 |
| Aug. 1806 | 90° | Index fell from +16 in Jan. to +12 in June |
| Oct. 1807 | 120° | Index +23 in January |
| Nov. 1809 | 180° | Embargo Depression; Index -10 in January |
| Jan. 1812 | 240° | Index above normal +4 |
| Apr. 1813 | 270° | War of 1812; Index below normal all year (-13 to -17) |
| July 1814 | 300° | Index rose from -11 in June to +14 in December |

Summation: 10 out of 32 aspects, or 31¼ percent, gave the wrong indications. 22 out of 32 aspects, or 68¾ percent, gave correct indications.

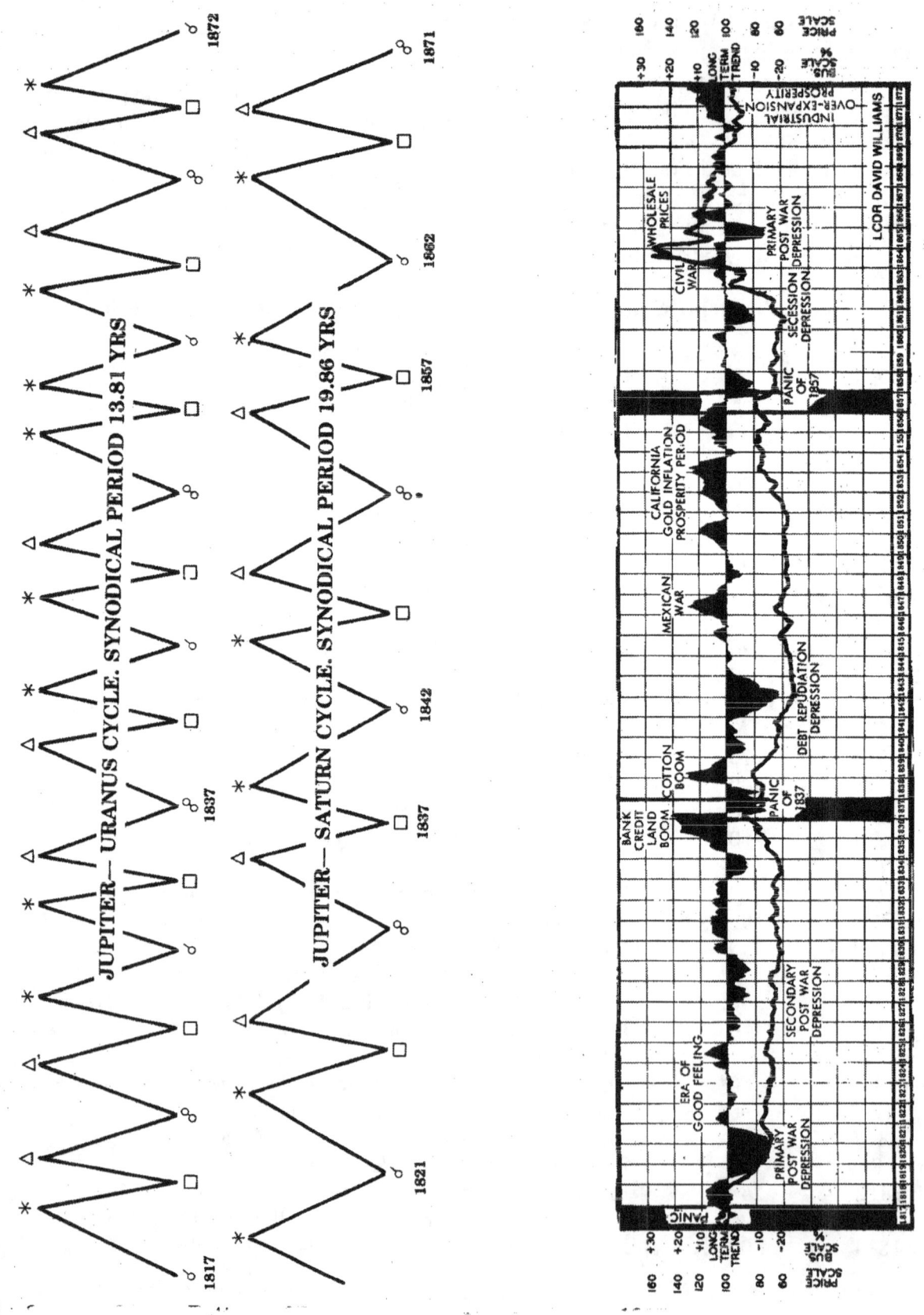

*Figure 24b. 56-Year Pattern of Business vs. Planetary Cycles 1817-1872.*

pita declined 48 percent and commodity prices declined 43 percent. By 1841, one-third of the banks of Ohio had failed, and riots occurred. Wisconsin, Tennessee, Kentucky, Indiana and Michigan had similar experiences. Many states omitted interest payments on their debts, while others repudiated their debts. Railroad stocks fell 75 percent and railroad bonds 50 percent. The assessed value per capita of New York City real estate fell 40 percent. The Jupiter-Saturn conjunction of April 21, 1841 saw the Business Index at 4 below normal, to be followed by a low of 19 below normal in January 1843 during the Debt Repudiation Depression. The Jupiter-Uranus conjunction of October 10, 1857 coincided with the Panic of 1857, which saw the Business Index fall to 13 below normal in January 1858.

*Panic of 1857.* The over-expansion of bank credit during the California Gold Inflation Prosperity Period came to an end with the failure of the Ohio Life Insurance Company in 1857. Failure of country banks in the West followed rapidly; 37 banks failed in the state of Maine alone; there were almost 5,000 business failures in 1857; land sales declined 84 percent; the number of incoming immigrants fell about 50 percent; wholesale prices of farm goods declined 33 percent; wholesale prices of all commodities fell 21 percent; railroad stocks fell 48 percent; railroad

**Table 10. Jupiter-Saturn Aspects vs Business Cycles, Second 56-Year Period.**

| Date | Aspect | Comment |
|---|---|---|
| Oct. 1818 | 300° | Index rose from +7 to +9 |
| Sept. 1821 | 0° | Primary post-war depression; Index bottomed at -16 in January and February |
| Jan. 1825 | 60° | Era of good feeling; Index rose from +2 in Feb. to +9 in June |
| Jan. 1827 | 90° | Secondary post-war depression; Index ranged from -5 in January to -1 in October |
| Feb. 1829 | 120° | INCORRECT |
| June 1832 | 180° | INCORRECT |
| May 1835 | 240° | Bank Credit Land Boom; Index rose from -6 in Jan. to +9 in Dec. |
| Jan. 1837 | 270° | Panic of 1837; Index fell from +21 in February to -13 in October |
| Oct. 1838 | 300° | Cotton Boom; Index rose from -12 in April to +14 in December |
| Mar. 1842 | 0° | Debt repudiation Recession; Index fell from -7 in January to -18 in December |
| Feb. 1845 | 60° | Index normal; rose from -2 in February to +4 in December |
| June 1846 | 90° | Index declined from +5 in February to -1 in June |
| Jan. 1848 | 120° | INCORRECT |
| Oct. 1851 | 180° | Index declined from +11 in January to +1 in December |
| May 1855 | 240° | California gold inflation prosperity period; Index rose from -3 in January to +5 in October |
| Dec. 1856 | 270° | Prelude to Panic of 1857 |
| July 1858 | 300° | INCORRECT (depression following Panic of 1857) |
| Jan. 1862 | 0° | Secession Depression; Index ran from -7 in January to 0 in October |
| Oct. 1865 | 60° | INCORRECT |
| Apr. 1867 | 90° | Primary post-war depression; Index was above normal only 2 months |
| Sept. 1868 | 120° | Index was above normal for 5 months |
| June 1871 | 180° | INCORRECT |

Summation: 6 out of 23 aspects, or 26 percent, gave the wrong indication. 17 out of 23 aspects, or 74 percent, gave the correct indication.

bonds fell 20 percent. The worst effects of the panic were felt by the labor classes as unemployment was widespread.

The dates of the Jupiter-Saturn aspects are shown in Table 10 and those of the Jupiter-Uranus cycle are shown in Table 11.

**Table 11. Jupiter-Uranus Aspects vs. Business Cycles–Second 56-Year Period.**

| Date | Aspect | Comment |
|---|---|---|
| Feb. 1817 | 0° | Panic of 1817; Index fell from +2 to -3, then rose to +4 in November |
| Dec. 1819 | 60° | INCORRECT |
| Jan. 1821 | 90° | Primary post-war depression; Index bottomed at -16 in January and February |
| Feb. 1822 | 120° | Era of good feeling; Index rose from +3 in February to +5 in April |
| Mar. 1824 | 180° | Era of good feeling; Index fell from -2 in February to -1 in May before rising |
| Aug. 1826 | 240° | INCORRECT |
| Dec. 1827 | 270° | Secondary post-war depression; Index fell from -5 in February to -1 in October |
| Mar. 1829 | 300° | INCORRECT |
| June 1831 | 0° | INCORRECT |
| July 1833 | 60° | Index above normal; between +2 and +5 |
| July 1834 | 90° | Index below normal; between -2 and -8 |
| Aug. 1835 | 120° | Bank Credit Land Boom; Index rose from -6 in Feb. to +9 in Dec. |
| Dec. 1837 | 180° | Panic of 1837; Index fell from +21 in Feb. to -13 in Oct. |
| June 1840 | 240° | INCORRECT |
| Sept. 1841 | 270° | Debt Repudiation Depression; Index ranged from -1 to -5 |
| Nov. 1842 | 300° | INCORRECT |
| Dec. 1844 | 0° | Debt Repudiation Depression; Index ranged from -4 to -5 |
| Dec. 1846 | 60° | Index rose during Mexican War; Index ranged from -1 to +5 |
| Feb. 1848 | 90° | Index fell at end of Mexican War from +3 to -5 |
| Apr. 1849 | 120° | INCORRECT |
| Oct. 1851 | 180° | Index fell from +11 to -1 |
| Mar. 1854 | 240° | California gold inflation prosperity period; Index ranged between +15 to -4 |
| Apr. 1855 | 270° | INCORRECT |
| May 1856 | 300° | California gold inflation prosperity period; Index ranged from +5 to +10 |
| June 1858 | 0° | Decline during the Panic of 1857; Index ranged between -13 and -4 |
| Sept. 1860 | 60° | Index rose from -1 to +5 |
| Nov. 1861 | 90° | Secession Depression; Index ranged from -2 to -10 |
| Mar. 1863 | 120° | Index rose during Civil War from 0 to +4 |
| Sept. 1865 | 180° | Primary post-war depression; Index fell from +4 to -14 |
| Dec. 1867 | 240° | INCORRECT |
| Dec. 1868 | 270° | INCORRECT |
| Dec. 1869 | 300° | Index rose from +1 to +5 |
| Mar. 1872 | 0° | INCORRECT |

Summation: 11 out of 33 aspects, or 33⅓ percent, gave the wrong indication. 22 out of 33 aspects, or 66⅔ percent, gave the correct indication.

### Third Period: 1873-1928 (Figure 24c)

The planetary pattern for this 56-year period shows the Jupiter-Saturn square of August 1896, and the Jupiter-Uranus square of October 1896 coinciding with the lowest point in the U.S. Wholesale Price Index in 200 years. (1780 = 3360 vs. 1896 = 23.9. The 1932 depression low was 33.6.) The Jupiter-Uranus opposition of May 1893 correctly indicated the PANIC of 1893 and the Jupiter-Uranus conjunction of May 3, 1914, coincided with the World War I depression.

The three major depressions that occurred during this period were:

*Panic of 1873.* In the fall of 1873, about crop-moving time, when credit tightened, a severe panic precipitated by the failure of Jay Cooke swept over the country. Wholesale prices of all commodities fell 39 percent, but prices of metals and textiles fell 50 percent; railroad stocks fell 50 percent; the number of incoming immigrants declined 70 percent; the tonnage of American vessels built fell 59 percent; production of pig iron declined 29 percent. The stock exchange and many banks were forced to close.

*Panic of 1893.* The weakening of the country's financial condition due to the outflow of gold occasioned, first, by the necessity for paying in gold for imports and interest on our debts, and second, by fears that silver was about to replace gold, brought on the Panic of 1893; 573 banks failed; one-fourth of the railroads went into the hands of receivers; pig iron production declined 27 percent; commercial failures trebled; unemployment was widespread; strikers and riots were numerous; Coxey's army of unemployed marched to Washington.

*Panic of 1913-1914.* The Balkan Wars of 1912-1913, foreshadowing an eventual armed conflict among the major European powers, caused the gradual liquidation by Europeans of billions of dollars worth of American securities in our markets. This liquidation reached its height in August 1914, when the New York Stock Exchange was forced to close. The Business Index fell to -14 in November and December of 1914.

*World War I (1914-1918).* This war between the Central Powers (Austria-Hungary, Germany, Bulgaria and Turkey) and the Allies (U.S., Britain, France, Russia, Belgium, Serbia, Greece, Romania, Montenegro, Portugal, Italy, Japan) resulted in the death of 10 million combatants and the wounding of another 20 million. The Business Index dropped from +1 in March to -14 in December 1914, and then climbed to +16 in October and November 1916 under the impetus of war orders from the Allies.

The dates of the Jupiter-Saturn aspects are shown in Table 12, and those for the Jupiter-Uranus cycle are shown in Table 13.

### Fourth Period: 1929-1984 (Figure 24d)

The planetary pattern for this 56-year period starts with the Jupiter-Uranus sextile aspect of November 17, 1929, which occurred during the 1929 Bull Stock Market. This was followed by the December 15, 1930 Jupiter-Saturn opposition and the December 22, 1930 Jupiter-Uranus square that ushered in the secondary post war depression. It is interesting to note that the Jupiter-Uranus sextile aspect coincided with four boom periods, viz, a) the 1929 Bull Market Boom; b) World War II Boom; c) Korean War Boom; d) Vietnam War Boom. The correlation between planetary aspects and the Business Cycle is shown in Tables 14, 15, 16, and 17.

The following is quoted from a lecture given by the author before the Henry George School of Social Science in New York on April 16, 1947.

*Panic of 1929.* In August 1929, began one of the greatest peace-time declines in prices of which the world has a record. The index of prices fell from 49.8 in July 1929 to 33 in June 1932 (Index 1967 = 100). Most measures of industrial activity were about 40 to 60 percent be-

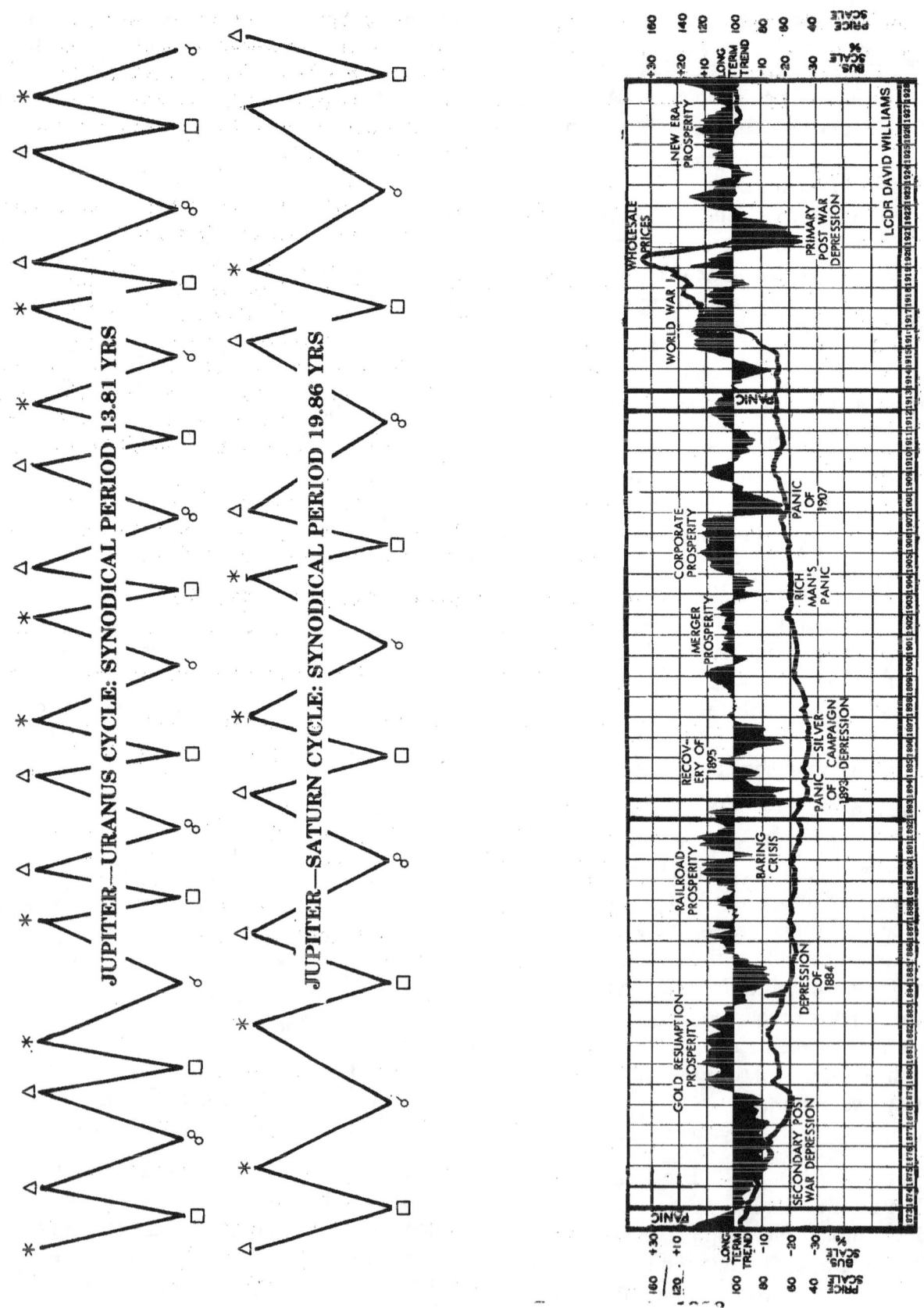

*Figure 24c. 56-Year Pattern of Business vs. Planetary Cycles 1873-1928.*

low normal. Honest men could not get work, creditors could not collect their debts, and "For Rent" signs appeared everywhere. Payments on reparations, war debts and other international debts were suspended; most countries of the world suspended specie payments. Banks closed; debt moratoriums were declared; the gold standard was abandoned; gold was confiscated; the dollar was devalued. Never before was such a prodigious destruction and transfer of wealth experienced by the world in times of peace.

*Panic of 1949.* What will be the aftermath of World War II? The late General Leonard P. Ayres of the Cleveland Trust Company in 1935 formulated the following generalized observation: "Great wars appear to produce regular sequences of economic results which we may identify as 1) commodity price inflation; 2) farm prosperity and farm land speculation; 3) price deflation and short primary post-war depression; 4) a period of city prosperity and widespread speculation; 5) secondary price deflation and a long secondary post-war depression." We are now (1947) going thru the third phase of Ayres's sequence. The fall of 1949 should usher in the fifth phase, if history repeats itself.

Wholesale commodity prices reached their peak during the Revolutionary War in 1780. Three 56-year periods brings us to 1948, in which year the peak of present day wholesale commodity prices will occur, if it has not already done so. (The peak actually came in 1948.) The peak in the Civil War occurred in

### Table 12. Jupiter-Saturn Aspects vs. Business Cycles, Third 56-Year Period.

| *Date* | *Aspect* | *Comment* |
|---|---|---|
| Oct. 1874 | 240° | INCORRECT |
| Sept. 1876 | 270° | Secondary post-war depression; Index ranged between -9 and -12 |
| May 1878 | 300° | INCORRECT |
| Apr. 1881 | 0° | INCORRECT |
| Aug. 1884 | 60° | INCORRECT |
| Sept. 1886 | 90° | Recovery from Depression of 1884, which bottomed in May 1885 at -13 |
| Oct. 1888 | 120° | Railroad prosperity; Index rose from -2 to +6 |
| Jan. 1892 | 180° | INCORRECT |
| Dec. 1894 | 240° | Recovery from Panic of 1893. Index rose from -20 to -4 |
| Aug. 1896 | 270° | Silver Campaign Depression. Index ranged between -2 and -18 |
| May 1898 | 300° | Recovery; Index ranged between +3 and -2 |
| 9/23/1901 | 0° | INCORRECT |
| 7/28/1904 | 60° | INCORRECT |
| 12/13/1905 | 90° | INCORRECT |
| 7/2/1907 | 120° | Corporate prosperity; Index ranged between +12 and -17 |
| 5/2/1911 | 180° | Depression; Index ranged between -8 and -5 |
| 12/16/1914 | 240° | INCORRECT; World War I |
| 6/28/1916 | 270° | INCORRECT |
| 1/13/1918 | 300° | WWI prosperity; Index ranged between +2 and +11 |
| 8/23/1921 | 0° | Primary post-war depression |
| 4/16/1925 | 60° | New era prosperity; Index ranged between +3 and +11 |
| 10/14/1926 | 90° | INCORRECT |
| 2/29/1928 | 120° | Bull Market Boom; Index ranged between +5 and +17 |

Summation: 11 out of 23 aspects, or 48 percent, gave the wrong indication. 12 out of 23 aspects, or 52 percent, gave the correct indication.

1864, and exactly 56 years later came the peak of World War I, in 1920. Because of price rigidities introduced by pressure from the farm and labor blocs, it is not expected that the decline in prices will be as violent as during the earlier deflations." (The outbreak of the Korean War in June 1950 resulted in an increase in prices, as shown in Figure 24d.)

The prediction made in April 1947 about the Panic of 1949 was fulfilled on schedule, as is proven by the following:

1a. The Cleveland Trust Co. Index of American Business Activity dropped from 32 percent above normal in February 1949 to 0.5 percent below normal in July 1949. (This index was revised in 1960.)

1b. The American Institute for Economic

### Table 13. Jupiter-Uranus Aspects vs. Business Cycle, Third 56-Year Period.

| Date | Aspect | Comment |
|---|---|---|
| Oct. 1874 | 60° | INCORRECT |
| Jan. 1876 | 90° | Secondary post-war depression; Index ranged between -9 and -12 |
| Apr. 1877 | 120° | INCORRECT |
| Aug. 1879 | 180° | Secondary post-war depression; Index below normal first 8 months |
| Aug. 1881 | 240° | Gold resumption prosperity; Index ranged between +8 and +12 |
| Oct. 1882 | 270° | INCORRECT |
| Nov. 1883 | 300° | Gold resumption prosperity; Index above normal first 10 months |
| June 1886 | 0° | INCORRECT |
| Jan. 1889 | 60° | Railroad prosperity; Index above normal for 11 months |
| Mar. 1890 | 90° | INCORRECT |
| Apr. 1891 | 120° | Index above normal for 8 months |
| May 1893 | 180° | Panic of 1893; Index fell from +10 to -20 |
| Aug. 1895 | 240° | Recovery of 1895; Index rose from -9 to +6 |
| Oct. 1896 | 270° | Silver Campaign Depression; Index fell to -18 |
| Jan. 1898 | 300° | Recovery; Index below normal only 3 months |
| Aug. 1900 | 0° | Index fell from +11 in January to -5 in October |
| 11/13/1902 | 60° | Merger prosperity; Index ranged between +2 and +5 |
| 12/1/1903 | 90° | Rich man's panic; Index dropped to -11 |
| 12/10/1904 | 120° | INCORRECT |
| 2/2/1907 | 180° | INCORRECT; Panic of 1907 didn't start until November 1907 |
| 7/1/1909 | 240° | Recovery; Index rose from +2 in July to +9 in December |
| 10/9/1910 | 270° | Decline from +9 in January to -6 in December |
| 1/10/1912 | 300° | Recovery; Index ranged between -3 and +8 |
| 5/3/1914 | 0° | World War I; Index ranged between +1 and -14 |
| 5/30/1916 | 60° | World War I prosperity; Index ranged between +12 and +16 |
| 6/9/1917 | 90° | INCORRECT |
| 7/2/1918 | 120° | World War I prosperity; Index ranged between +2 and +11 |
| 10/31/1920 | 180° | Primary post-war depression; Index declined from +15 to -16 |
| 5/7/1923 | 240° | Recovery; Index rose from +7 to +16 |
| 7/25/1924 | 270° | Index fell from +8 to -7 |
| 9/18/1925 | 300° | New era prosperity; Index ranged between +3 and +11 |
| 10/18/1927 | 0° | Index fell from +12 to +1 |

Summation: 8 out of 32 aspects, or 25 percent, gave the wrong indication. 24 out of 32 aspects, or 75 percent, gave the correct indication.

Research Index dropped from 12 percent above normal in February 1949 to 17 percent below normal in October 1949.

1c. An average of 5 Composite Indices of the Physical Volume of Business in the U.S. dropped from 132 percent in January 1949 to 104 percent in October 1949.

2. The U.S. Bureau of Labor Statistics Index of Commodity Prices showed a gradual decline from 160.6 in January 1949 to 151.3 in December 1949. But during this same time period 15 basic commodities dropped as follows: tallow, 51 percent; lead, 44 percent; copper, 43 percent; zinc, 42 percent; steel scrap (Phil.), 42 percent; cottonseed oil, 37 percent; flaxseed, 35 percent; steel scrap (Chic.), 29 percent; hogs, 25 percent; coco beans, 19 percent; tin, 17 percent; rosin, 15 percent; corn, 12 percent; rubber, 11 percent.

3. The Dow-Jones Index of Industrial Stocks made a new low in June 1949.

4. Dun and Bradstreet's Index of Commercial & Industrial Failures in the U.S. rose during 1949 to a total of 9246 with total liabilities of $308,109,000, the highest since 1945 when the comparable figures were 809 failures with liabilities of $30,225,000.

5. The *1950 World Almanac* reports: "September 18, 1949, Devaluation of Pound by Britain creates fiscal upset. Britain devalues Pound by 30 percent (from $4.03 to $2.80). The change caused a fiscal crisis in European states." 24 nations followed suit in 1949. Indonesia recently devalued her currency to 50 percent.

*Panic of 1969*. The casual observer of Figure 24d might well wonder why the author denoted 1969 as a PANIC period. While wholesale commodity prices continued their inflationary climb, the Business Index declined from its 1969 peak of +34 in August to a low of +21 in November 1970 (a decline of 38 percent), and the New York Stock Market declined 36½ percent in the 18 months between the Dow Jones Industrial high of 984.65 on December 2, 1968, and the low of 627.46 on May 26, 1970. This made it the worst Bear Market since that of 1937-1938 and represented a paper loss of 500 billion dollars.

Interest rates shot up to the highest levels since the Civil War, causing a severe decline in bond prices. Unemployment rose to 5.9 percent. The gross debts of the country increased from 484 percent of the value of commodity production in 1929 to 583 percent in 1969. In terms of dollars, the increase was from 215 billion in 1929 to 1,964 billion in 1969. This means that the financial resources of the U.S. economy were under a strain unprecedented in the financial history of the country.

The world's largest privately owned transportation company, the Penn Central Railroad, went bankrupt. Lockheed, the largest specialist munitions manufacturer, was only kept afloat by massive government subsidies. Many prominent stock brokerage houses went bankrupt. The dollar was devalued, as at the bottom of the Great Depression of the 1930s.

The aftermath of the misguided "guns and butter" policy of President Johnson during the Vietnam War resulted in a steady rise in the U.S. Wholesale Price Index which reached a level of 545 (1926=100) by the end of 1980, and 575 in 1981. Statistics for 1981 were not available at the time this was written (April 1982).

The correlations between the planetary aspects and the Business Cycle are shown in Tables 14-18.

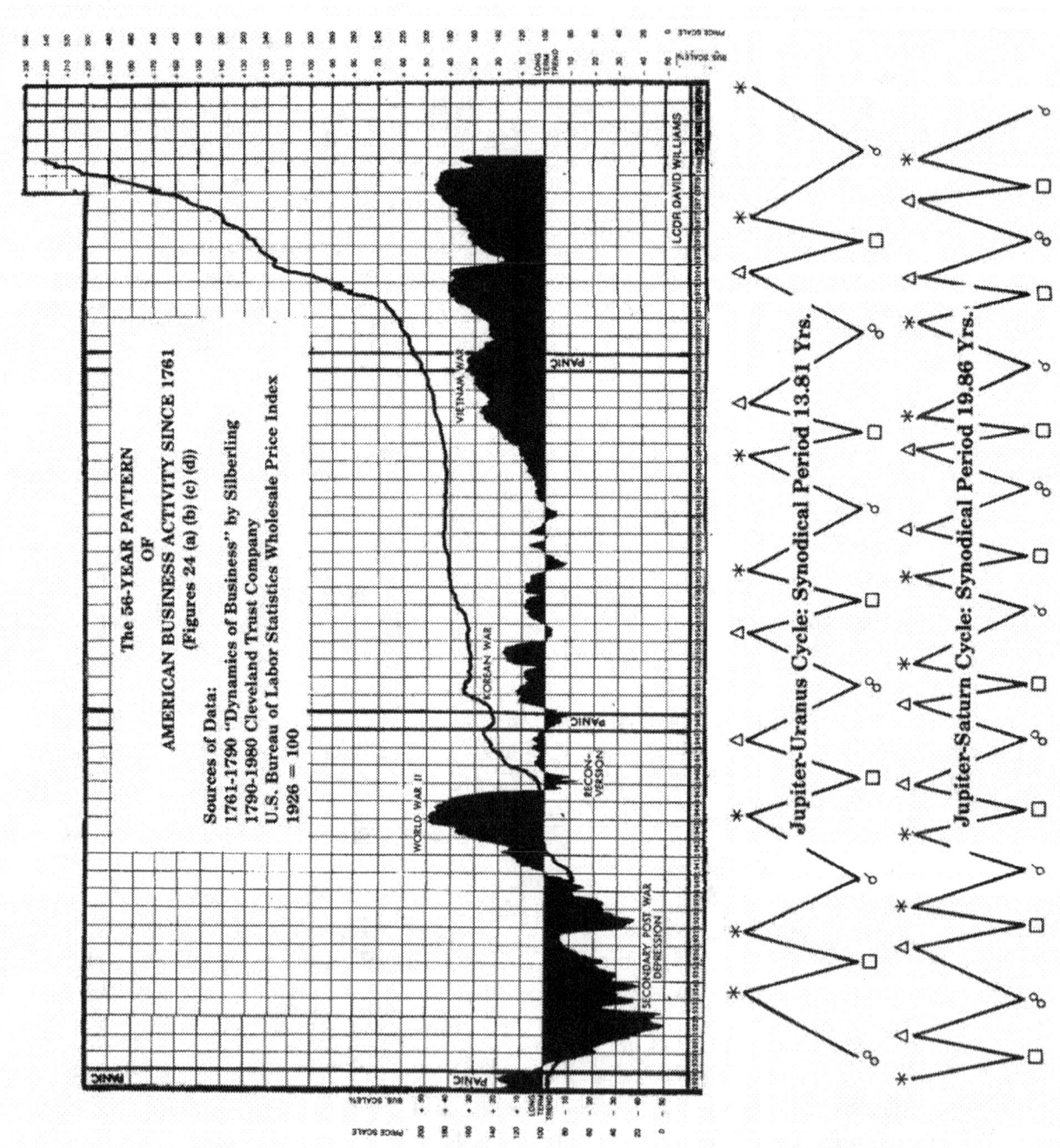

*Figure 24d. 56-Year Pattern of Business vs. Planetary Cycles 1929-1984.*

### Table 14. Jupiter-Saturn Aspects vs. Business Cycles, Fourth 56-Year Period.

| Date | Aspect | Comment |
|---|---|---|
| 12/15/1930 | 180° | Secondary post-war depression; Index fell from +4 in January to -21 in December |
| 6/1/1934 | 240° | INCORRECT |
| 3/28/1936 | 270° | Secondary post-war depression; Index varied between -25 and -7 |
| 11/25/1937 | 300° | INCORRECT |
| 11/15/1940 | 0° | Secondary post-war depression; Index varied between -17 and -2 |
| 5/1/1944 | 60° | World War II Boom; Index between +43 and +50 |
| 6/12/1946 | 90° | Reconversion; Index varied between -15 and +3 |
| 6/9/1948 | 120° | Index varied between +6 and +1 |
| 8/3/1951 | 180° | INCORRECT |
| 6/25/1954 | 240° | INCORRECT |
| 2/18/1956 | 270° | INCORRECT |
| 12/3/1957 | 300° | Index varied between +9 and -2 |
| 4/16/1961 | 0° | Index above normal only during last 3 months |
| 2/2/1964 | 60° | Index rose from +9 in February to +14 in December |
| 7/4/1965 | 90° | INCORRECT |
| 2/8/1967 | 120° | Index varied between +24 and +27 |
| 1/10/1971 | 180° | INCORRECT |
| 7/29/1974 | 240° | Index varied between +25 and +40 |
| 2/4/1976 | 270° | INCORRECT |
| 8/26/1977 | 300° | Index varied between +33 and +38 |
| 4/7/1981 | 0° | Index rose from +32 in January to +40 in June, then fell to +27 in December |
| 11/7/1984 | 60° | |

Summation: 8 out of 21 aspects, or 38 percent, gave the wrong indication. 13 out of 21 aspects, or 62 percent, gave the correct indication.

### Table 15. Jupiter-Uranus Aspects vs. Business Cycles, Fourth 56-Year Period.

| Date | Aspect | Comment |
|---|---|---|
| 11/17/1929 | 60° | Bull Market Boom; Index varied between +4 and +20 |
| 12/11/1930 | 90° | Secondary post-war depression; Index fell from +4 to -21 |
| 2/22/1932 | 120° | INCORRECT |
| 8/25/1934 | 180 | Secondary post-war depression; Index ranged between -29 and -40 |
| 1/30/1937 | 240° | INCORRECT |
| 3/13/1938 | 270° | Secondary post-war depression; Index ranged between -25 and -38 |
| 4/1/1939 | 300 | INCORRECT |
| 4/21/1941 | 0° | INCORRECT |
| 7/14/1943 | 60° | World War II Boom; Index ranged between -33 and +50 |
| 10/5/1944 | 90° | INCORRECT |
| 1/15/1946 | 120° | INCORRECT |
| 7/17/1948 | 180° | INCORRECT |
| 10/9/1950 | 240° | Korean War Boom; Index rose from -5 to +12 |
| 10/25/1951 | 270° | Index fell from +13 to +7 |
| 11/6/1952 | 300° | Korean War Boom; Index rose from +3 to +16 |
| 1/26/1955 | 0° | INCORRECT |
| 8/2/1957 | 60° | Index ranged from +8 to -2 |
| 11/21/1958 | 90° | Index fell from -4 to -10 |
| 2/23/1960 | 120° | Index peaked at +7 in January, then declined to -5 in December |
| 6/5/1962 | 180° | INCORRECT |
| 7/11/1964 | 240° | Index rose from +9 to +14 |
| 8/8/1965 | 270° | INCORRECT |
| 4/29/1966 | 300° | Vietnam War Boom; Index varied between +23 and +28 |
| 4/3/1969 | 0° | INCORRECT |
| 10/31/1971 | 60° | Index varied between +23 and +26 |
| 1/8/1973 | 90° | INCORRECT |
| 2/8/1974 | 120° | Index varied between +25 and +40 |
| 3/26/1976 | 180° | INCORRECT |
| 6/3/1978 | 240° | Index varied between +36 and +46 |
| 1/15/1979 | 270° | INCORRECT |
| 11/19/1980 | 300° | Index varied between +28 and +44 |
| 6/12/1983 | 0° | |
| 10/5/1985 | 60° | |

Summation: 14 out of 31 aspects, or 45 percent, gave the wrong indication. 17 out of 31 aspects, or 55 percent, gave the correct indication.

### Table 16. Saturn-Uranus Aspects vs. Business Cycles, 1761-1980

| Date | Aspect | Comment |
|---|---|---|
| Nov. 1761 | 0° | First commercial panic in America |
| Sept. 1768 | 60° | Index rose to +4 |
| June 1770 | 90° | Boston Massacre; Index fell. |
| June 1775 | 120° | INCORRECT |
| Feb. 1784 | 180° | INCORRECT |
| Jan. 1792 | 240° | Index ranged between +1 and +6 |
| June 1795 | 270° | INCORRECT |
| Aug. 1798 | 300° | INCORRECT |
| Jan. 1806 | 0° | INCORRECT |
| Mar. 1815 | 60° | Post-war prosperity; Index ranged between +13 and +24 |
| May 1819 | 90° | Primary post-war depression; Index fell from +5 in January to -11 in December |
| Nov. 1822 | 120° | Era of good feeling; Index was above normal first 9 months |
| Mar. 1829 | 180° | Secondary post-war depression; Index ranged between -4 and -8 |
| Mar. 1836 | 240° | Bank Credit Land Boom; Index ranged between +10 and +19 |
| Mar. 1840 | 270° | Debt Repudiation Depression; Index ranged between -1 and -7 |
| July 1844 | 300° | INCORRECT |
| Nov. 1851 | 0° | Index declined from +11 to -1 |
| May 1858 | 60° | Index rose from -13 to -4 |
| Sept. 1861 | 90° | Secession Depression; Civil War; Index ranged between -4 and -10 |
| Aug. 1865 | 120° | INCORRECT |
| Aug. 1874 | 180° | Secondary post-war depression; Index ranged between -3 and -6 |
| July 1882 | 240° | Gold Resumption Prosperity; Index ranged between +4 and +11 |
| Jan. 1886 | 270° | Index below normal first 5 months |
| June 1889 | 300° | Railroad Prosperity; Index ranged between 0 and +6 |
| Apr. 1897 | 0° | Silver Campaign Depression; Index was below normal first 10 months |
| 2/7/1906 | 60° | Corporate Prosperity; Index ranged between +6 and +13 |
| 10/20/1909 | 90° | Index below normal first 6 months. |
| 2/16/1913 | 120° | Index above normal first 10 months. |
| 6/7/1919 | 180° | Sharp decline first 5 months. |
| 10/24/1926 | 240° | New Era Prosperity; Index ranged between +8 and +13 |
| 1/10/1931 | 270° | Secondary post-war depression. Index ranged between -20 and -35 |
| 2/23/1935 | 300° | INCORRECT |
| 3/25/1942 | 0° | INCORRECT |
| 9/26/1948 | 60° | Index ranged between +1 and +6 |
| 6/8/1952 | 90° | INCORRECT |
| 9/24/1956 | 120° | Capital Goods Boom; Index ranged between +7 and +15 |
| 11/16/1965 | 180° | INCORRECT |
| 4/15/1973 | 240° | Index ranged between +38 and +41 |
| 2/19/1976 | 270° | INCORRECT |
| 2/4/1980 | 300° | Index ranged between +28 and +44 |

Summation: 12 out of 40 aspects, or 30 percent, gave the wrong indication. 28 out of 40 aspects, or 70 percent, gave the correct indication.

### Table 17. Summary of Three Planetary Cycles.

| Jupiter-Uranus 13.812 Years | | | Jupiter-Saturn 19.859 Years | | | Saturn-Uranus 45.362 Years | | |
|---|---|---|---|---|---|---|---|---|
| Table | Right | Wrong | Table | Right | Wrong | Table | Right | Wrong |
| 9 | 22 | 10 | 8 | 17 | 6 | 16 | 28 | 12 |
| 11 | 22 | 11 | 10 | 17 | 6 | | | |
| 13 | 24 | 8 | 12 | 12 | 11 | | | |
| 15 | <u>17</u> | <u>14</u> | 14 | <u>13</u> | <u>8</u> | | | |
| Total | 85 | 43 | Total | 59 | 31 | | | |

Summation:

| Cycle | Right | Wrong | Total Aspects |
|---|---|---|---|
| Jupiter-Uranus | 85 | 43 | 128 |
| Jupiter-Saturn | 59 | 31 | 90 |
| Saturn-Uranus | <u>28</u> | <u>12</u> | <u>40</u> |
| Totals | 172 | 86 | 258 |

The following breakdown by aspects shows that the most accurate correlation between planetary aspects and turning points in the Business Cycle were the Jupiter-Saturn conjunctions (83 percent accurate); the poorest were the Jupiter-Saturn oppositions (36 percent accurate).

### Table 18. Accuracy of Planetary Aspects at Business Cycle Turning Points.

| Aspect | Accuracy by Percent |
|---|---|
| Jupiter-Saturn Conjunctions | 83 |
| Saturn-Uranus Trines | 80 |
| Jupiter-Uranus Sextiles | 78 |
| Saturn-Uranus Sextiles | 70 |
| Saturn-Uranus Squares | 70 |
| Jupiter-Uranus Oppositions | 69 |
| Jupiter-Saturn Squares | 68 |
| Jupiter-Saturn Sextiles | 62 |
| Jupiter-Saturn Trines | 64 |
| Jupiter-Uranus Squares | 62½ |
| Jupiter-Uranus Trines | 62½ |
| Saturn-Uranus Oppositions | 60 |
| Jupiter-Uranus Conjunctions | 56 |
| Saturn-Uranus Conjunctions | 50 |
| Jupiter-Saturn Oppositions | 36 |

The dates of the planetary aspects were derived from the following: 1761-1800, *The Sun is Shining* by Michael Erlewine; 1800-1900, *The 200 Year Ephemeris* by Hugh MacCraig; and 1901-2000, *The American Heliocentric Ephemeris 1901-2000* by Neil F. Michelsen.

## Chapter 6

# The Theory of Unknown Causes

## Harmonic Analysis

Historically, the investigation of time series began with the astronomers, and it will be well for us to keep this fact in mind as we proceed. Their problem and that of the economists are essentially the same, and the methods which they have employed in untangling the complex motions and interactions of the heavenly bodies contain much that is illuminating in an analysis of the complicated behavior of economic time series.

H. T. Davis, in *The Analyses of Economic Time Series* (1941), discussed this matter as follows: "The problem of harmonic analysis, by which we mean the problem of discovering the constituent periodicities which enter into the construction of a given series of data arranged in a time sequence, probably begins with a memoir published by J. L. Lagrange in 1772. Although it was known to Leonard Euler (1707-1783) that an analytic function could be represented by means of a series of sines and cosines, the full significance of this development and its application to applied problems was not realized until the epoch-making work of J. B. Fourier (1768-1820).

"The most widely used method of harmonic analysis, however, is that which employs the idea of a *Periodogram.* This term was introduced in 1906 by Sir Arthur Schuster (1851-1934), who developed his theory in a number of papers and applied it successfully in the study of sunspots, the periodicity of earthquakes, terrestrial magnetism, etc.

"The economists were perhaps first introduced to periodogram analysis by H. L, Moore, whose classical study, *Economic Cycles Their Law and Cause,* published in 1914, contained an account of Fourier series and a periodogram of rainfall in the Ohio Valley (see Chapter 5).

"The idea of studying the harmonic behavior of time series by means of their auto-correlations apparently originated with H. H. Clayton in 1917, who used the method in a meteorological study. A similar application was made in 1927 by Dinsmore Alter, who recognized the importance pf the method in the analysis of time series and gave considerable currency to correlation periodograms.

"One of the most ambitious periodograms ever constructed is that due to Sir William Beveridge, who published his results in 1922.

This was a harmonic analysis of wheat prices in Western Europe over a range of approximately 300 years, from 1545 to 1845.

"One of the principal objections advanced to the use of harmonic analysis in economic data is that the cycles are necessarily very irregular, and hence that periodic, or almost, periodic movements observed in one era may fail to appear in another. Even though they may appear, their amplitudes will usually alter and the lengths of their period change.

"There is the strongest evidence to show that periods change from one era to another, and that significant amplitudes observed in one section of the data fail to appear in another. The periodogram is sometimes too rigid to reveal the nature of these changes. Its energies are only the average energies found in the whole of the data. Thus, in Sir Arthur Schuster's periodogram of sunspots from 1750 to 1900, about 35 percent of the total variation is accounted for by a single period of 11 to 25 years. But in the first half of the period (1750-1826) the importance of this period is entirely lost and we find a concentration of energy occurring at T equals 9.25 years and T equals 13.75 years. But in the second half of the period (1826-1900) nearly 85 percent of the variation is found in the 11-year component."

## Empirical Curve Fitting

We have previously noted Dr. Clarke's discovery of the 11-year cycle in 1847, Juglar's discovery in 1860 of the 9-year cycle, Professor Jevons's (the younger) 1909 discovery of the 3½-year cycle. Kitchin's 1923 discovery of the 3⅓-year (40-month) cycle, and Kondratieff's 1921 discovery of the Long Wave in Economics.

Although many economists deny the existence of any definite periodicity in economic variables, there is a strong temptation to construct periodic curves as a means of forecasting the business cycle. The *Sine Curve* is the commonest form used to represent periodicity in nature, e.g., light waves, sound waves, ocean waves, etc. One of the characteristics of a sine curve is that, when produced, it repeats the same pattern over and over again, indefinitely. Any curve which does this is said to be *periodic*. At this point, a word of caution is in order. Because of the elliptical shape of planetary orbits, the time elapsing between successive configurations of a given pair of planets, although predictable, is not uniform. Hence, it cannot be successfully represented by a sine curve.

Nevertheless, in *The Annalist* for May 1, 1931, Dr. Wilford I. King of New York University described a sine curve having a wave length of 39.56 months, which Mr. Saul Wallen fitted to the Quarterly Averages of the Axe-Houghton-Annalist Index of Business Activity for the years 1879 to 1931 (see Figure 25). From this curve Dr. King drew the assumption that "The major business cycle, at least in the United States, has a wave length of between thirty-nine and forty months—a wave length which has not changed appreciably in half a century." He then predicted: "According to the sine curve, the crest of the next boom should be reached about August 1932." Instead, business kept dropping until July 1932 and did not crest until December 1943.

In an attempt to avoid the criticism of those who do not believe in sine curves, Perry O. Crawford in 1934 published a skewed curve for *The Crawford Nine Year Cycle of Business Activity* superimposed on the Cleveland Trust Company Business Activity Index from 1832 to 1934. How poorly that curve fit the actual figures may be seen from Figure 26 and Appendix 4, which shows that out of 34 turning points from 1831 to 1980, only 38 percent were correct within 6 months, and 62 percent were wrong for periods ranging from 7 months to 3 years! Benner's 18-20-16 year series (see Chapter 5) is also essentially a 9-year cycle.

In 1941, Dr. King, in his book, *The Causes of Economic Fluctuations*, explains the failure of

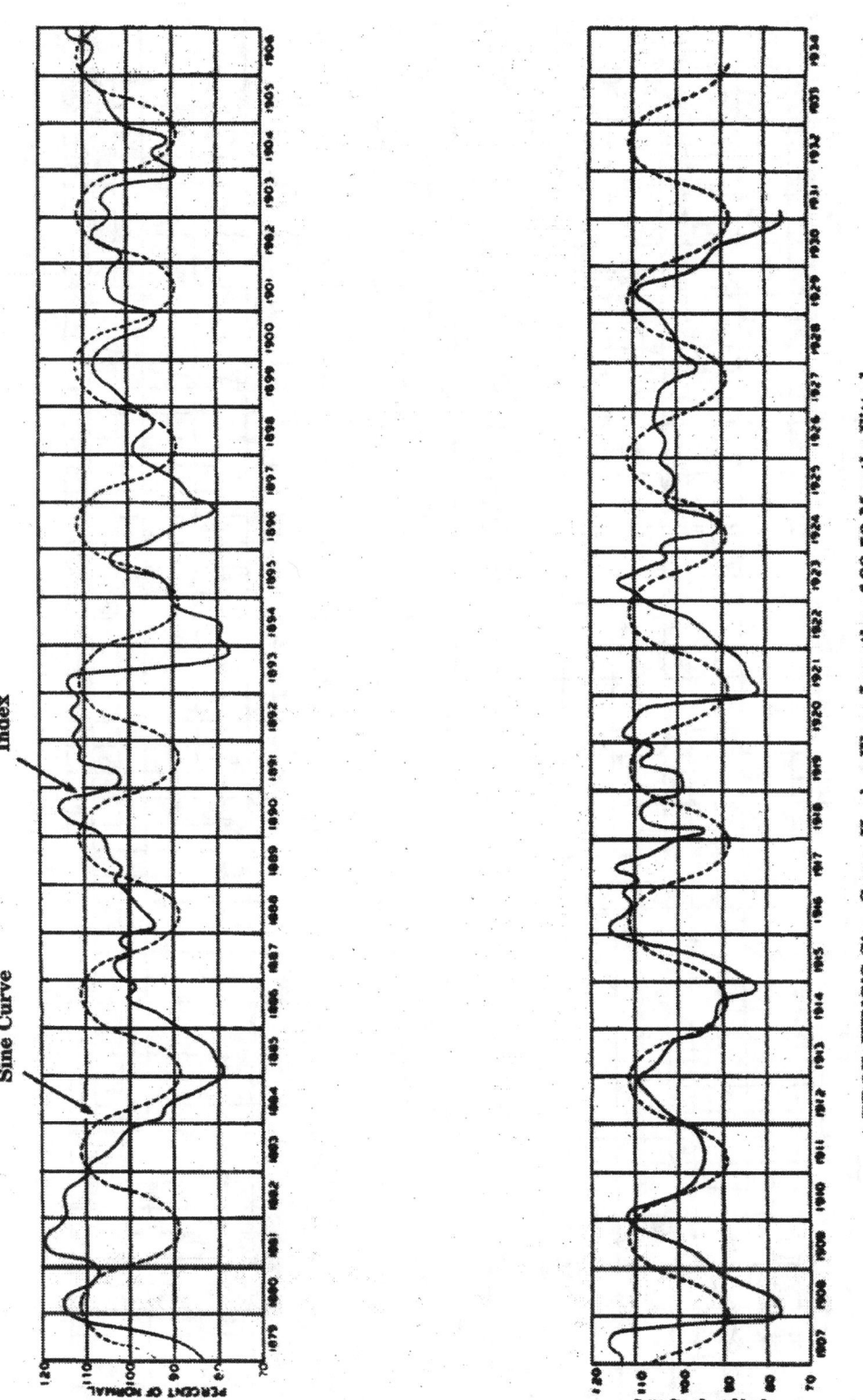

Figure 25. Professor King's Sine Curve vs. Houghton-Annalist Index of Business Activity.

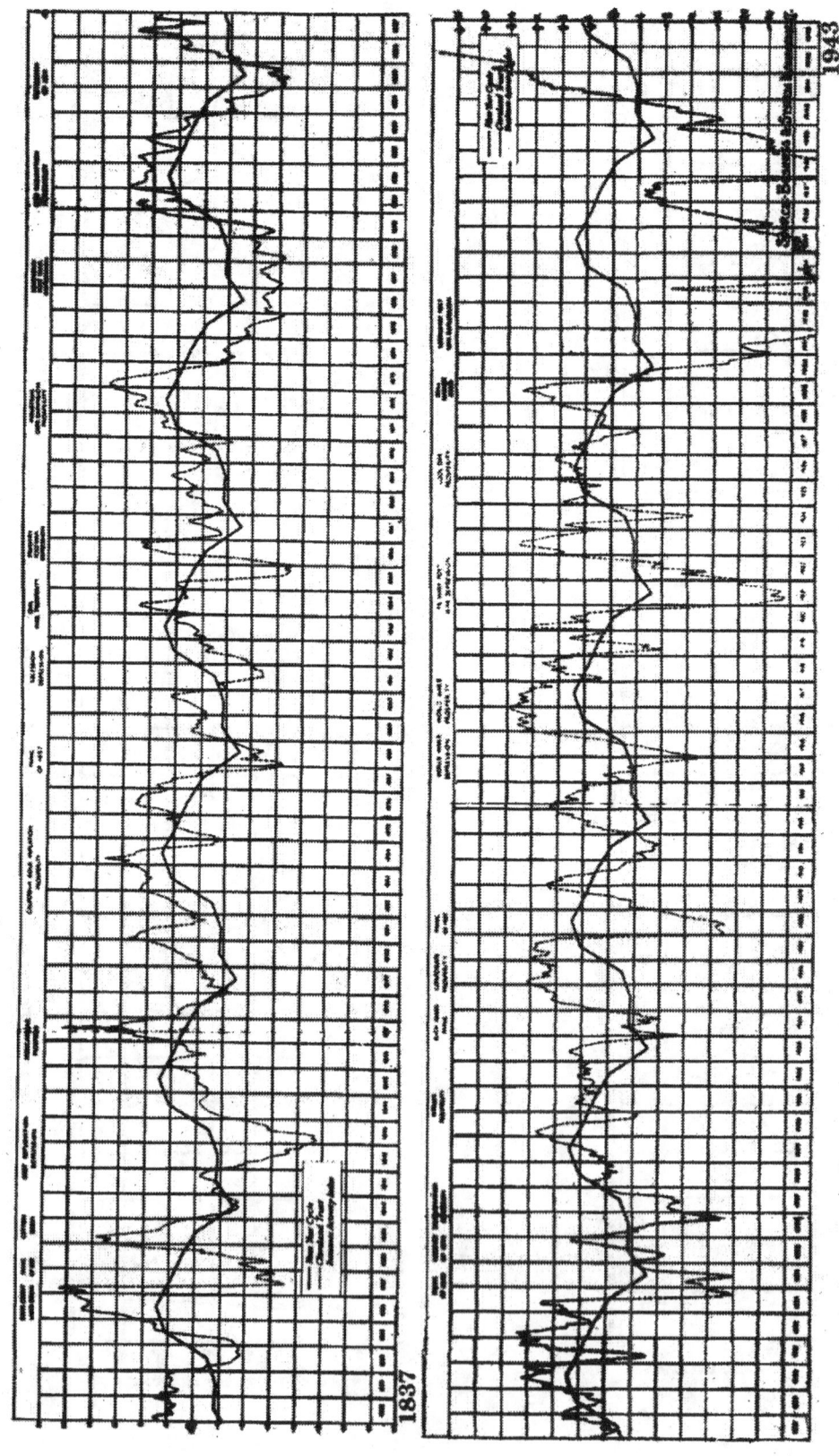

*Figure 26. The Crawford Nine Year Cycle of Business Activity.*

the 40-month sine curve to correctly forecast the future course of the business cycle, as follows: "The general appearance of the curve during the period 1930-34 suggests that some other overwhelming force crushed business down and prevented the influences producing the 40-month cycle from dominating the situation. Such an assumption would conform with the hypothesis that economic forces behave in the same way as physical forces and are governed by laws closely resembling Isaac Newton's laws of motion. If this hypothesis is correct, it might well follow that each force produces its own effect, regardless of other forces, and that the pattern of business as we know it is merely a composite of the individual effects of a considerable number of forces, each being weighted in proportion to its importance."

In 1953, Dr. King, having retired from his professorship at New York University, published a chart for the period 1945-1960, under the sponsorship of the Committee for Constitutional Government, Inc. Of this chart, Dr. King writes: "A painstaking analysis of the fluctuations of activity in mining, manufacturing and transportation during the period 1850 to 1938 was made by Simeon Hutner for his Ph.D. thesis. He showed that the oscillations were dominated by the composite of three sinusoidal curves having respective wave lengths of 3.35, 9.93, and 11.14 years. Minor forces having other wave lengths probably exist, but they have not been proved to be present.

"Cycles having wave lengths identical with the three mentioned above are also found in natural phenomena—the 3.35-year wave length occurring in magnetic fluctuations, and the 9.93 and 11.14 year wave lengths appearing in sunspot areas. This relationship is by no means surprising to anyone who realizes that, if the sun were to go out, all life and activity on earth would promptly disappear. But just why and how does solar activity affect business?

"The answer seems to be that the human organism responds to the solar rays—some producing *optimism* and others *pessimism*. And these changes in sentiment affect business mainly because optimism causes people to borrow to buy, while on the other hand, pessimism leads creditors to press for payment and borrowers to reduce their volumes of indebtedness. Such shifts in credit volume affect the *total* dollar demand for goods; and variations in total dollar demand are the *prime* forces for business ups and downs. However, total demand is also affected by governmentally generated inflation or deflation of the currency, by price and wage rigidity, by governmental or monopolistic interference with free competition. Labor union action is an important example of the last-mentioned force."

In the March 1960 *Cycles*, Gertrude Shirk, Editor, showed a curve prepared in 1952 by Dr. King showing the Hutner Cycle from 1952 through 1968, which has been combined by this author, with the earlier one covering the years 1945 through 1960, and a later one by Dr. King's son, Hugh P. King, published in the March 1975 issue of *Cycles*, which has been extended through 1980. All three segments are shown in Figure 27. Miss Shirk commented: "Hutner's work measuring optimism and pessimism is based on this assumption: optimism creates an expansion of credit, and pessimism leads to the contraction of indebtedness. These changes in the volume of credit produce changes in the demand for goods, and these variations in the dollar demand for goods are the main forces causing business ups and downs."

Commenting on the correlation of Hutner's curves with the three curves in solar activity, Hugh P. King states: "But the *real* question is just how and why does solar activity affect business?" He then repeats the arguments presented by his father in 1953, which have been mentioned previously. He concludes: "Because powerful interfering forces are nearly always present, business activity but rarely conforms closely to the composite of the three major cycle

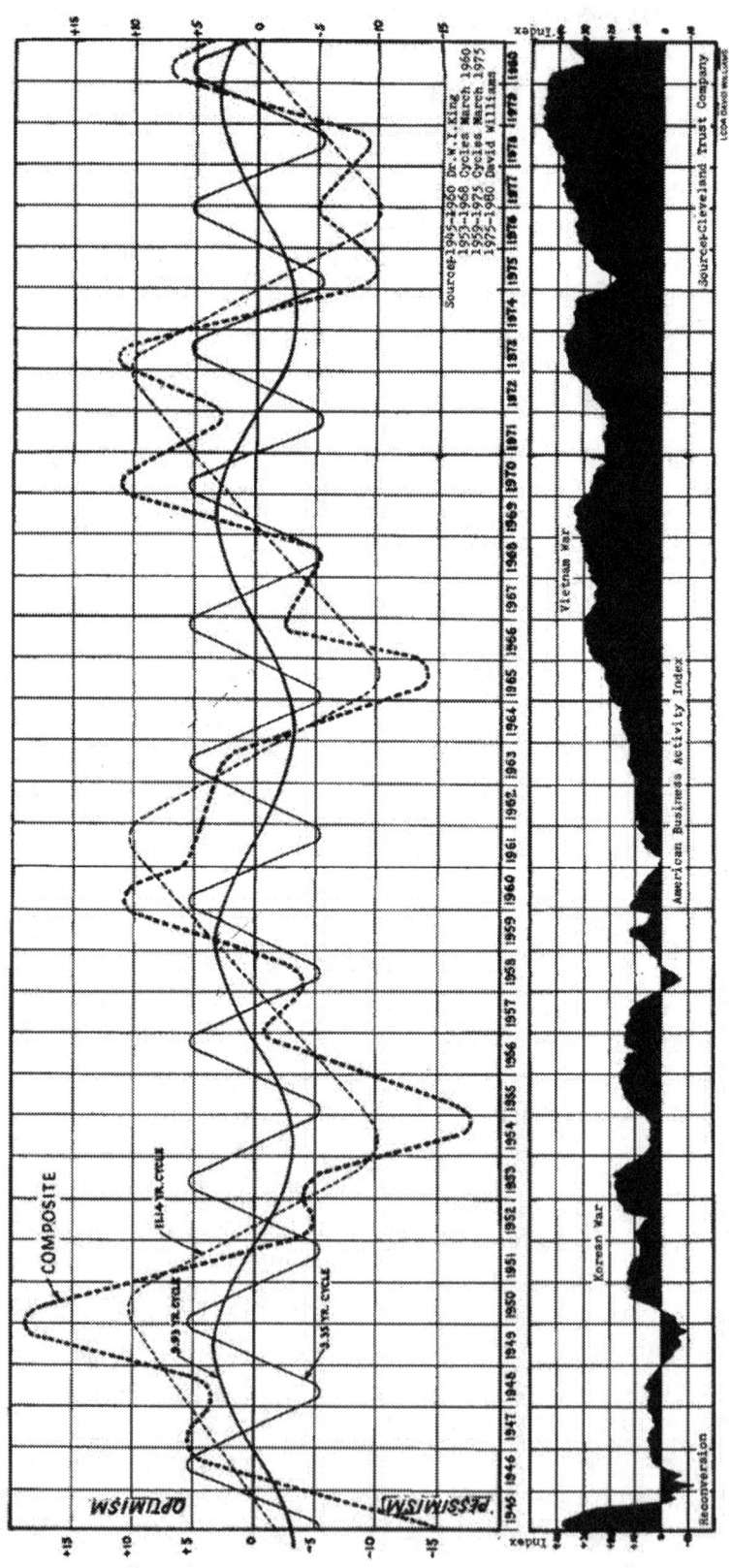

*Figure 27. Hutner's Cycles of Optimism and Pessimism vs. American Business Activity.*

waves described above. However, that composite practically always constitutes a force worthy of serious consideration, for it represents *changing human sentiment.*"

As Appendix 5 indicates, Hutner's composite curve correctly indicated the highs 81 percent and the lows 67 percent of the time from 1854 through 1980, for an overall accuracy of 76 percent! Contrast this with Crawford's 9-year cycle accuracy of only 38 percent. These two studies indicate that greater accuracy is obtained by including as many cycles as possible in the *composite,* thus confirming Professor King's statement that "The pattern of business as we know it is merely a composite of the individual effects of a considerable number of forces, each being weighted in proportion to its importance."

As yet we do not have a scientifically sound method for weighting the individual forces that affect the business cycle. But, with the aid of computers, we may soon be able to calculate reasonably approximate weighting values.

# Chapter 7

# Conclusion of Part I

*The roads you travel so briskly lead out of dim antiquity, and you study the past chiefly because of its bearing on the living present and its promise for the future.—Lt. Gen. James G. Harbord*

In the foregoing chapters we have traced the long and tortuous path trodden by eminent students of the physical and social sciences in the never-ending quest for an insight into the future. Despite the blind prejudice of materialistic scientists and economists who scoff at astrology, irrefutable evidence has been presented that planetary configurations can be successfully used to predict important turning points in the business cycle.

The lead article in the June 15, 1958, issue of *Forbes* magazine opens with the following unflattering statement: "If I were an anthropologist," a highly successful but largely self-educated businessman recently remarked, "I would say that modem business, as much as any primitive African tribe, has its own witch doctors and medicine men. I'm referring to the economists. We businessmen call them in to read the future, rationalize the past and justify the present to us. And like tribal medicine men, the economists don't have to produce results: only explanations and a kind of business cosmology."

Why are businessmen so skeptical of economists? The answer is given in the June 1958 issue of *Current Economic Trends* published by the American Institute for Economic Research, which states: "The science of economics is relatively immature. Much that is published on the subject, including supposed remedies for recessions, etc., has no more scientific standing than the notions of the itinerant medicine men who sold health elixirs to a gullible public a few decades ago."

What can economists do to improve their low estate? In 1930, Dr. E. R. Macaulay gave the following sound advice in his book, *The Movements of Interest Rates, Bank Yields, and Stock Prices Since 1856:* "Because economics is a study of the behavior of men, economists will probably never be able to make much use of the concept of necessity (or *invariable sequence*) which permeates the physical sciences. Economic 'laws' in the strict sense of the word will probably always be merely statements of more or less pronounced *'tendencies'*. Economics is one of the social sciences, and the chain of causation in all the social sciences is necessarily indirect rather than direct, mediate rather than immediate. The mind of man is always the connecting link—and the disturbing element. The obstacle that will always block the attainment of any such exactitude in economics as is possible in the physical sciences, is that the minds of men do not admit of the same definite analysis as do the events of the external world.

"Economic activities are peculiarly concerned with the future: forecasting is of the essence of such activities. But the economic future cannot be accurately known, and though it is conceivable that it could be forecast with a fairly high degree of *probability,* successful forecasting is now rare. Few men have either the necessary knowledge of the present or the technical equipment and ability to deduce the future from such knowledge. The first problem in economic reform involves a study of the problem of how to forecast the future. To the extent that the future can be foreseen, it can be prepared for. It is of course highly desirable to learn how things actually have occurred—and particularly how closely or distantly they have followed a 'rational' pattern; to study the problems of economic prediction even into the fields of 'irrational' sequences.

"With the growth of knowledge the accuracy of forecasting will increase, but this can bring about a pronounced decrease in the violence of economic disturbances only if it entails something more than mere 'speculative' forecasting. It must lead to a change in those present conditions that tend to produce untoward future results. *We must make the future and not merely foresee it. And that can only be done in the present.* The primary reason for the variableness of the economic future to which man must adjust himself lies in man himself. Without knowing what the future effects of his present acts will be, and often apparently caring less, he proceeds to *make* a future to which he will find he cannot adjust himself."

The correct relationship of man and the universe was expressed by Sir William Dampier in *A History of Science* (1946), as follows: "During the last hundred or hundred and fifty years, the whole conception of the natural universe has been changed by the recognition that man, subject to the same physical laws and processes as the world around him, cannot be considered separately from the world, and that scientific methods of observation, induction, deduction, and experiment are applicable, not only to the original subject matter of pure science, but to nearly all the many and varied fields of human thought and activity. Man from his strategic position midway between an atom and a star, has learned to study each in the light of information obtained from the other. As Eddington has pointed out, about $10^{27}$ atoms go to build a man's body, and $10^{26}$ times as many as that make an average star."

Since the controlling factor is the mind of man, economists should make a serious study of those extraterrestrial forces that affect man individually and in the mass. This means that they should drop the age-old prejudice against astrology a prejudice which J. G. Smith and A. J. Duncan expressed in *Elementary Statistics and Applications* (1944): "The human desire to look into the future led, even in ancient times, to the rise of various forms of pseudo-scientific forecasts. Astrologers were, and still are, consulted for what the stars have to say. It was partly to disprove some of these astrological notions that the statistical method was first undertaken on a scientific basis."

But, the statistical method is not necessarily synonymous with the scientific method, which Stuart Chase defined in *Power of Words* (1953) as follows: "Any activity that produces dependable, invariant knowledge, which all competent observers can agree has a high probability of being correct. Usually, the method involves three steps: 1) observation, 2) a hypothesis or theory to explain the observation, and 3) verification." The astrological tool described herein has been derived by the application of the scientific method, and is destined to become an important branch of the new science of astro-economics.

Even though the application of the scientific method to the field of economics may never provide answers to *all* economic problems, the American Institute for Economic Research is convinced that only those answers obtained through the application of the scientific method should be classified as "warranted assertions." Condemning astrology, without making an adequate investigation of the subject, is the utter negation of the scientific method. Economists who do so are guilty of "proceeding from an unwarranted assumption to a foregone conclusion."

The late Pulitzer Prize Winner, John J. O'Neill, formerly Science Editor of *The New York Tribune,* and one of the most brilliant of American men of science, stated on July 8, 1951: "Scientists today cannot look down on astrology; instead, they must raise their eyes to take in the higher horizons that astrologers have preserved for them. Astrology is one of the most important fields for scientific research today, and one of the most neglected. Astrology, properly defined, is the science of the relationship of man and his celestial environment; it is the accumulated and organized knowledge of the effect on man of the forces reaching the earth from surrounding space. The hypotheses of astrology are consistent with a vitalistic cosmogony. In this respect the astrological concept is much more modern than the astronomical."

Scientists are accustomed to living in a world where certainty is rarely found. They should realize that the most to be hoped for is confidence in a higher degree of probability that a theory is sound. However, this does not imply that practical application of such theories should wait until warranted assertibility has been superseded by certainty. Professor John Dewey defines "warranted assertibility" as "knowledge derived through application of the scientific method, knowledge that is highly probable to be sufficiently accurate for practical purposes."

It is firmly believed that the astrological technique described herein fully meets the requirements of Professor Dewey's definition, and it is earnestly hoped that sincere students will be encouraged to carry on further research in the much neglected field of astro-economics. It should, however, be realized that since no two events in nature are identical, scientific prediction must take the form of probabilities rather than complete certainties. But, no other branch of the social sciences can approach astrology in the percentage of predictions which have such a high probability of coming true. This is so because astrologers use the positions of the planets as calculated by the astronomers, who employ the most sophisticated electronic calculators to predict past, present and future planetary longitudes. And the predictions of no other science can compare with those of astronomy as far as accuracy is concerned.

As an illustration of the accuracy of the ancient Babylonian records of celestial events, Dr. P. H. Cowell of the Royal Observatory of England in 1905 found that by using the Babylonian records of the eclipses of 1062 B.C. and 762 B.C., he was able to obtain a more accurate value for the secular acceleration of the Moon's longitude and the Nodes of her orbit than any that could be obtained from modern observations made with instruments of the highest precession.

Furthermore, in 1962, Dr. Bryant Tuckerman of the International Business Machines Corporation published a two-volume book, *Planetary, Lunar and Solar Positions—601 B.C. to A.D. 1649.* The calculations were based on the naked eye observations of ancient Babylonian priest-astrologers from about 330 B.C. to the first century A.D. that were recorded on clay cuneiform tablets, which were discovered by Arabs in the middle of the 19th Century and eventually were acquired by the British Museum.

Additional tabulations were published in 1963 by William D. Stahlman and Owen Gingerich in *Solar and Planetary Longitudes for Years -2500 to +2000*. These tables have an accuracy of ±1 degree over a period of 4,500 years, and were computed with the aid of an IBM-7090 computer. The data are in substantial agreement with that in Dr. Tuckerman's books.

Since the Tuckerman and Stahlman-Gingerich tabulations of planetary positions is only given at 5 and 10 day intervals, the need for a daily tabulation soon became evident. This need was met by Neil F. Michelsen in 1976 by the publication of *The American Ephemeris, 1931-1980*. It not only gives the daily positions of the planets, but also contains an aspectarian, which lists the conventional aspects between any two planets.

All these books show the planetary positions in geocentric—Earth-centered—longitude. A heliocentric—or Sun-centered—ephemeris for the years 1653-2050 was recently published by Michael Erlewine. While a great step in the right direction, it is handicapped by the fact that the positions of the five outer planets are only given annually, while that of the inner planets must be calculated from Julian Day numbers. Furthermore, the book lacks an aspectarian. It is believed that these drawbacks are in the process of being remedied.

Robert Hand is also publishing a heliocentric ephemeris giving the daily positions of the inner planets and those of the outer planets at five-day intervals.

James T. Valliere has for several years plotted the daily geocentric positions of the planets in graphic form, and publishes same annually under the title *Valliere's Graphic Almanac*.

Neil F. Michelsen has recently published *The American Heliocentric Ephemeris 1901-2000*, which does contain a daily aspectarian. It is hoped that similar volumes will be prepared for the 18th and 19th centuries.

While much of the material in the preceding chapters has been largely historical and some of it somewhat technical, the author believes that all students of astrology should have some knowledge of what has transpired in the fields of science and economics, which have shown that the basic principles of the age-old art of astrology are just as valid in this technological world as they were in the ancient agricultural societies of 4,000-5,000 years ago.

In the second part of this book we shall see how these principles may be used in the stock market.

# Part II
# Stock Market Foreasting

## Chapter 8

# The Art of Prediction

*Prediction must inevitably fail unless we have lighted on the true cause of the phenomena; success is, therefore, a guarantee of the truth of the theory.—Professor G. H. Darwin*

## Introduction

The desire to predict the future is one of the characteristics of mankind. Everyone is continually making predictions, for every decision one makes involves a prediction. Most predictions made in the normal course of everyday living have a high degree of accuracy because they are short-term, such as making a luncheon or dinner engagement. The tremendous advances in science and technology have even made it possible for a person in New York to safely predict that he will have dinner in London or Hawaii that same day. Basically, it is experience which makes prophets of each of us. Most predictable events have become common knowledge, while others are known only to the specialists in a particular field. Thus man lives today in a world of predictions which have a high degree of probability for their fulfillment.

The dictionary defines *prediction* as the art of foretelling the future. It also lists as synonyms: *augury*—the art of foretelling the future from signs and omens; *prognostication*—the art of foretelling future events from observed signs, conditions or indications; *divination*—the art of foretelling the future by assumed supernatural aid; *prophesy*—the art of foretelling the future by supernatural or Divine aid; to prophesy in the Scriptural sense is to utter religious truth under Divine inspiration, not necessarily to foretell future events, but to warn, exhort, comfort, etc. by special impulse from God.

*Prediction* may be divided into two general classifications, viz: 1) *divination* through dreams, visions, inspiration, clairaudience, clairvoyance, or automatic writing; 2) *prognostication* from the interpretation of signs sent from the gods, such as the flight of birds, the patterns seen in the livers of animals, or the geometrical patterns formed by the heavenly bodies *(astrology)*. The first method usually manifested itself to individuals who were obviously in an abnormal state or during the dream state. The second method is based on elaborate intellectual systems, according to which the language of omens and the language of the stars is interpreted. These systems had been developed in the same way any other scientific knowledge is derived, namely by observation of uniformities extending over a sufficiently long period, and the inference from such uniformities of a general law. *Astrology,* for instance, is based on the observations made by the Babylonians over a period, it was claimed, of 470,000 years. (There is no historical basis for this fantastic period.)

## Prediction Through Dream Interpretation

In the early days of mankind, the ability to predict the future was reserved for the wise man, the Shaman, the sorcerer, or the witch-doctor of the tribe. The religious belief most commonly held by primitive societies was that known as Animism, i.e.; the belief that events are brought about through the agency of the innumerable spirits of the earth and the air, which can be controlled by the spells, exorcisms, and incantations of the Shaman or sorcerer. The Shaman could predict the future through dream interpretation and he also knew how to induce in himself a trance-like state, in which condition he was able to predict the future. These techniques were also practiced on a higher scale by more civilized races, such as the ancient Sumerians, the Hebrews and the Greeks.

The real founder of the art of divination and the codifier of the ancient rules of prophecy was believed to be Enmeduranki, the legendary King of Sumeria who was said to have lived before the flood. The religion of ancient Sumeria was Animism, and the oldest extant Sumerian prophecy involved the technique of dream interpretation. It is contained in the glorious Gilgamesh Epic, which is believed to have been originally written about 4000 B.C. and was extensively embellished by the Babylonians some 2000 years later. This epic, recorded on clay tablets, was found in A.D. 1851-1853 by the famous English archaeologist Sir Henry Layard in the ruins of the library of King Ashurbanipal (669-653 B.C.) at Nineveh, Assyria: In the epic, Gilgamesh—a Sumerian King—dreams that he will be attacked by his enemy Enkidu; but his mother predicts that they will eventually become good friends. The Babylonians used this story to stress the value of peaceful coexistence between themselves and the native Sumerians, whom they had conquered in the Second Millennium B.C.

*Divination* played a very important role in the development of the Hebrew race. One of the most famous predictions recorded in the Old Testament is that of Joseph (ca. 1800 B.C.), who correctly interpreted Pharaoh's dream of the seven fat kine being swallowed by seven lean kine as meaning that seven years of famine would follow seven years of plenty. Joseph was a born mystic, for it is recorded that he was a dreamer of dreams in boyhood. He came by his gift naturally, for his great grandfather—the patriarch Abraham—had been a native of the Sumerian city of Ur. Joseph's predictive powers manifested themselves through the visions he saw in his own dreams and in his interpretation of the dreams of others.

Beginning in the 8th Century B.C., there arose in Israel a succession of gifted individuals known as "the Prophets," whose predictive powers were manifested while they were in a self-induced trance state or through their highly developed intuitive faculties. These Hebrew prophets were not, however, primarily concerned with prediction or with working charms. They believed their divinely appointed mission to be the reformation of the moral order.

The Hebrews had been under strict orders not to engage in divination from the earliest days, for in the *Old Testament, Deuteronomy,* Chapter 18, we read: "When thou art come into the land which Jehovah thy God giveth thee, thou shall not learn to do after the abominations of those nations. There shall not be found with thee anyone that maketh his son or his daughter to pass through the fire, one that useth *divination,* one that practiceth *augury,* or an enchanter, or a sorcerer, or a charmer, or a consulter with a familiar spirit, or a wizard, or a necromancer."

The Hebrew prophets condemned the idolatrous practices of the heathen prophets. One of these forbidden practices was witchcraft—the technique of predicting the future by a medium (the witch) through whom the spirit of a dead person spoke. The most famous instance of this is recorded in the *Old Testament* story of King Saul (c. 1010 B.C.), who persuaded the Witch of Endor to summon the spirit of the prophet Samuel to predict the outcome of his forthcoming battle with the Philistines. The prediction was that Saul would be defeated by the Philistines and that he and his three sons would be slain, which prediction was fulfilled.

Thus, prophecy developed out of soothsaying; the Hebrew prophets purified the divinatory art and made it a powerful religious force. At first there were a few isolated spirits who fought to raise the standard of social righteousness and were undaunted by great names or great titles. Among them was Nathan, who rebuked King David (c. 1000 B.C.) for his affair with Bathsheba; and Elijah, who upbraided King Ahab (874-863 B.C.) for robbing Naboth of his vineyard. 2700 years ago, the prophet Amos thundered in the bazaars of Sumeria that if the Israelites did not repent of their wickedness, they would be destroyed. His prediction was fulfilled some 20 years later when the Assyrian King Sargon II destroyed the kingdom of Israel in 721 B.C.

The 6th Century B.C. produced such great religious leaders as Lao-Tse and Confucius in China, Gautama Buddha in India, Zoroaster in Persia, and the Prophet Jeremiah in Jerusalem. Throughout his life, Jeremiah was impelled by the prophetic fire within him to preach doom, to antagonize the people he loved, and to undermine their national existence. As a result, he was persecuted and imprisoned. Prophets of doom are likened to the demented Trojan princess Cassandra, who in 1000 B.C. predicted the fall of Troy, or to Jeremiah, who predicted the fall of Jerusalem, which was destroyed by Babylonian King Nebuchadnezzar in 586 B.C.

One of the greatest of the Hebrew prophets was Daniel, who became famous through his interpretations of two dreams of King Nebuchadnezzar. The first related to a dream which the King would not reveal. Daniel described the dream, which involved a colossus, the various parts of which were made of different metals, which Daniel interpreted as representing the successive kingdoms of Babylon, Medea-Persia, Greece, and Rome. *(Daniel* 11:1-16). The second dream contained the announcement of judgment upon the King from God. It was fulfilled when Nebuchadnezzar "was driven from men, acting like an animal, apparently suffering from the disease known as hycanthropy. At the end of the predicted time the King's reason returned to him, and from a heart of faith he praised the true God," according to *The New Bible Commentary* by Davidson, Kibbs and Kevan (1953).

The first recorded instance of a prediction made through *clairaudience* is that of Abraham, who was told, in 2085 B.C., by Jehovah, "Get thee out of thy country, and from thy kindred and from thy father's house unto a land that I will show thee; and I will make of thee a great nation" *(Genesis* 12:1-2).

The first recorded instance of a prediction made from *automatic writing* is that of the prophet Daniel, who in 539 B.C. interpreted the handwriting on the wall of King Belshazzar's palace, i.e., MENE. MENE, TEKEL, UPHARSIN, as predicting the end of the King's rule. That night, Belshazzar, the King of the Chaldeans, was slain and Darius, the Mede, took over the kingdom (*Daniel* 5:5-31). (Actually it was Cyrus the Great who conquered Babylon.)

Classical prophecy among the Jewish people was abolished toward the end of the 5th Century B.C., following the promulgation of the canonical *Book of the Torch* by the priest-scribe Ezra in 444 B.C. The training schools for prophets, which had sprung up during the preceding three centuries, were closed and prophesying was prohibited under pain of death in 400 B.C. The Rabbi or sage thus superceded the Nabi or prophet.

But prophetic activity did not altogether cease. Prophetic legends continued to be produced, some of which are preserved in the *Book of Daniel* and the *Books of Maccabees* in the *Old Testament* and the *Book of Revelations* in the *New Testament*. However, this prophetic literature took a new form, known as apocalyptic. The word apocalypse means a revelation of the unknown. But whereas the early prophets had been optimistic social reformers, the visionaries who wrote apocalyptic books were pessimists. They rarely dealt with events of their own day except in terms of images and prophecies now difficult to understand. Their theme was that since the world was going from bad to worse, there was only one way out, and that was for God Himself to miraculously intervene and save mankind. The authors of the apocalyptic literature seldom put their own names to their books, but ascribed them to one or the other of the ancients. The reason was self-preservation, for the lot of the prophet had never been an easy one. Even the great Isaiah was said to have been put to death by being sawn in twain!

In Greece, the divinatory art was manifested through the Sybils, certain women prophetesses or seers, two of whom were said to have predicted the Trojan War and the fall of Troy. Eventually, divination became an appendage of the Greek temples. The most famous of these was the Temple of Apollo at Delphi, where was located the world-renowned Oracle of Delphi, which endured for a thousand years. The technique employed here was to seat the priestess on a golden tripod set over a chasm from which emanated sulphurous fumes. These fumes put the priestess into a trance, during which she gave forth incoherent utterances; these were interpreted by the priests as the god's answer to the petitioner's request. But the answer was phrased so ambiguously that the oracle could always be proven to have been correct.

The classic example of this ambiguity was the case of Croesus, King of Lydia (560-640 B.C.), who inquired of the oracle whether or not he would be victorious in a war he proposed to wage against the Persians. The answer given was: "Croesus, having crossed the river Halys, will destroy a great kingdom." Croesus interpreted this to mean that he would destroy the kingdom of his enemy; but, instead he destroyed his own kingdom, for he was defeated by the Persians under Cyrus the Great and taken prisoner. When he was subsequently released, he complained to the priests of Delphi for having given him a prediction which had failed. The priests, however, maintained that the oracle had correctly predicted the result of his action—i.e., the destruction of a great kingdom—and that Croesus was at fault because he had misinterpreted the oracle! The Delphic Oracle grew immensely wealthy over the centuries, was plundered several times and was finally destroyed by Roman Emperor Theodosius the Great in 394 A.D.

Thus we have seen that the oldest form of divination—which means to divine the future, to foretell future events, to prophesy—was done by a revelation through the highly developed intuitive faculty of the diviner. This was true regardless of the nature of the diviner, be he the animistic sorcerer who invoked the power of the Nature spirits; the dreamer of dreams, like Gilgamesh, the Sumerian King; or Joseph, the Hebrew prophet who was inspired by a divine fervor; the Witch of Endor, who summoned the spirits of the dead; or the Greek priestess through whom the gods spoke.

But in the modern world, the exponents of this form of divination are variously called clairvoyants, mediums, mystics, psychics, or spiritualists. However, dream interpretation is no longer the sole prerogative of the mystics, for the followers of Freud and Jung have developed elaborate systems of interpretation based on inductive reasoning processes.

One of the greatest modern American mystics was Edgar Cayce (1876-1944) of Virginia Beach, Virginia. Thousands of well-attested cases of his healing ability while in a self-induced trance state are on record. But Cayce also was able to predict the future while in the trance state. Many of his predictions have already been fulfilled, while others are still in the future.

The most prominent living clairvoyants are the Dutchmen Peter Hurkos and Gerard Croiset and the American Jeane Dixon. The Dutchmen are famous for their ability to solve crimes, while the American is famous for her prediction of President Kennedy's death. The predictive powers of these clairvoyants are not constant. It is a well-known occult law that extrasensory or paranormal powers tend to diminish when the clairvoyant tries to use his rare abilities for personal gain.

## Prognostication from Omens

Although the oldest form of divination practiced by the ancient Sumerians and Babylonians was that of dream interpretation, the most common form was hepatoscopy—the reading of omens in the livers of freshly slain sheep. This method was in vogue for fully 3000 years and was used when great matters of state were involved, such as the dates and outcomes of future wars or revolutions. From Mesopotamia also came the art of reading the future in the intestines of animals; every turn had a special prophetic significance. The Romans established a College of Augurs, of which Julius Caesar was at one time the chief, to advise the rulers on matters of state through this divinatory part. The primitive races of Borneo, Burma, and Uganda still predict the future from the omens seen in the livers of animals and fowl.

Divination from the omens seen by the seer in an animal's liver was considered by the Christian church to be a pagan superstition, and materialistic science could not find any perceptive causal connection between the prophetic omen and the prophetic substance. But perhaps there was a connection, for in 1962, Professor Georgio Piccardi, Director of the Institute of Physical Chemistry, University of Florence, Italy, reported that thousands of tests by Italian, German and Japanese scientists over a period of 20 years indicated that organic and inorganic matter were affected by extraterrestrial forces. He further stated that living matter reacted to extraterrestrial forces exactly like non-living matter, because what reacted was its non-living or inorganic substructure. Thus the patterns or omens that the Babylonian or Roman seer saw in an animal's liver or intestines may have been caused by extraterrestrial forces. From past experience, certain omens were classified as favorable, while others were classified as unfavorable. After Christianity became the State religion of the Roman Empire, divination was prohibited in 392 A.D.

Nevertheless, divination from "omens" is still practiced in the Western world and in, of all places, Wall Street. However, the "omens" are not read in the entrails of slain animals, but in the patterns formed by charting the fluctuations in the prices of stocks or commodities. Such chart patterns as rounding tops, double tops, head and shoulders tops, or breaking a rising trend line are interpreted as foretelling the end of a Bull Market. Similarly, rounding bottoms, double bottoms, head and shoulder bottoms, or breaking through a declining trend line are interpreted as indicating the end of a Bear Market. Other chartist "omens" are ascending or descending triangles, flags or pennants, support levels and resistance levels. These chart patterns were first described by R. W. Schabacker, Financial Editor, *Forbes* magazine, in his book *Stock Market Theory and Practice* (1930). The 20th Century Wall Street chartist has learned from experience that his chart patterns convey a meaningful picture, yet no one would accuse him of indulging in a superstitious practise. See Figure 28 for typical patterns.

The rationale for using the "omens" seen in

the patterns of stock or commodity charts is explained by William L. Jiler, in *How Charts Can Help You in the Stock Market* (1962), as follows: "Now there is nothing mystical or hocus-pocus about chart reading. Stocks (and commodities) trace various patterns for reasons soundly based in human psychology—and it's psychology that determines stock (or commodity) movements. The tendency of stocks (or commodities) to move along straight line, for example, is not hard to explain. In physical terms, it often is likened to the Law of Inertia; that an object in motion will continue in motion in the same direction until it meets an opposing force. In human terms, an investor will resist paying more for a stock than the price other people have recently been paying for it—unless it continues moving up, which will give him some confidence or hope that it will keep going up. Conversely, an investor will resist selling a stock for less than the price other people have been getting for theirs—unless the price keeps declining, and he fears it will continue to decline."

Chart analysis is a study of market action, but it is an inexact science and considerable allowance must be made for errors. It is a market technique used by many speculators, commodity market analysts and others whose business necessitates anticipation of price trends. Its purpose is to measure the relative strength of buying and selling pressures. But there is no easy road to price forecasting and no single key that will open the door to complete accuracy. Readers should therefore avoid the error of adhering rigidly to charts to the exclusion of all other factors. Charts cannot guarantee a winner every time, but they can help determine when to buy and when to sell.

## Prognostication from Astrology

When the Babylonians, under Sargon of Akkad (c. 2360 B.C.), conquered Sumeria, they replaced the Sumerian animistic religion with their own system of astrotheology, and the Babylonian priest replaced the Sumerian Shaman. *Astrology,* the belief that the future can be read in the stars, is now believed by scientists to have originated in Babylonia about 3000 B.C., and was transmitted via Assyria to Egypt, Greece and Rome in the West and Persia, India and China in the East.

In fact, one French savant—Paul Couderc—asserted in 1951 that the astrological prophecies discovered in China seem to be mere copies from the library of the Assyrian King Ashurbanipal (669-693 B.C.) in Nineveh, Assyria. The standard work on ancient Babylonian astronomy and astrology is recorded on 70 clay tablets called the "Illumination of Bel," which were found in 1851-1853 by Sir Henry Layard in the ruins of King Ashurbanipal's library. These tablets are believed to have been copied from originals ascribed to Sargon of Akkad (ca. 2360 B.C.) in the Temple Library of Nippur in Chaldea dating back to the 3rd Century B.C., the ruins of which were discovered in 1900 by Professor H. V. Hilprecht of the University of Pennsylvania Babylonian Expedition.

A. H. Sayce, Deputy Professor of Comparative Philology, Oxford University, in *The Religion of the Ancient Babylonians* (1887), believed this work, which was attributed by tradition to Sargon of Akkad, to be "not so much a treatise on astronomy, as on the pseudo-science (astrology) that had been evolved out of the observations of astronomy. Babylonia was really the cradle of astronomical observations."

Morris Jastrow, Jr., Professor of Semitic Languages, University of Pennsylvania, in *Religion of Babylonia and Assyria* (1898), added confirmation by stating: "The zodiacal system as a whole is the product of the Babylonian schools of astronomy." He summarized as follows: "The chief motive in the development of astronomy in the Euphrates Valley was the belief that the movements of the heavenly bodies portended something that was important for man to know. Scientific observations were but means to an end; and the end was invariably the deriva-

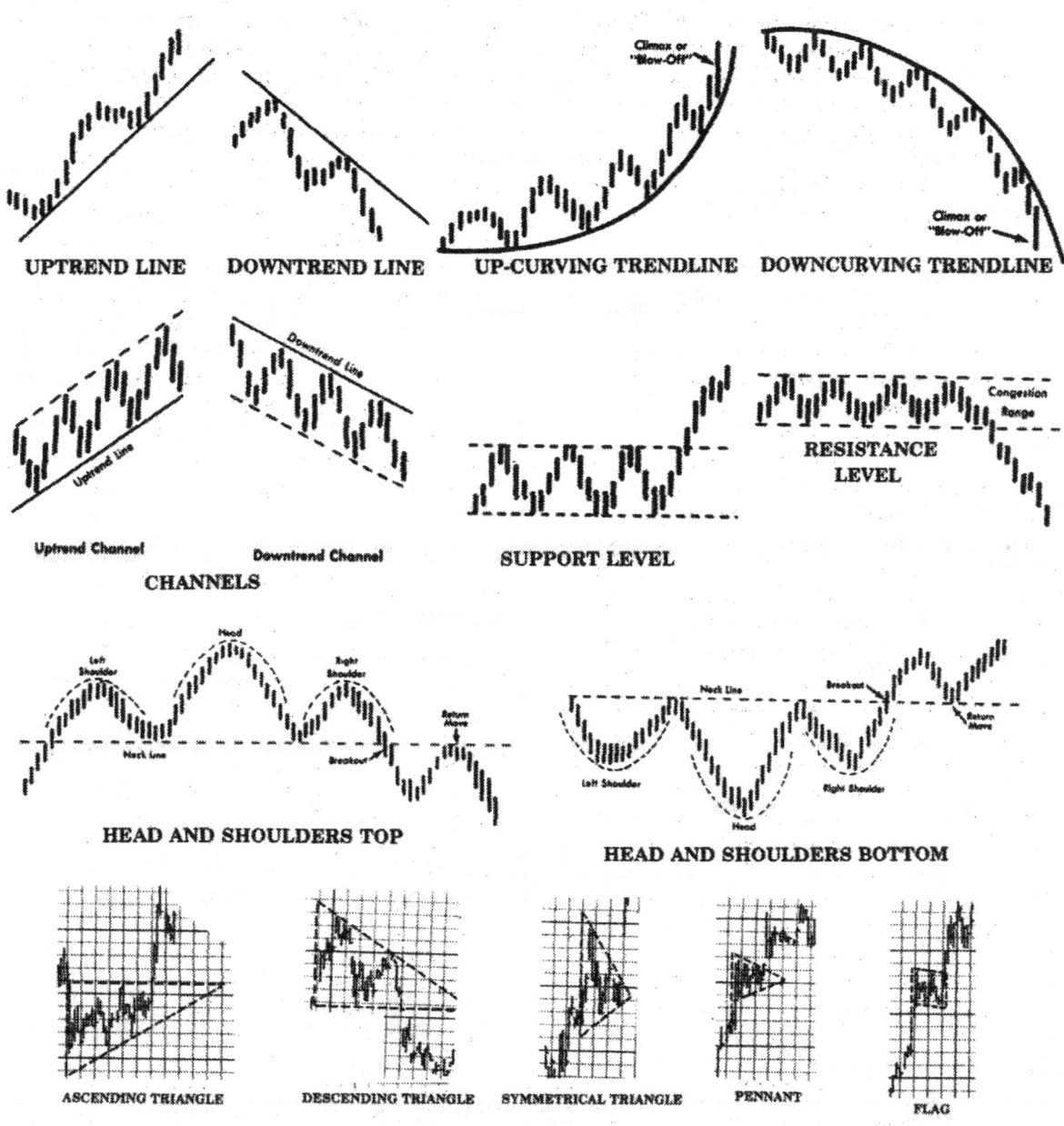

*Figure 28. Typical Stock and Commodity Chart Patterns.*

tion of omens from the movements and positions of the planets, stars, and the vernal equinox. The omens usually referred to rain, crops, war, distress, the country's prosperity, and the king's welfare or misfortune. Lists of omens derived from eclipses, works on the planets and stars, and the calendars, all have the same origin due to observation of coincidences, to past experience, and to a variety of combinations, some logical and some fanciful, of supposed relationships between cause and effect."

Professor Giorgio Abetti, in *The History of Astronomy* (1952), stated: "Astrology was the main goal of the Babylonian astronomers. They have the great merit of not having relied upon pure fantasy or simple deception, as did other peoples later in the Middle Ages, but upon accurate and systematic celestial observations extending throughout many years. The priests of Egypt also were concerned with astronomy. They tried jealously to keep hidden from the public at large their doctrines and results acquired from observations, in order to use them later for their own astrological deductions."

Professor O. Neugebauer, in *The Exact Sciences in Antiquity* (1952), wrote: "To the historian of civilization, astrology is not only one of the significant phenomena of the Hellenistic world, but an exceedingly helpful tool for the investigation of the transmission of Hellenistic thought. Compared to the background of religion, magic and mysticism, *the fundamental doctrines of astrology are pure science.*"

The Babylonian priests had developed the daring belief that events are natural occurrences, caused and determined by other natural occurrences, which could be discovered and noted by a trained observer. They reasoned that by keeping exact records of the movements of the planets and of terrestrial events that occurred under certain planetary arrangements, that the future could be predicted much more logically and accurately than by any other predictive method. Hence, the priests prepared long lists in which all possible phenomena connected with the planets and the stars were noted and their meaning indicated. The larger the number of observations, the greater the possibility of finding an answer to a particular problem. Similarly, the interpretation of the phenomena were founded on the actual occurrence of certain events at certain times when the conditions indicated actually existed. Therefore no important enterprise was undertaken without first ascertaining what phenomena might be looked for on the day fixed for any action, and what these phenomena portended.

The oldest Babylonian predictions were meteorological, i.e., they had to do with the weather — rain, storm, drought, etc. But the rulers were not only concerned with the effects of the weather on the crops, but also with the outcome of their future military campaigns and with their enemies' plans. So the scope of the astrological predictions was broadened. Hence, if a war with Elam had followed an eclipse of the Sun on a particular day, it was assumed that a recurrence of the eclipse on the same day would be followed by a recurrence of a war with Elam. Thus was mundane, or political, astrology born. But just as the gods were held chiefly responsible for the larger affairs of this world, so the planets and stars, as symbols of the gods, were regarded as auguries for the chief or ruler of the country—the vicar of the deity on Earth—rather than for the miscellaneous population, and more for the general welfare than for individual prosperity. Thus was natal, or personal, astrology born. It was to reach its highest development under the Greeks and was transmitted to the West through the Arabs.

But while the Babylonian priest, as the servant of the gods, used his astrological knowledge to foretell the future, he was honest enough to recognize his own limitations. For Professor George Rawlinson, in *The Five Great Monarchies* (1862), writes: "Curiously enough, it appears that they regarded their art as locally limited to the regions inhabited by themselves and their kinsmen, so that while they could boldly predict storm, tempest, failing or abundant crops, war, famine, and the like, for Syria, Babylonia, and Susiana, they could venture on no prophecies with respect to other neighboring lands as Persia, Media, Armenia."

Why was this so? The answer is clearly given by Thomas Brown, Professor of Moral Philosophy, Edinburgh University, Edinburgh, Scotland, in his book, *The Relation of Cause and Effect* (1835): *"Experience* is, in every case, necessary, for strict undoubting belief of the future sequences of phenomena; and, even after experience, the relation of cause and effect, as extending beyond the particular facts observed, cannot be discovered by reason. *Experience*, then, is necessary for anticipating the phenomena of matter; and it is not less necessary for anticipating the successions which may be expected in the phenomena of the mind. It is *experience*, therefore, which in every case enables us to be prophets."

The Babylonian astrologer would only predict in those areas in which he had experience. Modern astrologers could well emulate this sensible practice instead of attempting to "cover the waterfront." For it must be remembered that astrology is an empirical art, and as Richard Lewinsohn states in *Science, Prophecy and Prediction* (1961), "All non-inspirational or non-intuitive attempts to look into the future are necessarily based on experience, i.e., on the past, and on the assumption that like causes will have like effects."

The conquests of Alexander the Great, who captured Babylon in 331 B.C., brought the Babylonian and Greek astrologers into closer contact. In 280 B.C., the Babylonian priest Berosus founded a school for the study of oriental astronomy and astrology on the Greek island of Cos, the seat of the famous medical school which produced the great Hippocrates. Since the Greeks were better mathematicians than the Babylonians, they soon outstripped their teachers, and the first Greek horoscopes were composed about 250 B.C. The Greek scientist Hipparchus (ca. 161 B.C.), who made a major contribution towards turning astronomy into an exact science by cataloguing the stars, was a master of astrology as well. It was from him that Ptolemy (ca. A.D 150) (who codified ancient astrology for the Western world) and later Greek astrologers derived much of their wisdom.

While astrology had a somewhat checkered career among the Romans, it eventually became an official Roman science, with a special school and state subsidies during the reign of the Emperor Alexander Severus (A.D. 223-235), who was of Phoenician origin. After the Emperor Constantine the Great proclaimed Christianity to be the State Religion of the Roman Empire in 325 A.D., the Catholic Church put an end to all other methods of divination except astrology. Although the church never issued a formal condemnation of astrology, it condemned astrological superstitions. The greatest collection of ancient manuscripts on astrology is in the Vatican Library.

Astrology in the Roman Empire nevertheless fell into a decline that lasted for centuries, because of the abuses of charlatans. More ethical astrologers took refuge in the courts of the East, and when Persia was conquered by the Arabs in 651 A.D., astrology spread throughout the Arab world. Thus it was a brilliant Arab mathematician, Albategnius (A.D. 850-929) who was the first to introduce "houses" into astrology, thus making it possible to construct charts which simplified the process of predicting the future of an individual. The Arab system of house interpretation eventually became the basis of Western astrological predictions.

During the Middle Ages, astrology was held in such high repute in the West that chairs of astrology were established in Italian and French universities, and several Popes even employed personal astrologers. With the rise of materialistic science in the 18th and 19th Centuries, astrology again went into a decline. But the 20th Century has seen a remarkable revival of the ancient art. The revolutionary discoveries of atomic scientists have shattered many a scientific dogma and have created a more unbiased intellectual climate for the investigation of ancient philosophies.

What makes astrology work? Please read the following chapter for answers.

# Chapter 9

# The Rationale of Astrological Prediction

*Do not be afraid to challenge authority at any time, if a search for truth is in question. Truth is mt found behind a man's reputation. Truth appears only through the search for answers to questions by a free mind.*—Vincenzo Galilei (Father of Galileo)

What makes astrology tick? Here are some answers:

In 1898, Swedish scientist Svante Arrhenius published a paper, "Cosmic Influences of Physiological Phenomena," which, although ignored at that time by most of the scientific world, astrophysical as well as biophysical, is considered as marking the beginning of the scientific study of man in the universe. Arrhenius noted a distinct correlation between the lunar cycle and menstruation, births, epileptic attacks, deaths and atmospheric-electrical potential. On the sixtieth anniversary of Arrhenius's paper, Drs. Walter Menaker and Abraham Menaker reported the results of a statistical analysis of over 500,000 live births in New York City hospitals between January 8, 1948, and January 26, 1957, which confirmed Arrhenius's findings that more births occur around a Full Moon than around a New Moon. The Menaker paper was published in the April 1959 *American Journal of Obstetrics and Gynecology*.

Having been born under a celestial pattern, when does the newborn infant become affected by extraterrestrial forces? The answer, according to W. J. Tucker, in his book, *The Principles, Theory and Practice of Scientific Prediction* (1939), is as follows: "At the moment of birth certain resultant magnetic conditions are present which produce a type of sensitivity and selectivity in the individual then born, and when an electrically charged body (the transiting planet) again enters the area which held the original electrically charged body (the natal planet) magnetic effects are produced which operate as a cause affecting the individual with whom they are synchronized."

Again, in *The Principles of Scientific Astrology* (1938), Tucker writes: "Self-animation enters into the child at the moment of drawing its first breath. This, then, is the critical moment in which the lines of force of the resultant magnetic field of the Sun, Moon and stars, running through the child's body, fix and determine the relative positions of the electrons and protons in the atoms of the child's flesh, blood, and bones for the duration of its life. That is why the child will behave in a characteristic manner as it progresses through life, and why certain configurations of the heavenly bodies appear to affect him. The type of magnetic field set up by existing configurations (of transiting planets) is the actuating medium."

The importance attached by astrologers to the moment of birth, i.e., when the child takes its first breath of air, may be grasped from the fact that Dr. O. R. Wait of the Department of Terrestrial Magnetism of the Carnegie Institute of Washington, D. C. demonstrated in a series of extremely delicate experiments that every human breath contains at least 700,000,000 electrically charged particles, which are produced by the collision of cosmic rays and uranium and thorium emanations from the soil with atmospheric molecules. The electrical charge of the air we breathe is affected by changes in the electro-magnetic field surrounding the Earth, and thus we are affected biologically.

Furthermore, Miss M. Gosh, in the March 1953 *Journal of Geophysical Research,* stated: "The ionizations of the different ionospheric regions are known to vary not only with the hour of the day and the season of the year, but also with the phase of sunspot activity." These variations in the intensity of the electromagnetic field surrounding the earth are believed to be due to the geometrical configurations of the planets and the movement of the Earth around the Sun. Since planetary movements can be accurately predicted, we thus have a most valuable tool with which to work.

One of the clearest explanations of the astrological theory was given by Elbert Benjamine in *Beginner's Horoscope Reader* (1943). He stated that, in the physical world, energies are limited by Einstein's Special Theory of Relativity to the speed of light (186,000 miles per second.) But, in the inner world, which is variously termed the subconscious mind, the unconscious mind, or the soul, there are energies with velocities exceeding the speed of light. Among these energies are those known as astrological energies, which influence not only electromagnetic energies in space having approximately the velocity of light, but also electromagnetic energies within a living organism having velocities slower than that of light. Thus it is through the medium of electromagnetic energies that the outer plane affects the inner plane of man and, conversely, the inner plane affects the outer plane.

Each planet radiates astral energy of a different frequency, and hence has a different effect upon the astral form of things, just as each different musical tone or pitch has a definite vibratory frequency and each different color has a definite electromagnetic frequency. The planetary energies converge upon the Earth from different angles, and these angles determine the manner in which the energies combine into harmony or discord. From time immemorial, it has been found that the following angles or aspects between planets are harmonious in their effects: 60 degrees, or sextile, and 120 degrees, or trine. Found to be inharmonious are 0 degrees, or conjunction, 90 degrees, or square, and 180 degrees, or opposition.

The characteristic effect of a planetary configuration or angle may vary within certain limits from perfect. These limits are known as orbs of influence and are usually of the following order of magnitude: conjunction, 10 degrees; sextile, 6 degrees; square, 6 degrees; trine, 8 degrees; and opposition, 10 degrees. The potency of an aspect rises slowly as the planets enter the orb of influence and accelerates rapidly during its approach to exactitude. It then declines in like manner as the planets move apart. The potency of the aspect at various points within orb may be represented by a symmetrical sine curve, which shows that an aspect which is one-third of its distance to exact has only one-fourth of its ultimate value. At the half-way mark, it reaches half of its potential, and at two-thirds of exactitude it exerts three-fourths of its total potential.

The planets whose geometrical configurations appear to affect the business cycle the most are Jupiter, Uranus and Saturn. Jupiter, the largest of our planets, makes one complete revolution around the Sun in 11.86 years, while Uranus, more remote from the Sun, requires 84.02 years to complete its circuit. The time required for these two planets to complete a circle of 360 degrees with respect to each other is 13.81 years and is known as their synodical period.

Saturn requires 29.46 years to complete its solar revolution; its synodical period with respect to Jupiter is 19.86 years, and with respect to Uranus is 45.36 years.

One of the strongest endorsements by a non-astrologer of the truth lying back of astrology is contained in the following letter written by the late John J. O'Neill, Science Editor of the *New York Herald Tribune*, on July 8, 1951, to Astrologer Sydney Omarr saying, "The hypothesis of the astrologers that *forces are transmitted to the earth without attenuation with increasing distance, and do not vary with respect to the differences in masses of the Sun, Moon, and planets on which they originate,* was totally inconsistent with the old style Newtonian mechanics; but today is in complete accord with the much more recent Einstein photoelectric theory, which demonstrates that the effect of a photon does not diminish with distance, and which has been universally adopted by scientists to supplant the Newtonian mechanics in that field. The hypothesis of the astrologers that different effects will be produced by different configurations of the heavenly bodies is entirely consistent with the modern developments in the field of chemistry, in which the properties of substances are stated in terms of the architectural configurations of the atoms within the molecules, and with the theories of the atomic scientists that the properties of the atoms are associated with the orbital architecture of the electrons."

The truth of the *italicized* portion of the foregoing has been amply demonstrated by John Nelson, the Radio Wizard, in his thirty years of successfully forecasting radio disturbances from planetary configurations. Nelson gives Pluto, one of the smallest planets, the same weight as Jupiter, the largest planet.

Astrologer Tucker's 1930 theory that individuals are affected by changes in the interplanetary electromagnetic field was corroborated by non-astrologer Professor Ellsworth Huntington of Yale University, who stated in the December 1944 issue of *The Frontier* published by the Armour Research Foundations that "Studies such as those begun by Adrian and continued by Burr indicate that the human body has its own definite electrical field. If that is the case, variations in the external electrical field must inevitably influence the internal human field. It is likewise obvious that, if the electrical field of the Sun or of the solar system as a whole undergoes variations there must be corresponding disturbances in the field of the earth. Thus, there is a logical connection between solar activity, the earth's atmosphere, man's psychological reactions, prices on the stock market, and the ups and downs of business. Thus far this whole matter is in the stage of an hypothesis. Nevertheless, the hypothesis seems to fit a great number of facts which were previously inexplicable."

Furthermore, Dr. W. F. Peterson, in *Man, Weather and Sun* (1947), stated: "All life is rhythmic in some fashion, and all life is meshed into the inorganic rhythm of the universe. The immediate state or 'constitution' of the atmosphere is of paramount importance. This is a terrestrial matter involving time, place, and amplitude. Cosmic forces (the Sun and possibly planetary effects on the Sun) govern the play of the atmosphere. Weather is conditioned by variations in force that modify the electronic and lower gaseous layers of the atmosphere, and these forces must come from the Sun and the changes induced therein by planetary motions. The individual is weather-conditioned; we respond to every whim of the air mass in which we exist. Directly or indirectly, the human will respond and swing in harmony with these major forces which are solar and far back of these remote cosmic forces.

"If we wish to evaluate the present and project the future, we can do so only in the framework of the past. Patterns of human reaction are expressions of reaction to major cosmic forces that directly or indirectly govern the state of the organic world as they do the inorganic, govern the individual as they do the mass; govern not only man today but have governed man in the past and will govern man in the future, despite all imaginable controls that we may devise."

Dr. Peterson further stated: "The seemingly insignificant impact of the moment may, if occurring for some short period of time during the earliest stages of development, leave its imprint fixed for the duration of the life of the individual. So the simple tides of the inorganic forces of the world and the universe—reflected and amplified—dampened and stemmed in flesh and blood, in brain and marrow, may, in the final analysis, be of supreme importance, not only for the individual, but for the mass of mankind, as long as mankind is led (or misled) by the individual."

In addition to solar radiation, scientists have detected radiation from the stars, which is called sidereal radiation. Garfield A. Drew, in *New Methods for Profit in the Stock Market* (1948), stated: "The Townsend Brown Foundation in Los Angeles, California has made a study of sidereal radiation for the past twenty-five years, recording the impulses by an instrument developed some twenty years ago. Complete records, however, have only been kept since 1937, except for the World War II period when the equipment was taken over by the Naval Research Laboratory.

"The conclusion of the Brown Foundation is that sidereal rays are not electromagnetic in nature, but are 1) tremendously penetrating and 2) are subject to decisive changes in intensity in an irregular wave-like pattern. Their studies indicate a correlation between the intensity of sidereal radiation and various records of human expression, including the trends of stock prices—not of course, with absolute perfection, but to a degree suggesting that more than chance is involved."

Stuart Chase, in *Power of Words* (1953) concluded: "Cosmic rays, by hitting the genes, may cause sudden biological mutations. We are drilled by about 100 cosmic rays every minute of our lives. According to the physiologists, every one of us creates the patterns in his brain, beginning with the day he is born. The world he apprehends at any given time is shaped by those patterns. He has, moreover, the power deliberately to seek new experiences, create new patterns, and even change the shape of his world."

Rodney Collin, in *The Theory of Celestial Influence* (1954), put things in a nutshell, when he stated: "All phenomena in nature are the product of three forces—Sun, planets, Earth. If the Sun is the source of life and energy, and Earth the quarry of raw material, planets are the creators of form and function. The result is the whole world of nature. All rotating bodies in the universe create and are surrounded by a magnetic field. All magnetism affects all other magnetism. The true influence of the planets upon Earth is almost certainly of a magnetic nature."

This interaction of magnetic fields was explained by David Dietz, Scripps-Howard Science Editor, on June 14, 1958, as follows: "The Sun is a great shotgun, spraying the earth with showers of sub atomic bullets. Blasts from the solar shotgun are heralded by the appearance of bright outbursts of ultraviolet light on the surface of the Sun—the so-called solar flares. A cloud of hydrogen gas is thereby released, which becomes electrified or ionized and the atoms of hydrogen separate into their constituent particles, namely protons and electrons.

"The spray of protons and electrons encounters the earth's magnetic field and is bent into a circle around the earth. But the protons, being positive, move in one direction, and the electrons, being negative, move in the other. This sets up a tremendous electric current which flows in a ring around the earth. A magnetic field is generated by this ring of current, and it is the interaction of this magnetic field that results in magnetic storms."

Collin further stated: "If the possibility exists that a planet may stimulte an organ in one particular man, it seems indisputable that the same conjunction could activate this organ in millions of men, producing waves of business activity or depression, cycles of wars, periodic fluctuations in birth rate and so on."

While astrologers have stressed the importance of the moment of birth as the determining factor in the establishment of certain planetary patterns, they also recognize the power of free will. This theme of *free will* is emphasized by the great American psychic, Edgar Cayce, who, in one of his readings is quoted as follows: "The strongest force affecting the destiny of man is the Sun first, then the closer planets to Earth, or those that are coming to ascension at the time of the birth of the individual. Just as the tides are ruled by the Moon in its path about the earth, just so is the higher creation ruled by its actions in conjunction with the planets about the earth.

*"But let it be understood here: no action of any planet or the phases of the Sun, the Moon, or any of the heavenly bodies, surpasses the rule of man's own willpower;* the power given by the Creator to man in the beginning, when he became a living soul with the power of choosing for himself..." *(Vide, Edgar Cayce on Reincarnation* by Noel Langley, 1968).

Similarly, G. de Purucker, in *The Esoteric Tradition* stated: "Storms, wars, local or widespread outbreaks of disease, blights on crops, etc. all have their causal origins in the cyclically recurring movements of the Astral Light. But the primal or ultimate causes arise in the cosmic spheres of the Sun, Moon, and the so-called Seven Sacred Planets, which affect and work through the mediate or effectual causes aroused in the regions of the Astral Light.

"The statement that the two luminaries and the Seven Sacred Planets are the causative agents in the production of effects on Earth, while perfectly true, must not be misunderstood to mean that human beings are but helpless and irresponsible victims of cosmic fatality, for this is emphatically not the teaching. *The stars impel but do not compel.* Thus, any human being possessing the divine inherent principle or faculty of free will in whatever manner or degree, can at any moment direct his own life, and can, in proportion to the development in him of his spiritual intellect, rise superior to the cosmic karmic urges or impulses brought about by the influences of the celestial bodies. The Divine Spirit, in man's breast, is incomparably superior even to any cosmic force that can bring about results on Earth; and while a human being can at no time escape his karma or the karmic consequences of his former thoughts and deeds, he can at every instant of his life modify for better and change to the good all new situations in which he may be placed. Thus it is that little by little, by so following the inner light, he can build up a store of karmic consequenses which, when they reach him in future ages, will be like incoming angels of light and mercy."

In a somewhat similar vein, Sir James Jeans, the eminent British scientist, says in substance that it may be that the gods determining our fate are our own minds working on our brain cells, and through them on the world about us. Scientists have even invented a machine that records the force of our thoughts, for, every thought expressed by the mind of man radiates energy as it passes through the brain cells, and this radiation is measurable. University of Chicago scientists are using a thought-wave measuring device as an aid in selecting business executives for promotion.

Mention has been made earlier of Professor Ellsworth Huntington's reference to the work of Adrian and Burr regarding the discovery of an electrical field in human beings. As a follow-up, in the April 1959 issue of *The American Journal of Clinical Hypnosis,* Dr. Leonard J. Ravitz, one of Burr's most prominent followers, reports having obtained experimental proof of the validity of the 1935 Burr-Northrop Electrodynamic Theory of Life, stating: "When finally put into operation, what theory predicted, the instruments found; in their theoretic component, living things are electrodynamic systems exhibiting reproducible force field properties continuously in four dimensional spacetime. . . . In human subjects within any twelve month span, the most pronounced electric tides comprise diurnal, fortnightly, monthly, seasonal and semi-annual variations. . . . On inspection, geomagnetic tides likewise seem to correspond to these electric rhythms. Moreover, annual variations in the force field pattern of trees have paralleled the sunspot cycle, and evidence has been collected which suggests similar trends in human subjects."

An interesting sidelight is contained in the April 28, 1962 *Le Concours Medical,* in which Frank Ivan Lenart published a paper, "Biometeorological Influences on Life and Death," giving the results of a statistical study of 7,695 deaths over the 10-year period of May 1945 to May 1955, which confirmed the findings of American scientists that 1) most deaths occur in the early morning hours and 2) that they are governed by extraterrestrial forces emanating from the Sun, Moon, stars, or cosmic rays from outer space.

Even the staid medical profession is beginning to admit the validity of some astrological teachings, for the February 15, 1965 issue *of Hospital Focus* in its lead article, "Astrology and Biology" stated: "The central thesis may be simply stated: the heavenly bodies have distinguishable effects on biologic materials. At the present stage of knowledge, this thesis has become testable, and has apparently been verified, at least in broad outline. . . . The case for celestial influence rests on several pillars: Electromagnetic phenomena can be shown to be associated in some ways with biologic processes; the terrestrial environment is rich in electromagnetic phenomena (and secondary effects from these); and the terrestrial electromagnetic environment is subject to variations induced by other electromagnetic events in the solar system." The article concludes: "If it is verified that human processes are affected by the magnetic field interactions and celestial bodies, and if the Babylonians and Harappans knew nothing at all about wave mechanics or the solid state, how were they able to conceive of astrology?" To which we answer, "There are more things in heaven and earth, Horatio, than are dreamt of in your philosophy."

Finally, reference has been made in Chapter 1 to Arne Fisher's *Law of Causality,* which forms the basis of all intelligent forecasting. Fisher stated: "Everything that happens, and everything that exists, necessarily happens or exists as the consequence of a previous state of things." Furthermore, Dr. David F. Jordan has stated: "Since everything that happens necessarily occurs as the result of a previous state of things, the pre-determination of economic developments is predicated upon adequate knowledge of existing conditions."

Statisticians become so engrossed with their statistics that they often fail to see the forest for the trees. Thus, Smith and Duncan, in *Elementary Statistics and Applications* (1944), stated: "The human desire to look into the future led, even in ancient times, to the rise of various forms of pseudo-scientific forecasts. Oracles were frequently consulted as to the outcome of a contemplated military campaign, business venture, or love affair. Among the most famous of these was the Delphian Oracle. Astrologists were, and still are, consulted for what the stars have to say. It was partly to disprove some of these astrological notions that statistical method was first undertaken on a scientific basis." These writers then stated: "Business forecasting is one of the most important uses of statistics."

But the human element has also to be taken into consideration. The importance of the human element was recognized by Dr. Warren M. Persons, Professor of Economics, Harvard University, who stated in *Forecasting Business Cycles* (1931): "The world of affairs in which we live is not a mechanistic world; it is a bewildering world of multiplicities, complexities, interactions, repercussions, and the vagaries of human wants, fears and hopes. It is a world in which, at times, facts and logic become subordinated to human emotions. At such times individuals, who by themselves are rational, join with other rational individuals to form an unreasoning mob. The business world then suffers from an epidemic of optimism, with hope, recklessness and indolence as its leading symptoms, or from an epidemic of pessimism, with fear, timidity and inertia as its leading features. It is also a world of wars, droughts, floods, earthquakes, and monetary changes. In such a world there can be neither a sure fire system nor a reliable trick method of forecasting business cycles."

Similarly, Dr. Frederick R. Macauley, in *The Movements of Interest Rates, Bank Yields and Stock Prices in the United States Since 1856* (1938), stated: "The very essence of economics is that it is a study of human behavior, of the life of man, and basically of the *mental* life of man. It takes cognizance of facts in the external world, not for their own sakes, but only because of their relations to the mind of man. It is a study of some of the *causes and effects* of those conscious or unconscious decisions that men inevitably make in their rational or instinctive struggle to earn a living and to satisfy at least some of their desires by adjusting the external world to themselves and—perhaps—thereby securing happiness and well-being." Change the word "economics" in the foregoing to "astrology" and you have a perfect definition of the modern art of astrology.

Not only does economic forecasting recognize a cause and effect relationship, but it also employs the principle of historic analogy, just as does astrology. Thus, Professor S. J. Maisel of the University of California states, in *Fluctuations, Growth and Forecasting* (1957), that "Successful forecasting is intricate. Forecasts deal in probabilities. Most forecasters make use of *historical* and *statistical* patterns. It is almost impossible to work without them. The procedures assume that there are certain uniformities in the economy which can be discovered by an analysis of *past experience.* By means of statistics, observation or theory, it is discovered that a certain situation A in the past has always been followed by another situation B. Assuming that this results from a relationship in the economy which will not change, it can be predicted that the next time A occurs, B will ensue."

Reference has been made to the *Law of Causality* or the *Law of Cause and Effect.* Just what is this Law? One of the earliest and clearest explanations was given about 150 years ago by Thomas Brown, Professor of Moral Philosophy, University of Edinburgh, Scotland, in his book, *Inquiry Into the Relation of Cause and Effect* (1835), in which he stated: "We observe the varying phenomena, as they are continually taking place around us and within us, and the observation may seem to be, and truly is, of a single moment; but the knowledge which it gives us is far more extensive; it is, virtually, information of the past and of the future, as well as of the present. The future, when it arrives, we find to be only the past under another form.

"We are truly, then, prophets of the future, while we may seem to be only observing what is before us, or remembering what has been formerly observed; and, in whatever way this prophetic gift may have been conferred on us, it must be regarded as the most valuable of all gifts, since without it, every other gift would have been profitless.

"It is not to science only, then, but to all the practical acts of life, and consequently to the preservation of life itself, that the faith is essential which converts the passing sequences of phenomena into signs of future corresponding sequences.

"A *cause* may be said to be that which *immediately precedes any change,* and which, *existing at any time in similar circumstances, has been always, and will always, be immediately followed by a similar change.*

"We do not give the name of cause to that which we suppose to have once preceded a particular event, *but to that which we believe to have been in all past time, as much as in the present, and to be equally in all future time, followed, uniformly and immediately, by a particular change, which we therefore denominate its effect.*

"It is experience which, in every case, enables us to be prophets. Experience, then, is necessary for anticipating the phenomena of matter; and it is not less necessary for anticipating the successions which may be expected, in the phenomena of mind.

*"Experience is, in every case, necessary for strict undoubting belief of the future sequences of phenomena; and, even after experience, the relation of cause and effect, as extending beyond the particular facts observed, cannot be discovered by reason."*

How planetary movements may be used to successfully forecast the general trend of the stock market are discussed in Chapter 10.

## Chapter 10

# Rhythmic Stock Market Cycles

*By the Law of Periodical Repetition, everything which has happened once
must happen again and again and again—and not capriciously,
but at regular periods, and each thing in its own period, not another's,
and each obeying its own law . . . and the same Nature which delights in
periodical repetition in the skies is the Nature which orders the affairs
of the earth. Let us not underrate the value of that hint.—Mark Twain*

## Introduction

What are cycles? *Funk & Wagnall's Practical Standard Dictionary* gives the following definitions: "1. A period of time, at the end of which certain aspects or motions of the heavenly bodies repeat themselves. 8. A series that repeats itself." Edward R. Dewey, for many years Executive Secretary and then President of The Foundation for the Study of Cycles, gave this definition in *Cycles, The Mysterious Forces that Trigger Events* (1971): "Cycle comes from the Greek word for circle. Actually, the word cycle means coming around again to the place of beginning. . . . When there is a fairly regular period of time, the correct word to use is 'Rhythm,' from another Greek word meaning measured time. . . . Rhythmic cycles are almost universal in nature. . . . When the wave lengths of natural science cycles are the same as the wave length of cycles in the social sciences, we have reason to believe that we are approaching the very heart of the mystery."

Dewey found that stock prices, like most other phenomena, fluctuate in cycles. The practical use to which a knowledge of such cycles may be put is related by Dewey as follows: "The late General Charles Gates Lawes, former Vice President of the United States, former Chairman of the Board of the City National Bank and Trust Company of Chicago, and until his death a member of the Board of Directors of The Foundation for the Study of Cycles, once told me that he and his brother had made over a million dollars in the stock market solely as a result of his knowledge of cycles. He showed me brokerage statements that indicated more than this amount in clear profit."

In his classic book, *Cycles—The Science of Prediction* (1947), written in collaboration with

Edwin F. Dakin, Dewey stated: "The student of periodic rhythms in human affairs has a tool which the Law of Averages itself puts into his hands. If trends have continued for decades, or if the oscillation of cycles around the trend have repeated themselves so many times and so regularly that the rhythm cannot reasonably be the result of chance, it is unwise to ignore the probability that those behaviors will continue.... The result is not prediction, in the sense in which the word is ordinarily understood.... It is in effect, the probability of tomorrow."

Dewey's original technique was based on smoothing the cycle by the use of *moving averages*, which is a flexible mathematical method of smoothing the data. The data so smoothed are often used as a trend. Figure 29 shows what happens to an ideal 9-year rhythm when the curve of which it is a component is smoothed by moving averages.

When the author first met Dewey in 1948, the latter was skeptical about astrology for he stated in the Introduction of *Cycles—The Science of Prediction:* "When people find that predictions of many financial advisers, statesmen, historians, and other proclaimed experts are seldom better than the predictions of the astrologers, our social sciences have demonstrably not been earning their way."

Dewey cautioned in the February 1952 *Cycles* that "You must always be on the lookout for compound cycles. There is reason to believe that the well-known 41-month cycle and the 9.2 year cycle may be compound, and may be reversing at the present time, but a great deal more work needs to be done before we can be sure."

Hence, Dewey recommended in the April 1952 *Cycles:* "In my opinion, the way to make money with cycles in the stock market is to determine some short-term cycles that have repeated themselves so often and over so long a period of time that they cannot reasonably be the result of chance, and then to play these short-term cycles on an actuarial basis, expect-

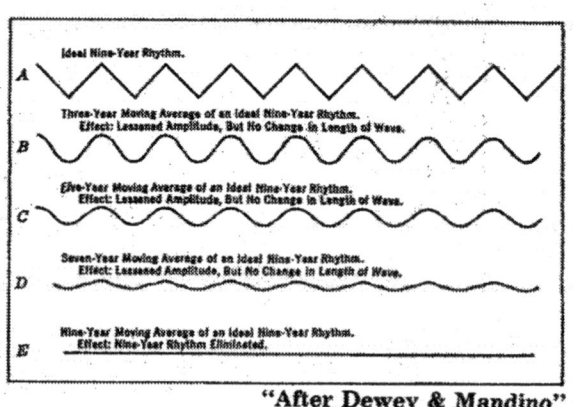

*Figure 29. Effect of Moving Average of Different Lengths Upon an Ideal 9-Year Rhythm.*

ing losses and runs of losses, but expecting—or at least hoping—that on the average and in the long run the gains will exceed the losses, just as they do in fire insurance."

In the December 1965 *Cycles,* with the aid of electronic computers, hints were found of 37 possible cycles in stock market prices, ranging in length from 2½ to nearly 11 years during the period 1937-1965. The most important of these were 9.2 years and 38 months in length. The former is similar to the 9-year Juglar Cycle and the latter to the 3½ year Kitchin Cycle found in business, which were discussed in Part I of this book.

## The 9.2-year Stock Market Cycle

Dewey's 9.2-year cycle in stock prices from 1930 to 1966 is shown in Figure 30. He stated in his 1971 book that "according to the Bartel's test of probability, the 9.2-year cycle *could not occur by chance more than once in 5,000 times."* As the chart shows, tops were correctly indicated 100 percent, while lows were indicated 12 out of 14 times, or were 86 percent correct.

Gertrude Shirk, in *Cycles* of March 1973, stated that on the basis of the most recent measurements, the 9-year cycle in stock prices is more precisely 9.225 years in length from crest to crest. The ideal form of this cycle has a crest at 1965-1966, followed by a trough at 1970-1971. The latter was predicted by Dewey in his 1971

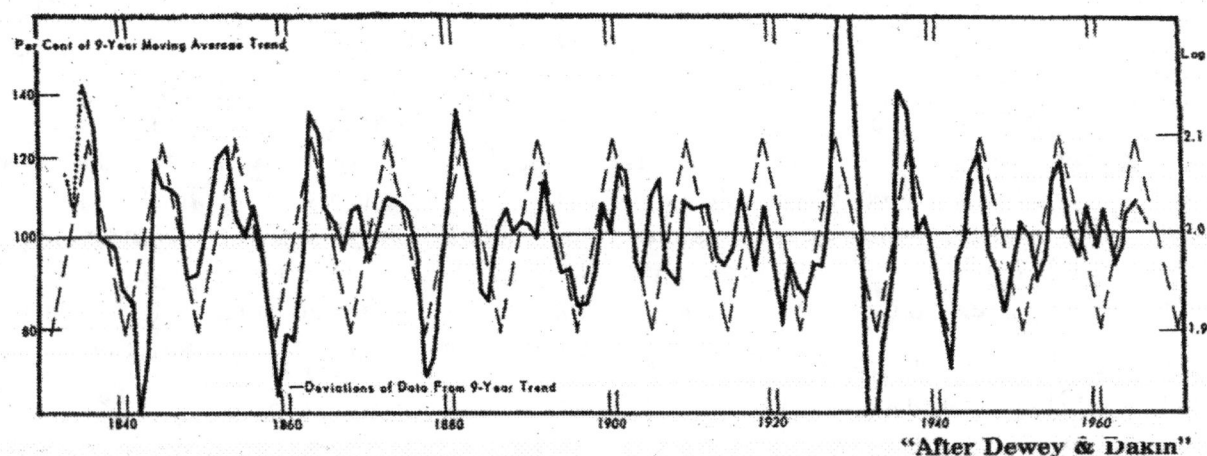

*Figure 30. Dewey's 9.2-Year Cycles in Stock Prices 1830-1966.*

book. Shirk forecast the next turning point in the cycle as a crest in 1974-1976, which was wrong, for the market bottomed that year. Shirk qualified her forecast by stating: "The last statement does not say that stock prices are going up to 1974. The comment is about one cycle, and there are many cycles in stock prices." The reader may recall from Figure 26 in Chapter 6, how poorly Crawford's 9-year Business Cycle behaved.

James E. Vaux, in *Cycles* of May/June 1976, updated the studies of the 9.2-year cycle in the Standard & Poor's 500 stock price average (1831-1976), which correctly indicated tops 100 percent of the time and lows 14 out of 15 times, or 93 percent correct, and stated that "The cycle is statistically significant with a 99 percent confidence that it is not the result of chance. . . . The important 9.2-year cycle in stock prices is only one of several such cycles in this series; however, over the time span from 1831 to date, it has been the most dominant and most regular cycle present in stock prices. The theoretical next time of crest for this cycle is early 1983 and a *low* is due in mid-1978." The predicted *low* came on schedule on February 29 to March 6 of 1978.

Shirk, in *Cycles* of April/May 1977, updated Vaux's studies and reiterated her 1973 statement that the ideal cycle has an ideal crest at 1974.64, and that the cycle in the long (1789-1976) record of the Dow-Jones Industrial Average also shows a crest in 1974. Actual stock prices in 1974 were down, the Standard & Poor's Combined Index dropped 23 percent and the Dow-Jones Industrial Average dropped 18 percent from the 1973 high. Shirk predicted that the next ideal turning point of this cycle would be a low, due ideally at 1979-26 vs. Vaux's "mid-1978 low." Shirk stated, "At various times the description of this cycle in stock prices has varied slightly, depending on the data being used and the period of time covered by the analysis."

## The 38- to 41-month Cycle in Stock Prices

In his 1971 book, Dewey gave the following interesting account of the discovery in 1912 by a New York group of investors of a 40.68-month cycle that had been present in industrial common stock prices since 1871: "These gentlemen had learned that the Rothschilds had analyzed British Consols [government obligations] and had broken up the price fluctuations into a series of repeating curves that had been combined and used for forecasting. The New York group hired a mathematician to discover the secret formula of the Rothschilds and, working with the Dow-Jones Railroad Averages, he discovered a 41-month cycle; plus three others, which his employers used to help them invest in the market. Apparently they were very successful around World War I.

"Some ten years after the original discovery, Professor W. L. Crum of Harvard, noted a cycle of '39-, 40-, or 41-months' in monthly commercial-paper rates in New York. Almost simultaneously, Professor Kitchin, also of Harvard, discovered a cycle that he called forty months in six economic time series, bank clearings, commodity prices, and interest rates in both Great Britain and the United States from 1890 to 1922."

Twenty-three years after the original discovery, Chapin Hoskins, in 1935, noticed this cycle in stock prices. There was an amazing correspondence with an ideal 40.68-month wave from 1868 through 1945, through wars and peace, good times and depression. But, in 1946, the cycle got out of step until 1956. (It actually reversed direction during that period.) The following explanation for this extraordinary behavior was given by Gertrude Shirk in *Cycles* of April 1969, March 1970 and February 1973. In April 1969, from a study of the data from 1930 through 1968, it was concluded that the average length of the cycle had changed from 40.68 months, after 19 successive repetitions, to one of 38 months since the low of 1932.

Shirk, in *Cycles* of March 1974, indicated that the 38-month cycle appeared to have become less reliable. The difficulty in assessing the current situation of any cycle—actual vs. ideal—is because a cycle is a function of two factors, the past and the future. Using data through January of 1974 gave results only through September of 1968. Using a filtering technique of calculating the departures of the original data from a 41-month moving average, smoothed by a 17-month moving average of the data through January of 1974 gave results through May of 1972. A third technique indicated that the ideal peak of the 38-month cycle would come in November 1971, about a year early; similarly the ideal low of June 1973 would also appear to be too soon. (The actual stock market peak occurred in January of 1973 and the lows in September and December of 1974.)

The foregoing analysis of the 41- to 38-month cycle indicates the danger of using an average cycle length of past data to predict the future. A similar situation is the prediction of sunspots. Most people have heard of the 11-year sunspot cycle (discussed in Chapter 2) but few know that the length has varied from a minimum of 8 years to a maximum of 16 years! Accordingly, scientists do not attempt to forecast the sunspot cycle from the 11-year average.

## Combination of Cycles in Stock Market Prices

In 1943, Jacques Coe, a New York stock broker, devised a simple technique for combining the 3⅓-year Kitchin Cycle with the 9-year Juglar Cycle to indicate turning points in the Dow-Jones Industrial Stock Average from 1897, which has been brought up to date by the author in Figure 31. He drew up ideal 3⅓- and 9-year cycles and stated: "When both lines are in gear, stock market continues that way until both lines are in gear in opposite direction." As the chart shows, downward movements from a top were correctly indicated 100 percent of the time, and upward movements from a low 9 out of 10 times, or 90 percent correct. The only exception was the 1921 stock market bottom which came about one and a half years too soon.

In *Cycles* of July 1978, Gertrude Shirk found a 10.36-year cycle in stock price annual averages for the period 1789 through 1977, the longest data record thus far studied. The 10.36-year cycle showed an ideal peak at 1979.8. When the 9.225-year cycle and the 10.36 year cycle are combined, there are times when they enhance each other, and other times when they offset each other. Thus, the ideal 9.225-year cycle was going down to an ideal low at 1979.1, while the ideal 10.36-year cycle was going up to an ideal high at 1980.1. Shirk cautions that "these cycles are only two of the many possible components that help to explain the past behavior of stock price averages." The combined chart of the two cycles is shown in Figure 32 for the period

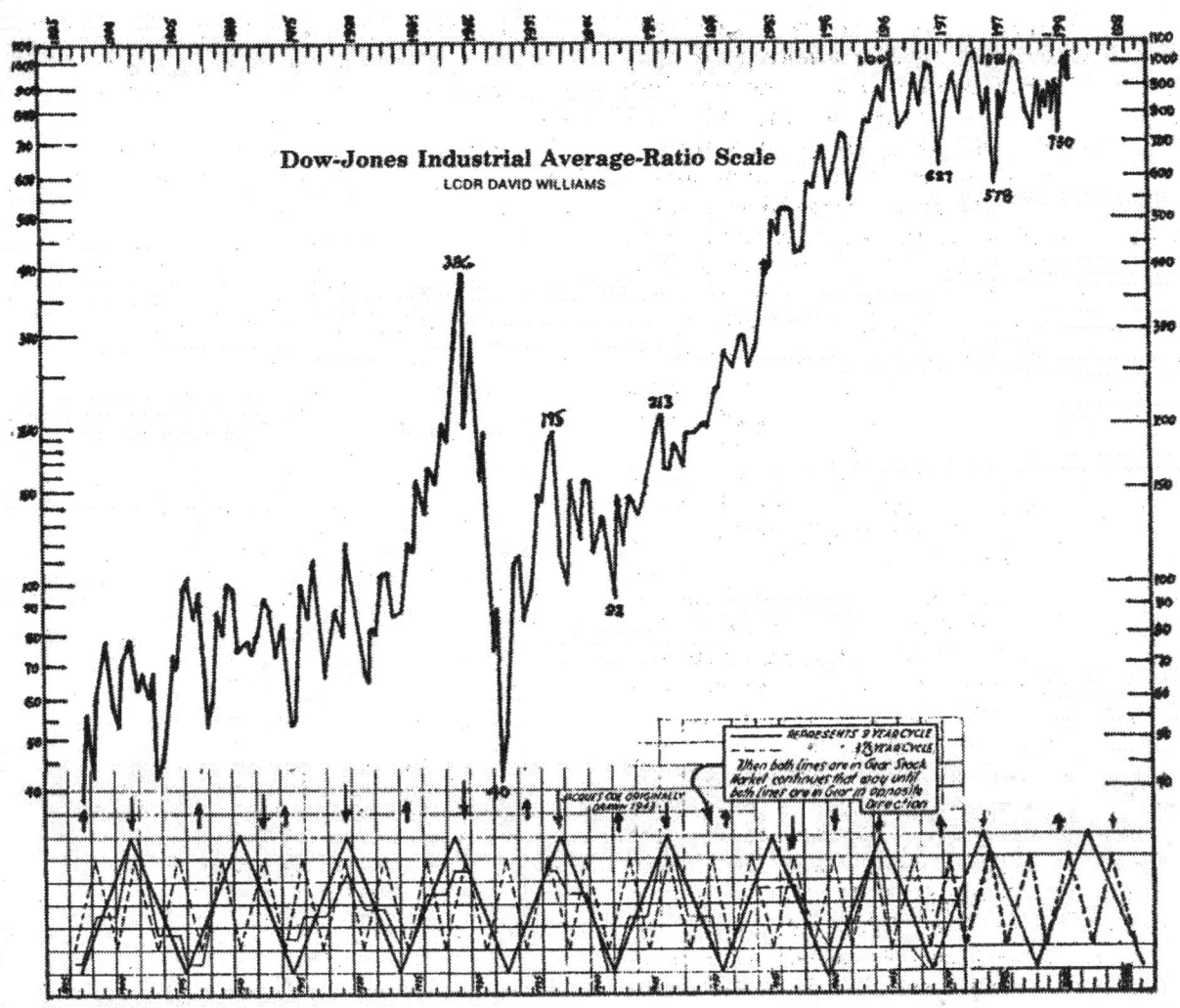

*Figure 31. Coe's Coordinated 3⅓- and 9-Year Cycles vs. DJI Average.*

1789-2000. Tops and bottoms were correctly indicated 86 percent of the time.

In January 1944, Dewey made his first stock market forecast, based on annual data from 1854 to 1944, using 10 cycles varying in lengths from 4.89 to 21 years, with a forecast to 1954. This 10-year forecast correctly indicated the highs of 1946 and 1954 and the intervening low of 1949, for a gain-loss ratio of 185 to 1. But, thereafter, the forecast went awry. Dewey cautioned in the *Cycles* report for June 1953: "It is the simplest of all mathematical tricks to reproduce any time series to any degree of accuracy you wish by combining enough perfectly regular cycles of well-defined properties. That is why, in 1944, even though the combination of 10 cycles and trends fairly well corresponded to the actual values, I was not too impressed with the results. Neither was the New York financial house for which I did the work. I put it away and forgot all about it. Then one day, in 1951, I think, I happened to come across it. I compared the projection with actual behavior, from 1943 forward and was highly gratified with the result.

"If the rhythms are significant, they can be expected to continue. Being 'significant' means that they are the result of periodic forces, not the result of random forces which just happen to occur at rhythmic intervals. . . . As for 1954 being *the* year of crest, it would be surprising and a matter of pure luck if it should turn out so. You simply cannot ignore all cycles under 4½ years and hope to hit the target on the button every time. By luck I did it twice. Do not count on my being able to do it again."

This study was updated by Dewey in *Cycles* of July 1962, for the period 1871-1962, which the author has extended to 1981, as per Figure 33. As the chart shows, the forecast since 1956 has gone haywire.

## The Decennial Pattern in Stock Prices

One of the more important tools in reaching decisions as to the stock market or the business outlook, is the Decennial Pattern formed by three overlapping 10-year cycles. While Vice President of the New York Chapter, Foundation for the Study of Cycles, the author had the pleasure of meeting Anthony Gaubis, an Investment Counselor, who, in a lecture at the December 14, 1960 meeting of the chapter (subsequently published in *Cycles* of February 1961) gave the following account of the origin of the Decennial Pattern.

Gaubis began his research in stock market cycles in 1924, when he joined the Business Forecasting Division of the American Telephone & Telegraph Co. (A. T. & T.) In 1928, he became Research Assistant to Edgar Lawrence Smith, the author of *Common Stocks as Long Term Investments* (1924), and President of two mutual investment trusts he had organized on the basis of his book. In the spring of 1929, Smith started to drastically reduce his holdings of the equities in the investment trusts but, when the Directors refused to go along with him, Smith sold out to the Irving Trust Company in September 1929—at the market top!

Gaubis had become head of Smith's research department and on July 12, 1930, called Smith's attention to the Decennial Pattern, which nine years later became the basis of Smith's book, *Tides in the Affairs of Men* (1939). Gaubis ventured the opinion "that there were weather cycles which influenced the size of our crops and thereby had an important bearing on the cost and supply of certain raw materials used in industry, as well as on the cost of food."

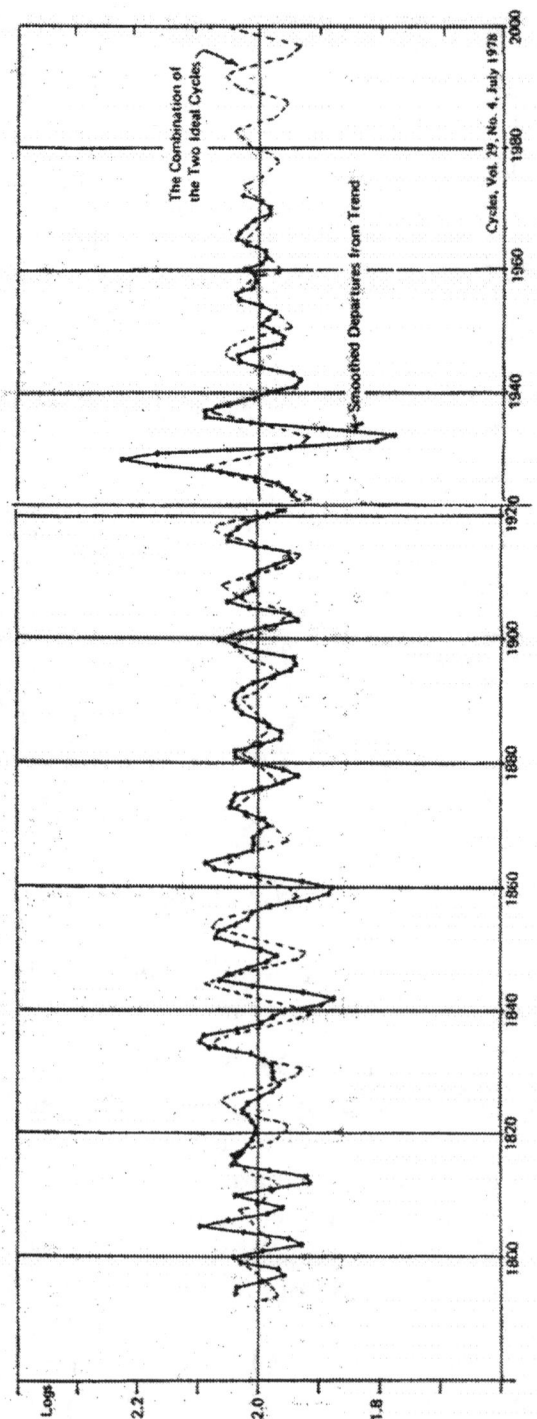

*Figure 32. Smoothed Detrended Stock Prices vs. the 9.225- and 10.36-Year Cycles Combined.*

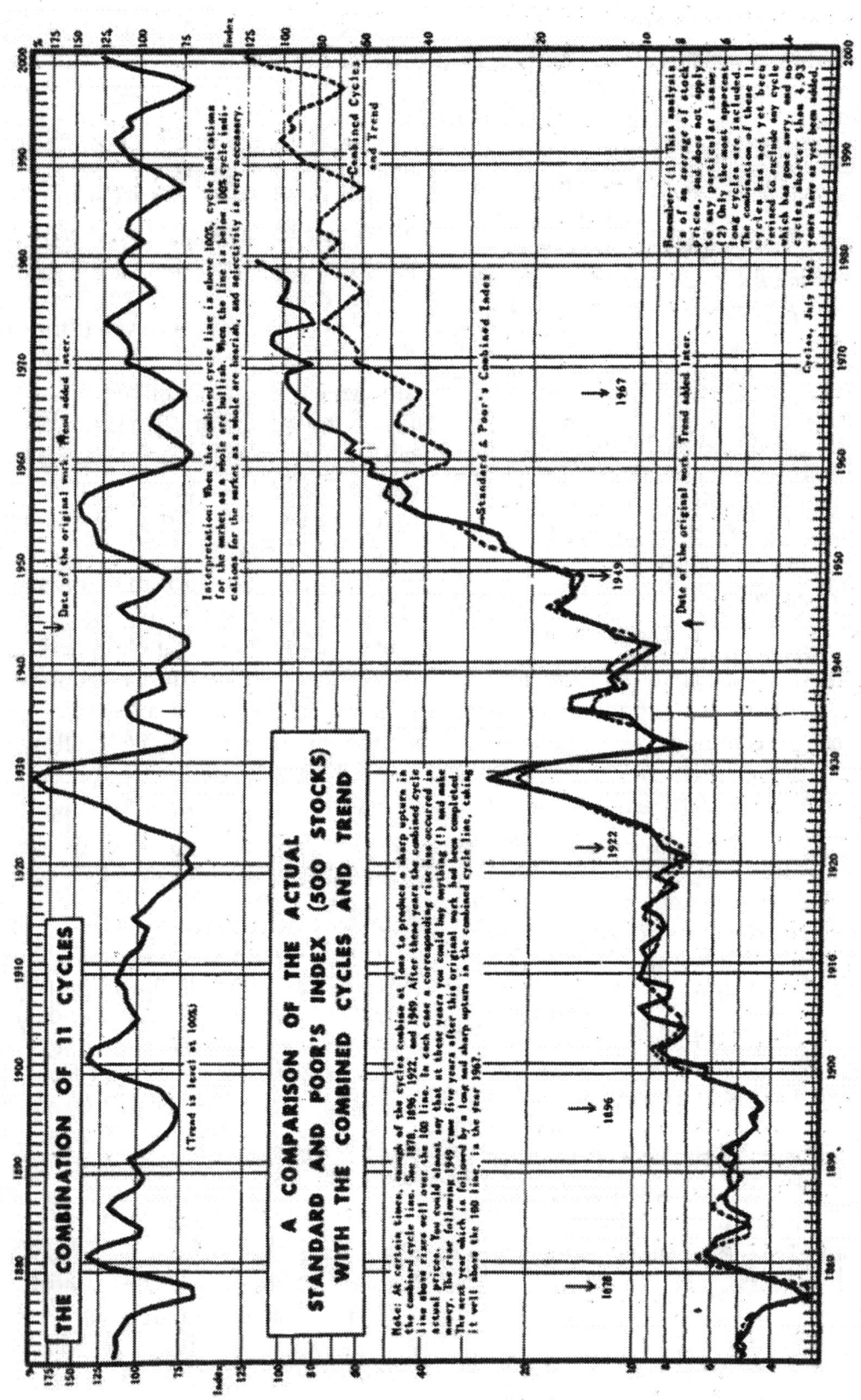

Figure 33. Dewey's 11-Cycle Combination vs. the S&P 500 Stock Index.

When Smith retired from the Irving Trust Company in 1931, he began to make his own researches into the *why* of the timing cycles that Gaubis had called to his attention in 1930. When he discovered that weather affects the chemistry of the blood, and therefore tends to influence the psychology of the more sensitive individuals, he concluded that *"Price movements of any importance upon the stock exchange are an expression of current mass psychology."* Smith and Gaubis agreed, in 1960, that the Decennial Pattern had a batting average of better than 80 percent. Indeed, Smith told Gaubis that in actual practice, this timing technique "had by far the highest batting average of any of the market forecasting methods he had studied in his forty years of research on the cycle." Gaubis cautioned that this technique should be considered, "as merely one of a handful of approaches in reaching decisions as to the stock market or business outlook."

How is the Decennial Pattern formed? It is very simple: just tabulate the price index of the stock market (or commodity or weather) by years beginning say with 1881 to 1890, then 1891 to 1900, 1901 to 1910, etc. List the value for each year ending with one index the heading I, then do the same for the rest of the 9 years in that decade, index the headings II, III, IV, etc. Tabulate the values for succeeding decades, add the values under I and get the average. Do the same for the balance of the data. You will then get a curve for the Decennial Pattern for the period 1881-1936, which shows a tendency for prices to *decline* in the third, seventh, and tenth years, and to *rise* in the second, fifth and eighth years of the decade, as shown at the bottom of Figure 34. The pattern changes slightly as more decades are included, per the curves for 1871-1994 and 1871-1970 shown at the bottom of Figure 34.

When *monthly* data are used, there is a further distortion of the pattern as shown in the middle of Figure 34 for the S & P Industrial Average 1871-1950 and the DJI Average 1951-1960. The last two decades in the Dow Jones Average are shown at the top of the chart. Another distortion occurs when the starting point is shifted to July instead of December.

In a follow-up at the December 12, 1961 meeting of the New York Chapter of the Foundation for the Study of Cycles, published in *Cycles* in February 1962, Gaubis stated: "The apparent existence of three intermediate cycles in every decade means, of course, that the duration of these cycles on a round-trip basis must *average about forty months.* Those who originally developed and publicized the concept of a 40-month cycle overlooked the fact that averages can be misleading. . . . There is a major difference in the conclusions that can be drawn from the concept of three overlapping ten-year cycles than from the observation that cycles have an average duration of 40 months." Gaubis then predicted that "the probabilities are in the nature of about 8 to 1 that the underlying trend of stock prices will continue to be irregularly upward until the fall of 1962, and quite possibly into the early months of 1963, followed by a decline." This was incorrect, as shown on the upper part of Figure 34. Gaubis cautioned about "the risks in using any single stock market cycle or valuation theory as a basis for determining investment policy."

The failure of the Decennial Pattern 1881-1936 (at the bottom of Figure 34) to continue when additional decades of data are added is shown by a comparison with the S & P Industrial Average 1871-1950, the DJI Monthly Averages 1951-1960, 1961-1970, 1971-1980.

## Cycles—Real and Synthetic

In a lecture at the January 13, 1960, meeting of the New York Chapter, Foundation for the Study of Cycles, the author pointed out that cycles can be found in random numbers. This was first emphasized by Dewey in *Cycles* in January of 1952, when he stated: "The cycles you find in random numbers are perfectly *real*, but they have *no significance*. That is, they are not the re-

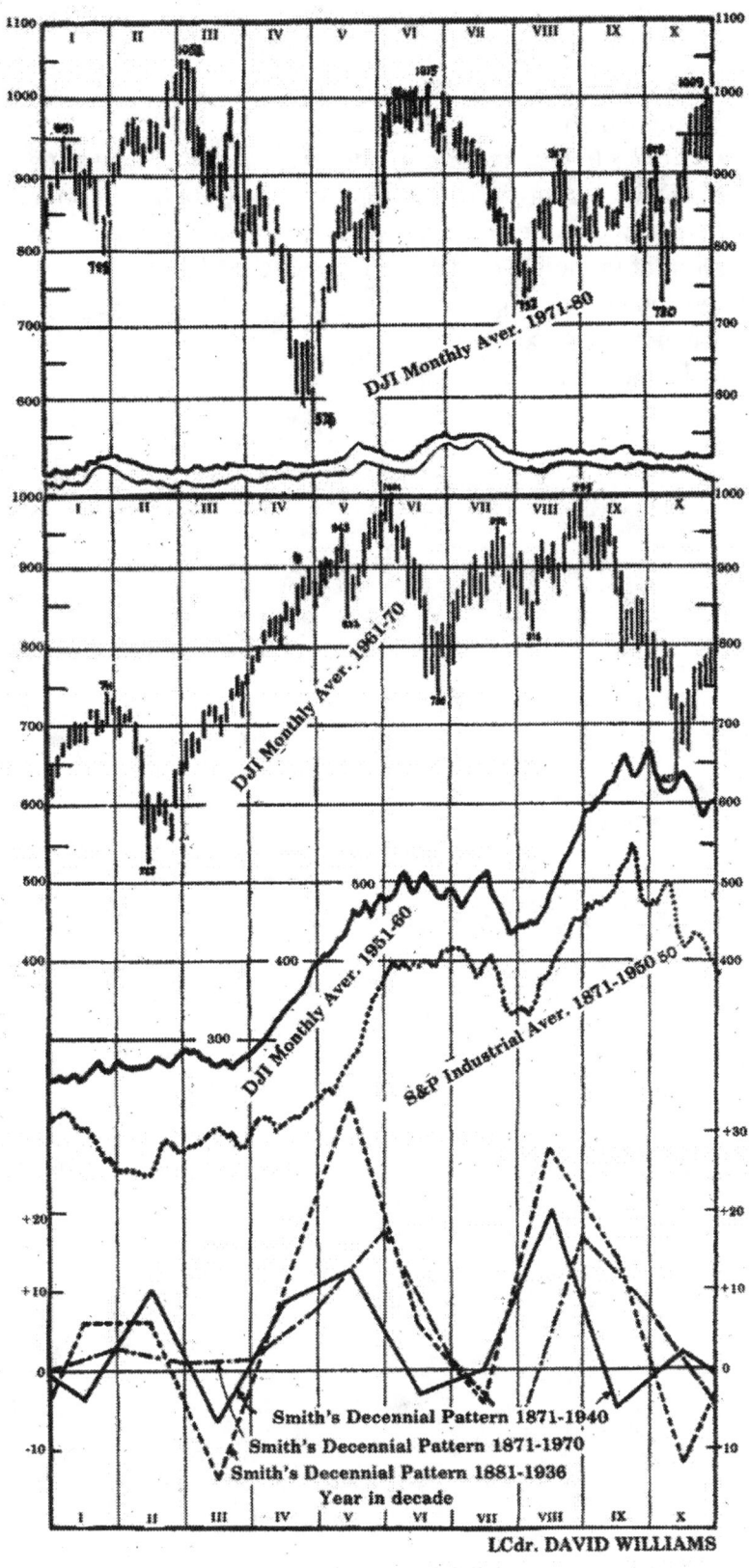

*Figure 34. The Decennial Pattern in Stock Prices.*

sult of any cyclic cause and there is no reason to expect them to continue." Referring to Professor Harold T. Davis's study of three cycles derived from random numbers, published in 1941 as *Monograph No. 6 of the Cowles Commission for Research in Economics,* Dewey continued: "It will bear repeating that these cycles merely happen to be in this succession of random numbers; that they have absolutely no forecasting value whatever. That is, there is not a chance in a million (to speak figuratively and not mathematically) that the next 204 random numbers drawn out of a hat would show a continuation of these three cycles.... It means that every cycle should be looked upon with suspicion unless the cycle shows *enough* regularity and *enough* dominance and *enough* repetitions so that the observed behavior cannot reasonably be the result of chance (most cycles do not)."

To learn what cycles are *real is* the subject of the next chapter.

*Chapter 11*

# Planetary Cycles in the Stock Market

## Introduction

Frequent reference was made in the previous chapter to the Dow-Jones Industrial Average and the Standard & Poor's 500 Stock Average. What do these mean? They are simply an index of the price of a group of stocks at any particular time. The most widely used index is the Dow Jones Average, which began in 1884 as a simple arithmetic average of one industrial and 10 railroad stocks. As time went on, the list was increased to 20 stocks. With the growth of industry it became necessary to add the stocks of industrial companies, so on June 5, 1896, *The Wall Street Journal* printed two lists of stocks, 20 railroad and 12 industrial stocks. The average for each list was still obtained by calculating a simple average of the closing daily prices.

Between January 1897 and July 1926, 28 substitutions were made in the railroad list. In the industrial list, 18 substitutions were made from January 1897 to September 1916, when the number of stocks was increased from 12 to 20 and only 8 of the original stocks were included in the revised list, the other 12 being new stocks. A further change had been made on October 13, 1916, when the computation of the averages was changed from a percentage basis to a dollar basis. Since 1915, there have been about 15 changes in the original list of 20 stocks during the following 10 years. The list was expanded to 30 stocks on October 1, 1928.

While these 30 stocks comprise only 1.5 percent of the total of 2,000 stocks listed on the New York Stock Exchange, they account for about one-third of the total market value. As a result of stock splits, recapitalizations, substitutions, etc. the divisor which originally was 30 has dropped to 1.314 as of August 17, 1981. The 30 stocks currently used in the DJI Average are shown on Appendix 6. The arithmetical average of these stocks at the close of the market on August 14, 1981, was $41.05 and $40.579 on August 18, 1981 versus the quoted values in *The Wall Street Journal* of 936.93 and 926.75, respectively.

The Standard & Poor's 500 Stock Price Index consists of 400 industrial, 20 transportation, 40 utility, and 40 financial stocks, beginning on

March 1, 1957. It is a capitalization weighted index, which measures the total market value of the stocks included in the index. The market value of a stock is calculated by multiplying the number of common shares outstanding by the current price per share. The values for individual stocks are then added to determine the total market value of all the stocks in the index. The Standard & Poor's Index is based on the total market value of the 500 stocks for the years 1941-1943 and the base number =10. The S & P Index has been linked to other indices for the period 1873-1917 by the Cowles Commission, and the end product is a continuous market index record for over a century.

Since the Standard & Poor's Index is based on the number of shares of individual issues that are outstanding, the stock of a company having, say a 300 million share capitalization, has 300 times the influence on this average than does the issue of a company with only one million shares outstanding. Thus, while the S & P Index is superior to the DJI Index as a measure of the fluctuations in the total value of the stocks listed on the New York Stock Exchange, there are times when an unusual degree of popularity of the 15 or 20 stocks with the largest capitalizations can give a misleading picture of what is going on in the market as a whole. These two averages are shown in Figure 35 for the period 1789-1980 (originally published in *Cycles,* May 1962).

In 1966, the New York Stock Exchange began the publication of a stock index for every stock listed on the Exchange, with a base of 50 as of December 31, 1965. It is a capitalization weighted index of some 2000 stocks, whereas the Standard & Poor's comprises only 500 stocks.

To avoid the distortions that have arisen in the Dow Jones Industrial Stock Average and the overemphasis on the capitalization weighting method of the S & P and New York Stock Exchange Index, several other methods of constructing stock indexes have evolved. Thus, in January 962, the Value Line Average was established for some 1,600 stocks on the basis of geometrically averaging the daily percent change in the monitored stocks. For example, if the geometric average percent change of the 1,600 stocks on a given day is +2 percent and the previous day's reading of the Value Line Average was 100, then the average increases by 2 points (2% x 100), resulting in a new reading of 102. The Value Line Average thus assigns each of the stocks contained therein equivalent percentage weights. IBM, which is quoted at a price in hundreds of dollars and has a market value in the tens of billions, is treated no differently than a stock quoted at $2.00 a share and with a total market value of $20 million (see Figure 36).

A serious flaw in the Value Line method is that the percentage changes are averaged geometrically, i.e., by averaging the logarithms of each item and then finding the anti-logarithm of the average, which produces a result that is less than the true answer. The cumulative consequence is that the Value Line Average is so biased *downward* that its current level is deceptively low. The publishers nevertheless state: "The Value Line Averages, which are geometrically averaged and equally weighted, provide a superior picture of the price action of the typical stock."

In the past decade or so, a number of other unweighted averages have been developed in which each stock is given equal weight. For example, if a stock goes up from $10 to $20, it has gained 100 percent. But a stock which goes from $100 to $110 has only gained 10 percent. After calculating the average percent change of each stock on a given day, for example 1 percent, the new index value is 1.01 times the base. If the base were 50, the new value would be 50 x 1.01 = $50.50. The average percent changes of all New York and American Stock Exchange stocks are published in several weekly financial periodicals, notably *Barron's* and Media General's *Financial Weekly.* The most widely known of the unweighted averages is the Indica-

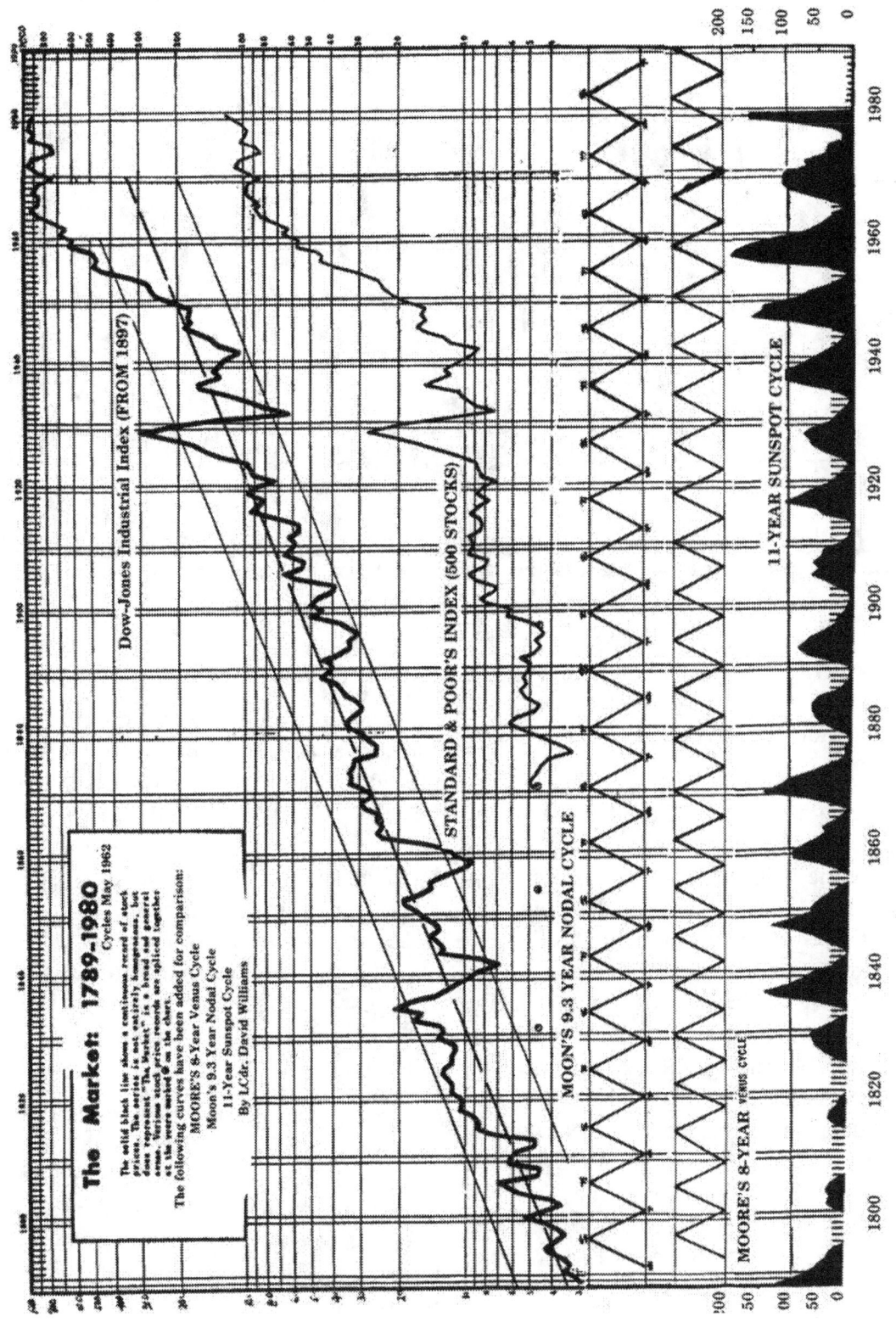

*Figure 35. The Market 1789-1980.*

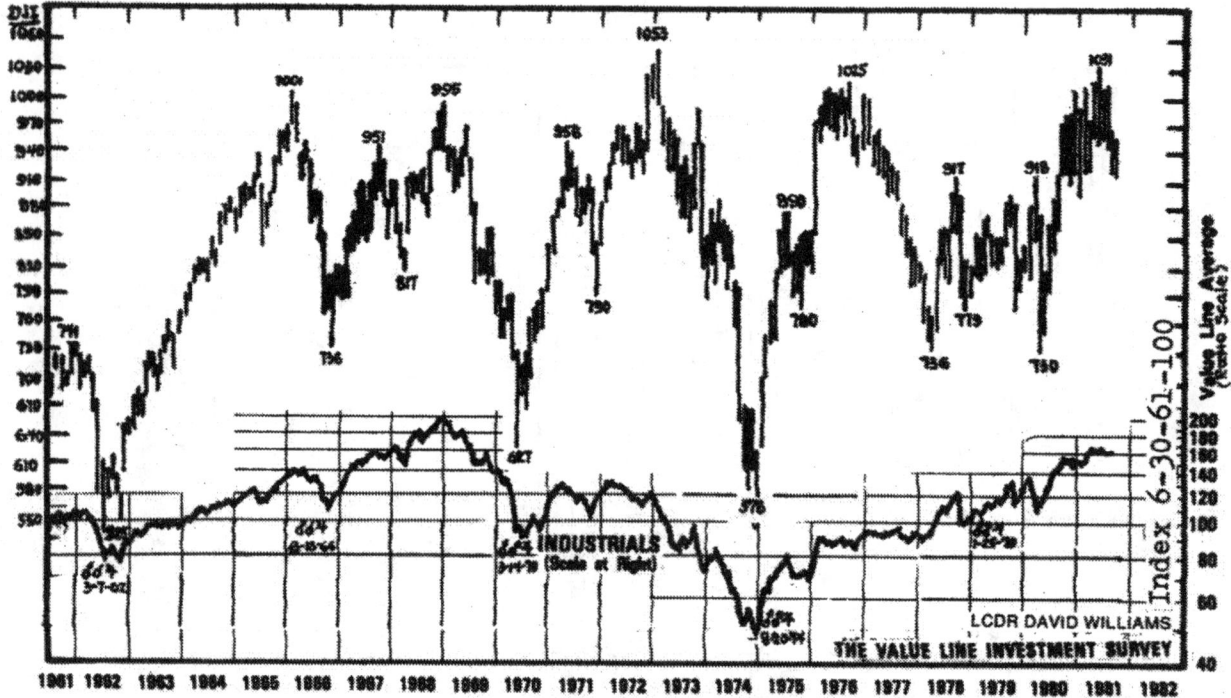
*Figure 36. DJI vs. Value Line Industrial Averages.*

tor Digest Average. Figure 37 shows a comparison of the Indicator Digest Average with the Dow-Jones Industrial Average from 1968 to 1981.

The unweighted averages are also flawed by having a *downward* bias. For example, a stock which has gone from $10 to $20 has increased 100 percent in price. However, the computer used (Quotron Systems, Inc.) calculates the percent change by dividing the $10 increase by the $20 ending price, which gives a percent change of 50 percent, instead of by dividing the $10 increase by the $10 starting price, which correctly gives an increase of 100 percent. This seems incredible, but it is a fact, according to Norman G. Fosback, in *Stock Market Logic* (1976). While the extent of the downward bias may be relatively insignificant from day to day, it becomes considerable over a span of years. For example, the Quotron based indexes of New York Stock Exchange stocks should have been approximately twice their December 31, 1975 level to properly reflect the returns including dividends of their component stocks during the previous 10-year period!

An improved index, called the Total Return Index, was developed by the Institute for Econometric Research, Inc., Ft. Lauderdale, Florida. It has the following two advantages: 1) it gives equal arithmetic weight to the correctly calculated daily percent change of every common stock, regardless of whether its price is $1 or $100, or whether the company is large or small; and 2) it includes dividend return as well as price changes (over half the total return of all common stocks throughout history has been from dividends).

While no index can be perfect, it is believed that the Total Return Index is the broadest and most accurate gauge of daily stock market behavior in existence. Analysis of the trend and cyclical patterns shown in this index provide an unparalleled technical view of the U. S. stock market. It is also shown in Figure 37 for the years 1968-1981 on Ratio Scale, in which equal percentage changes occupy equal distances on the chart.

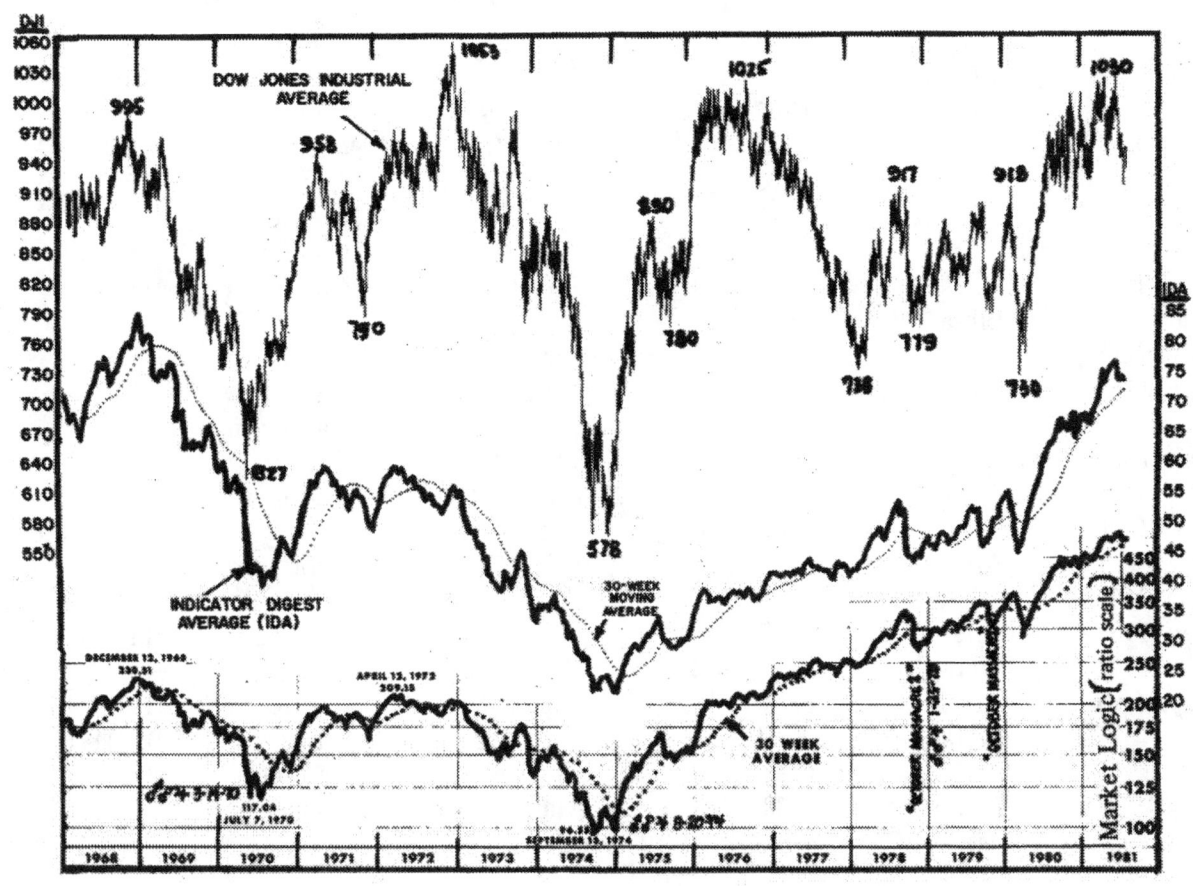

*Figure 37. DJI Average vs. Indicator Digest Average and Market Logic Index.*

A comparison of the curves in Figure 37 shows that whereas the Market Logic Total Return Index of all New York Stock Exchange common stocks has gone up 436 percent (517.51 ÷ 96.55 = 436%) between the September 13, 1974 low of $96.55 and the June 15, 1981 high of $517.51, the Indicator Digest Average has only gone up 267 percent (77 ÷ 21 = 267%), while the Dow Jones Industrial Average has gone up a mere 78 percent (1030 ÷ 578 = 78%) during the same period of time. The S & P 500 Index has risen 134 percent (157 ÷ 67) between the December 1974 low of 67 and the January 1981 high of 157. The superiority of the Market Logic Index as a true measure of what the average stock is doing is self-evident.

## The Planetary Cause of the 9.225-year Stock Market Cycle

We have seen from the previous chapter that the 9.226-year stock market cycle during 1830-1966 correctly indicated tops 100 percent and bottoms 86 percent of the time (see Figure 30). What is the cause of this remarkably accurate cycle? The author believes that the answer may very well lie in the backward movement of the Moon's North Node through the zodiac over a period of 18.6 years.

Figure 35 shows the 18.6-year Nodal Cycle divided into 9.3-year segments, beginning with the Moon's North or Ascending Node at 0° Libra in March 1792 and regressing during the ensuing 9.3-years to 0° Aries in July 1801. The signs Aries and Libra are indicated at 18.6-year inter-

**Table 19. The 9.3 Year North Node Cycles vs. Stock Market Lows and Highs.**

| Date | North Node 0 Degrees | Low | Date | North Node 0 Degrees | High |
|---|---|---|---|---|---|
| Mar. 1792 | Libra | 1792 | Jan. 1797 | Cancer | 1795 |
| July 1801 | Aries | 1802 | May 1806 | Capricorn | 1806 |
| Nov. 1810 | Libra | 1812 | Aug. 1815 | Cancer | 1815 |
| Mar. 1820 | Aries | 1820 | Jan. 1825 | Capricorn | 1824 |
| July 1829 | Libra | 1829 | Apr. 1834 | Cancer | 1834 |
| Nov. 1838 | Aries | 1842 | July 1843 | Capricorn | 1844 |
| Mar. 1848 | Libra | 1848 | Oct. 1852 | Cancer | 1852 |
| July 1857 | Aries | 1859 | Mar. 1862 | Capricorn | 1863 |
| Dec. 1866 | Libra | 1866 | Aug. 1871 | Cancer | 1872 |
| Jan. 1876 | Aries | 1877 | Oct. 1880 | Capricorn | 1881 |
| June 1885 | Libra | 1884 | Mar. 1890 | Cancer | 1889 |
| Nov. 1894 | Aries | 1896 | May 1899 | Capricorn | 9/7/99 |
| Jan. 1904 | Libra | 3/12/1904 | Sept. 1908 | Cancer | 1906-1909 |
| July 1913 | Aries | 6/11/1913 | Feb. 1918 | Capricorn | 11/3/1919 |
| Aug. 1922 | Libra | 8/24/1921 | Apr. 1927 | Cancer | 9/23/1929 |
| Dec. 1931 | Aries | 7/8/1932 | Sept. 1936 | Capricorn | 11/17/1936 |
| May 1941 | Libra | 4/28/1942 | Dec. 1945 | Cancer | 12/11/1945 |
| July 1950 | Aries | 6/13/1949 | Apr. 1955 | Capricorn | 12/30/1955 |
| Dec. 1959 | Libra | 2/9/1959 | Aug. 1964 | Cancer | 11/18/1964 |
| Apr. 1969 | Aries | 6/26/1970 | Oct. 1973 | Capricorn | 1/11/1973 |
| July 1978 | Libra | 2/28/1978 | Mar. 1983 | Cancer | ? |
| Dec. 1987 | Aries | ? | | | |

Summation:

| | Correct | % | Incorrect | | Total |
|---|---|---|---|---|---|
| Lows | 17 | 81 | 4 | 19 | 21 |
| Highs | 16 | 80 | 4 | 20 | 20 |
| Totals | 33 | 80½ | 8 | 19½ | 41 |

Nodal positions from 1852 to 1978 are from *True Lunar Nodes 1850-2000* (1975) by Digital Research Corporation. Extrapolation backward to 1792 by LCdr. David Williams. Stock market highs and lows (DJI) by LCdr. David Williams.

vals at the bottom of the curve. In the depression year of 1932 the North Node was in Aries. It was also in that sign during 1969, when the stock market was through its worst decline since the Great Depression. In each case, the nodal position was reached several months before the stock market Low, viz: December 27, 1931 versus the July 18, 1932 stock market Low, and April 18, 1969 versus May 26, 1970. Thus, the position of the Moon's North Node may be said to be an "advance warning indicator" of an important stock market low.

The author thus predicted at the September 12, 1974 meeting of the Society for the Investigation of Recurring Events (SIRE) that the next low of the 9.3-year cycle would come following the Moon's North Node entry into Libra on July 4, 1978. The "October 1978 Massacre I" occurred during the month of October 1978, when the Dow Jones Industrial Average fell from 909.59 on October 13 to 782.06 on October 31, a decline of 14 percent in two weeks.

As Table 19 shows, out of a total of 41 highs

### Table 20. Moore's 8-Year Venus Cycle vs. Stock Market Highs and Lows.

| Date of Conjunction | Date of Market Low | Date of Cycle High | Date of Market High |
|---|---|---|---|
| 6/5/1761 | | | |
| 6/3/1769 | | | |
| 1777 | | | |
| 1785 | | | |
| 1793 | 1792 | 1797 | 1795 |
| 1801 | 1802 | 1805 | 1806 |
| 1809 | 1812 | 1813 | 1815 |
| 1818 | 1820 | 1822 | 1824 |
| 1826 | 1829 | 1830 | 1834 |
| 1834 | 1842 | 1838 | 1844 |
| 1842 | 1842 | 1846 | 1847 |
| 1850 | 1848 | 1854 | 1852 |
| 1858 | 1859 | 1862 | 1863 |
| 1866 | 1866 | 1870 | 1872 |
| 12/8/1874 | 1877 | 1878 | 1881 |
| 12/6/1882 | 1884 | 1886 | 1889 |
| 12/4/1890 | 1896 | 1894 | 1899 |
| 12/2/1898 | 1896 | 1902 | 1906 |
| 12/6/1906 | 3/12/04 | 1910 | 1909 |
| 11/28/1914 | 6/11/13 | 1918 | 1919 |
| 11/25/1922 | 8/24/21 | 1926 | 1929 |
| 11/22/1930 | 7/8/32 | 1934 | 1936 |
| 11/19/1938 | 4/28/42 | 1942 | 1945 |
| 11/16/1946 | 6/13/49 | 1950 | 1955 |
| 11/13/1954 | 2/9/59 | 1958 | 1964 |
| 11/11/1962 | 2/9/59 | 1966 | 1965 |
| 11/9/1970 | 5/26/70 | 1974 | 1973 |
| 11/7/1978 | 2/28/78 | 1982 | ? |
| 11/5/1986 | ? | 1990 | ? |

| Summation | Correct | % | Incorrect | % | Total |
|---|---|---|---|---|---|
| Lows | 10 | 42 | 14 | 58 | 24 |
| Highs | 7 | 30 | 16 | 70 | 23 |
| Totals | 17 | 36 | 30 | 64 | 47 |

and lows, the 9.3-year Nodal Cycle has correctly indicated the stock market turning points 80 percent of the time.

## Moore's 8-Year Venus Cycle

Another alleged planetary indicator is Professor Moore's 8-year Venus Cycle discussed in Chapter 5. This is based on the astronomical fact that at approximately 8-year intervals Earth, Venus and the Sun are in a straight line at about the same degree of longitude. The relationship of this cycle to the business cycle is shown in Figure 20, while its relationship to the stock market cycle is shown in Figure 35. As indicated in Table 20, this cycle has had a very poor record for accuracy, having been correct only 36 percent of the time.

### Table 21. Sunspot vs. Stock Market Highs and Lows.

| | Lows | | | Highs | |
|---|---|---|---|---|---|
| Sunspot | Stock Market | | Sunspot | Stock Market | |
| 1798 | 1798 | | 1804 | 1806 | |
| 1810 | 1812 | | 1816 | 1815 | |
| 1823 | 1820 | | 1830 | 1834 | |
| 1833 | 1829 | | 1837 | 1834 | |
| 1843 | 1842 | | 1848 | 1852 | |
| 1856 | 1859 | | 1860 | 1863 | |
| 1867 | 1866 | | 1870 | 1872 | |
| 1878 | 1877 | | 1883 | 1881 | |
| 1889 | 1884 | | 1893 | 1889 | |
| 1901 | 3/12/04 | | 1905 | 1/19/06 | |
| 1913 | 6/11/13 | | 1917 | 11/3/19 | |
| 1923 | 8/24/21 | | 1928 | 9/23/29 | |
| 1933 | 7/08/32 | | 1937 | 11/17/36 | |
| 1944 | 4/28/42 | | 1947 | 12/11/45 | |
| 1954 | 2/09/59 | | 1957 | 12/30/55 | |
| 1964 | 5/26/70 | | 1968 | 11/18/64 | |
| 1976 | 5/28/78 | | 1979 | 4/27/81 | |

*Summation*

| | Correct | % | Incorrect | % | Total |
|---|---|---|---|---|---|
| Lows | 8 | 47 | 9 | 53 | 17 |
| Highs | 4 | 24 | 13 | 76 | 17 |
| Totals | 12 | 35 | 22 | 65 | 34 |

## The 11-year Sunspot Vs. The Stock Market Cycle

Much has beep written about the Sunspot Theory of the Business Cycle (see Chapter 1), but little about sunspots and the stock market. Figure 35 shows these two cycles from 1789 to 1981. A comparison of the highs and lows is shown in Table 21.

This tabulation indicates that the 11-year Sunspot Cycle was correct in calling stock market turns only 35 percent of the time, and it is therefore no more reliable than Moore's 8-year Venus Cycle as a means of forecasting the stock market.

## The Planetary Cause of the 4-4½ Year Cycle in Market Lows

Dr. Louis H. Bean, a former government economist who was once called "the best-known prophet since Daniel," described, in his book, *How to Predict the Stock Market* (1962), a "seven-come-eleven" formula for predicting stock market lows, which prevailed from 1878 to 1932. It involved an alternating sequence of 7- and 11-year intervals in market lows. But, after 1949, the intervals were approximately 4 years long. He concluded: "Since World War II, the New Dealers, with their Employment Act of 1946 and other economic stabilizers, together with the perpetual cold war, have served to destroy this seven-come-eleven rhythm."

But Bean did not know that his "seven-come-eleven" rhythm was due to the influence of the Mars-Jupiter *opposition,* as per the tabulation in Table 22.

It will be noted that there were four repeti-

**Table 22. Bean's "7 Come 11" Rhythm and Mars-Jupiter Oppositions.**

| Date of Market Low | Interval Between Succeeding Lows | Date of Aspect | Aspect | Interval between Aspect and Low |
|---|---|---|---|---|
| June 1878 |  | 7/01/78 | 180° | 1 month |
| Feb. 1885 | 7 years | 2/21/85 | 180° | Exact |
| July 1896 | 11 years | 3/02/96 | 180° | 4 months |
| Nov. 1903 | 7 years | 2/25/04 | 180° | 3 months |
| July 1914 | 11 years | 6/12/14 | 180° | 1 month |
| Aug. 1921 | 7 years | 1/28/21 | 180° | 7 months |
| July 1932 | 11 years | 2/09/32 | 180° | 5 months |
| Mar. 1938 | 6 years | 9/01/38 | 180° | 6 months |
| June 1949 | 11 years | 8/29/49 | 180° | 2 months |

**Table 23. 4-Year Cycle in Market Lows from 1949 to 1978.**

| Date of Market Low | Date of Aspect | Aspect | Interval Between Aspect and Low |
|---|---|---|---|
| June 1949 | 8/29/49 | 180° | 2 months |
| Sept. 1953 | 4/27/53 | 0° | 5 months |
| Oct. 1957 | 10/16/57 | 0° | Exact |
| June 1962 | 3/07/62 | 0° | 3 months |
| Oct. 1966 | 8/13/66 | 0° | 2 months |
| May 1970 | 3/14/70 | 180° | 2 months |
| Dec. 1974 | 8/20/74 | 180° | 4 months |
| Oct. 1978 | 1/25/79 | 180° | 3 months |
| Aug. 9, 1982 | 8/08/82 | 0° | Exact |

tions of Bean's seven-come-eleven rhythm, but in one case—July 1932 to March 1938—the interval between market lows was 6 years instead of 7.

Table 23 shows the 4-year cycle of market lows after 1949.

The synodical period of the Mars-Jupiter cycle is 2.2353 years and the stock market lows come at alternating conjunctions or oppositions. It will be noted that there is a transition from the Mars-Jupiter *opposition* of August 29, 1949 to a Mars-Jupiter conjunction on April 27, 1953. There were four such conjunctions between August 29, 1949 and March 14, 1970, when the Mars-Jupiter *oppositions* resumed their influence.

In the hundred years between 1878 and 1978, there were only four stock market lows that did not fit into the "7-come-11" or 4-year patterns shown in Table 24.

In addition, there were 11 stock market lows between 1785 and 1878 that were also related to Mars-Jupiter aspects, as per Table 25.

The stock market lows and corresponding Mars-Jupiter aspects from 1962 to 1978 are indicated in Figures 36 and 37. It will be noted that while all four market averages—DJI, Indicator Digest, Market Logic, and Value Lows—bottomed together in 1970 and 1974, there was a decided divergence in 1978. While the DJI average bottomed at 736 on March 2, 1978, the three unweighted averages continued their rise until the "October Massacre #1." All four averages declined again in October 1979 ("October Massacre II"). Then followed the March 1980 "Hunt Debacle."

The divergence between the Dow Jones Industrial Average and the unweighted averages

### Table 24. Other Stock Market Lows Between 1878 and 1978.

| Date of Market low | Date of Aspect | Aspect | Interval Between Aspect and Low |
|---|---|---|---|
| Aug. 1893 Panic | 12/21/93 | 180° | 4 months |
| Dec. 1901 | 12/17/01 | 0° | Exact |
| Nov. 1907 Panic | 6/21/07 | 180° | 5 months |
| Apr. 1942 | 4/04/42 | 0° | Exact |

### Table 25. Market Lows vs. Mars-Jupiter Aspects Prior to 1878.

| Date of Market Low | Date of Aspect | Aspect | Interval Between Aspect and Low |
|---|---|---|---|
| 1785 Crisis | 6/11/85 | 0° | ? |
| 1792 Panic | 8/03/92 | 0° | 5 months |
| 1808 Crisis | 1/18/08 | 0° | ? |
| Dec. 1819 Crisis | 2/14/19 | 0° | 10 months |
| Oct. 1825 Crisis | 10/10/25 | 0° | Exact |
| Apr. 1837 Panic | 3/21/37 | 0° | 1 month |
| Jan. 1847 Panic | 1/09/47 | 180° | Exact |
| Oct. 1857 Panic | 3/14/57 | 0° | 7 months |
| Apr. 1861 Panic | 11/14/60 | 180° | 5 months |
| Sept. 1869 Crisis | 10/04/69 | 180° | 1 month |
| Oct. 1973 Panic | 2/10/74 | 180° | 3 months |

since 1974 is believed to be due to the passage that year of a law which made managers of pension funds liable for losses suffered by clients because of over-concentration of funds in the "blue chips" stocks included in the DJI Average. Pension fund managers and other institutional fund managers sold the DJI stocks and invested the money in the so-called "second-tier" stocks, which rose while the DJI stocks fell.

The remarkable record of accuracy in pinpointing stock market lows during almost two centuries by the Mars-Jupiter conjunctions or oppositions at approximately four-year intervals indicates that this phenomenon must be taken seriously. As Table 23 indicates, the next Mars-Jupiter conjunction is due on August 8, 1982. Since the previous adverse aspect occurred on January 25, 1979, and was preceded by the "October 1978 Massacre I," it would be foolhardy to ignore the likelihood that the next major stock market low could come during the summer of 1982.

Mars and Jupiter are in conjunction every 2.2353 years; every other conjunction thus occurs at 4.4706 years (say 4½ years), which equals 232½ weeks, or close enough to the Fibonacci Number 233—a highly significant number. Leonardo Fibonacci or Leonardo of Pisa (A.D. 1175) was a famous Italian mathematician, who, in A.D. 1202, devised a series of numbers, in which each number is the sum of the two preceding numbers, viz:

| | | |
|---|---|---|
| 1 | 13 | 144 |
| 2 | 21 | (233) |
| 3 | 34 | 377 |
| 5 | 55 | 610 |
| 8 | 89 | 987 |

This series of numbers is found in such natural phenomena as the shape of the shell of the chambered nautilus, the offspring of bees and rabbits, the petals of such flowers as iris, primrose, ragweed, daisy, sunflower. The series has been called *The Divine Proportion of the Golden Section*. The symmetry embodied in the Fibonacci Numbers was known by the priests of

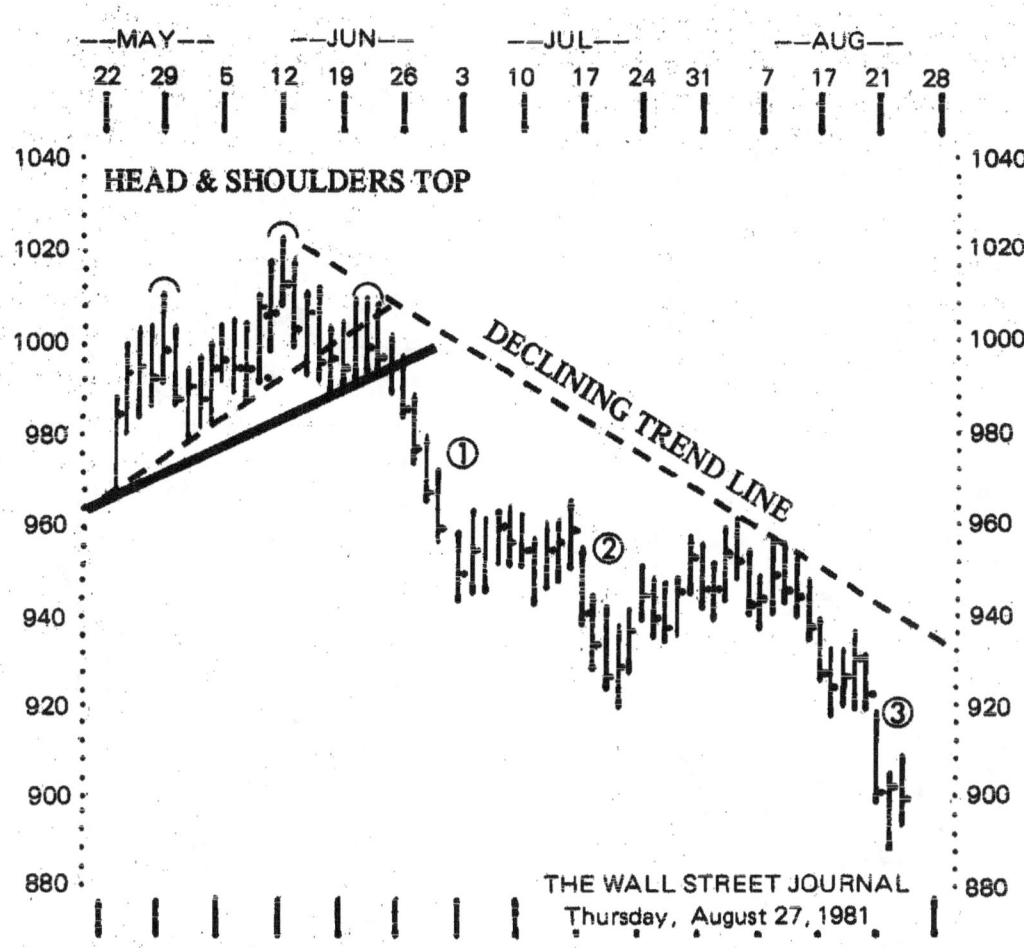

*Figure 38. Indications of 1981 DJI Market Top.*

Ancient Egypt as early as 3000 B.C., according to John Crawford Pierce in *The Fibonacci Series* (1954).

The indications that the stock market was topping out are shown on Figure 38 of the Dow Jones Industrial Average for the period May 22 through August 25, 1981. The familiar "Head and Shoulders Top," the "Declining Trend Line" (see Figure 38) and the 3-stage decline from the June 12, 1981 high are clearly indicated. Investors should have sold on rallies and put the proceeds of such sales into money market funds, which were then paying better than 17½ percent.

## Stock Prices and Planets in the Tenth House

Edward R. Dewey (a non-astrologer) of the prestigious Foundation for the Study of Cycles wrote a trail-blazing article, "Stock Prices and Space," in the October 1969 issue of *Cycles*. From a study of the Dow Jones Industrial Averages 1897-1961, he found a significant correspondence between monthly price changes and the positions of Mercury, Mars and Jupiter. Specifically, geocentric (Earth-centered) conjunctions of Mars and the Sun, Jupiter and the Sun, superior and inferior conjunctions of Mercury and the Sun, occurring in the tenth segment of the celestial sphere (270°-300°, Capricorn) were associated with rises in stock prices as compared with stock prices 30 days previous. See Figure 39, which shows the percentage that stock price advances are of stock price advances and declines from 30 days prior to the day of geocentric conjunctions and oppositions to the day of such conjunctions or oppositions, by planet and by

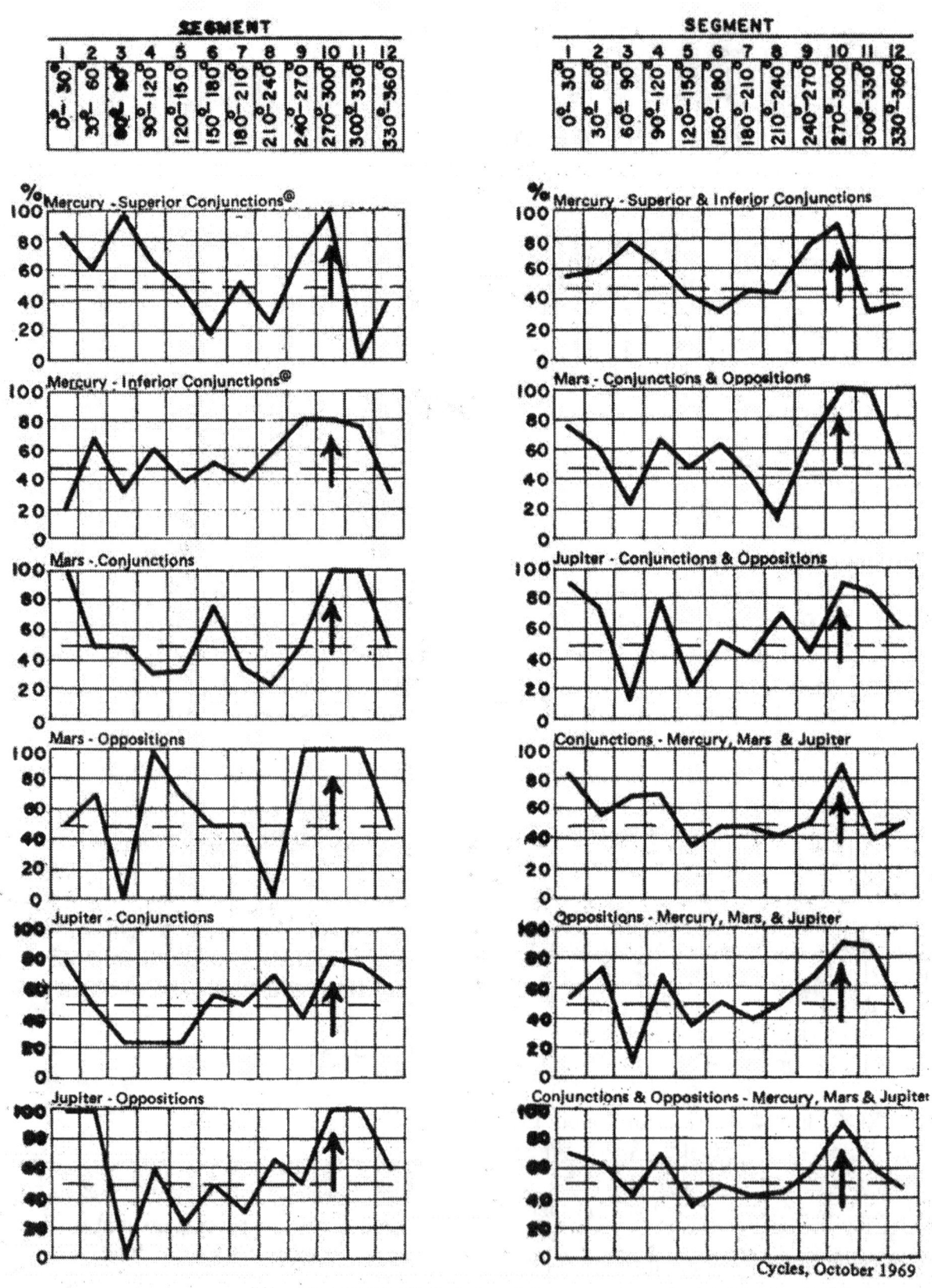

Figure 39. Percentage Rise in Stock Prices 30 Days Prior to Tenth House Aspects.

**Table 26. Daily Stock Prices 1897-1961**

| Segment | Degrees | Advances | Declines | Total Percentages | Advances Are of Total |
|---|---|---|---|---|---|
| 1 | 0-30 | 17 | 7 | 24 | 71 |
| 2 | 30-60 | 15 | 8 | 23 | 65 |
| 3 | 60-90 | 9 | 12 | 21 | 43 |
| 4 | 90-120 | 18 | 8 | 26 | 69 |
| 5 | 120-150 | 9 | 15 | 24 | 38 |
| 6 | 150-180 | 16 | 17 | 33 | 48 |
| 7 | 180-210 | 13 | 17 | 30 | 43 |
| 8 | 210-240 | 13 | 15 | 28 | 46 |
| 9 | 240-270 | 13 | 9 | 22 | 59 |
| 10 | 270-300 | 22 | 2 | 24 | 92 |
| 11 | 300-330 | 11 | 7 | 18 | 61 |
| 12 | 330-360 | 12 | 13 | 25 | 48 |
| | Totals | 168 | 130 | 298 | |

The number of advances, the number of declines, and the total number of advances and declines, from 30 days prior to the day of geocentric planetary conjunctions and oppositions to the day of such conjunctions and oppositions for Mercury, Mars and Jupiter, combined, together with the percentages that the advances are of the total number of advances and declines combined by longitude and segment.

Mercury has no oppositions. It has superior conjunctions and inferior conjunctions, both of which have been included for the period 1943 to 1961.—*Cycles,* October 1969

celestial longitude 1897-1961. The broken lines on the chart show chance expectations.

Dewey stated: "The consistency with which stock prices tend to advance during the 30 days prior to conjunctions or oppositions of Mars, and Jupiter, and the superior and inferior conjunctions of Mercury, *when in the same segment of space,* is truly remarkable, and is surely not chance."

Dewey reported that the relationship between planets, the Sun, and space was first observed in the 1950s by a member of the Foundation for the Study of Cycles who wished to remain anonymous. Dewey's work, which confirmed the member's findings, was first done in 1962. In the late 1950s, the author was told by the late Hamilton Bolton, one of the nation's most brilliant economic forecasters, that while he was only a dilettante in the field of astrology, he had noticed a significant relationship between stock prices and planets in the tenth house.

Dewey further stated that the relationship that prevailed for Mercury, Mars, and Jupiter did not prevail for Saturn or Uranus, because those planets were farther from the Sun. There were no conjunctions or oppositions of Venus or Neptune and the Sun at 270° to 300° during the period under review. Nor were there any conjunctions of Pluto and the Sun at 270° to 300°.

While oppositions of Pluto and the Sun occurred between September 1912 and April 1939, they were not investigated because data for Pluto were not available prior to 1951. As Table 26 shows, advances in stock prices occurred 92 percent of the time that conjunctions or oppositions of Mercury, Mars and Jupiter occurred in the tenth house (Capricorn), 71 percent in Aries, and 69 percent in Cancer.

Dewey noted that 270° to 300° of the celestial sphere is the general area where the celestial equator intersects the galactic equator (the Milky Way), or 281° of celestial longitude. He concluded that if the coincidences "are more than mere statistical curiosa—the implications are profound. They would suggest the possibility of extra solar-system forces (galactic?) or possibly the very structure of space itself."

Nicholas DeVore, in the *Encyclopedia of Astrology* (1947), described the galactic center as "The gravitational center around which the Sun revolves. Astrology has hypothetically placed this at 0 degrees of Capricorn (270° celestial longitude), which is exactly confirmed by recent published results of thousands of calculations of spectroscopic radial velocity measurements and other thousands by the parallax method of .determining proper motion. In consequence, the astronomers have arrived at a position of the center of the Milky Way Galaxy at R.A. 270°, Decimation + 29.7°. Therefore, at the time of the Winter Solstice, the galactic center is a few degrees south of the Sun. The plane of the Sun's orbit is presumed to be approximately that of the galactic center, which is inclined to the Earth's orbit by about 50 degrees."

More recent authorities, give the following values for the Galactic Center:

*Larousse Encyclopedia of Astronomy* (1967)—R.A. $17^h42.4^m$=266° or 26° Sagittarius

*Van Nostrand's Scientific Encyclopedia* (1968)—R.A. $17^h42.4^m$=266° or 26° Sagittarius

*The Cambridge Encyclopedia of Astronomy* (1977)—R.A. $17^h42^m37^s$=266° or 26° Sagittarius

What does all this mean? If you look up at the sky on a clear night you will see a luminous white band stretching across the heavens. This is known as the Milky Way, or our galaxy. It consists of a disc-shaped collection of billions of stars, gas and dust in which our own solar system is embedded, as shown in Figure 40 (GNP is the Galactic North Pole, GSP is the Galactic South Pole) from *Astronomy, Maps and Weather* by C. O. Wylie (1942). Our Sun moves in an almost circular orbit around the center of the galaxy at a speed of about 150 miles per second. A system of coordinates has been devised with the plane of the galaxy as the equator. Galactic longitudes are reckoned from 0° to 360°, starting from the galactic center, a point at R.A. $17^h42.4^m$ (266° or 26° Sagittarius), declination 28°55". Galactic latitudes run from 0° (the galactic equator or median line of the Milky Way) to +90° in the northern and from 0° to 90° in the southern hemisphere; the north galactic pole is situated at R.A. $12^h49^m$ (192°), declination +27.4°.

The galactic center is the source of powerful x-rays and infrared rays, and when our solar system enters that area of influence, stock prices rise, as Dewey has shown. Since Gemini is the area opposite Sagittarius, we now have an explanation of why the transit of Uranus through Gemini, the ruling sign of the United States, has been accompanied by the historical events shown in Table 27.

In the next chapter we will review some of the planetary systems of forecasting the stock market.

### Table 27. Uranus in Gemini.

| Date | Comment |
|---|---|
| 1607 | First successful English settlement founded at Jamestown, Virginia |
| 1691 | Colonial Revolution establishes religious freedom |
| 1775 | Revolutionary War establishes political freedom |
| 1858 | Civil War establishes personal freedom |
| 1942 | World War II establishes economic freedom |

Since Dewey's research included the entire 30° segment from 270° to 300° of longitude, the author made a survey of what happened when the planetary conjunctions and oppositions occurred at 266° for the period 1897 to date, as per Table 28. The results were inconclusive.

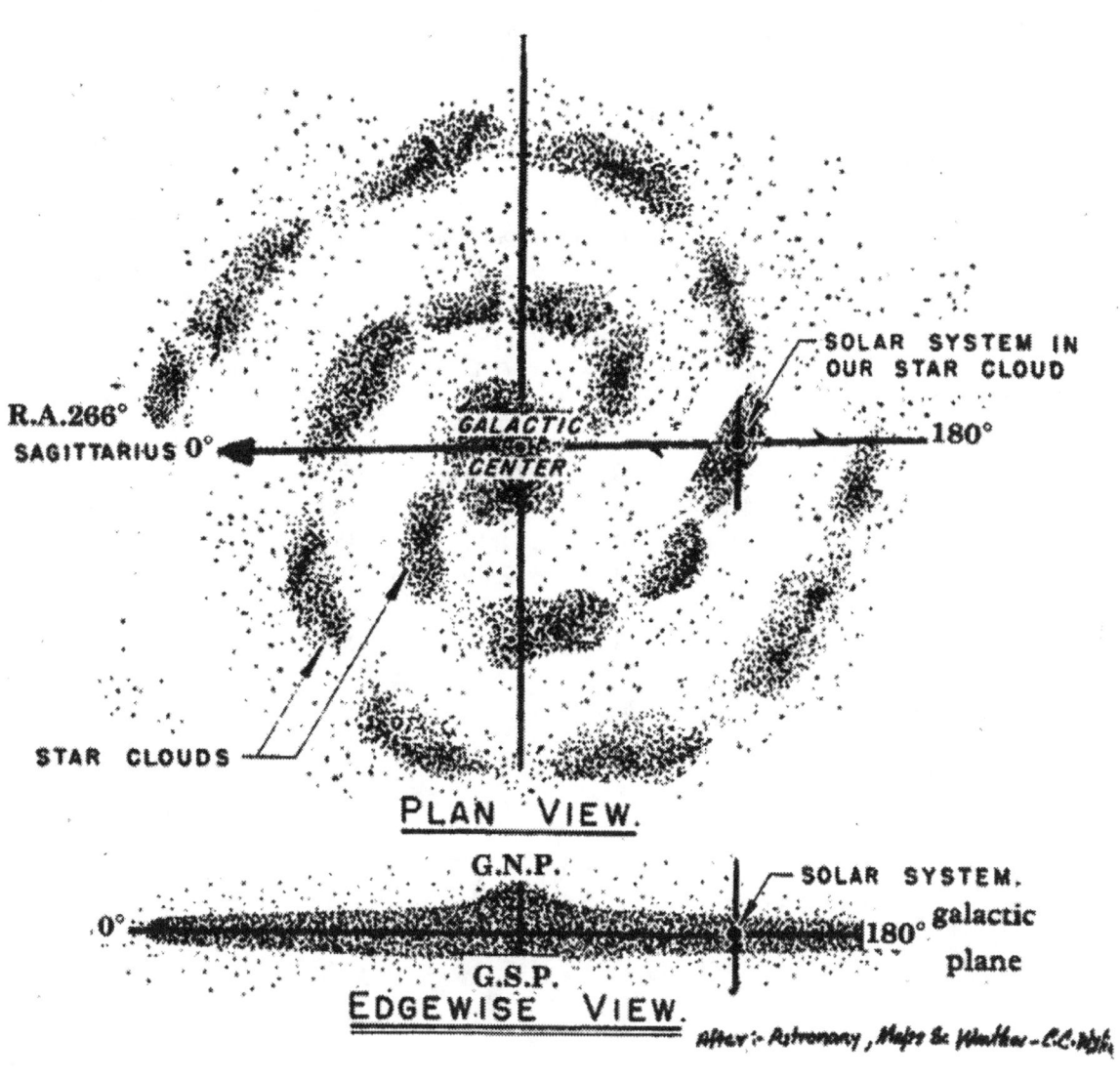

*Figure 40. Our Solar System in the Milky Way Galaxy.*

## Table 28. Conjunctions and Oppositions to 266° Longitude.

| Date of Aspect | Aspect | Date | DJI Average Range Low | Date | High | Remarks |
|---|---|---|---|---|---|---|
| | | | *Pluto Aspects to 266°* | | | |
| 7/13/09 | 180° | 2/23 | 80 | 11/19 | 101 | No significance |
| | | | *Neptune Aspects to 266°* | | | |
| 7/29/1899 | 180° | 12/18 | 58 | 9/7 | 78 | No significance |
| 1/25/82 | 0° | | ? | | ? | |
| | | | *Uranus Aspects to 266°* | | | |
| 9/13/04 | 0° | 3/12 | 46 | 12/5 | 73 | No significance |
| 6/12/48 | 180° | 3/16 | 165 | 6/15 | 193 | Incorrect |
| 9/9/88 | 0° | ? | | ? | | |
| | | | *Saturn Aspects to 266°* | | | |
| 12/17/1899 | 0° | 12/18 | 58 | 9/7 | 78 | Correct |
| 7/17/14 | 180° | 7/30 | 71 | 3/20 | 83 | Correct |
| 1/22/29 | 0° | 11/13 | 199 | 9/03 | 381 | Incorrect |
| 5/20/44 | 180° | 2/07 | 134 | 12/16 | 153 | Rose during preceding 30 days |
| 12/3/58 | 0° | 2/25 | 437 | 12/31 | 584 | Incorrect |
| 6/30/73 | 180° | 12/5 | 788 | 1/11 | 1052 | Temporary low |
| 1/6/88 | 0° | | ? | | ? | |
| | | | *Jupiter Aspects to 266°* | | | |
| 1/1/01 | 0° | 12/24 | 62 | 6/17 | 78 | Rose during preceding 30 days |
| 7/12/06 | 180° | 7/13 | 85 | 1/19 | 103 | Correct |
| 12/16/12 | 0° | 2/10 | 80 | 9/30 | 94 | Correct |
| 6/25/18 | 180° | 1/15 | 73 | 10/18 | 89 | Rose during preceding 30 days |
| 11/30/24 | 0° | 5/20 | 88 | 12/31 | 121 | Incorrect |
| 6/9/30 | 180° | 12/16 | 158 | 4/17 | 294 | Incorrect |
| 11/14/36 | 0° | 1/6 | 143 | 11/17 | 185 | Incorrect |
| 5/24/42 | 180° | 4/28 | 93 | 12/26 | 120 | Correct |
| 3/2/48 | 0° | 3/16 | 165 | 6/15 | 193 | Correct |
| 5/5/54 | 180° | 1/11 | 280 | 12/31 | 404 | Rose during preceding 30 days |
| 4/13/66 | 180° | 10/7 | 744 | 2/9 | 995 | Incorrect |
| 1/18/72 | 0° | 1/26 | 889 | 12/11 | 1036 | Rose during preceding 30 days |
| 7/31/77 | 180° | 11/2 | 801 | 1/3 | 1000 | Incorrect |
| 9/2/84 | 0° | | ? | | ? | |

## Chapter 12

# Stock Market Forecasting Systems

## Introduction

In Chapter 10, we learned that the Rothschilds had discovered a secret method for forecasting the price fluctuations in British Consols (government 3 percent perpetual bonds) by breaking up the price data into a series of repeating curves, which when recombined were used to forecast the future movements of the security. A New York group of investors followed the Rothschild technique in 1912 and derived a 40.68-month cycle for forecasting stock price movements, which worked for a while and then went awry after 1946.

What happens when an apparent cycle is broken down into several component cycles, which are then recombined, is shown graphically in Figure 41 (according to Dewey in *Cycles* in 1971). He chose, as an example, a 5.7-year cycle which appeared in stock prices from 1884 through 1896, and then disappeared. Dewey stated: *"Our 5.7-year cycle was never a cycle with a life and beat of its own!* It was a combination of three other cycles closely related: A is 4.89 years, B is 5.50 years and C is 6.07 years long. The 5.7-year cycle vanished after 1896, and when it reappeared in 1918, it was *upside down!"* This is exactly what happened to the 40.68-month cycle previously mentioned.

For almost 30 years, the author has remonstrated with Dewey that his cycle technique created synthetic cycles, which while "perfectly real and statistically significant, will not continue." This is the danger inherent in all mathematically derived cycles.

We will now discuss other methods of stock market forecasting.

## The Dow Theory

Readers of the author's article, "Autumn Business and Stock Trends," published in the October 1966 issue of Dell *Horoscope* magazine, were informed that the oldest stock market forecasting system in the United States is known as the Dow Theory, after its originator, Charles A. Dow, founder of Dow, Jones & Company and *The Wall Street Journal*, of which he became the first editor. It was based on Dow's interpretation

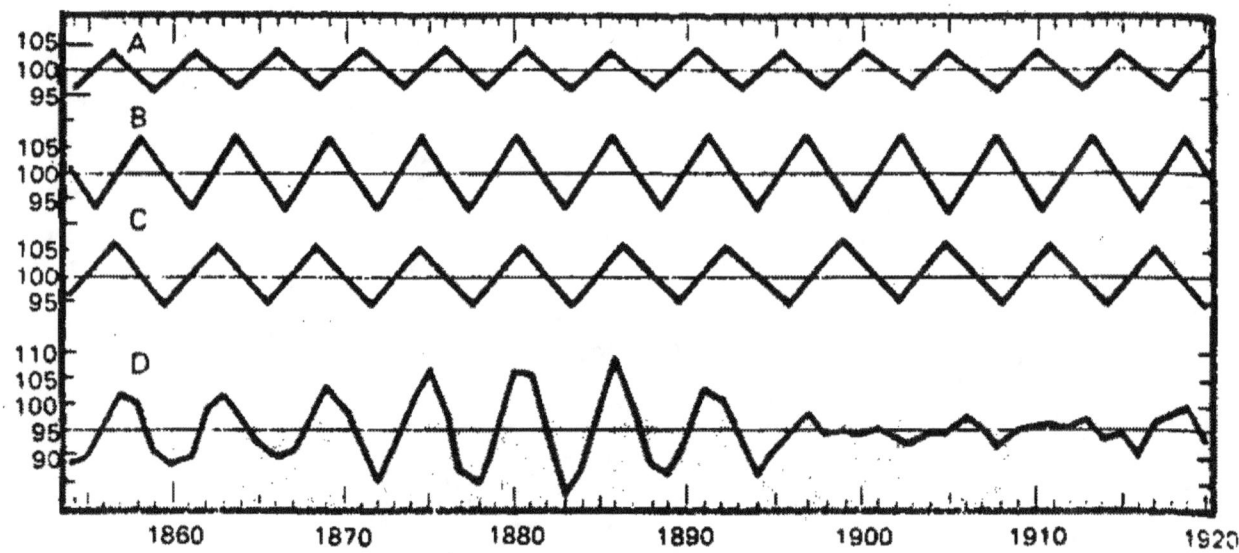

*Figure 41. Three Cycles and Their Combiantions. A is a 4.89-year cycle, B is a 5.50-year cycle, C is a 6.07-year cycle, D is how all three look when combined. A false cycle is created and eventually disappears.*

of the 1901 and 1902 stock markets.

After Dow's death in 1902, it was further developed by Dow's successor on *The Wall Street Journal*, W. P. Hamilton, famous as the man whose October 25, 1929 *The Wall Street Journal* editorial, "The Turn of the Tide," correctly identified the end of the great Bull Market of the 1920s. Although Dow never intended his theory to be used as an instrument for forecasting the stock market, but rather as a method of interpreting stock price averages with reference to fluctuations in business, many Dow theorists used the theory to forecast major turns in the stock market.

Thus, Richard Russell, the dean of present day Dow theorists stated in the May 9, 1966, issue of *Barron's*, that when the Dow Industrial and Transportation Averages both penetrated their March 15, 1966 Lows, the Bull Market which had made an all time high of 1001.11 on the DJI Average on February 9, 1966, turned into a Bear Market (see Figure 42). Russell also correctly recognized the Dow Theory SELL signal of July 2, 1981 (see Figure 43) as marking the end of the 1980-1981 Bull Market. But he was wrong on the June 25, 1965 Dow Sell signal.

Although different Dow theorists have in the past devised radically different criteria for Dow Theory Buy and Sell signals, most analysts seem to agree on the following:

1. Both the Industrial and Transportation Averages must confirm one another.

2. After an extended market advance, a BEAR market is signaled when each of the averages declines to points substantially below their major highs; then an advance by each of the averages that does not surpass their previously established highs, followed by a decline from this record top to a new cyclical low.

Perhaps the first investment advisor to recognize the possibility of a 1981 Dow Theory Sell signal was Norman G. Fosback, who stated in the June 26, 1981 issue of *Market Logic:* "The Dow Jones Industrial and Transportation Averages could yield a Dow Theory Sell signal by closing below 963.44 and 410.28, respectively." Then, in the July 10 issue *of Market Logic*, Fosback stated: "The Dow Theory has flashed a major SELL signal, contravening the bullish trend that has been in force since March 26, 1979. The latest signal occurred on July 2, when the Dow Industrial Average closed at 959.19 and

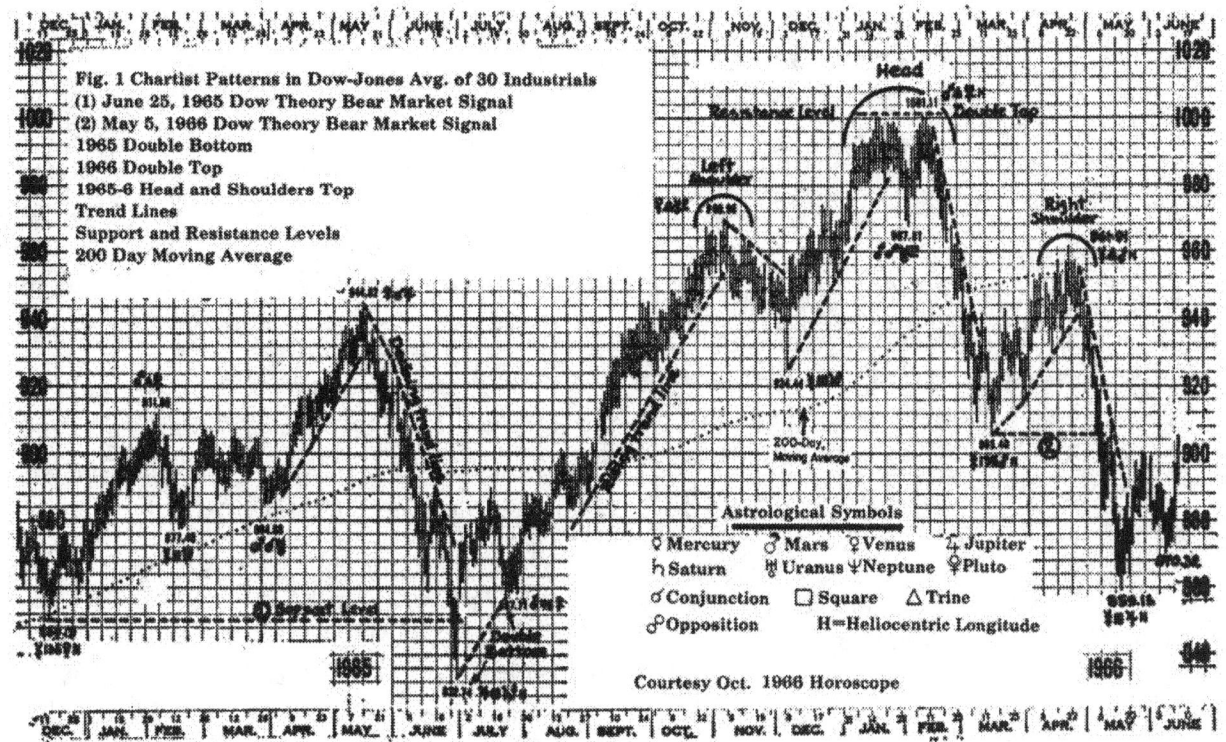

*Figure 42. End of 1966 Bull Market.*

the Dow Jones Transportation Average closed at 409.60, completing the formal requirements for a full SELL signal (see Figure 43).

Finally, in the July 24 issue of *Market Logic*, Fosback stated: "As noted here two weeks ago, the Dow Theory flashed a major SELL signal on July 2, when the Dow Jones Industrial and Transportation Averages dropped to new intermediate lows, completing a bearish pattern. The theory will remain bearish until both averages trace the following pattern: Establishment of a low, ascent to an intermediate high, correction to a second intermediate low that does not drop below the first low, and finally, rally to a new high above the previous intermediate peak. Obviously, such a pattern will take weeks, and probably months, to complete, so investors can count on Dow theorists holding to their bearish market outlook for some time to come."

Yet Fosback had earlier stated in *Stock Market Logic* (1976): "On the basis of rigorous and objective analysis, it is not possible to assign any significant forecasting value to the Theory."

Russell made the following qualification in the June 28, 1965 issue of *Barron's*: "A word of caution might be injected at this point. Primary movements (whether Bull or Bear) are a law unto themselves; neither their duration nor extent can forecast in advance. Thus, all that can be said of a BEAR market is that it is usually a protracted period of declining values and falling prices. A BEAR market will continue until the worst that can be seen ahead is fully discounted in the price structure."

Donald J. Hoppe, in his July 20, 1981 letter, confirmed the validity of the July 2, 1981 Dow Theory SELL signal by stating: "The oldest and perhaps most widely known technical indicator, the Dow Theory, gave a primary bear market signal on July 2, when both the Dow Jones Industrials and the Dow Transportation Average declined below their prior intermediate lows. . . . I admit that the Dow Theory does not have the most enviable record for accuracy. Often the signals are late and sometimes they are quickly reversed. But this one I am inclined to think is the real thing, not only because it is being ignored (more of that dangerous complacency again), but also because it is strongly supported by other technical evidence."

## Chartist Indications for Major Market Turning Points

In addition to the Dow theorists, there is a school of Wall Street market technicians who see other patterns in charts of stock market prices from which they predict which way the market will go. The pioneer in this field was R. W. Schabacker, financial editor of *Forbes* magazine, whose book *Stock Market Theory and Practice* (1930), has for many years been the most authoritative work on this subject. Figure 28 of Chapter 8 shows a number of price formations that have been found to be very helpful in detecting major market turning points.

Figure 42, from the October 1966 issue of Dell *Horoscope*, shows the Dow Jones Average of 30 Industrials for the period December 1965 to June 1966, prepared monthly by Trendline, a division of Standard & Poor's Corporation. On it the author has indicated the astrological aspects calculated in *advance of* certain turning points and some of the omens that chartists see in the patterns formed by the daily price range *after* the patterns have been formed. Reading from left to right, the following patterns are shown: Support Level, Declining trend line, Double Bottom, Rising trend line, Left Shoulder, Resistance Level, Head, Double Top, Right Shoulder, and 200-day Moving Average.

The most important of the foregoing patterns is the Head and Shoulders Top of February 9, 1966, with the DJI at 1001.11, which signaled the end of the previous Bull Market. It will be noted that the Head actually consisted of a Double Top, the first top having been made at 1000.55 on January 19, 1966, and the second top at 1001.11 on February 9, 1966. The Bear Market ended at 735.7 on October 7, 1966.

The latest Head and Shoulders Top formation in the DJI Average is shown in Figure 38 of Chapter 11 and in Figure 44, which shows it within the context of the DJI daily averages from January 1, 1981 to and including December 31, 1981. It also shows the premature SELL signal issued on January 6, 1981 by Joseph Granville, a prominent investment advisor, whose overnight advice caused a 45-billion dollar decline in the stock market the next day.

Now, how far will the decline go? One method for estimating the extent of the decline is to measure the distance from the HEAD on June 15, 1981, at 1023, to the NECKLINE that day at 985, which amounts to 38 points. This amount is then subtracted from the NECKLINE on the day (June 29) that the DJI broke below the NECKLINE at 993, giving a reading of 955, which was reached on July 2, when the Dow Sell signal was given (see Figure 44). But, this only gives the extent of the *initial* decline.

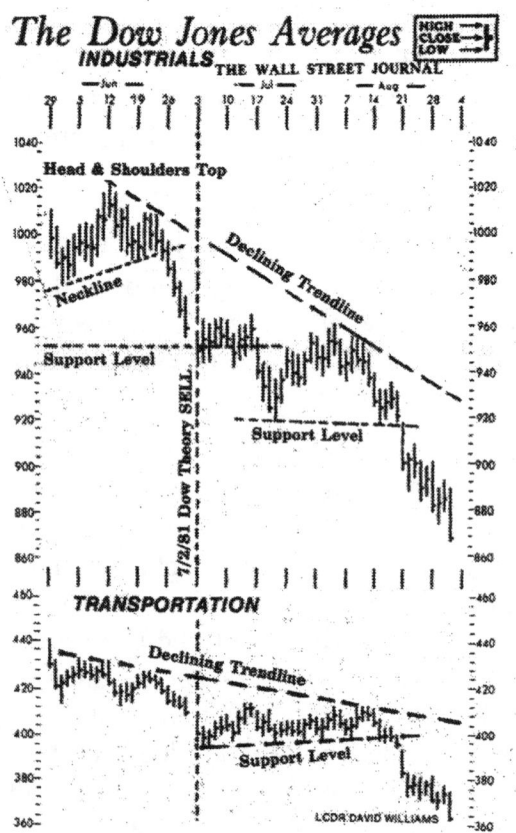

*Figure 43. Dow Theory Sell Signal July 2 1981.*

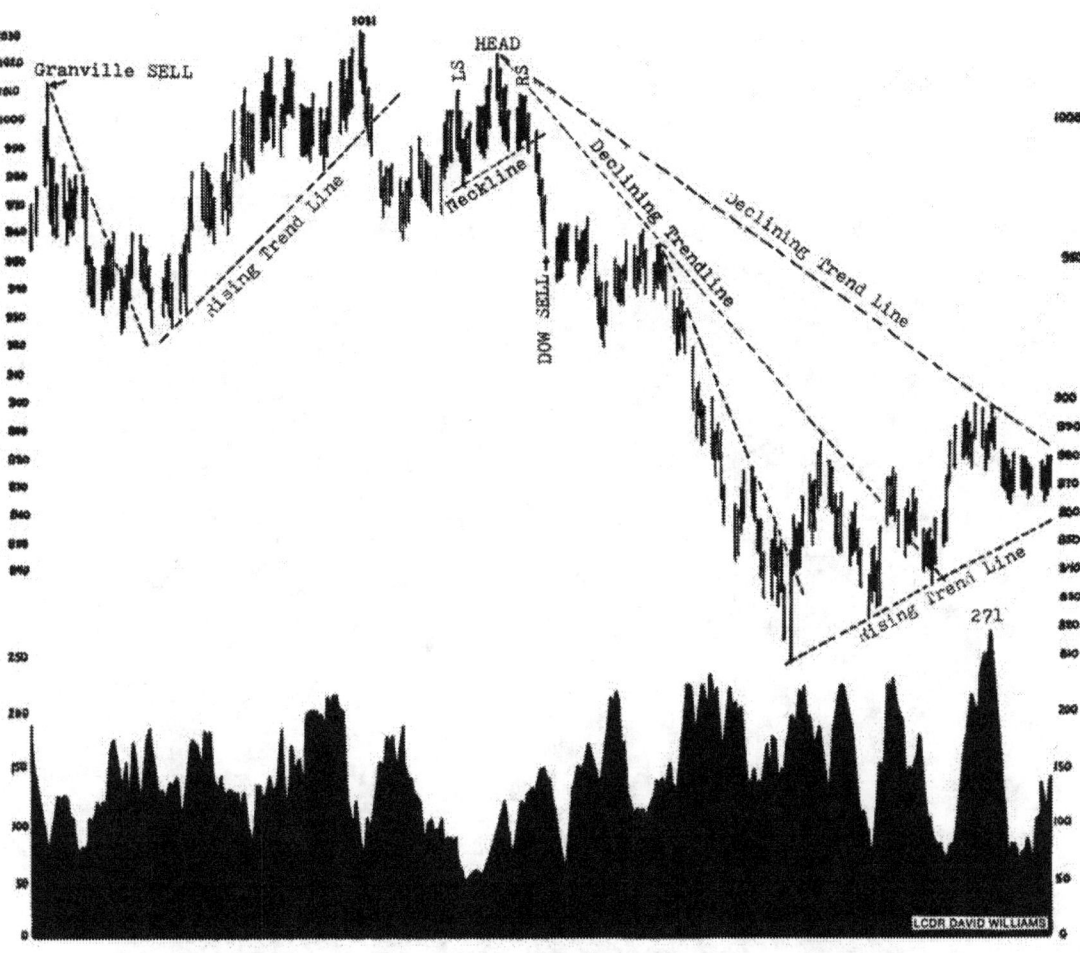

*Figure 44. Daily Range of 1981 DJI Average vs. Zurich Sunspot Numbers.*

A second method is to subtract the mid-December 1980 Low of 894 from the April 27, 1981 Top of 1031, which gives 137 points. This figure is then subtracted from 894, giving 757 as the target Low for this Bear Market. Allowing for the effects of momentum, the decline could continue to the area of the February 1978 low of 736 and the March 1980 low of 730. By a curious coincidence, Robert Bleiberg, the distinguished Editor and Publisher *of Barron's National Business and Financial Weekly,* in a talk at the Vista International Hotel in New York on September 19, 1981, entitled "The Financial Markets and Business," estimated that the decline would end in March 1982 with the DJI at *732!* The American stock market guru, Joseph Granville, is reported to have stated that if this target were broken, the DJI could drop to the 650-550 level, which would bring the decline to the level of the 1974 Bear Market (578)!

What are the astrological indications as to when the current Bear Market might end? There are two possibilities: 1) as Table 23 shows, the Mars-Jupiter *opposition* of January 25, 1979 came 3 months after the Lows recorded by the unweighted averages of Market Logic, Indicator Digest, and Value Line at the end of the "October 1978 Massacre," per Figures 36 and 37. The next Mars-Jupiter opposition occurs on May 25, 1983; therefore, the Low might occur 2-3 months prior to that date, based on past experience shown in Table 20. Thus, the Low in the unweighted averages could come in February or March 1983.

The second possibility is based on the DJI

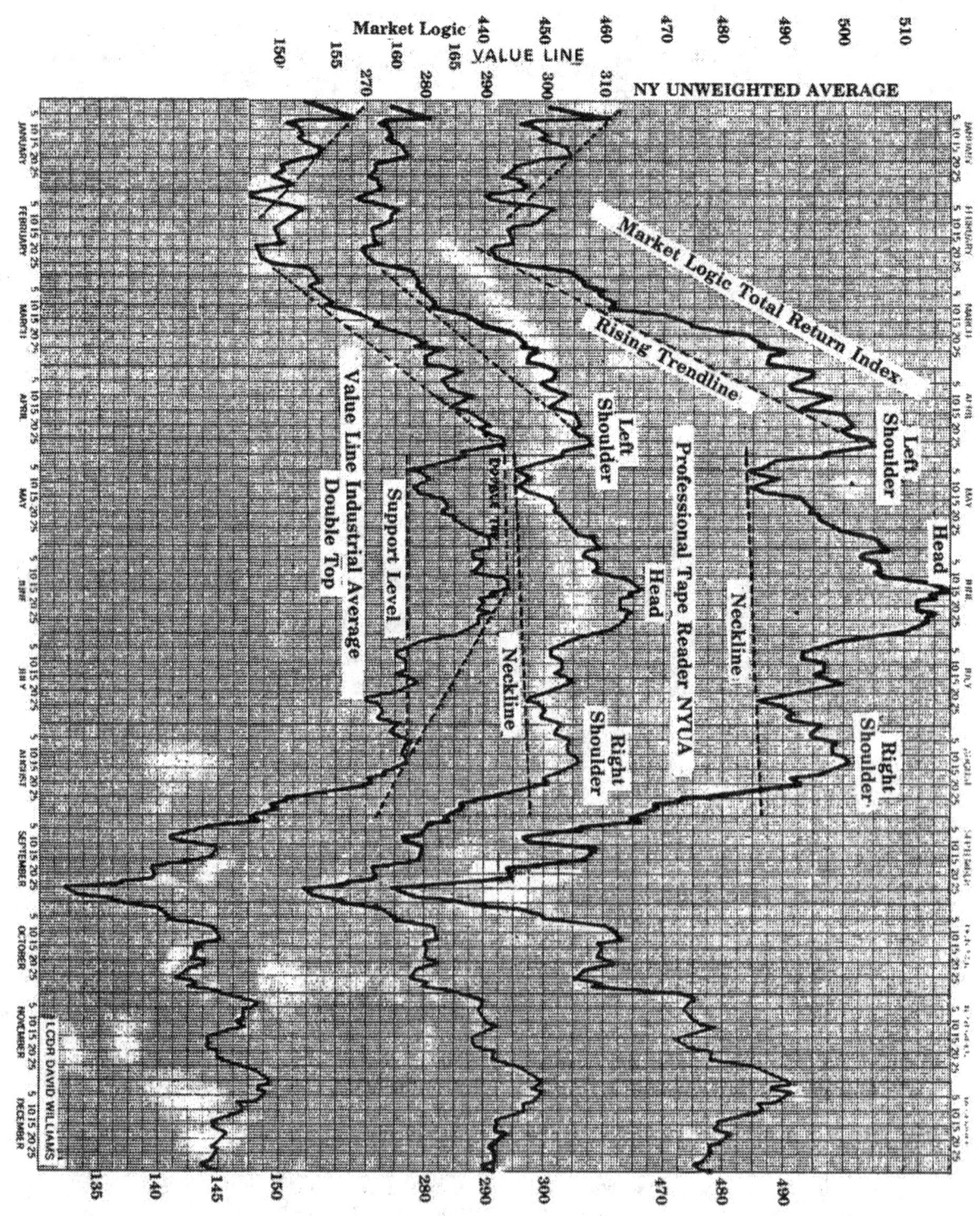

*Figure 45. End of 1981 Bull Market.*

Average, which made its Low of 736 on February 28, 1978, as shown in Figures 36 and 37. This Low was made 6 months after the Mars-Jupiter *conjunction* of September 4, 1977, which indicates a reversal of the Mars-Jupiter aspects. Such a reversal took place from the Mars-Jupiter *opposition* of August 29, 1949 to the Mars-Jupiter *conjunction* of April 27, 1953, which respectively indicated the DJI Lows of 1949 and 1953. Similar reversals are shown in Tables 24 and 25. Since the DJI Average made a Double Bottom at 730 in March 1980, preceding the Mars-Jupiter *conjunction* of May 5, 1980 by 2 months, the current Bear Market could end several months prior to the Mars-Jupiter *conjunction* of August 8, 1982, which would come near Robert Bleiberg's forecast of March 1982 for the DJI Low.

(Editor's Note: The first low of the "double bottom" came on March 9, 1982 and the second low actually came on August 9, 1982.)

The Head and Shoulders Top formation is more noticeable in the charts of such unweighted averages as those of Market Logic and The Professional Tape Reader, shown in Figure 45. Both averages topped on June 15, the same day as the DJI average. In the case of Market Logic, the distance from the Head at 517.5 to the Neckline on June 15, 1981 is 32.5 points, which, subtracted from the August 24 value of 478, when the Neckline was broken, would indicate a decline to 445, which has not as yet been reached (September 8, 1981). A similar count for the Professional Tape Reader Index would give a Low of 277, which has not as yet been reached.

A third unweighted stock average shown on Figure 45 is the Value Line Industrial Average, which made a Double Top on March 25 and June 15, 1981. This formation has also been found to be a reliable indicator of market tops. In this case, the extent of the decline is obtained by measuring the distance from the Double Top of 169 on June 15 to the Support Level at 162, or 7 points, which, subtracted from 162 gives 155, which occurred on August 23, 1981. But, the Index has dropped still lower, because it includes some more volatile stocks listed on the American Stock Exchange and Over the Counter Market (OTC).

Reference to Figure 43 shows the possibility of considering the April 27, 1981 Top of 1031 and that of June 15, 1981, at 1023, as forming a Double Top. In this case the countdown would be 1027 (average of 1031 and 1023) to the Support Level at 957, or 70 points, which, subtracted from 957 gives 887 as a *temporary* Low, which was reached on August 25, 1981.

### The McWhirter Theory

What is said to be "The most reliable method for forecasting monthly trends on the New York Stock Exchange" is described in *McWhirter's Theory of Stock Market Forecasting* (1938), by Louise McWhirter, a financial and economic analyst. The technique consists of analyzing the aspects made to a chart of the New York Stock Exchange at the time of the lunation (New Moon) of the previous month.

Figure 46 shows the planetary positions at the lunation of March 2, 1938, which forecast a *Down Turn* in the stock market. The following analysis was given:

1. "The first factor is that the depressing planet Saturn is placed in the Midheaven or tenth house of the chart.

2. Mars, one of the planetary rulers of the Midheaven of the chart, is in the tenth house or Midheaven.

3. The aspects in force at the lunation showed no aspects to either Mars or Saturn, but the lunation did show Neptune in opposition aspect to the lunation (conjunction of the Sun and Moon). "Neptune is one of the rulers of the Midheaven of the New York Stock Exchange horoscope, and the fact that the lunation formed an unfavorable opposition aspect to it showed a slump in stock prices. Since the lunation made

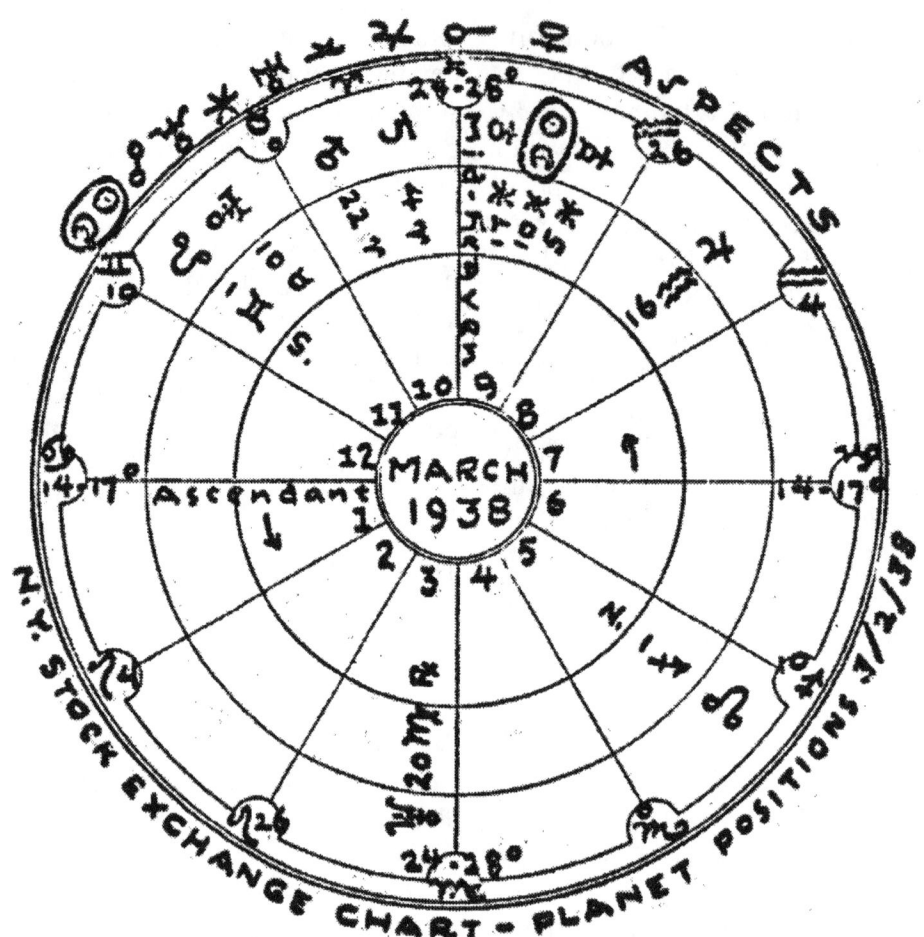

*Figure 46. New York Stock Exchange Chart, Planetary Positions, March 2, 1938. Forecasts a Downturn in the Stock Market. Aspects or angles in force at this lunation are: Venus, Sun and Moon opposition Neptune unfavorable; Sun and Moon sextile Uranus; Sun and Moon semi-sextile Jupiter; Sun and Moon conjunction Venus and Mercury.*

no aspect to either Mars or Saturn, their influence would not be brought into effect at this time. Unfavorable aspects to Neptune at a lunation, especially if no favorable aspect between Saturn and Uranus was in force at the same time, usually indicates a sharp break in stock market prices.

"Saturn and Uranus, although one sign apart, were not in orb of aspect for a semi-sextile aspect since they were six degrees apart. Three degrees apart is the maximum orb for this aspect."

Figure 47 shows the planetary positions at the lunation of May 29, 1938, which forecast an *Up Turn* in the stock market. The following analysis was given:

"1. The lunation (conjunction of the Sun and Moon every 28 days) made no aspect to Neptune or Mars, the two planetary rulers of the New York Stock Exchange chart's Midheaven or tenth house.

"2. The two planets which point out major trends in the stock market, Saturn and Uranus, were in close semi-sextile aspect (30°), which is favorable.

"3. At the same time Mercury was in conjunction with Uranus, and both Mercury and Uranus were in a very favorable trine (120°) aspect with Neptune. Mercury also was in favorable semi-sextile aspect to the very powerful planet Saturn.

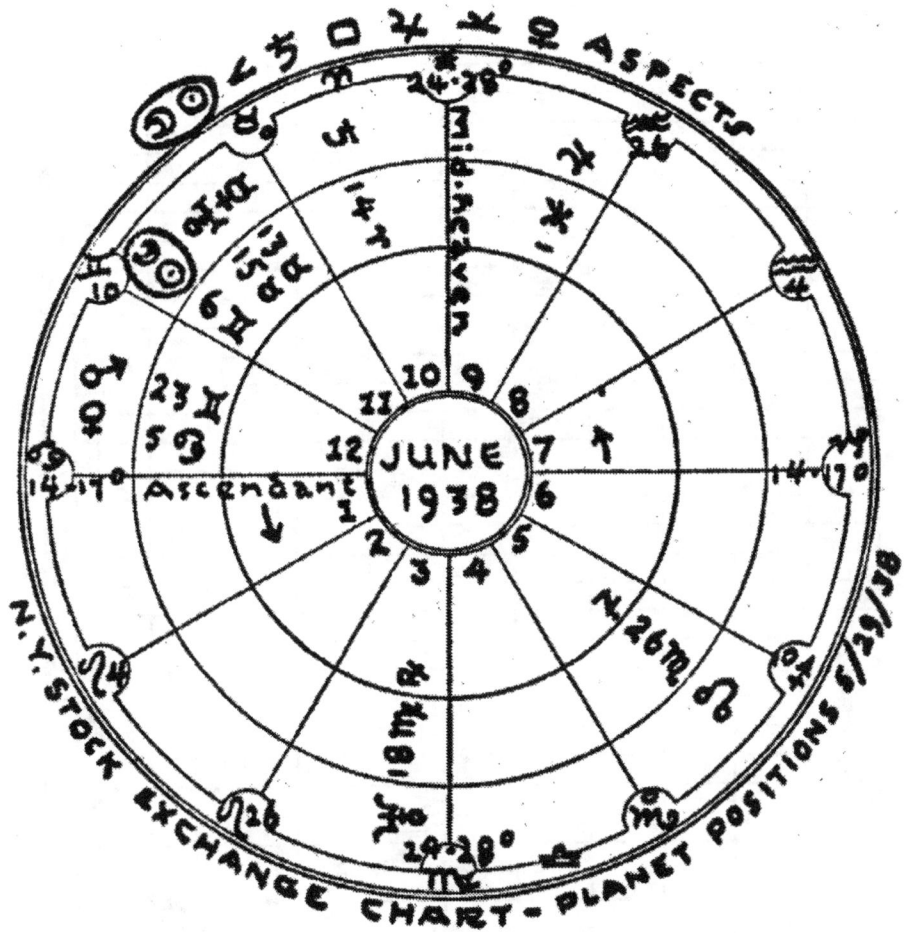

*Figure 47. New York Stock Exchange Chart, Planetary Positions, May 29, 1938. Forecasts an Upturn in the Stock Market. Aspects in force at this lunation are: Saturn Semi-sextile Uranus and Mercury—favorable; Sun and Moon semi-square Saturn; Sun and Moon square Jupiter; Sun and Moon semi-sextile Venus; Mercury and Uranus trine Neptune—favorable.*

"Favorable aspects between Saturn and Uranus always indicate an upturn in the stock market, which will last as long as the aspect is in force. All aspects between Saturn and Uranus are very significant in studying stock market trends. The semi-sextile aspect did not come into effect between these two planets until they had become almost exact due to the fact that the semi-sextile aspect is only a minor favorable aspect and the orb of its influence does not extend beyond an area of three degrees."

The extent of the *Downward and Upward* movements of the Dow Jones Industrial Average for the foregoing two forecasts are shown on Figure 48.

Figure 49 shows the planetary positions at the lunation of May 4, 1981, which forecast an *Upturn* in the stock market for the month of June 1981, when the DJI Average rose from 957 to 1023 on June 15.

The favorable aspects were 1) the stellium of Mars, Sun, Moon, Venus, and Mercury in the money sign of Taurus in the eleventh house of the New York Stock Exchange horoscope; 2) Mercury conjunct Venus and sextile Pluto; and 3) the Jupiter-Saturn conjunction was sextile the North Node in Leo, the sign of speculation in the second house (money) of the New York Stock

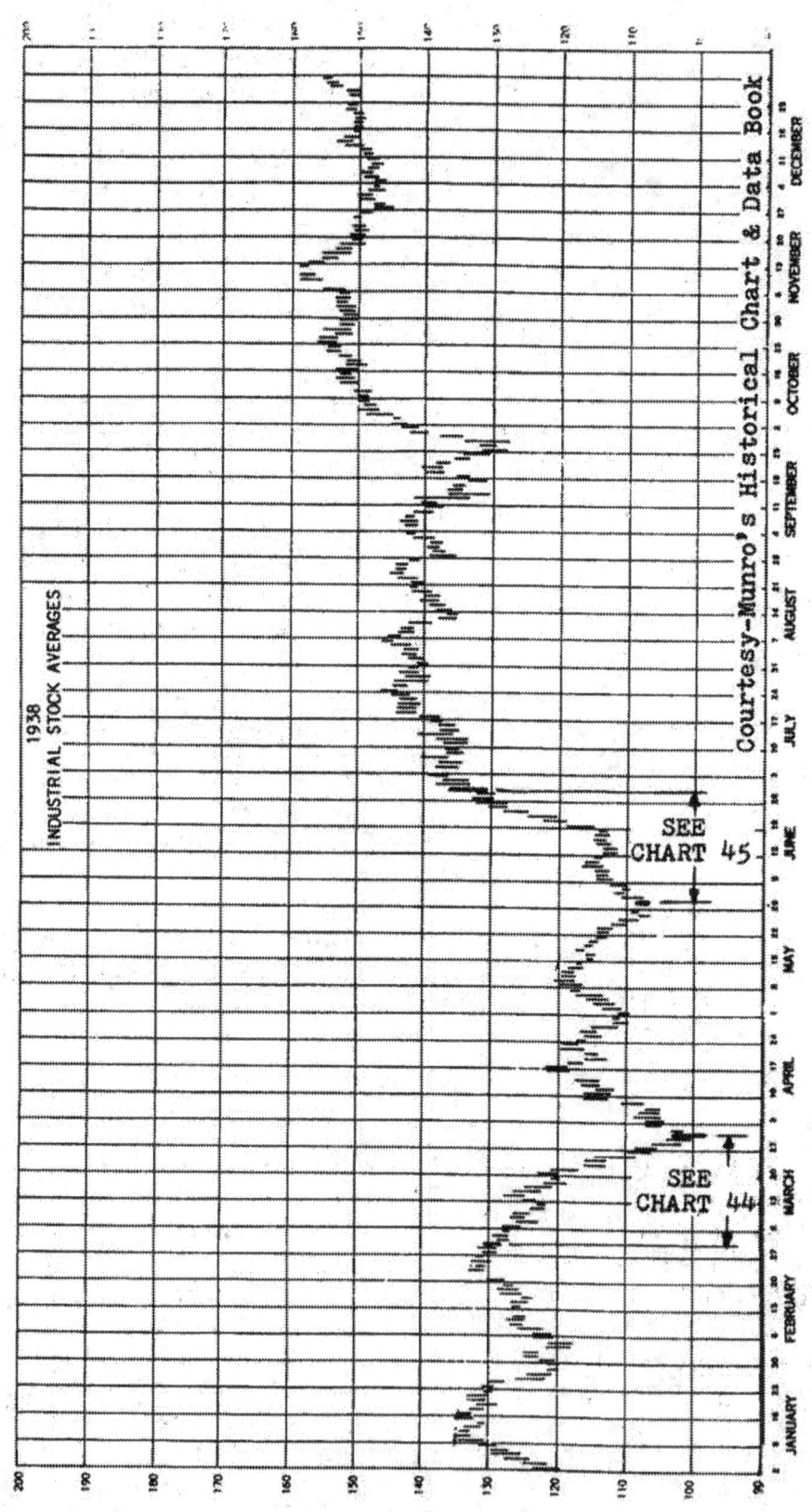

*Figure 48. Movements of DJI Average During March and May 1938.*

Table 29. Summation of Aspects to N.Y.S.E. Horoscope on June 17, 1981.

| POSITIVE | VALUE | NEGATIVE | VALUE |
|---|---|---|---|
| Tr. ♃ △ N. ☉ | 6 | Tr. ♅ ☍ N. ☉ | 8 |
| Tr. ♆ △ N. ☽ | 6 | Tr. ♀ ☍ N. ☽ | 8 |
| Tr. ☿ ✶ N. ♀ | 4 | Tr. ♅ ☍ N. ☿ | 8 |
| Tr. ☉ △ N. ♃ | 6 | Tr. ♆ □ N. ♂ | 4 |
| Tr. ☽ ✶ N. ♃ | 4 | Tr. ♀ ☌ N. ♃ | 10 |
| Tr. ♆ ✶ N. ♃ | 4 | Tr. ♀ ☍ N. ♄ | 8 |
| Tr. ☉ ✶ N. ♄ | 4 | Tr. ♀ ☌ N. ♆ | 10 |
| Tr. ☽ △ N. ♄ | 6 | Tr. ♅ □ N. ♇ | 4 |
| Tr. ♆ △ N. ♄ | 6 | Total | −60 |
| Tr. ☉ △ N. ♆ | 6 | | +80 |
| Tr. ☽ ✶ N. ♆ | 4 | Net Aspect Value | +20 |
| Tr. ♆ ✶ N. ♆ | 4 | Therefore Sell | |
| Tr. ☉ △ N. ♇ | 6 | | |
| Tr. ☽ ✶ N. ♇ | 4 | | |
| Tr. ♆ ✶ N. ♇ | 4 | | |
| Tr. ♀ △ N. ♇ | 6 | | |
| Total | +80 | | |

The minor aspects such as 30°, 45°, 135°, 150° shown on the speculum are not included in the above tabulation because their values canceled out.

**FAVORABLE ASPECTS**
1) The stellium of Mars, Sun, Moon, Venus & Mercury in the money sign of Taurus in the 11th house of the N.Y.S.E. Natal chart.
2) ☿ ☌ ♀ 150° ♇
3) ♃ ☌ ♄ ✶ ☊ in ♌

New Moon 5/4/81
Indicates Rising Market
DJI Rose from 957 to 1023.

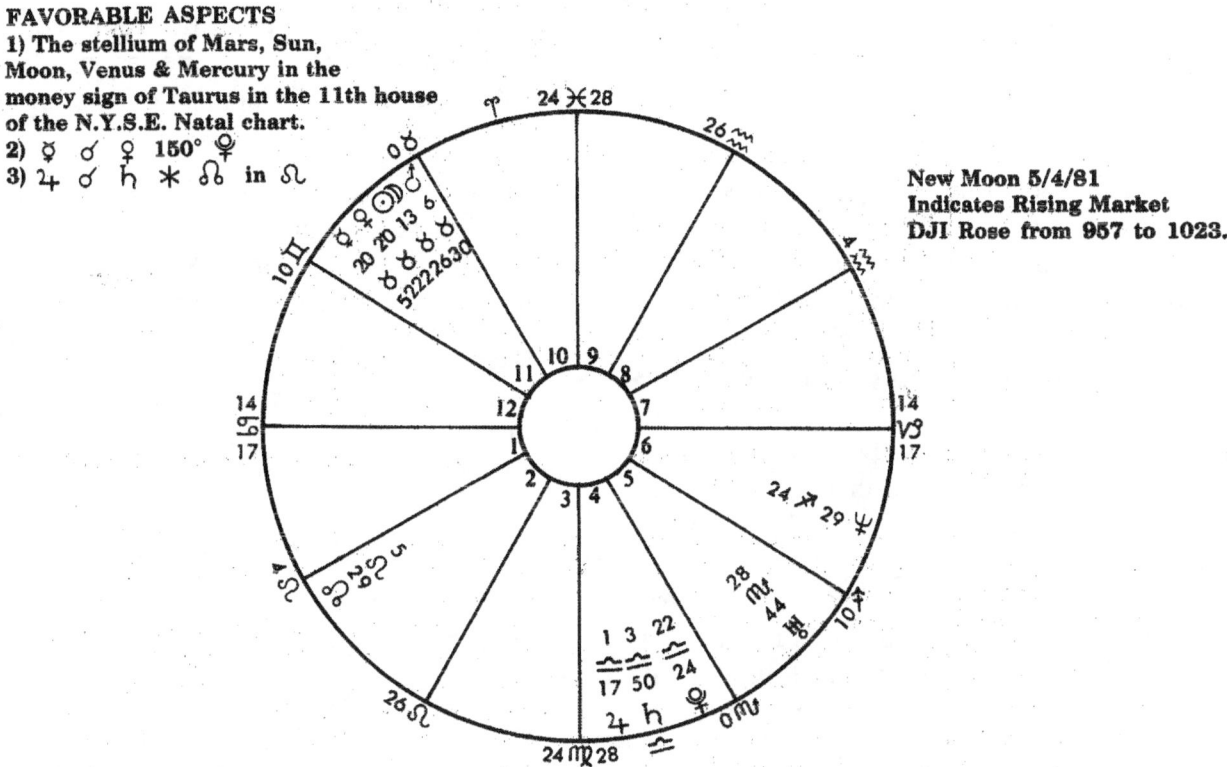

Figure 49. McWhirter Theory Forecast for June 1981.

Exchange chart.

Contemporary astrologers use the more accurate natal chart of the New York Stock Exchange, set for 8:52 a.m. May 17, 1792 at New York City, per Figure 50. The end of the 1980-1981 stock market was forecast by the planetary pattern at the time of the Full Moon of June 17, 1981. The DJI declined from the 1023 High of June 15, 1981 to a Low of 815 on September 25, 1981. The aspects shown on the speculum of Figure 49 are summarized in Table 29.

## The Williams Solar Ingress Method

Several years after the favorable reception accorded the author's book, *Astro-Economics*, which was published in April 1959, he was asked to write stock market forecasts for several popular astrological magazines. But, since stock price fluctuations are more violent than the ups and downs of the business cycle, which was the subject of *Astro-Economics*, it was found necessary to take into account the influence of the faster moving planets, such as Mars, Venus and Mercury, plus the Sun and Moon.

Research covering the period 1897-1964 had shown that Bull Markets were characterized by a planetary pattern that was decidedly different from that which indicated Bear Markets. Forecasts were made at quarterly intervals, based on the author's interpretation of the planetary patterns shown in the heavens above our national capital, Washington, D.C., at the time of the Sun's entry into the cardinal signs of Aries, Cancer, Libra and Capricorn, which respectively denote the beginning of spring, summer, autumn, and winter. But since our calendar year begins on January 1, the forecasts for the year ahead begin with the three months following the Sun's entry into the sign of Capricorn, at the Winter Solstice on December 22 of each year. Although New York is the financial center of the United States, Washington is the seat of our government and has been playing an ever-increasing role in the economic life of the nation since the days of President Franklin D. Roosevelt's "New Deal."

The basis for the author's forecasting technique, as published in Dell *Horoscope*, are the planetary patterns shown on the Solar Ingress charts for each year. The following steps are taken:

1. Convert the sign of the planet's position into degrees and minutes of longitude as shown in Table 30.

2. Calculate the degrees of separation between each pair of planets and record.

3. Circle in red the negative aspects and in green the positive aspects, allowing the following orbs: conjunction, 10 degrees; oppositions, 8 degrees; sextiles, square and trines, 5 degrees.

4. Use Table 31 for the polarities of conjunctions.

5. Use the following polarities for the other aspects: sextiles are positive, trines are positive, squares are negative, and oppositions are negative.

6. Tabulate the positive and negative aspects, assigning the following values to them: conjunctions, 10; oppositions, 8; trines, 6; sextiles and squares, 4.

7. Add up the values of the positive and negative aspects. The excess of the sum of the aspect values is called the Net Aspect Value and determines the general direction of the stock market for the 3 months following the Solar Ingress (Up, if positive; Down, if negative).

The complete record of the author's Solar Ingress forecasts is shown in Table 32.

Figure 51 shows the planetary pattern in the heavens above Washington, D.C. at the time of the Winter Solstice of December 22, 1966, the speculum which records the longitude of the planets and the angular separation between any pair of planets, the aspects and their values, and

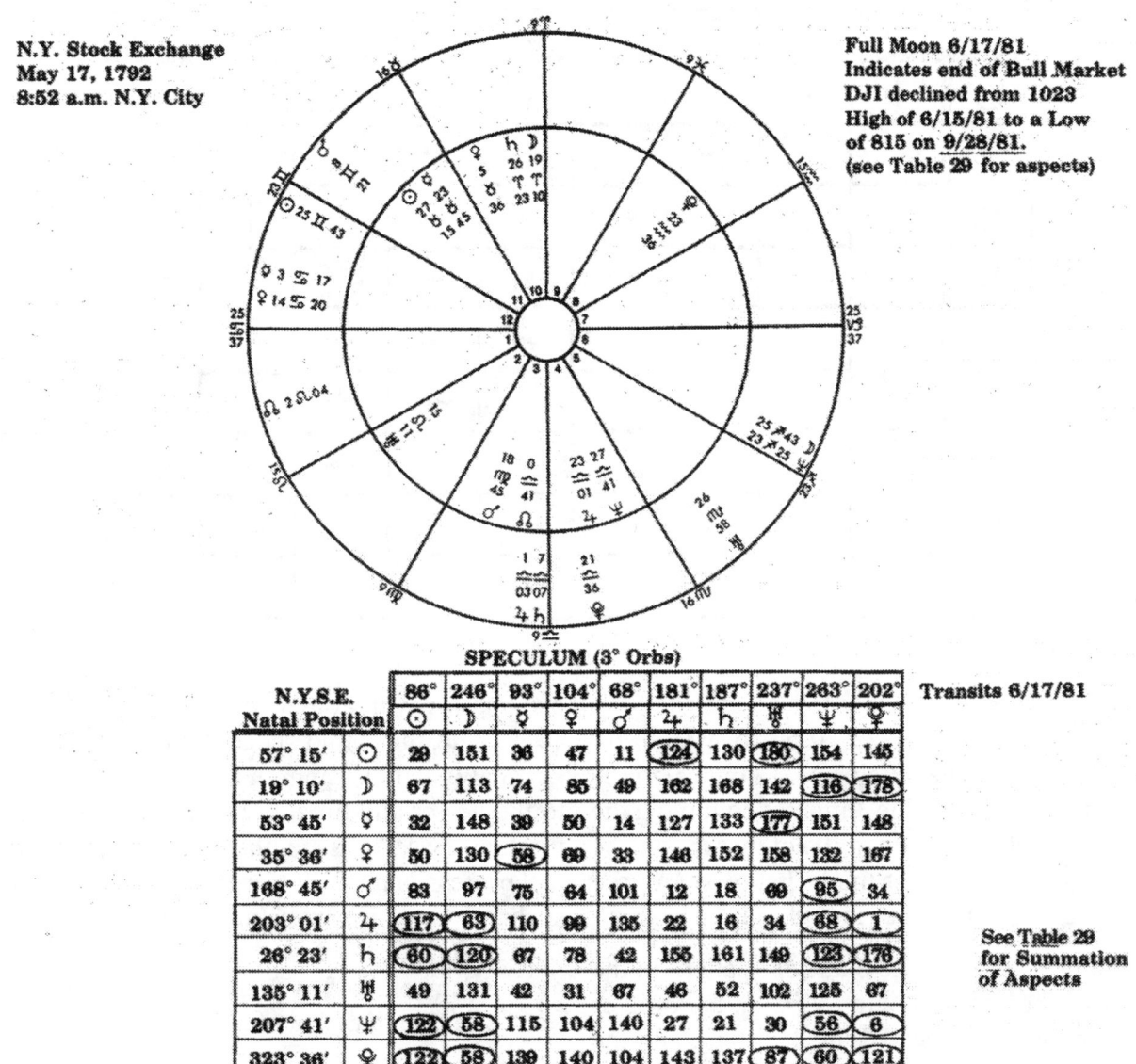

*Figure 50. Aspects Made by Transiting Planets on June 17, 1981 to Natal Positions of N.Y.S.E. Chart of May 17, 1792.*

| Table 30. Conversion of Signs into Longitude | | | |
|---|---|---|---|
| Sign | Degrees | Sign | Degrees |
| ♈ Aries | 0-30 | ♎ Libra | 180-210 |
| ♉ Taurus | 30-60 | ♏ Scorpio | 210-240 |
| ♊ Gemini | 60-90 | ♐ Sagittarius | 240-270 |
| ♋ Cancer | 90-120 | ♑ Capricorn | 270-300 |
| ♌ Leo | 120-150 | ♒ Aquarius | 300-330 |
| ♍ Virgo | 150-180 | ♓ Pisces | 330-360 |

Table 31. Polarity of Conjunctions.

| | ☽ | ☿ | ♀ | ♂ | ♃ | ♄ | ♅ | ♆ | ♇ |
|---|---|---|---|---|---|---|---|---|---|
| ☉ | + | + | + | − | + | − | + | − | − |
| ☽ |   | + | + | − | + | − | − | + | − |
| ☿ |   |   | + | − | + | − | + | + | − |
| ♀ |   |   |   | − | + | − | + | + | + |
| ♂ |   |   |   |   | − | − | − | − | − |
| ♃ |   |   |   |   |   | − | + | + | − |
| ♄ |   |   |   |   |   |   | − | − | − |
| ♅ |   |   |   |   |   |   |   | − | − |
| ♆ |   |   |   |   |   |   |   |   | − |

a diagram of the daily Dow Jones Industrial Average from December 22, 1966 to March 20, 1967. The Net Aspect Value of -12 indicated declining prices during the 3 months following the Winter Solstice, which did not occur, as the daily average record of the DJI shows. (A case of "the exception proves the rule.")

Figure 52 shows the planetary pattern in the heavens above Washington, D.C. at the time of the Summer Solstice of June 21, 1969, and the interpretation was for declining prices during the following three months, which came to pass as the daily average record of the DJI indicates. The most important negative element was the eleventh house Sun square the stellium of Pluto, Jupiter and Uranus in the second house of money.

Readers of the author's articles in Dell *Horoscope*, may recall that in the January 1965 issue of that magazine, he reported, "Although the Dow Jones Industrial Stock Average, which is made up of only thirty stocks, is the most widely used index of stock market activity, it is at best a somewhat imperfect measure of financial mass psychology." Again, in the January 1969 issue, the author stated: "Professional market analysts are beginning to pay more attention to the newer and broader averages." Finally, in the January 1974 issue, the author stated: "Several professional stock market advisory services, such as Value Line Investment Survey, Indicator Digest, and The Professional Tape Reader, have devised unweighted averages that more truly reflect what the majority of stocks are doing."

To make matters worse, Congress passed a law in 1974 making it mandatory for managers of pension funds, institutional funds, and mutual funds to discontinue putting the bulk of their clients' money into the 30 Dow Jones Industrial Stocks and to diversify their holdings over a wider range of stocks. Therefore, as the funds sold their Dow stocks and put the proceeds into the so-called "second-tier" stocks, the market price of the DJI Average declined, while those of the unweighted averages, which included all the stocks listed on the New York Stock Exchange, ROSE. This disparity is clearly indicated on Figures 36 and 37 of Chapter 11. Table

### Table 32. Record of Quarterly Stock Market Forecasts vs. DJI Averages.

| Solar Ingress | Net Aspect Value | Forecast | Results Correct | Incorrect |
|---|---|---|---|---|
| 3/20/64 | -4 | Up & Down | X | |
| 6/21 | +4 | Decline | | X |
| 9/22 | +10 | Rise | X | |
| 12/21 | +4 | Decline | | X |
| 3/20/65 | -34 | Decline | X | |
| 6/21 | -12 | Down & Up | X | |
| 9/23 | +34 | Rise | X | |
| 12/21 | -32 | Up & Down | X | |
| 3/22/66 | -76 | Decline | X | |
| 6/21 | +8 | Rise | | X |
| 9/23 | +26 | Down & Up | X | |
| 12/22 | +8 | Rise | X | |
| 3/21/67 | +32 | Up & Down | X | |
| 6/21 | +12 | Rise | X | |
| 9/23 | +2 | Decline | X | |
| 12/22 | -14 | Decline | X | |
| 3/20/68 | +2 | Rise | X | |
| 6/21 | +2 | Rise | X | |
| 9/22 | +18 | Rise | X | |
| 12/21 | -14 | Decline | X | |
| 3/20/69 | -40 | Decline | X | |
| 6/21 | -28 | Decline | X | |
| 9/23 | -24 | Decline | X | |
| 12/21 | +20 | Rise | | X |
| 3/20/70 | -36 | Sideways | | X |
| 6/21 | +16 | Rise | X | |
| 9/23 | +34 | Rise | X | |
| 12/22 | -26 | Decline | | X |
| 3/21/71 | -10 | Decline | X | |
| 6/22 | +12 | Rise | X | |
| 9/23 | +48 | Rise | X | |
| 12/22 | +38 | Rise | X | |
| 3/20/72 | -10 | Decline | X | |
| 6/20 | -10 | Decline | X | |
| 9/22 | -34 | Decline | | X |
| 12/21 | +30 | Rise | | X |
| 3/20/73 | +12 | Rise | | X |
| 6/21 | -8 | Decline | X | |
| 9/22 | +12 | Rise | | X |
| 12/21 | +34 | Rise | X | |
| 3/20/74 | +28 | Rise | | X |
| 6/21 | -8 | Decline | X | |
| 9/23 | -12 | Decline | X | |
| 12/22 | +16 | Rise | X | |
| 3/21/75 | +28 | Rise | X | |
| 6/22 | -12 | Decline | X | |
| 9/23 | +24 | Rise | X | |
| | | Totals | 36 | 11 |
| *Percentage of Total (47)* | | | 77% | 23% |

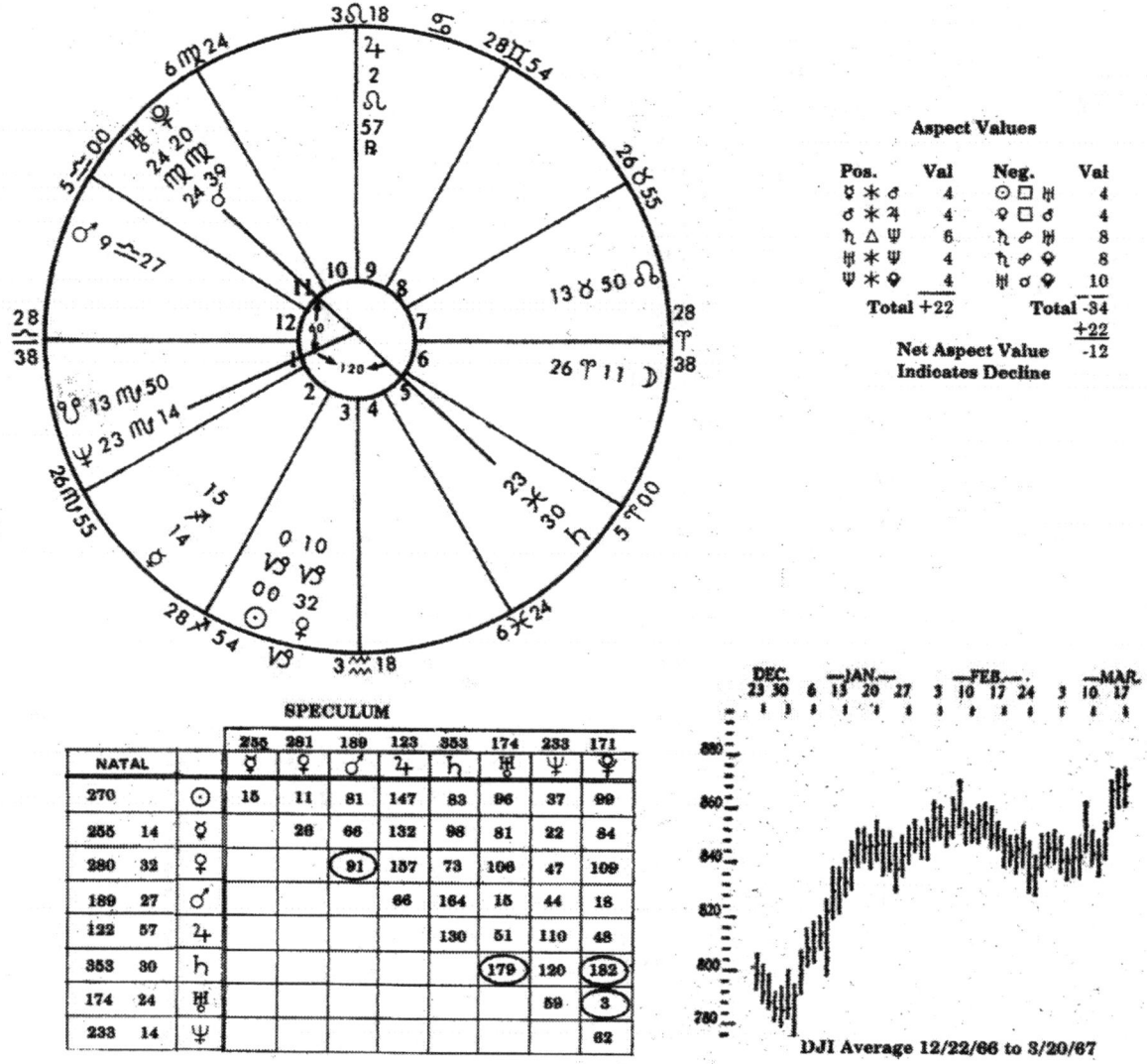

*Figure 51. Winter Solstice December 22, 1966 Forecasts Rising Prices.*

33 shows how accurate the author's forecasts have been since the Winter Solstice of December 22, 1975.

## The Williams Running Total Aspect Method

In an effort to be of service to those readers of Dell *Horoscope* who wished to know the probable direction of stock prices on a monthly instead of a quarterly basis, the author began such forecasts in the January 1980 issue of Dell *Horoscope*. The technique consisted of adding up the Net Aspect Value of the major aspects, viz: conjunction, sextile, square, trine and opposition that were listed in the Daily Aspectarian of *The American Ephemeris*. A sample calculation, for January 1980 is shown in Table 34. The results for the year are shown in Figure 53.

The results of the published forecasts for 1980 and 1981 are shown in Table 35.

Because the author feels that his 1981 forecast published in Dell *Horoscope* was misused, he will no longer publish annual stock market forecasts. However, for the benefit of readers of this book, the forecast for 1982 is in Table 36.

## Conclusion

The most important lesson to be learned

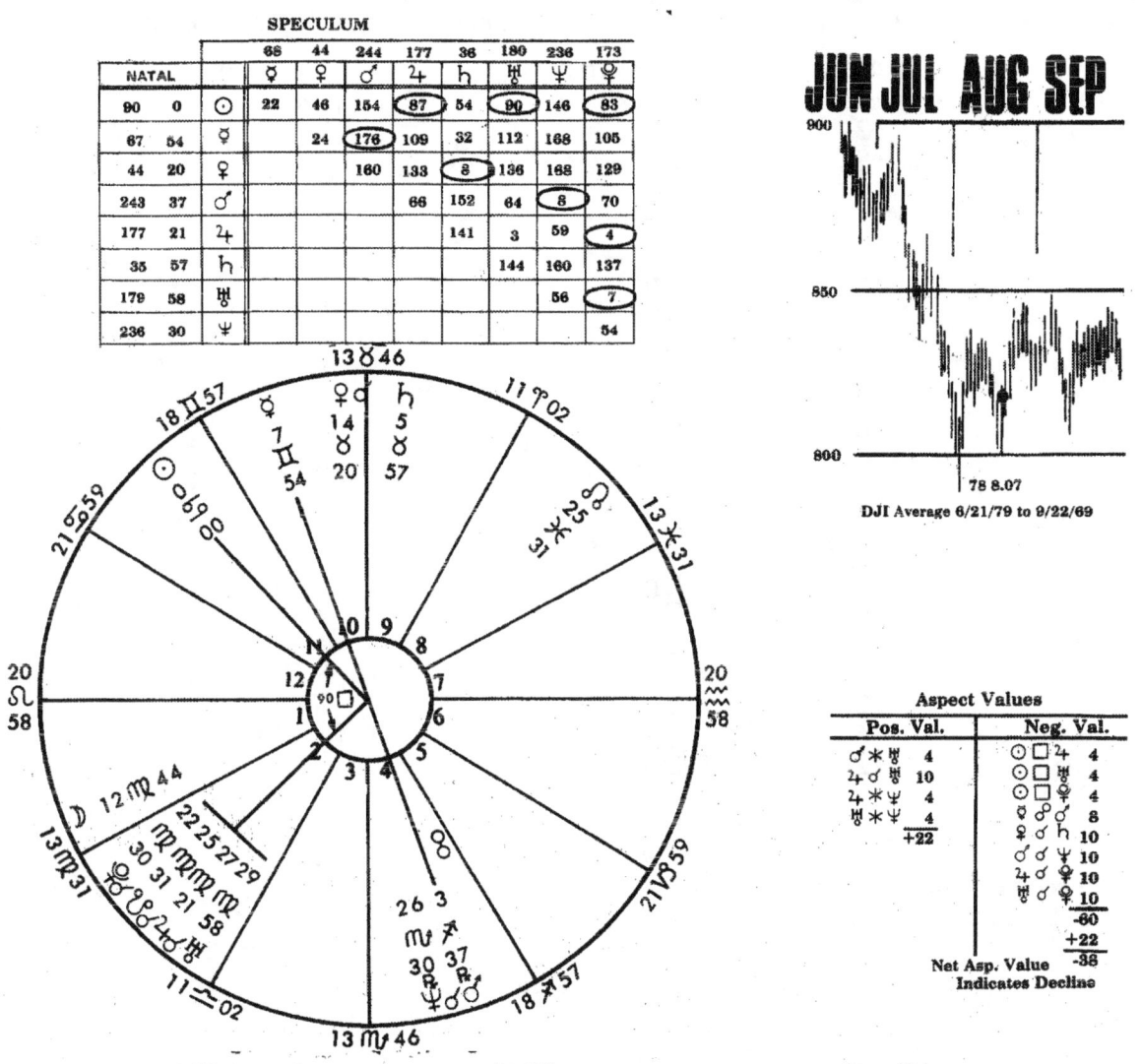

*Figure 52. Summer Solstice June 21, 1969 Forecasts Declining Prices.*

from this chapter is the absolute necessity of avoiding reliance on any one particular method or technique to the exclusion of others. Most professional stock market technicians have a battery of indicators to help them gauge what the market may do—one internationally famous advisor boasts of some 50 technical aids. But the layman hasn't the time nor the inclination to spend on such a vast array of indicators. In this chapter the author has described two of the most important chartist indicators, viz, the Dow Theory, and the Head and Shoulders Top, plus the Double Top pattern.

In the October 1966 issue of Dell *Horoscope*, the author introduced the Dow Theory to his readers, as follows: "A modern version of the age-old technique of divination from the observation of omens is practiced, in, of all places, the canyons of Wall Street. The Babylonian baru or seer and the Roman haruspice or augur have been replaced by the Wall Street technical analyst, who predicts the future course of stock prices from the patterns he sees in the charts of stock price movements. The oldest method of such stock market forecasting is known as the Dow Theory. . . ." This theory correctly signaled the end of the 1980-1981 Bull Market on July 2, 1981, as shown in Figure 43.

**Table 33. Record of Quarterly Stock Market Forecasts vs. Unweighted Averages.**

| Solar Ingress | Net Aspect Value | Forecast | Results Correct | Incorrect |
|---|---|---|---|---|
| 12/22/75 | +2 | Up | X | |
| 3/20/76 | +8 | Up | | X |
| 6/21 | +16 | Up | X | |
| 9/22 | +12 | Up | X | |
| 12/21 | +8 | Up | X | |
| 3/20/77 | +14 | Up | X | |
| 6/21 | -18 | Down | X | |
| 9/22 | +6 | Up | X | |
| 12/21 | +43 | Up | X | |
| 3/20/78 | +10 | Up | X | |
| 6/21 | +14 | Up | X | |
| 9/23 | 0 | Down | X | |
| 12/22 | +14 | Up | X | |
| 3/21/79 | +28 | Up | X | |
| 6/21 | +20 | Up | X | |
| 9/23 | +38 | Up | | X |
| *12/22 | -24 | Down | X | |
| *3/20/80 | -6 | Down | | X |
| *6/21 | +2 | Up | X | |
| *9/22 | -22 | Down | X | |
| *12/21 | +16 | Up | X | |
| *3/20/81 | -12 | Down | | X |
| *6/21 | +8 | Up | | X |
| *9/22 | -8 | Down | | X |
| | | Total | 18 | 6 |
| Percentage of Total (24) | | | 75% | 25% |

*Unpublished forecasts

**Table 34. January 1980 Running Total Aspects.**

| Date | Aspect | Positive | Negative |
|---|---|---|---|
| 1 | ☉△♃ | 6 | - |
| 5 | ☉△♂ | 6 | - |
| 8 | ☿△♃ | 6 | - |
| | ♀✶♆ | 4 | - |
| 9 | ♀△♇ | 6 | - |
| 11 | ♀□♅ | - | 4 |
| 12 | ☿△♂ | 6 | - |
| | ☉□♀ | - | 4 |
| 16 | ☿□♀ | - | 4 |
| 17 | ☉△♄ | 6 | - |
| | ☿✶♅ | 4 | - |
| 19 | ☿△♄ | 6 | - |
| 21 | ☉☌☿ | 10 | - |
| 23 | ♀☍♃ | - | 8 |
| 26 | ♆✶♀ | 4 | - |
| 28 | ♀☍♂ | - | 8 |
| | Total | +64 | 28 |
| | Net Aspect Value | -28 | |
| | | +36 | |

Indicate Rising Market

(see Figure 53 for the year's results)

**Table 35. Record of Running Total Aspects vs. Unweighted Averages.**

| | | *1980* | | | | | *1981* | | |
|---|---|---|---|---|---|---|---|---|---|
| Mo. | Net Val. | Forecast | Result Correct | Incorrect | Mo. | Net Val. | Forecast | Result Correct | Incorrect |
| Jan. | +36 | Up | X | | Jan. | +44 | Up | | X |
| Feb. | -34 | Down | X | | Feb. | +44 | Up | X | |
| Mar. | +10 | Up | | X | Mar. | -52 | Down | | X |
| Apr. | +10 | Up | X | | Apr. | -32 | Down | X | |
| May | -2 | Down | | X | May | +14 | Up | X | |
| June | +12 | Up | X | | June | +4 | Down | X | |
| July | +24 | Up | X | | July | -2 | Up | | X |
| Aug. | +44 | Up | X | | Aug. | +44 | Up | | X |
| Sept. | 0 | Sideways | X | | Sept. | -4 | Up | | X |
| Oct. | +6 | Up | | X | Oct. | +64 | Up | X | |
| Nov. | +6 | Up | X | | Nov. | +30 | Up | X | |
| Dec. | -12 | Down | X | | Dec. | +14 | Up | X | |
| | | Total | 9 | 3 | | | Total | 7 | 5 |
| | | | 75% | 25% | | | | 58% | 42% |

**Table 36. Williams Forecast for 1982.**

| Month | Net Value | Running Total Forecast | Solar Ingress Period | Forecast |
|---|---|---|---|---|
| Jan. | +22 | Up | 1 Q | Up |
| Feb. | +28 | Up | | |
| Mar. | +42 | Up | | |
| Apr. | -14 | Down | 2 Q | Up |
| May | -12 | Down | | |
| June | +32 | Up | | |
| July | -16 | Down | 3 Q | Up |
| Aug. | +20 | Up | | |
| Sept. | -4 | Down | | |
| Oct. | +20 | Up | 4 Q | Down |
| Nov. | +54 | Up | | |
| Dec. | +40 | Up | | |

In the same *Horoscope* article, the author introduced the subject of other chart patterns as follows: "In addition to the Dow Theorists, there is a school of Wall Street market technicians who see other patterns in charts of stock market prices, from which they predict which way the market will go." And then, in the January 1967 issue of Dell *Horoscope*, after describing the Head and Shoulders Top pattern that correctly indicated the end of the 1965-1966 Bull Market, per Figure 42, the author continued, "Thus do modem stock market professionals apply a technique which was developed by the wise men of ancient Babylonia some 5,000 years ago. The only essential difference is the medium in which patterns of future occurrences are seen by the seer. The Babylonian baru saw his patterns in the flight of birds or the entrails of sacrificial animals, whereas the modern stock market technician sees his patterns in stock market charts.

"However, the technique of the ancient Babylonian seer and his modern stock market counterpart has one basic defect. No prediction can be made until *after* a pattern has been formed. This deficiency is not present in the other predictive technique that was also developed by the an-

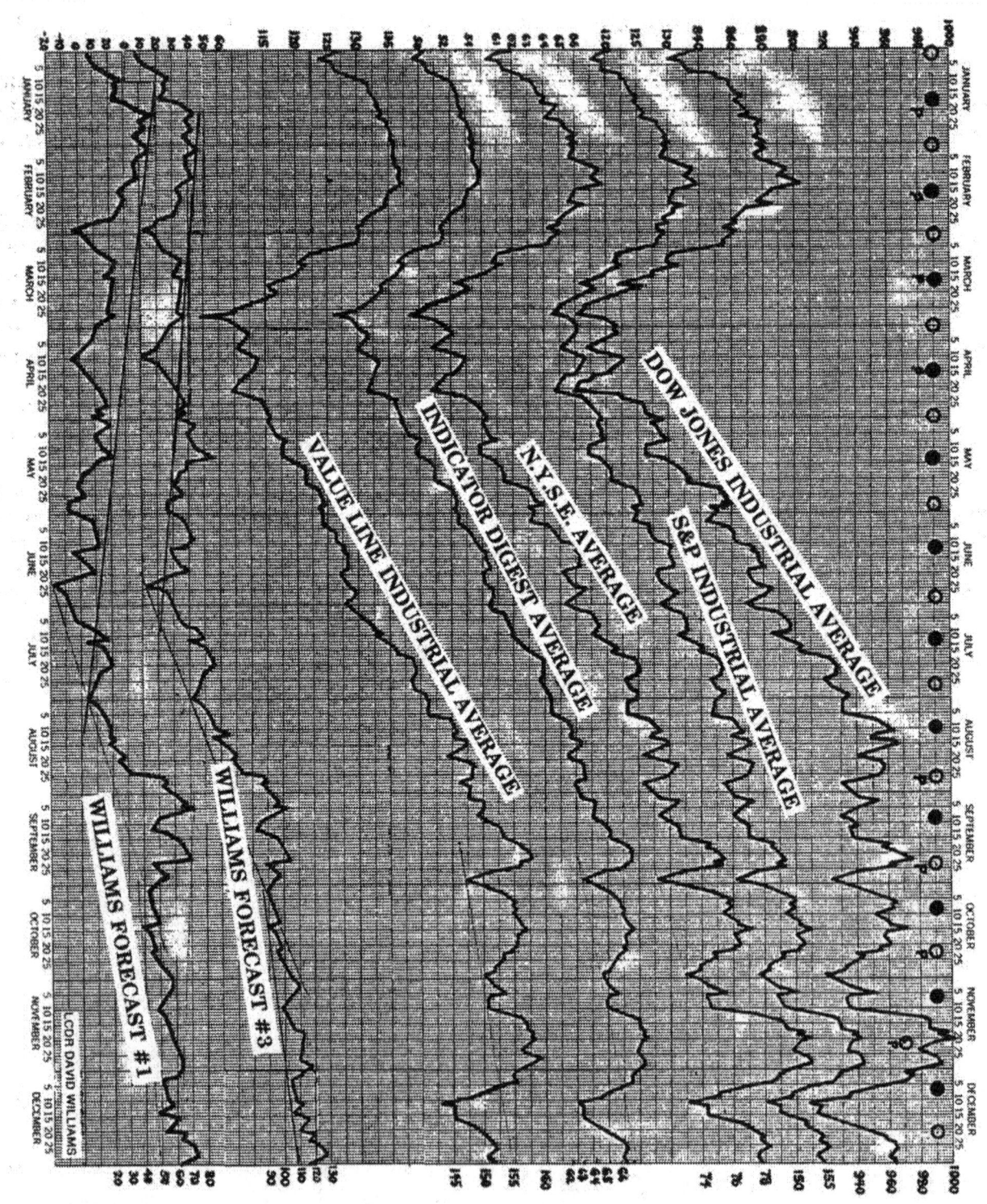

Figure 53. 1980 Williams Forecast vs. Stock Market Averages.

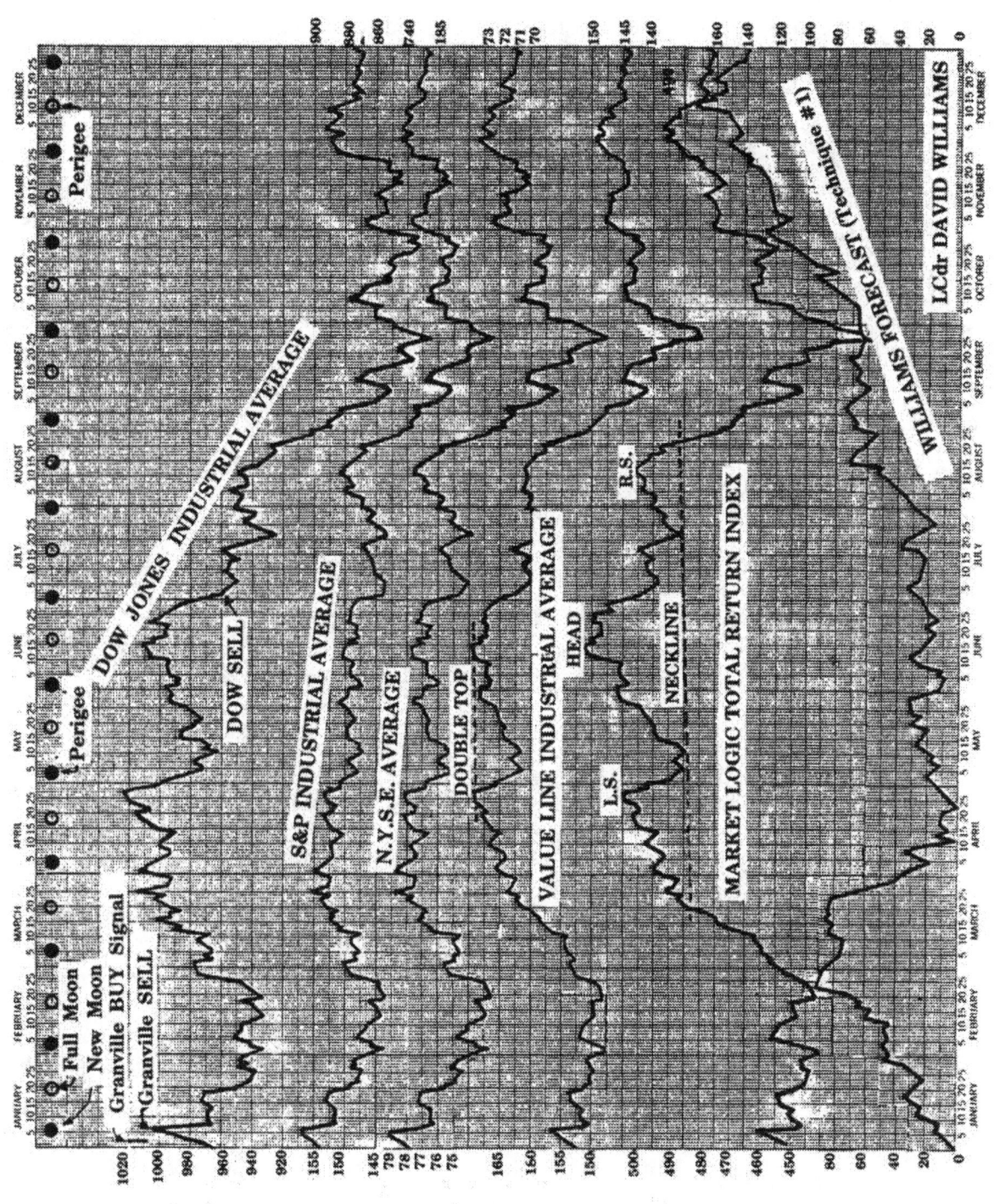

*Figure 54. 1981 Williams Forecast vs. Stock Market Averages.*

cient Babylonians, i.e., predicting the future from the patterns formed by the planets. Since the positions of the planets could be calculated for years in advance, it was, therefore, possible to predict in *advance* of the formation of the actual pattern."

Thus, as Tables 32 and 33 indicate, the author's advance forecasts since the Solar Ingress of March 20, 1964 to September 23, 1981 (a total of 71) have been accurate 76 percent of the time. Nevertheless, as the actual market unfolded in 1981, it soon became apparent that the forecast shown in Figure 54 was not being realized. First came the distortion caused by *guru* Joseph Granville's January 6, 1981 Sell signal. Then came the Head and Shoulders Top pattern in the DJI Average shown in Figure 38 of Chapter 11 and Figure 44 of this chapter, when the Neckline was broken on June 29, 1981, followed by the Dow Theory Sell signal of July 2, 1981.

The end of the Bull Market in the unweighted averages shown in Figure 45 came later than in the DJI Average. The Neckline of the Head and Shoulders Top in the Market Logic Total Return Index and The Professional Tape Reader (NYUA) was not broken until August 22, 1981, and the Support Level of the Value Line Industrial Average Double Top was not violated until July 18, 1981. The chart patterns that were developing gave such strong indications that the stock market was headed for trouble that the author sold a number of his stocks on July 2, 1981, to realize long-term capital gains (the very day that the Dow Theory Sell signal was given). See Table 36 for the 1982 forecast.

There is an old saying on Wall Street: "Don't get married to any stock." This may also be paraphrased: "Don't get hung up on any one forecasting technique."

In the next chapter we will review the important subject of personal investments.

## Chapter 13

# Personal Investing

### Introduction

In the April 1964 issue of Dell *Horoscope*, the author stated: "A keen student of market conditions, who is a professional market analyst recently published the results of a study which indicated that the observed correlation between the trends of business activity and the stock market during the past 50 years has only been about 15 percent. The stock market sometimes correctly anticipates a turn in the business cycle by from six to nine months. At other times, as in the spring of 1962, the stock market decline had no appreciable repercussion on the business cycle.

"The same stock market analyst stated that 80 percent of market trends are caused by fluctuations in investor psychology—fear, excitement, greed and overoptimism. In answer to the writer's question whether investor psychology was measurable, he answered yes, but declined to reveal how it was done. It is apparent that it is one of the "trade secrets" he was not inclined to reveal. But students of astrology are familiar with Dr. Carl G. Jung's statement: "Astrology represents the summation of all the psychological knowledge of antiquity."

A more recent investment advisor stated: "Despite all the computers and all the fundamental and technical analysis, investor psychology is still the most significant factor in market behavior. Actually, so-called technical analysis, whether based on computer studies or not, is simply an attempt to measure and evaluate on a mathematical basis, the psychological condition of the market."

Napoleon once said that greed and fear were the two levers by which men are controlled. The most common manifestation of greed in the marketplace is the refusal of most speculators to sell out and take their profits at market tops. Fear, of course, is the cause of panics and crashes. Only by keeping your emotions under control can you increase your real wealth by sound investments.

The story is told that during 1848, the Yyear of Revolution, Baron Rothschild was buying French bonds. A friend asked him why he was buying bonds when the streets of Paris were running red with blood. The Baron replied: "That's why I am buying." But it takes courage to buy during a panic and it takes strength of character to sell at the top of a boom. *Therefore buy during panics and sell during booms!*

## Who Should Invest or Speculate

The dictionary gives the following definitions: "Invest—to lay out money or capital in the purchase of property for permanent use as opposed to speculation. Speculate—to make an investment involving a risk, but with hope of gain." Disregarding real estate, bonds have for centuries been considered to be the safest investments, but in recent years, with interest rates fluctuating wildly between 10 and 20 percent, bonds have become just as speculative as stocks. While falling interest rates result in rising bond prices, stocks will outperform bonds. What then is a conservative individual to do with his or her surplus funds in order to build up a nest-egg for the future? Here is where natal astrology provides the answer, through the following:

1. One must have an accurate natal chart.

2. Look to the second house of the natal chart, which indicates money to be made by the native through his own efforts, i.e., through investment in conservative or growth stocks. He will succeed if the Sun, Moon, Venus or Jupiter are in the second house or rule the sign that is on the cusp of the second house. He will have difficulties if Mars, Saturn, Uranus, Neptune or Pluto are involved.

3. Look to the fifth house of the natal chart, which indicates money to be made through speculation. Successful results will be obtained if the Sun, Moon, Venus, Jupiter or Neptune (the planet of speculation) are in the fifth house or on its cusp. Losses will occur if Mars, Saturn, Uranus or Pluto are involved.

4. However, an afflicted Jupiter or Neptune in the fifth house is indicative of bad judgment, due to overoptimism, while a well-aspected Saturn in the fifth house would indicate caution.

5. The conservative investor will probably have Saturn in either the second or fifth houses. Such an individual should put his or her surplus funds into Certificates of Deposit, which are guaranteed by the U. S. Government, or in the higher interest paying Money Market Funds, which, although not guaranteed by the government, are practically risk free.

## Which Stock Should Be Bought

Main Street is full of investors who complain that "everything is going up, except my 'cats and dogs'." Why should this happen? Many years ago, a retired vice president of one of the nation's largest banks gave the author the following formula for picking stocks: "Buy only those stocks whose natal chart harmonizes with your own natal chart." He stated that he had gone broke in the 1929 Stock Market Crash, but subsequently became acquainted with an astrologer, who was the widow of a New Jersey banker, and thus was acquainted with the stock market. Under this astrologer's guidance, he recouped his losses and became a millionaire. When his wife died, he married his astrologer!

Some stocks are said to be "ruled" by certain planets, viz, iron and steel by Mars, copper by Venus, oil by Neptune, electric utilities by Uranus, agriculture and real estate by Saturn, underground mining by Pluto. Jupiter is considered to be the planet of optimism or expansion; Saturn, the planet of pessimism or contraction; Neptune, the planet of illusion (speculation is an illusion). Astrologers who deal in commodities are not in agreement as to which planets rule silver, gold, wheat, corn, pork bellies, etc.

Figure 55, which is the natal chart of the author, illustrates some of the principles herein discussed. For example, the Sun is conjunct Jupiter in the second house of money, indicting gain through his own efforts and from investments. Jupiter is also the ruler of the fifth house of speculation, indicating gain from the purchase of speculative stocks. Jupiter's sextile to Saturn and Uranus, indicates gain from conservative investments and real estate (the sale of a home). Saturn shows gainful employment in electrical utility industry (the author spent 43 years with one of the largest public utility com-

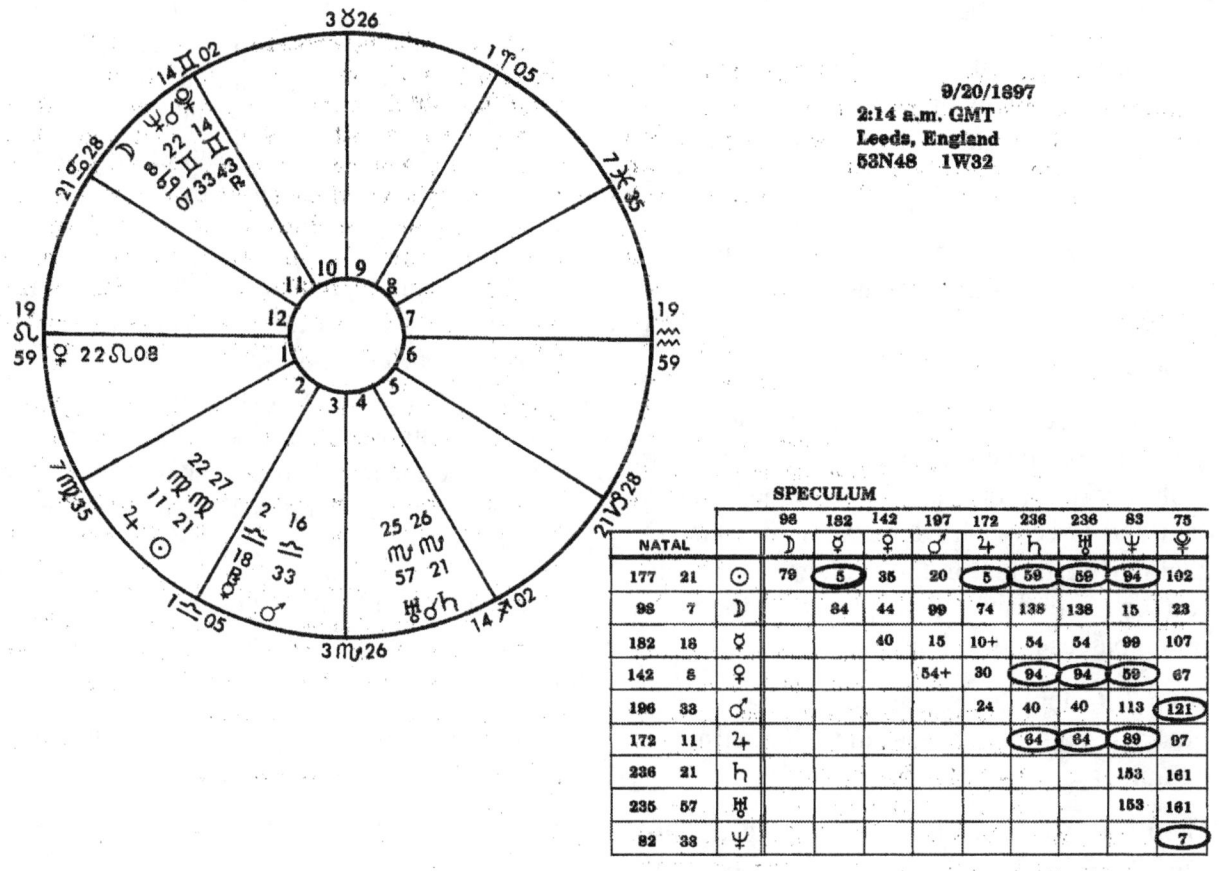

*Figure 55. Natal Chart of Author.*

panies in the U.S.) and Uranus shows gain from investments in the electric utility and electrical manufacturing stocks. But Jupiter's square to Neptune in the eleventh house of friends indicated losses in oil stocks purchased on the advice of a broker "friend."

How did the foregoing work out in the author's life? He earned his livelihood for 43 years with Con-Edison of New York, and gained from the purchase of stocks in electric utilities and electrical manufacturing companies (Jupiter sextile Uranus). He sold his home in New York for four times what he paid for it (Jupiter sextile Saturn). However, the natal square of Jupiter to Neptune was activated on July 1, 1969, when, on the advice of a broker friend, he purchased stock in two oil and gas drilling companies sponsored by a Denver promoter. Transiting Saturn was semi-square (45°) from natal Neptune and sesquiquadrate (135°) from natal Jupiter, indicating that this purchase would result in loss. Both companies went bankrupt following the bankruptcy of the Denver promoter. One stock was reorganized and bought out by a larger company to whom the stock was sold on December 5, 1977, for a loss of $14,380 (original cost $20,000). Because the triggering adverse aspects (45° and 135°) were minor, the loss was indicated to be minor. In fact, the $14,380 long-term capital loss was used to offset a similar amount of long-term capital gains in the author's 1977 federal income tax return. So the net loss was about $7,000. The second company in which the author also invested $20,000 has recently been reorganized and was sold December 15-18, 1981 for $20,320, giving a gain of 1.5 percent.

## Corporation Horoscope Analysis

Business corporations are living entities created by men and run by men. The life of a corporation begins with the date of incorporation, when the corporation thus becomes a living entity. It has been found from experience that the lives of corporations are affected by planetary influences, just as are the lives of individuals. The technique for erecting the horoscope of a corporation is as follows:

Step 1: Since the time of incorporation is seldom given, you must set up a solar chart for the date of incorporation, using the Equal House System and Greenwich Meridian Time (GMT) with Noon positions of the planets. Place the Sun on the Ascendant and the planets in their appropriate places in the chart.

Step 2: Calculate the angular separation between each pair of planets and record in the speculum.

Step 3: Encircle in RED the negative aspects and in GREEN or BLUE the positive aspects, allowing the following orbs: conjunctions, 10 degrees; oppositions, 8 degrees; sextiles, squares and trines, 5 degrees.

Step 4: Determine the aspects formed by the transiting planets Pluto, Neptune, Uranus, Saturn, Jupiter, Mars, Venus, and Mercury to the natal planets. This will indicate when big up or down movements in the company's stock will occur.

Step 5: Before making a final judgment on what the stock may or may not do in the future, always take into consideration any aspects to the company's ruler. This is always the planet which rules the sign in which the Sun is placed, viz. Sun in Virgo, the ruler is Mercury; Sun in Sagittarius, the ruler is Jupiter, etc.

Having done all of the above, you are now ready to interpret the horoscope according to the following rules:

1. The position of the Sun in any company's chart is the most important planetary position to be considered, for it represents the company, its organization, its management and aims. Hence, the Sun is placed on the Ascendant and aspects to it from the major planets, both at the time of incorporation and at later dates by transit, are of major importance.

2. The Moon represents the public and the attitude of people toward the company or its products or services. Aspects to the Moon are second in importance to those made to the Sun. Thus, a company which is incorporated at a time when the Moon is in favorable aspect to the Sun, will have a long life and will usually be most successful.

3. Mercury indicates the commercial and scientific abilities of the company's management.

4. Venus indicates the company's acquisition or merger potentials.

5. Mars governs the activity of the company's stock. Whenever Mars, at the time of incorporation or by transit, strongly aspects the Sun, Moon, Jupiter or its own place at the time of incorporation, the price of the stock will fluctuate strongly while under such influence.

6. Jupiter indicates the money-making possibility of the company and shows the money behind the company and its chances for expansion.

7. Saturn indicates the limitations and restrictions placed on the company.

8. Uranus indicates the management's ability to exploit new ideas or inventions, as well as sudden, unexpected events.

9. Neptune indicates management's vision or liability to illusion or delusion.

10. Pluto represents mass production, mass consumption and mass psychology.

11. The trend will be UPWARD if Jupiter and Uranus are in a favorable aspect to the Sun or Moon, viz: forming angles of 0, 60, or 120 de-

grees. Always invest in a stock which is coming under a favorable aspect from Jupiter or Uranus singly, or when both planets are in favorable aspect to each other and are aspecting the Sun or Moon of the company by transit.

12. The trend will be DOWNWARD if Saturn and Uranus are in unfavorable aspect to the Sun or Moon, viz: forming angles or 90 or 180 degrees, and in the case of Saturn, 0 degrees. Do not invest in a stock which is coming under an unfavorable aspect to the Sun or Moon from Saturn or Uranus singly, or when both planets are in unfavorable aspect to each other and are aspecting the Sun and Moon of the company by transit.

13. *Buy* the stocks of companies whose natal Venus or Jupiter is conjunct, sextile, or trine to your own natal Sun, Moon or Ascendant.

14. Do *not* buy the stocks of companies whose negative planets (Mars, Saturn, Neptune or Pluto) are conjunct, square or opposition your own natal Sun, Moon or Ascendant.

## Fairchild Camera and Instrument Corp.

To illustrate some of the foregoing principles we will now study Figure 56, the natal chart of Fairchild Camera and Instrument Corp., the third largest worldwide supplier of semi-conductor devices, and a prominent manufacturer of cameras and computers for the defense industries. This was one of the glamour stocks of the 1960s, having had a phenomenal rise of 20-fold during the 23 months from July 1958 to June 1960. The price of the stock had been fluctuating between a high of $6.6 in 1954 to a low of $2.7 in 1957, and a 5-year base had been formed from the following lows: 1954, $3.3; 1955, $3.5; 1956, $3.3; 1957, $2.7; 1958, $3.3. The planetary pattern during the July 1958 low is shown in Table 37.

Following the 6-year base, the stock skyrocketed to a high of $67 in June 1960, under the influence of the planetary pattern shown in Table 38.

The stock then declined during the next four years until June 1964, when it hit bottom at $14 a share. The planetary pattern for the month of June 1964 is shown in Table 39.

From the 1964 low of $14, the stock skyrocketed to an all-time high of $144 in February 1966, or 10 times its 1964 low, under the influence of the planetary pattern shown in Table 40.

After a series of violent downward swings during the next four years, the stock made a double bottom at 18 in August and October 1970 under the influence of the planetary pattern shown in Table 41.

The stock rose to $50 in June 1971, then dropped back to the $18 low of August 1970, in November 1971, and, from the double bottom of 1970-1971, rose to $92 in October 1973, under the influence of the planetary pattern shown in Table 42.

From the October 1973 high of $92, the stock plummeted to a low of $16 in December 1974, under the influence of the planetary pattern shown in Table 43.

From the December 1974 low of $16, the price rose to $60 in June 1975, fell to $30 in December 1975, rose to $54 in January and September 1976, and fell to $20 in October 1977. Fairchild was finally bought out by a much larger company, Schlumberger, Ltd., on June 19, 1979, for $66 per share. For the price gyrations in Fairchild see Figure 57.

The reason for devoting so much space to Fairchild was that on January 20, 970, the author gave the following analysis of the company to a client, who had purchased the stock at about $85 a share, upon the advice of her broker. At the time, the Value Line Investment Survey of January 16, 1970 rated the stock as AVERAGE for the year ahead, with a POTENTIAL value of $138 in 1972-1974.

1. The Sun was in a favorable relationship to

Originally incorporated 2/9/1920
Reorganized 11/23/1927*
Noon GMT Equal Houses
*This is the date used.

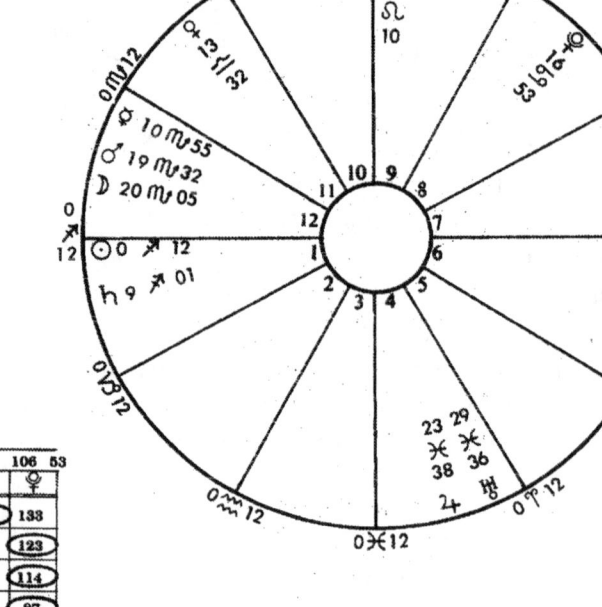

Figure 56. Natal Chart of Fairchild Camera and Instrument Company.

Table 37. Major Aspects Between Transiting and Fairchild Natal Planets July 1958 Low.

| | Positive | Value | | Negative | Value |
|---|---|---|---|---|---|
| July 3 | Tr. Sun trine N. Mercury | 6 | July 1 | Tr. Pluto conjunct N. Neptune | 10 |
| July 5 | Tr. Mercury trine N. Sun | 6 | | Tr. Pluto square N. Sun | 4 |
| July 8 | Tr. Venus trine N. Venus | 6 | | | |
| July 10 | Tr. Mercury conjunct N. Neptune | 10 | | Tr. Mars square N. Pluto | 4 |
| July 13 | Tr. Mercury sextile N. Venus | 4 | July 4 | Tr. Sun conjunct N. Pluto | 10 |
| | | | | Tr. Venus opposition N. Saturn | 8 |
| July 13 | Tr. Sun trine N. Moon | 6 | July 6 | Tr. Sun square N. Venus | 4 |
| July 17 | Tr. Venus sextile N. Neptune | 4 | July 9 | Tr. Sun conjunct N. Pluto | 10 |
| July 21 | Tr. Venus trine N. Mercury | 6 | July 11 | Tr. Mercury square N. Mercury | 4 |
| July 20 | Tr. Mars trine N. Neptune | 6 | July 15 | Tr. Uranus square N. Mercury | 4 |
| | | | July 18 | Tr. Mercury square N. Moon | 4 |
| July 24 | Tr. Sun trine N. Sun | 6 | July 27 | Tr. Mercury square N. Sun | 4 |
| | | Total +60 | | | Total -66 |
| | | -66 | | | |
| | Net Aspect Value | -6 | | | |
| | Therefore Buy | | | | |

174

**Table 38. Major Aspects Between Transiting and Fairchild Natal Planets June 1960 High.**

| | Positive | Value | | Negative | Value |
|---|---|---|---|---|---|
| June 1 | Tr. Saturn sextile N. Mars | 4 | June 2 | Tr. Mars square N. Pluto | 4 |
| June 2 | Tr. Mercury sextile N. Neptune | 4 | June 5 | Tr. Venus opposition N. Saturn | 8 |
| June 4 | Tr. Sun trine N. Venus | 6 | June 12 | Tr. Mercury square N. Venus | 4 |
| June 5 | Tr. Mercury trine N. Jupiter | 6 | | Tr. Saturn opposition N. Pluto | 8 |
| June 8 | Tr. Mercury trine N. Mars | 6 | June 13 | Tr. Jupiter square N. Neptune | 4 |
| | Tr. Venus trine N. Venus | 6 | June 18 | Tr. Venus opposition N. Mercury | 8 |
| June 9 | Tr. Mercury trine N. Uranus | 6 | | Total | −36 |
| June 16 | Tr. Jupiter trine N. Neptune | 6 | | | +70 |
| June 19 | Tr. Mars trine N. Neptune | 6 | | *Net aspect value* | +34 |
| June 20 | Tr. Sun sextile N. Neptune | 4 | | *Therefore Sell* | |
| June 21 | Tr. Venus sextile N. Neptune | 4 | | | |
| June 30 | Tr. Venus trine N. Mercury | 6 | | | |
| | Tr. Mercury trine N. Sun | 6 | | | |
| | *Total* | +70 | | | |

**Table 39. Major Aspects between Transiting and Fairchild Natal Planets June 1964 Low.**

| | Positive | Value | | Negative | Value |
|---|---|---|---|---|---|
| June 1 | Tr. Pluto sextile N. Mercury | 4 | June 1 | Tr. Pluto square N. Saturn | 4 |
| | Tr. Mercury sextile N. Pluto | 4 | June 3 | Tr. Mercury opposition N. Mars | 8 |
| June 4 | Tr. Sun trine N. Venus | 6 | June 9 | Tr. Mercury square N. Neptune | 4 |
| June 19 | Tr. Venus sextile N. Neptune | 4 | June 14 | Tr. Mercury opposition N. Mars | 8 |
| June 20 | Tr. Sun sextile N. Neptune | 4 | June 18 | Tr. Mars opposition N. Sun | 8 |
| June 24 | Tr. Mercury sextile N. Neptune | 4 | June 30 | Tr. Mars opposition N. Saturn | 8 |
| June 30 | Tr. Mercury trine N. Neptune | 6 | | Total | −40 |
| | *Total* | +32 | | | +32 |
| | | | | *Net aspect value* | −8 |
| | | | | *Therefore Buy* | |

**Table 40. Major Aspects Between Transiting and Fairchild Natal Planets February 1966 High.**

| | Positive | Value | | Negative | Value |
|---|---|---|---|---|---|
| Feb. 1 | Tr. Pluto sextile N. Mars | 4 | Feb. 1 | Tr. Mars square N. Sun | 4 |
| | Tr. Uranus sextile N. Mars | 4 | Feb. 3 | Tr. Mercury square N. Mercury | 4 |
| | Tr. Mercury sextile N. Saturn | 4 | Feb. 13 | Tr. Mercury opposition N. Neptune | 8 |
| Feb. 3 | Tr. Sun trine N. Venus | 6 | Feb. 18 | Tr. Mercury square N. Saturn | 4 |
| Feb. 7 | Tr. Venus sextile N. Uranus | 4 | Feb. 28 | Tr. Sun square N. Saturn | 4 |
| Feb. 12 | Tr. Mars trine N. Mercury | 6 | Feb. 31 | Tr. Mars conjunct N. Jupiter | 10 |
| Feb. 14 | Tr. Mercury trine N. Mercury | 6 | | Total | −34 |
| Feb. 17 | Tr. Neptune trine N. Neptune | 6 | | | +60 |
| Feb. 18 | Tr. Neptune conjunct N. Mercury | 10 | | *Net aspect value* | +26 |
| Feb. 24 | Tr. Mercury trine N. Mars | 6 | | *Therefore Sell* | |
| Feb. 30 | Tr. Pluto sextile N. Pluto | 4 | | | |
| | *Total* | +60 | | | |

### Table 41. Major Aspects Between Transiting and Fairchild Natal Planets August 1970 Low.

| | Positive | Value | | Negative | Value |
|---|---|---|---|---|---|
| Aug. 1 | Tr. Sun trine N. Saturn | 6 | Aug. 1 | Tr. Pluto opposition N. Jupiter | 8 |
| Aug. 2 | Tr. Mars trine N. Saturn | 6 | Aug. 2 | Tr. Venus opposition N. Jupiter | 8 |
| Aug. 8 | Tr. Mercury sextile N. Mercury | 4 | Aug. 4 | Tr. Mars square N. Mercury | 4 |
| | Tr. Mars trine N. Venus | 6 | Aug. 8 | Tr. Venus opposition N. Uranus | 8 |
| Aug. 15 | Tr. Mercury sextile N. Mars | 4 | Aug. 17 | Tr. Mars square N. Mars | 4 |
| Aug. 21 | Tr. Venus conjunct N. Venus | 10 | Aug. 20 | Tr. Mercury opposition N. Jupiter | 8 |
| Aug. 31 | Tr. Neptune trine N. Jupiter | 6 | Aug. 21 | Tr. Sun conjunct N. Neptune | 10 |
| | Total | +42 | Aug. 24 | Tr. Sun square N. Sun | 4 |
| | | -68 | Aug. 31 | Tr. Neptune square N. Neptune | 4 |
| | Net aspect value | -26 | | Tr. Mars conjunct N. Neptune | 10 |
| | Therefore Buy | | | Total | -68 |

### Table 42. Major Aspects Between Transiting and Fairchild Natal Planets Oct. 1973 High.

| | Positive | Value | | Negative | Value |
|---|---|---|---|---|---|
| Oct. 1 | Tr. Venus conjunct N. Moon | 10 | Oct. 1 | Tr. Venus square N. Neptune | 4 |
| | Tr. Sun sextile N. Saturn | 4 | Oct. 10 | Tr. Sun conjunct N. Pluto | 10 |
| Oct. 2 | Tr. Mercury sextile N. Neptune | 4 | Oct. 19 | Tr. Mercury conjunct N. Mars | 10 |
| Oct. 3 | Tr. Venus trine N. Jupiter | 6 | Oct. 30 | Tr. Venus square N. Jupiter | 4 |
| Oct. 9 | Tr. Venus trine N. Uranus | 6 | | Total | -28 |
| Oct. 11 | Tr. Mercury conjunct N. Pluto | 10 | | | +90 |
| | Tr. Venus conjunct N. Sun | 10 | | Net aspect value | +68 |
| | Tr. Mercury conjunct N. Mercury | 10 | | Therefore Sell | |
| Oct. 20 | Tr. Mercury conjunct N. Moon | 10 | | | |
| Oct. 23 | Tr. Mercury trine N. Jupiter | 6 | | | |
| | Tr. Sun sextile N. Neptune | 4 | | | |
| Oct. 27 | Tr. Venus sextile N. Venus | 4 | | | |
| Oct. 31 | Tr. Mars trine N. Neptune | 6 | | | |
| | Total | +90 | | | |

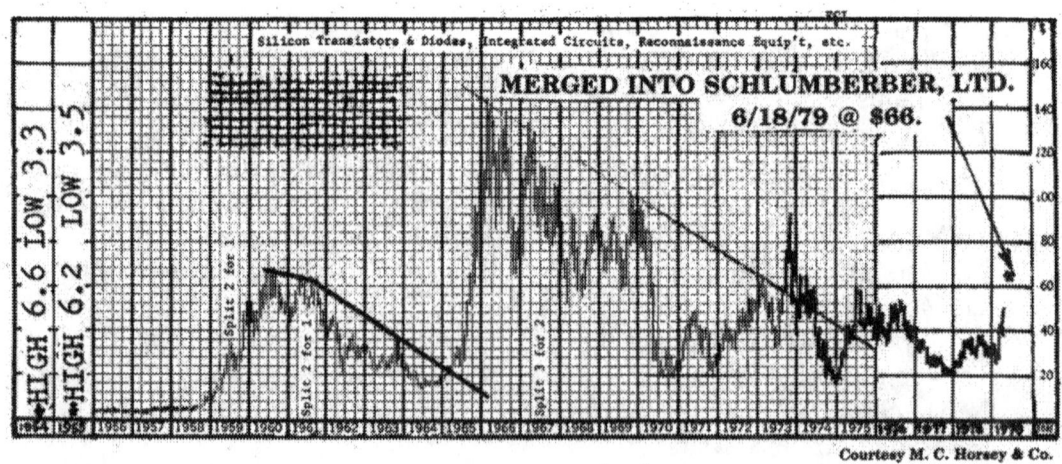

*Figure 57. Fairfield Camera and Instrument Company.*

**Table 43. Major Aspects Between Transiting and Fairchild Natal Planets December 1974 Low.**

| | Positive | Value | | Negative | Value |
|---|---|---|---|---|---|
| Dec. 1 | Tr. Mars trine N. Neptune | 6 | Dec. 1 | Tr. Neptune conjunct N. Saturn | 10 |
| | Tr. Venus sextile N. Venus | 4 | | Tr. Jupiter square N. Saturn | 4 |
| | Tr. Uranus sextile N. Neptune | 4 | | Tr. Sun conjunct n. Saturn | 10 |
| Dec. 2 | Tr. Mercury trine N. Uranus | 6 | Dec. 6 | Tr. Mercury conjunct N. Saturn | 10 |
| Dec. 3 | Tr. Mercury conjunct N. Sun | 10 | Dec. 10 | Tr. Mars square N. Neptune | 4 |
| Dec. 6 | Tr. Sun sextile N. Venus | 4 | Dec. 12 | Tr. Mars conjunct N. Sun | 10 |
| Dec. 10 | Tr. Mars trine N. Uranus | 6 | Dec. 16 | Tr. Sun square N. Jupiter | 4 |
| Dec. 11 | Tr. Mercury sextile N. Venus | 4 | Dec. 17 | Tr. Mercury square N. Jupiter | 4 |
| Dec. 13 | Tr. Venus trine N. Neptune | 6 | Dec. 19 | Tr. Saturn conjunct N. Pluto | 10 |
| Dec. 14 | Tr. Pluto sextile N. Saturn | 4 | Dec. 21 | Tr. Mercury square N. Uranus | 4 |
| Dec. 16 | Tr. Jupiter trine N. Mercury | 6 | Dec. 22 | Tr. Sun square N. Uranus | 4 |
| Dec. 21 | Tr. Mercury trine N. Neptune | 6 | Dec. 24 | Tr. Mars conjunct N. Saturn | 10 |
| | Tr. Sun trine N. Neptune | 6 | Dec. 26 | Tr. Venus opposition N. Pluto | 8 |
| | Total | +72 | Dec. 30 | Tr. Venus square N. Venus | 4 |
| | | −104 | Dec. 31 | Tr. Mercury opposition N. Pluto | 8 |
| | *Net aspect value* | −32 | | Total | −104 |
| | *Therefore Buy* | | | | |

Uranus, indicating that the company would be successful in a highly original and scientific field.

2. The Sun was in an unfavorable relationship to Neptune and Saturn, indicating that management's visionary ideas would be slow to materialize because of financial difficulties.

3. The company's ruling planet, Jupiter, was in a very favorable relationship to Mars and Uranus, indicating success in a scientific field and rising stock prices.

4. The Moon was widely conjunct the Sun, which was mildly favorable.

5. The Moon was favorably related to Mercury, Jupiter and Pluto, indicating favorable acceptance of the company's products.

6. The Moon and Mercury were unfavorably related to Mars, indicating friction between the business and scientific elements of management.

7. Venus was favorably related to Saturn, but unfavorably to Pluto, indicating success with conservative products, but losses on mass produced products.

## Summary

The planetary pattern at the time this company was reorganized (November 23, 1927) indicated that it would be successful in a highly technical field *that did not involve the production of products for the masses,* that its growth would be slow, and that the price of its stock would rise. The company consequently became a leader in the manufacture of highly sophisticated precision instruments and optical products for specialized applications.

## Postscript on October 31, 1981

Reference has been made to the January 20, 1970 target price of $138 for 1972-1974 by *Value Line*. This forecast was reiterated in *Value Line's* May 29, 1970 issue, but was reduced to $63 for 1974-1976 in the August 27, 1971 issue. (The stock had collapsed to $18 during the 1970 Bear Market.) The $63 target was maintained for 1976-1977 in the August 25, 1972 and November 24, 1972 issues, but was raised to $141 in the February 21, 1975 issue, $139 in the November 18, 1977 issue and $140 in the February 18 and May 18, 1979 issues. But these values never materialized, because the Sun square Neptune aspect in the natal chart indicated that management would have delusions of grandeur and Venus square Pluto indicated losses on mass-produced products, i.e., transistors, and digital watches, which required large capital investments in a highly competitive field.

Finally, it should be noted that the client purchased this stock before requesting an astro-analysis from the author. Should the client have purchased this stock? The answer is NO, for the following reasons:

a. The company's Saturn was *conjunct* the client's natal Sun.

b. The company's Uranus was *conjunct* the client's natal Moon.

c. The company's Uranus was *square* the client's natal Ascendant.

d. The company's Neptune was *square* the client's natal Sun.

Unfortunately, the author did not have the courage to break the bad news to the client. Whether the client took her loss before the 1970 debacle, the author does not know, because he moved to Florida the following year. This case illustrates the dilemma that astrological counselors have to face at times. Should you be an optimist and refrain from telling the client the bad news or should you give the client the bad news? This is something each astrologer must decide for himself or herself.

## Consolidated Edison Co. of N.Y.

This company is one of the premier electric utility companies in the world. The author had spent seven years in its Engineering Department and the next 36 years in its Purchasing Department before retiring in February 1963. It was incorporated in Albany, N.Y. on December 17, 1880 as The Edison Electric Illuminating Company of New York, at which time the planetary pattern was as shown in Figure 58. The analysis of the planetary pattern is as follows:

1. The Sun trine Saturn indicated the success of a new and long-term enterprise.

2. Jupiter, the company's ruling planet was in favorable aspect to Mercury, the planet of inventions, Venus, the planet of acquisitions, and Mars, the planet of energy, all of which were favorable to the success of the company and its growth through mergers (see Note 1).

3. Jupiter square the Moon, indicated opposition to the company's expansion, viz: public opposition to the 2,000,000 kilowatt pumped storage plant at Cornwall, New York, forced its abandonment after 10 years of controversy, and then the city of New York prohibited the building of any more power plants within the city limits.

4. Venus sextile Mars indicated successful mergers (see Note 1).

5. Mercury sextile Venus indicated success from inventions and business acumen.

6. Mercury conjunct Mars indicated breakdowns due to equipment malfunction (see Note 2).

7. Mars square Uranus indicated electrical failures (see Note 2 on page 179).

8. Uranus trine Neptune indicated success

---

Note 1. The history of the company indicated its successful acquisition of competing companies, beginning in 1895, when it absorbed three smaller companies; in May 1901 when it absorbed four more competitors and changed its name to The New York Edison Company; and on March 23, 1936, when all of the gas and electric companies in New York City and Westchester County were merged to form The Consolidated Edison Company of New York. (The gas business was started in 1825 by The New Amsterdam Gas Company, which ultimately became part of The Consolidated Gas Company, which also acquired its electric competitors.) But in the 1936 merger, it was the Edison Company which came out on top, because the revenues from electric service far surpassed that from gas.

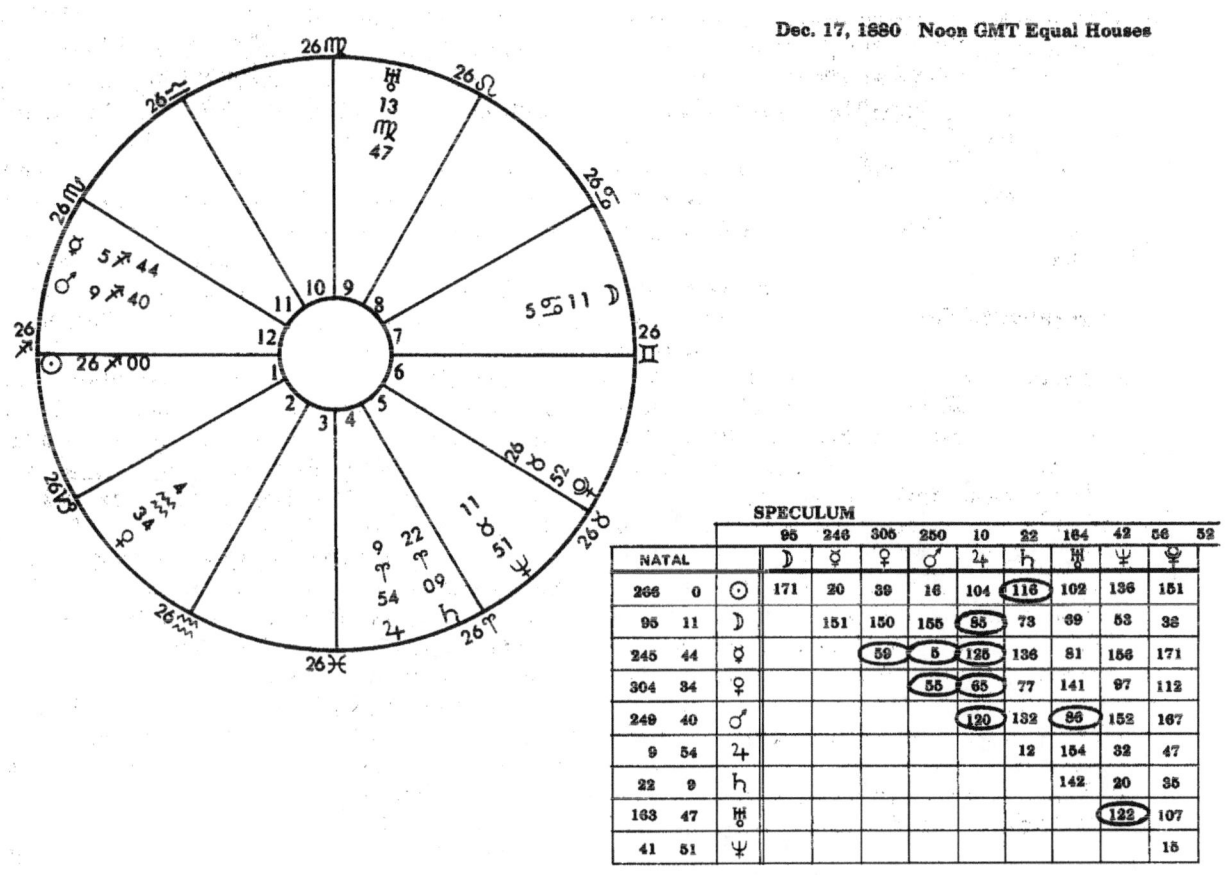

*Figure 58. Natal Chart of Consolidated Edison Company of New York.*

through new and original ideas and vision.

The *first* serious interruption of electric service occurred at 6:10 a.m. on January 2, 1890, when the original Pearl Street Station, which had been in continuous service since it was opened on September 4, 1882, was partially destroyed by fire.

The *second* major interruption of service and the most serious breakdown in more than half a century of operation occurred at 4:15 p.m. on January 15, 1936, when a short-circuit caused a fire in the Hell Gate Generating Station, resulting in loss of electric service to a large part of Manhattan north of 59th Street.

The *third* major service interruption was caused by the hurricane of September 21, 1938, and affected both gas and electric service. A tidal wave roared up the East River and flooded the basements of both electric and gas generating stations.

The *fourth* major interruption of electric service occurred at 2:56 p.m. on August 17, 1959, when 500,000 people in the Central Park area of Manhattan were affected. This was caused by the successive failures of 7 out of 20 underground cables supplying high voltage electricity

---

Note 2. In the early days of the company's history there were many electrical failures because the capacity of the fuses in the underground junction boxes fell to one-half or less than normal when subjected to the accumulated heat in the confined space of the underground "catch boxes." Thus, when a big thunderstorm arose and day was suddenly changed into night, the resulting overload when everyone turned on their lights, blew the fuses. In recent years, the fantastic growth of air conditioning has so overloaded the company's facilities as to cause brownouts and blackouts of electric service.

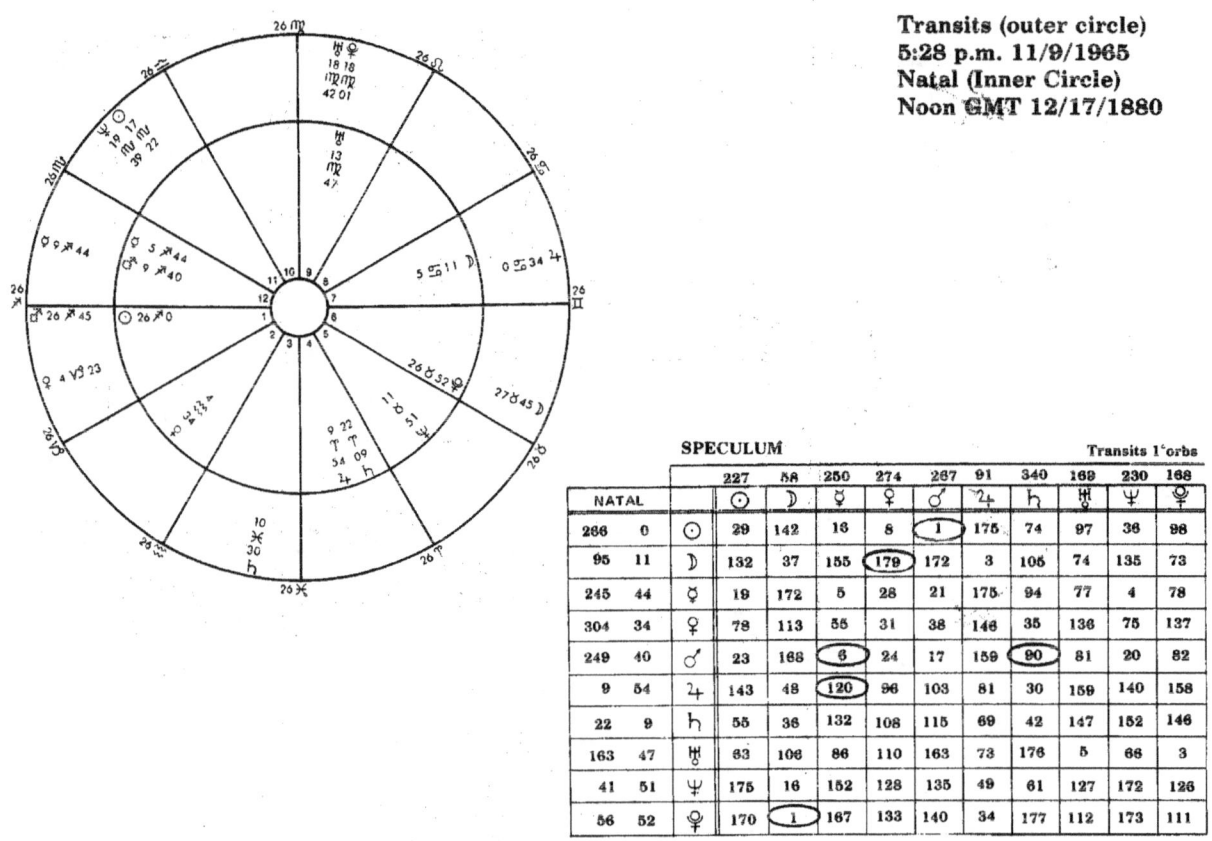

*Figure 59. Transits to Edison Natal Chart on November 9, 1965 Blackout.*

to the area during a violent geomagnetic storm, which also disrupted long distance radio transmission and triggered the disastrous earthquake in Yellowstone National Park.

*The fifth* major interruption of service occurred at 5:05 p.m. on June 13, 1961, blacking out a substantial part of mid-town Manhattan due to equipment failure in two substations,

The *sixth* major interruption of service occurred as a result of the biggest power failure in North America on November 9, 1965, which affected 30,000,000 people in an 80,000 square mile area of the northeastern United States and Canada. It originated in a substation of the Ontario Hydroelectric Commission near its Niagara Falls Hydroelectric Station. The Con-Edison System was shut down because of its System Operator's tardiness in disconnecting Con-Edison from the Niagara-Mohawk Electric Corporation, which was tied into the Ontario System.

This disaster led to a major shake-up in Con-Edison's top management, which is reflected in Figure 59.

As the speculum of Figure 59 shows, there were the following major aspects between the transiting planets of November 9, 1965 and the natal planets of December 17, 1880:

1. Transiting Mars conjunct natal Sun indicated damage to the company's reputation and to management. Top management was completely replaced shortly thereafter.

2. Transiting Moon conjunct natal Pluto indicated mass public inconvenience.

3. Transiting Mercury conjunct natal Mars indicated equipment damage. When power failed, the electric motor-driven oil pumps supplying oil to the generator bearings failed. Hence, the generator rotor, spinning at 3,600 revolutions per minute, burnt out the bearings,

and the heat generated at the bearings so distorted the generator shaft that the unit (the largest on the Edison System) was never able to furnish more than 80 percent of its capacity.

4. Transiting Venus opposition natal Moon indicated financial losses to the public.

5. Transiting Saturn square natal Mars, long-term or lasting damage to equipment.

6. The only positive aspect was transiting Mercury's trine to natal Jupiter, indicating that management's scientific expertise would foster the company's growth.

The *seventh* and most disastrous power blackout in the 95-year history of Con-Edison in terms of people involved (9,000,000) and potential claims for property damage, occurred at 9:34 p.m. EDST on the hot, humid night of July 13, 1977. It was triggered by a series of severe lightning strikes that took place during a violent thunderstorm that was moving across northern Westchester County, which knocked out several 345,000 volt overhead transmission lines that were supplying 40 percent of Con-Edison's load at the time.

The price history of this stock from 1941 to date (October 1981) is shown in Figure 60. Public utility stocks are for the conservative investor and the price fluctuations are not as violent as in more speculative stocks such as Fairchild, which we have previously reviewed. Thus, it took 23 years for Con-Edison's stock to rise from its World War II low of $5.75 in April 1942, to its high of $49 in January-February 1965. The planetary pattern for the December 1941 low is shown in Table 44.

The price of the stock then climbed to a post-World War II high of $18 in February 1946, reacted to $10.5 in 1947-1949, rose to a new high of $26 in August 1955, reacted to $20.5 in November 1957, and then climbed to an all-time high of $49 in January-February 1965. The planetary pattern for January 1965 is shown in Table 45.

After the peak in prices had been reached, a long-term decline started until April 23, 1974, when Con-Edison passed its quarterly dividend for the first time in its 83-year history. Panic selling ensued and the price of Con-Edison stock crashed from a high of 20 to a low of 9¾ during the month of April and sank to a low of 6 in June and September 1974 from which level the price began to rise in December 1974, as shown on Figure 60. The entire Public Utility Industry also "fell out of bed." The planetary pattern during December 1974 is shown in Table 46.

From the 1974 lows of $6, the price of the stock rose steadily for the next three years to $26 in January 1978, moved sideways for the following three years and is currently (November 2, 1981) selling for $32⅞ a share. The price will continue to rise as interest rates decline, but will fall again when interest rates go up.

Should the author have invested in this stock? Reference to Rule 16 gives a YES answer, for the midpoint of Edison's natal Venus-Jupiter was trine the author's Ascendant. On the other hand, Edison's natal Neptune, the planet of speculation, was opposition the author's natal Ascendant, a clear warning NOT to speculate in this stock! How did the author make out in his purchases of this stock? His first purchase was on September 17, 1973, of 200 shares at $21⅞. Succeeding purchases were made on a scale down until December 26, 1974, for a total of 1,000 shares at a cost of $11,263. Sales were made during the following year on a scale up, for a long-term capital gain of $3137 or 27.85 percent, plus $640 in dividends for a total return of $3777 or 33½ percent on the invested capital. All purchases were made for cash.

## Asarco (Formerly American Smelting & Refining Co.)

Although Asarco is primarily a producer of copper, lead and zinc, it is also the largest producer of silver in the United States, even though

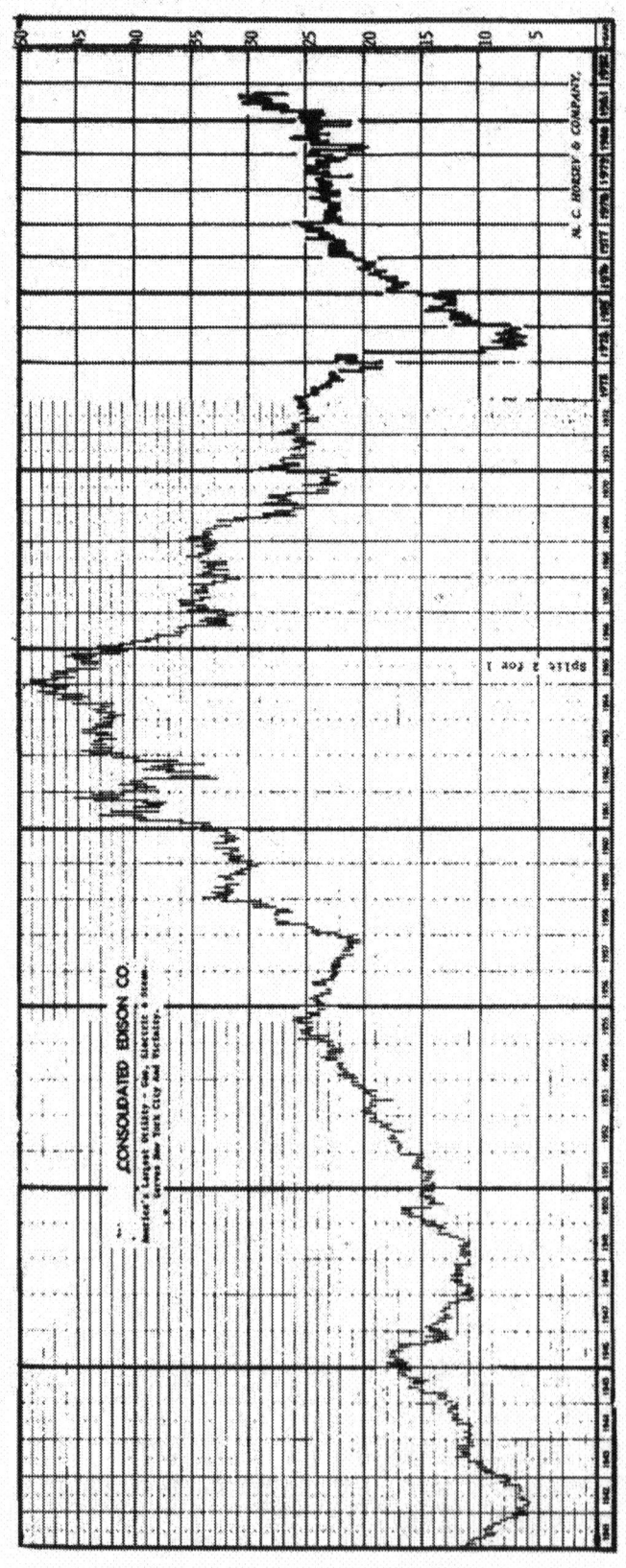

*Figure 60. Consolidated Edison Company Prices.*

**Table 44. Major Aspects Between Transiting and Natal Edison Planets Dec. 1941 Low.**

| | Positive | Value | | Negative | Value |
|---|---|---|---|---|---|
| Dec. 1 | Tr. Pluto trine N. Mercury | 6 | Dec. 1 | Tr. Sun opposition N. Sun | 8 |
| Dec. 6 | Tr. Mercury conjunct N. Mercury | 10 | Dec. 2 | Tr. Sun conjunct N. Mars | 10 |
| | | | Dec. 6 | Tr. Sun square N. Uranus | 4 |
| Dec. 11 | Tr. Venus conjunct N. Venus | 10 | Dec. 9 | Tr. Mercury conjunct N. Mars | 10 |
| Dec. 17 | Tr. Venus sextile N. Mars | 4 | Dec. 11 | Tr. Mercury square N. Uranus | 4 |
| Dec. 19 | Tr. Mercury conjunct N. Sun | 10 | Dec. 19 | Tr. Venus square N. Neptune | 4 |
| | Tr. Sun conjunct N. Sun | 10 | Dec. 23 | Tr. Mars conjunct N. Saturn | 10 |
| Dec. 30 | Tr. Mercury trine N. Uranus | 6 | Dec. 27 | Tr. Sun opposition N. Moon | 8 |
| | Total | +56 | Dec. 30 | Tr. Jupiter square N. Uranus | 4 |
| | | −72 | Dec. 31 | Tr. Uranus conjunct N. Pluto | 10 |
| | *Net aspect value* | −16 | | Total | −72 |
| | *Therefore Buy* | | | | |

**Table 45. Major Aspects Between Transiting and Natal Edison Planets January 1965 High.**

| | Positive | Value | | Negative | Value |
|---|---|---|---|---|---|
| Jan 1 | Tr. Uranus conjunct N. Uranus | 10 | Jan. 10 | Tr. Mars square N. Sun | 4 |
| Jan. 4 | Tr. Sun trine N. Uranus | 6 | Jan. 17 | Tr. Venus opposition N. Moon | 8 |
| Jan. 9 | Tr. Venus conjunct N. Sun | 10 | Jan. 18 | Tr. Mercury opposition N. Moon | 8 |
| | Tr. Mercury conjunct N. Sun | 10 | | Total | −20 |
| Jan. 15 | Tr. Mars trine N. Pluto | 6 | | | +62 |
| Jan. 23 | Tr. Venus trine N. Uranus | 6 | | *Net aspect value* | +42 |
| | Tr. Mercury trine N. Uranus | 6 | | *Therefore Sell* | |
| Jan. 26 | Tr. Sun sextile N. Mercury | 4 | | | |
| Jan. 30 | Tr. Sun sextile N. Mars | 4 | | | |
| | *Total* | +62 | | | |

**Table 46. Major Aspects Between Transiting and Edison Natal Planets Dec. 1974 Low.**

| | Positive | Value | | Negative | Value |
|---|---|---|---|---|---|
| Dec. 5 | Tr. Mercury sextile N. Venus | 4 | Dec. 1 | Tr. Venus square N. Uranus | 4 |
| Dec. 10 | Tr. Venus conjunct N. Sun | 10 | | Tr. Mercury conjunct N. Mercury | 10 |
| Dec. 11 | Tr. Mars sextile N. Venus | 4 | | Tr. Mercury opposition N. Pluto | 8 |
| Dec. 15 | Tr. Sun trine N. Saturn | 6 | Dec. 6 | Tr. Sun square N. Uranus | 4 |
| | Tr. Neptune trine N. Jupiter | 6 | | Tr. Jupiter square N. Mars | 4 |
| Dec. 18 | Tr. Sun conjunct N. Sun | 10 | Dec. 8 | Tr. Mercury conjunct N. Mars | 10 |
| Dec. 19 | Tr. Mercury conjunct N. Sun | 10 | Dec. 10 | Tr. Neptune conjunct N. Mars | 10 |
| Dec. 31 | Tr. Pluto sextile N. Mars | 4 | Dec. 11 | Tr. Mercury square N. Uranus | 4 |
| | Tr. Mercury trine N. Uranus | 6 | Dec. 18 | Tr. Venus opposition N. Moon | 8 |
| | *Total* | +60 | Dec. 25 | Tr. Mercury opposition N. Moon | 8 |
| | | | Dec. 28 | Tr. Sun opposition N. Moon | 8 |
| | | | Dec. 30 | Tr. Mars square N. Uranus | 4 |
| | | | Dec. 31 | Tr. Pluto opposition N. Jupiter | 8 |
| | | | | Tr. Jupiter opposition N. Uranus | 8 |
| | | | | Total | +60 |
| | | | | | −98 |
| | | | | *Net aspect value* | −38 |
| | | | | *Therefore Buy* | |

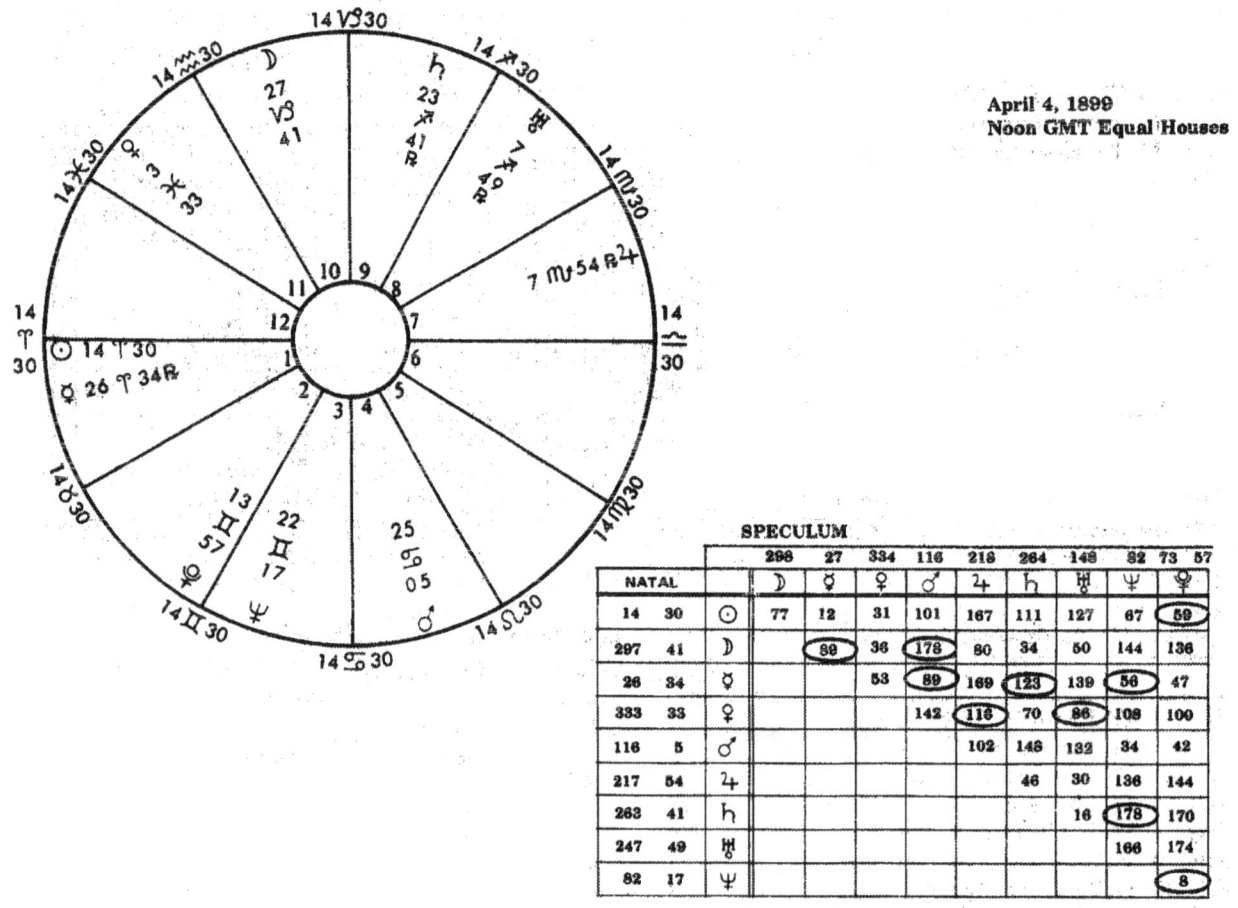

Figure 61. Natal Chart of Asarco.

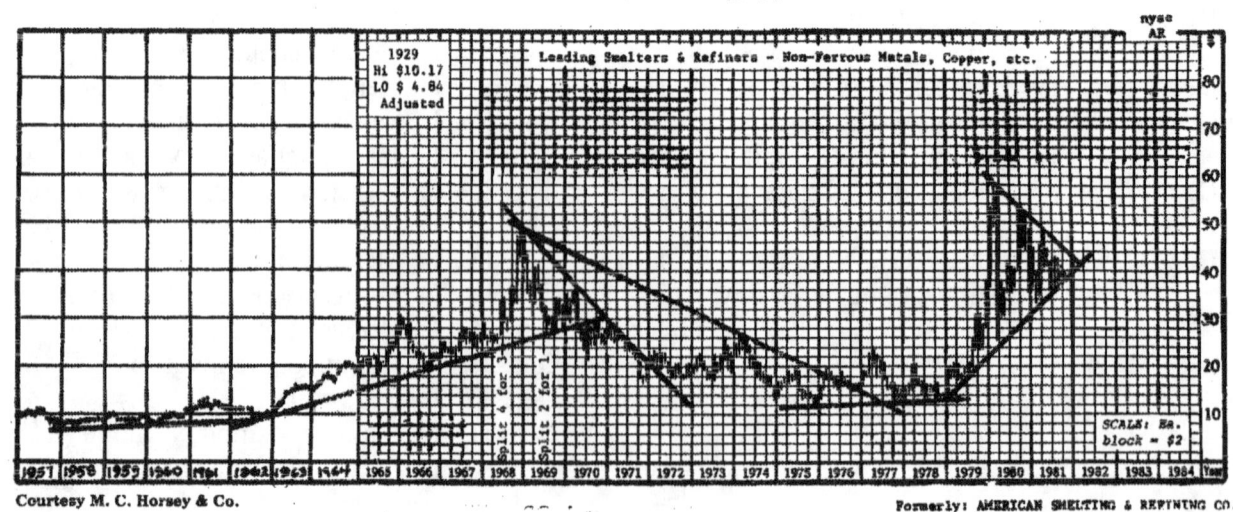

Figure 62. Asarco Prices.

**Table 47. Major Aspects Between Transiting and Natal Asarco Planets July 1962 Low.**

| | Positive | Value | | Negative | Value |
|---|---|---|---|---|---|
| July 1 | Tr. Pluto square N. Pluto | 4 | July 1 | Tr. Pluto sextile N. Jupiter | 4 |
| | Tr. Uranus trine N. Mercury | 6 | July 4 | Tr. Mercury opposition N. Saturn | 8 |
| July 4 | Tr. Mars sextile N. Mars | 4 | July 16 | Tr. Venus opposition N. Venus | 8 |
| July 6 | Tr. Mercury conjunct N. Venus | 10 | July 20 | Tr. Mars opposition N. Venus | 8 |
| July 7 | Tr. Venus trine N. Saturn | 6 | | Tr. Sun conjunct N. Mars | 10 |
| July 9 | Tr. Mercury sextile N. Mercury | 4 | July 21 | Tr. Sun opposition N. Moon | 8 |
| July 30 | Tr. Mercury trine N. Saturn | 6 | July 22 | Tr. Mercury opposition N. Moon | 8 |
| July 31 | Tr. Sun trine N. Uranus | 6 | July 24 | Tr. Venus square N. Pluto | 4 |
| | Total | +46 | July 25 | Tr. Mercury conjunct N. Mars | 10 |
| | | −76 | July 30 | Tr. Mercury square N. Jupiter | 4 |
| | Net aspect value | −30 | July 31 | Tr. Sun square N. Jupiter | 4 |
| | Therefore Buy | | | Total | −76 |

**Table 48. Major Aspects Between Transiting and Asarco Natal Planets Dec. 1968 High.**

| | Positive | Value | | Negative | Value |
|---|---|---|---|---|---|
| Dec. 1 | Tr. Pluto sextile N. Sun | 4 | Dec. 1 | Tr. Pluto square N. Saturn | 4 |
| | Tr. Neptune sextile N. Moon | 4 | Dec. 4 | Tr. Mars opposition N. Sun | 8 |
| | Tr. Neptune trine N. Mars | 6 | Dec. 12 | Tr. Mercury conjunct N. Saturn | 10 |
| | Tr. Sun conjunct N. Uranus | 10 | Dec. 15 | Tr. Sun conjunct N. Saturn | 10 |
| Dec. 2 | Tr. Mars trine N. Pluto | 6 | Dec. 26 | Tr. Mars square N. Moon | 4 |
| | Tr. Mercury conjunct N. Uranus | 10 | | Total | −36 |
| Dec. 8 | Tr. Venus conjunct N. Moon | 10 | | | +66 |
| Dec. 13 | Tr. Mars sextile N. Saturn | 4 | | Net aspect value | +30 |
| Dec. 29 | Tr. Sun sextile N. Jupiter | 4 | | Therefore Sell | |
| Dec. 30 | Tr. Venus sextile N. Saturn | 4 | | | |
| | Tr. Pluto sextile N. Mars | 4 | | | |
| | Total | +66 | | | |

this precious metal is obtained as a by-product of the production of the baser metals. The company is also the largest custom smelter of non-ferrous ores in the United States. It was incorporated on April 4, 1899 in Trenton, New Jersey, and its natal planetary pattern is shown in Figure 61. The analysis of this chart is as follows:

1. The Sun sextile Pluto indicated the success of the company in underground mining.

2. The Moon square Mercury indicated financial loss due to public antagonism. (The company had to spend enormous sums to meet government pollution standards.)

3. The Moon opposition Mars indicated public opposition to some of the company's actions.

4. Mercury square Mars indicated losses due to equipment breakdowns.

5. Mercury trine Saturn indicated financial gain through conservative business practices.

6. Mercury sextile Neptune indicated success in speculative enterprises.

7. Venus trine Jupiter indicated a successful financial future for the company.

8. Venus square Uranus indicated unexpected losses. (Pollution control expenditures.)

9. Mars, the ruling planet in Aries, indicated that the company would be a pioneer in its field.

10. Saturn opposition Neptune indicated a clash of views regarding speculative ventures.

**Table 49. Major Aspects Between Transiting and Asarco Natal Planets Dec. 1978 Low.**

| | Positive | Value | | Negative | Value |
|---|---|---|---|---|---|
| Dec. 1 | Tr. Sun conjunct N. Uranus | 10 | Dec. 3 | Tr. Mars opposition N. Neptune | 8 |
| Dec. 4 | Tr. Venus conjunct N. Jupiter | 10 | | Tr. Sun opposition N. Pluto | 8 |
| Dec. 23 | Tr. Jupiter trine N. Uranus | 6 | Dec. 4 | Tr. Mars conjunct N. Saturn | 10 |
| | Tr. Mars sextile N. Saturn | 4 | Dec. 16 | Tr. Sun conjunct N. Saturn | 10 |
| | Tr. Mars sextile N. Jupiter | 4 | Dec. 22 | Tr. Jupiter square N. Jupiter | 4 |
| Dec. 30 | Tr. Sun sextile N. Jupiter | 4 | | Tr. Saturn square N. Pluto | 4 |
| | Total | +38 | | Total | -44 |
| | | | | | +38 |
| | | | | Net aspect value | -6 |
| | | | | Therefore Buy | |

**Table 50. Major Aspects Between Transiting and Asarco Natal Planets Feb. 1980 High.**

| | *Positive* | *Value* | | *Negative* | *Value* |
|---|---|---|---|---|---|
| Feb. 1 | Tr. Pluto trine N. Neptune | 6 | Feb. 1 | Tr. Mars square N. Pluto | 4 |
| | Tr. Saturn trine N. Moon | 6 | Feb. 4 | Tr. Jupiter square N. Uranus | 4 |
| | Tr. Jupiter sextile N. Jupiter | 4 | Feb. 16 | Tr. Neptune opposition N. Neptune | 8 |
| Feb. 3 | Tr. Mercury sextile N. Saturn | 4 | Feb. 27 | Tr. Sun square N. Uranus | 4 |
| Feb. 8 | Tr. Saturn sextile N. Mars | 4 | Feb. 30 | Tr. Saturn square N. Saturn | 4 |
| Feb. 9 | Tr. Mercury conjunct N. Venus | 10 | Feb. 31 | Tr. Neptune conjunct N. Saturn | 10 |
| Feb. 12 | Tr. Mercury trine N. Jupiter | 6 | | Total | -34 |
| Feb. 13 | Tr. Sun sextile N. Saturn | 4 | | | +76 |
| Feb. 22 | Tr. Venus conjunct N. Sun | 10 | | Net aspect value | +42 |
| Feb. 23 | Tr. Sun conjunct N. Sun | 10 | | Therefore Sell | |
| Feb. 25 | Tr. Sun trine N. Mars | 6 | | | |
| Feb. 28 | Tr. Sun trine N. Jupiter | 6 | | | |
| | Total | +76 | | | |

11. Neptune conjunct Pluto indicated the speculative nature of underground mining.

As Figure 62 indicates, the price of this stock moved in a narrow channel, from a low of $7 in 1957, to a high of $13.5 in 1961, and then began a meteoric rise from a low of $9.5 in July 1962, to a high of $49.5 in December 1968. The planetary pattern for July 1962 is shown in Table 47, and for December 1968, in Table 48.

During the next seven years the price of Asarco stock declined from the December 1968 high of $49.5 to a low of $12 in November and December 1975, and then spent the next three years moving sideways between a low of $12 and a high of $23 until January 1979, when it began an explosive rise that carried the price from a low of $13 in December 1978, to a high of $58 in February 1980. (Silver made its all-time high of $48 on January 21, 1980.) The planetary pattern for December 1978 is shown in Table 49 and that for February 1980 in Table 50.

With the collapse of the silver market, the price of Asarco plummeted from the February 1980 high of $58 to a low of $26 in March 1980, recovered in September 1980 to $53 and then dropped to a low of $25⅝ in October 1981 (see Figure 62). The Bear Market in this stock is expected to end during the summer of 1982, when silver will bottom.

Should the author have invested in Asarco stock? Reference to Rule 13 gives a YES answer, for Asarco's natal Jupiter was trine the author's Moon. How well did he make out in his purchases of Asarco? He purchased 800 shares for cash in July 1979 at a cost of $18,173, and sold in December 1980 for a profit of $10,506 or a gain of 58 percent, plus $2,192 in dividends, for a total return of $12,698 or 70 percent on the invested capital! He did not sell at the February 1980 top, as that would have made his gains *short term* instead *of long term*, and would therefore have involved a higher federal income tax.

The observant reader may note that the author's purchase of Asarco stock was financially more rewarding than his earlier purchase of Con-Edison stock (70% vs. 33½%). The astrological reason for this is that in the case of Asarco, its natal Jupiter was trine the author's natal Moon, while in the case of Con-Edison, it was Edison's midpoint of natal Venus-Jupiter that was trine the author's natal Ascendant. The planetary pattern involving Asarco was much more favorable than that of Edison.

## Homestake Mining Company

Homestake Mining Company, the largest gold producer in North America, was incorporated at Sacramento, California on November 5, 1877, and the planetary pattern at that time is shown in Figure 63. The analysis of this pattern is as follows:

1. The Sun conjunct the Moon and Mercury indicated that the company would be a favorite with the public and be well-managed. It is considered to be the premier gold mining company in America and has been very successful. The company profits by using the latest and most efficient processes to work its low-grade ores.

2. The Sun trine Mars indicated favorable activity in the company's stock.

3. The Sun trine Saturn indicated that its management was conservative.

4. The Sun opposition Neptune indicated losses through speculative enterprises.

5. The Moon conjunct Mercury indicated that the public would profit. The price of the company's stock (prior to splits) climbed to $400 in 1934. The stock was split several times thereafter.

6. The Moon trine Mars and Saturn indicated that company would be a favorite with the public because of its conservative management and the rising prices of its stock.

7. Mercury opposition Neptune indicated losses through speculative enterprises. The company in recent years has branched out into oil and gas (ruled by Neptune) explorations.

8. Venus conjunct Jupiter indicated great success for the company.

9. Venus trine Uranus indicated the successful use of new and original ideas. The company will profit from an unexpected discovery of gold in a California mine.

10. Mars conjunct Saturn indicated the difficulty in profiting from low-grade ores.

11. Jupiter trine Uranus and Neptune indicated success through the application of new and original ideas, and eventually from oil and gas exploration.

12. Uranus square Pluto, the company's ruling planet, indicated that unexpected problems would arise in the production of uranium, whose price has fallen from $43 to $23.50 a pound, a six-year low.

As Figure 64 shows, the company's stock formed a 10-year base between a low of $5.2 in December 1956 to a high of $10 in July 1962, and back to a low of $5.8 in October 1966. It then rose to $14.9 in March 1968, tumbled down to $5.3 in December 1969, rose again to $10.55 in May 1971, dropped to $5.7 in November 1971, from whence it climbed to $46 in August 1974, concurrently with the rise in gold prices. The planetary pattern during the November 1971 low is shown in Table 51, while that during the August 1974 high is shown in Table 52.

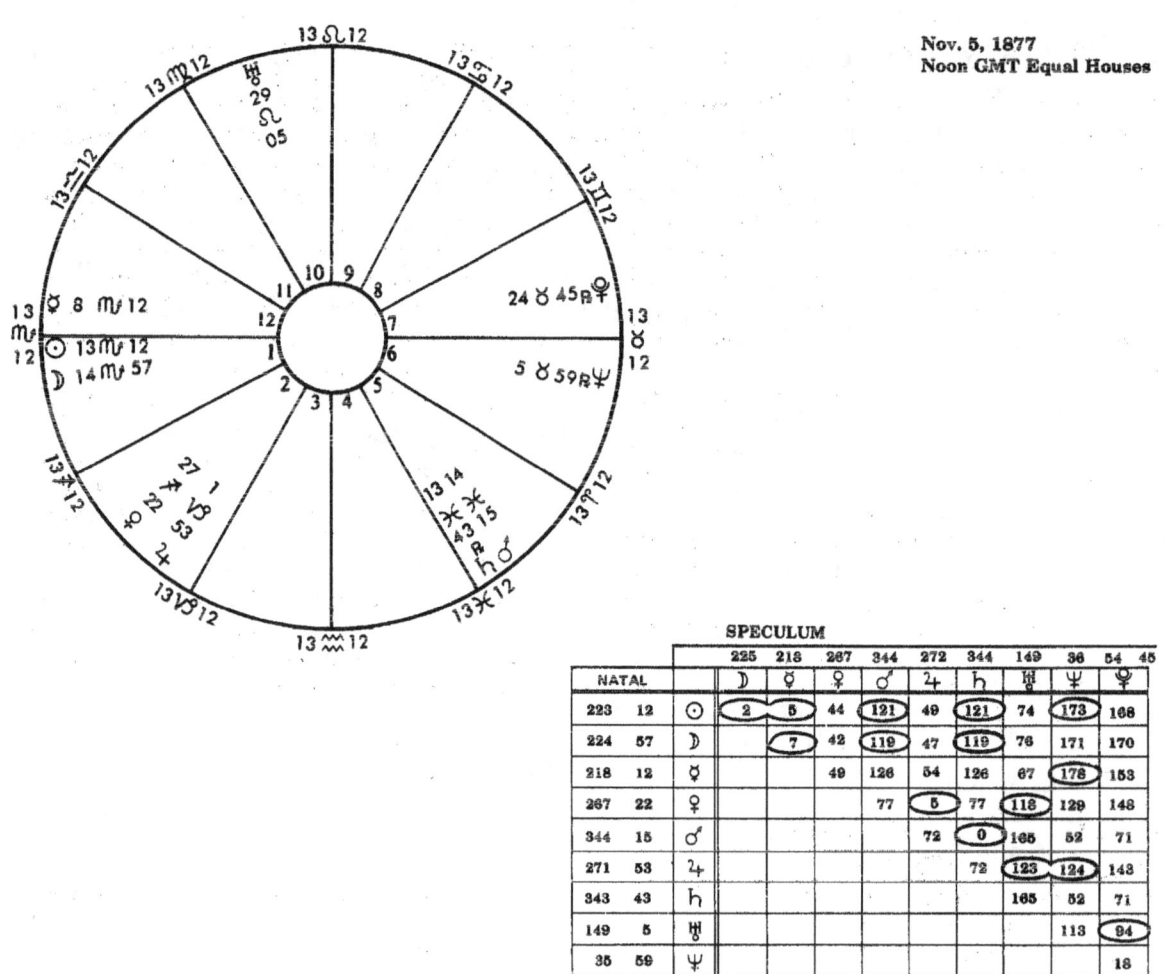

*Figure 63. Natal Chart of Homestake Mining Company.*

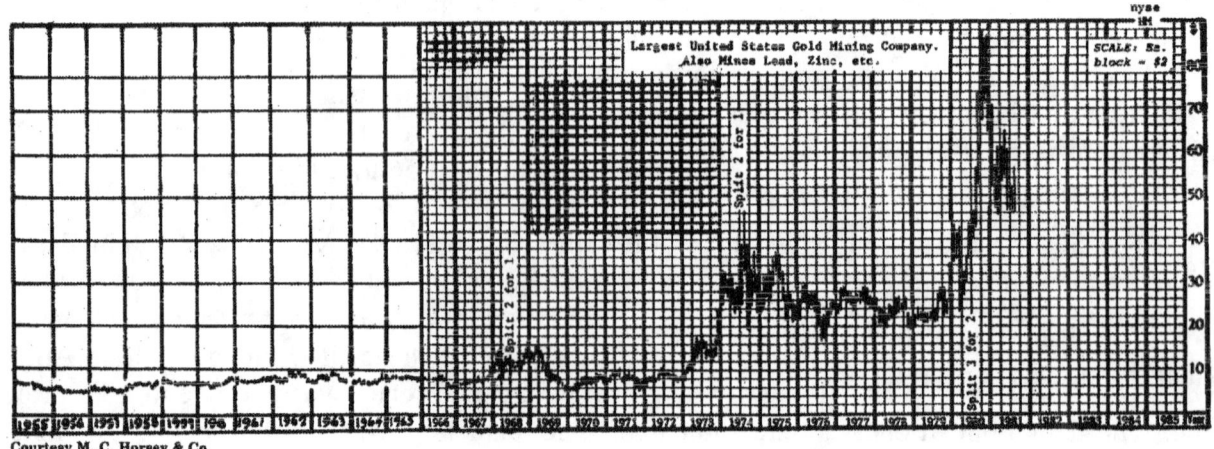

*Figure 64. Homestake Mining Company Prices.*

### Table 51. Major Aspects Between Transiting and Homestake Natal Planets Nov. 1971 Low.

| Date | Positive | Value | Date | Negative | Value |
|---|---|---|---|---|---|
| Nov. 1 | Tr. Mars sextile N. Venus | 4 | Nov. 1 | Tr. Pluto square N. Jupiter | 4 |
| | Tr. Sun conjunct N. Mercury | 10 | | Tr. Uranus conjunct N. Uranus | 10 |
| Nov. 7 | Tr. Sun conjunct N. Sun | 10 | | Tr. Venus opposition N. Pluto | 8 |
| Nov. 8 | Tr. Sun conjunct N. Moon | 10 | Nov. 2 | Tr. Mercury opposition N. Pluto | 8 |
| Nov. 10 | Tr. Mars sextile N. Jupiter | 4 | Nov. 4 | Tr. Mars opposition N. Uranus | 8 |
| Nov. 21 | Tr. Mars trine N. Mercury | 6 | Nov. 5 | Tr. Venus square N. Uranus | 4 |
| Nov. 27 | Tr. Venus conjunct N. Venus | 10 | Nov. 8 | Tr. Sun opposition N. Pluto | 8 |
| Nov. 29 | Tr. Venus trine N. Uranus | 6 | Nov. 17 | Tr. Mercury square N. Mars | 4 |
| Nov. 30 | Tr. Venus conjunct N. Jupiter | 10 | | Tr. Mercury square N. Saturn | 4 |
| | Tr. Mercury conjunct N. Venus | 10 | Nov. 22 | Tr. Sun square N. Uranus | 4 |
| | Total | +80 | Nov. 23 | Tr. Jupiter square N. Saturn | 4 |
| | | −90 | Nov. 28 | Tr. Jupiter square N. Mars | 4 |
| | *Net aspect value* | −10 | Nov. 30 | Tr. Mars conjunct N. Mars | 10 |
| | *Therefore Buy* | | | Tr. Mars conjunct N. Saturn | 10 |
| | | | | Total | −90 |

### Table 52. Major Aspects Between Transiting and Homestake Natal Planets Aug. 1974 High.

| Date | Positive | Value | Date | Negative | Value |
|---|---|---|---|---|---|
| Aug. 1 | Tr. Moon trine N. Jupiter | 6 | Aug. 1 | Tr. Sun square N. Mercury | 4 |
| | Tr. Venus trine N. Sun | 6 | Aug. 6 | Tr. Sun square N. Sun | 4 |
| Aug. 2 | Tr. Venus trine N. Moon | 6 | Aug. 7 | Tr. Sun square N. Moon | 4 |
| | Tr. Venus sextile N. Pluto | 4 | Aug. 8 | Tr. Mercury square N. Neptune | 4 |
| Aug. 3 | Tr. Mercury sextile N. Pluto | 4 | Aug. 10 | Tr. Mercury square N. Mercury | 4 |
| Aug. 6 | Tr. Saturn trine N. Moon | 6 | Aug. 11 | Tr. Mercury square N. Sun | 4 |
| Aug. 8 | Tr. Saturn trine N. Sun | 6 | Aug. 12 | Tr. Mercury square N. Moon | 4 |
| | Tr. Sun sextile N. Uranus | 4 | Aug. 18 | Tr. Mars opposition N. Mars | 8 |
| Aug. 9 | Tr. Mars sextile N. Mercury | | | Tr. Sun square N. Pluto | 4 |
| Aug. 12 | Tr. Mars sextile N. Sun | 4 | | Tr. Mercury square N. Pluto | 4 |
| Aug. 13 | Tr. Mercury sextile N. Uranus | 4 | Aug. 19 | Tr. Mars opposition N. Jupiter | 8 |
| Aug. 17 | Tr. Mars sextile N. Moon | 4 | | Tr. Venus square N. Neptune | 4 |
| Aug. 19 | Tr. Mercury trine N. Venus | 6 | Aug. 22 | Tr. Venus square N. Mercury | 4 |
| Aug. 21 | Tr. Sun trine N. Venus | 6 | | Tr. Mercury opposition N. Saturn | 8 |
| | Tr. Mercury trine N. Jupiter | 6 | | Tr. Mercury opposition N. Mars | 8 |
| | Tr. Jupiter trine N. Moon | 6 | Aug. 26 | Tr. Venus square N. Sun | 4 |
| Aug. 25 | Tr. Sun trine N. Jupiter | 6 | | Tr. Jupiter conjunct N. Mars | 10 |
| | Tr. Mercury sextile N. Mercury | 4 | Aug. 27 | Tr. Venus square N. Moon | 4 |
| Aug. 27 | Tr. Mercury sextile N. Sun | 4 | Aug. 30 | Tr. Jupiter conjunct N. Saturn | 10 |
| Aug. 28 | Tr. Mercury sextile N. Moon | 4 | | Total | −104 |
| | Tr. Sun trine N. Neptune | 6 | | | +116 |
| | Tr. Venus sextile N. Uranus | 4 | | *Net aspect value* | +12 |
| Aug. 31 | Tr. Jupiter trine N. Moon | 6 | | *Therefore Sell* | |
| | Total | +116 | | | |

**Table 53. Major Aspects Between Transiting and Homestake Natal Planets Aug. 1976 Low.**

| | *Positive* | *Value* | | *Negative* | *Value* |
|---|---|---|---|---|---|
| Aug. 1 | Tr. Mars sextile N. Moon | 4 | Aug. 1 | Tr. Saturn square N. Neptune | 4 |
| | Tr. Mercury trine N. Neptune | 6 | | Tr. Mars opposition N. Mars | 8 |
| Aug. 2 | Tr. Mercury trine N. Venus | 6 | | Tr. Mars opposition N. Saturn | 8 |
| Aug. 9 | Tr. Mercury sextile N. Mercury | 4 | Aug. 4 | Tr. Venus square N. Pluto | 4 |
| Aug. 12 | Tr. Mercury sextile N. Sun | 4 | Aug. 8 | Tr. Mercury square N. Venus | 4 |
| Aug. 13 | Tr. Mercury sextile N. Moon | 4 | Aug. 11 | Tr. Saturn square N. Mercury | 4 |
| Aug. 15 | Tr. Mars trine N. Sun | 6 | Aug. 12 | Tr. Mercury opposition N. Saturn | 8 |
| | Tr. Venus sextile N. Mercury | 4 | | Tr. Mercury opposition N. Mars | 8 |
| Aug. 19 | Tr. Mercury sextile N. Sun | 4 | Aug. 14 | Tr. Jupiter square N. Mercury | 4 |
| | Tr. Mercury sextile N. Moon | 4 | Aug. 17 | Tr. Sun square N. Pluto | 4 |
| Aug. 20 | Tr. Sun trine N. Venus | 6 | Aug. 19 | Tr. Venus opposition N. Saturn | 8 |
| Aug. 23 | Tr. Uranus sextile N. Jupiter | 4 | | Tr. Venus opposition N. Mars | 8 |
| Aug. 28 | Tr. Venus trine N. Pluto | 6 | Aug. 30 | Tr. Venus square N. Mercury | 4 |
| Aug. 29 | Tr. Sun trine N. Neptune | 6 | | *Total* | −76 |
| | *Total* | +68 | | | +68 |
| | | | | *Net aspect value* | −8 |
| | | | | *Therefore Buy* | |

**Table 54. Major Aspects Between Transiting and Homestake Natal Planets Oct. 1980 High.**

| | *Positive* | *Value* | | *Negative* | *Value* |
|---|---|---|---|---|---|
| Oct. 1 | Tr. Mercury sextile N. Jupiter | 4 | Oct. 3 | Tr. Mercury opposition N. Neptune | 8 |
| | Tr. Sun sextile N. Venus | 4 | Oct. 4 | Tr. Mars opposition N. Pluto | 8 |
| Oct. 2 | Tr. Jupiter trine N. Pluto | 6 | Oct. 7 | Tr. Saturn square N. Jupiter | 4 |
| Oct. 3 | Tr. Venus trine N. Venus | 6 | Oct. 17 | Tr. Venus opposition N. Mars | 8 |
| Oct. 7 | Tr. Venus trine N. Neptune | 6 | | Tr. Venus opposition N. Saturn | 8 |
| | Tr. Mercury conjunct N. Mercury | 10 | Oct. 27 | Tr. Sun Oppositon N. Neptune | 8 |
| Oct. 11 | Tr. Venus trine N. Jupiter | 6 | Oct. 28 | Tr. Venus square N. Venus | 4 |
| Oct. 12 | Tr. Venus sextile N. Mercury | 4 | Oct. 31 | Tr. Uranus opposition N. Pluto | 8 |
| | Tr. Sun sextile N. Jupiter | 4 | | Tr. Jupiter square N. Jupiter | 4 |
| | Tr. Mercury trine N. Mars | 6 | | Tr. Mars square N. Saturn | 4 |
| | Tr. Mercury trine N. Saturn | 6 | | Tr. Venus square N. Jupiter | 4 |
| | Tr. Mercury conjunct N. Sun | 10 | | *Total* | −68 |
| Oct. 13 | Tr. Mercury conjunct N. Moon | 10 | | | +110 |
| Oct. 16 | Tr. Venus sextile N. Sun | 4 | | *Net aspect value* | +42 |
| Oct. 17 | Tr. Venus sextile N. Moon | 4 | | *Therefore Sell* | |
| Oct. 26 | Tr. Venus trine N. Pluto | 6 | | | |
| Oct. 31 | Tr. Sun conjunct N. Mercury | 10 | | | |
| | Tr. Mars sextile N. Uranus | 4 | | | |
| | *Total* | +110 | | | |

During 1974, gold had risen from $114.75 an ounce on January 2, to $197.50 an ounce on December 30, in anticipation of the U.S. Government action on January 1, 1975 to permit American citizens to own gold for the first time since 1934, when President Franklin D. Roosevelt prohibited such ownership. But, when the public did not rush to buy gold after January 1, 1975, the price of gold dropped to $103.50 an ounce on August 25, 1976. The price of Homestake stock followed the price of gold and dropped from the August 1974 high of $46 to a low of $16.6 in August 1976 per Figure 64. It moved sideways during the next three years and then skyrocketed from a low of $19.8 in January 1979 to a high of $88 in October 1980 under the influence of frenzied buying. The planetary pattern during the August 1976 low is shown in Table 53, and that for the October 1980 high in Table 54.

From its October 1980 high of $88, Homestake dropped to a Double Bottom of $46 in March and September 1981. *The Wall Street Journal* of November 6, 1981 gave the past 52 weeks range as 86⅞ High 42¼ Low. The closing price on November 5, 1981 was 43⅜. Since gold is in a Bear Market until the summer of 1982, it is expected that Homestake will continue its decline until that time.

## Conclusion

In this chapter, the reader has been taught how to determine who should invest or speculate in the stock market, which stocks to BUY, when to BUY and when to SELL, illustrated by four sample corporations, viz:

1. A typical highly speculative and volatile stock—Fairchild Camera & Instrument Corp.

2. A conservative Public Utility company—Con-Edison of New York.

3. The largest U.S. silver producer, Asarco.

4. The largest U.S. gold producer, Homestake.

All aspects between transiting and natal planets allow for a 1.5 degree orb. Only the five major aspects, viz: conjunction, sextile, square, trine, and opposition are considered. The minor aspects, such as 30, 45, 135, 150 degrees, are omitted, since experience has shown that they tend to offset each other. The transiting Moon is omitted; its action is too fleeting since it moves so fast.

The basic thought to keep in mind is that there is a preponderance of positive aspects at market highs, when everyone is optimistic and expects that the sky is the limit—that is the time to SELL and take your profit. Do not let greed cheat you out of your hard-won gains. Conversely, there is a preponderance of negative aspects at market lows, when everyone is pessimistic and expects the bottom to fall out of the market—that is the time to have the courage to BUY.

By following the simple rules described herein, the author has, over the past 23 years, made average gains of 25 percent annually by purchasing stocks for cash only. The reader can probably do even better. But—don't gamble.

## Chapter 14

# Epilogue

### Review of Parts I and II

Part I traced the slow progress of scientific acceptance of the theory advanced by Sir William Herschel in 1801 that sunspot activity affected the yield of agricultural products in England and thus their prices. In the 180 years that have elapsed since then, scientists and economists have finally accepted the evidence that sunspot activity is caused by planetary patterns, which can be predicted in advance. The correlation of certain planetary patterns, with the ups and downs of the American Business Cycle, has provided a more accurate means of forecasting turning points in business activity.

Part II dealt in detail with the correlation between certain planetary cycles and the stock market cycle. In addition to teaching the reader how to forecast the stock market cycle, he or she has been taught how to determine which stock to buy, as well as when to buy and sell. Several examples have been exhaustively analyzed. Now for a word of caution.

### Buying on Margin

The author does not recommend buying stocks on *margin*, i.e., borrowing money from the broker for the difference between the amount deposited and the price of the stock, including the broker's commission. While buying on margin offers unlimited potential for profit if the speculator guesses right, it also offers unlimited potential for losses if he guesses wrong. Never gamble with more than you can afford to lose. When the author first began to buy stocks in 1924, the margin (or deposit) required was only 10 percent of the purchase price of the stock. During the next 22 years, the margin varied from a minimum of 10 percent to a maximum of 50 percent. After 22 years of buying on margin through one brokerage house, the author closed out his account with a net loss of $620.75! The capital employed rose from $390 on February 27, 1924 to $12,199 on May 17, 1943. The author considers himself lucky with having lost only $620 over a period of 22 years. The margin requirement for 5,000 ounces of silver worth $42,900 (silver at $8.58 per oz.) is $3,000. For a 100 Troy ounce of gold worth $411.50 (gold at $411.50 per oz.) it is $1,500.

### Short-selling

Short-selling is selling something you do *not* own in hope of buying it back at a lower price. If the price goes below the selling price, the short-seller has made a profit; if it goes above the selling price and the short-seller is forced to buy back the stock at the higher price, he suffers a loss. The author has never sold short and does *not* advise short-selling since he considers such action as unethical. While short-selling is legal in the U.S., it is illegal in West Germany. *The Wall Street Journal* of November 10, 1981, stated: "Germany, for one, is straitlaced about the perfectly respectable American practice of short-selling, or selling borrowed stock in hope of replacing it with stock acquired later at a lower price. When Merrill Lynch & Co. tried to collect money owed it by a German customer who ran up losses, a German court ruled that his short-selling was nothing more than gambling, a debt for which is legally uncollectible. The Court even ordered Merrill Lynch to return the customer's collateral." In the U.S. there is a saying: "He who sells what isn't his'n, must pay or go to pris'n."

## Stock Options (Puts and Calls)

A call option is a contract permitting the holder to buy a set amount of a stock at a fixed price within a particular period of time. A put option is a contract that permits the holder to sell a set amount of a stock within a given time period. The call option buyer makes money when the price of the stock rises, while the put option buyer only makes money when the stock price declines. For example, suppose a stock is selling for $20 a share and you think the price is going higher. So you buy a call option at $20, which may cost you $2 share. If the price of the stock goes up to $30 (for a gain of 50 percent), you exercise your option to buy at $20 and then sell it at $30 for a gain of $10 less the $2 cost of the option, for a gain of 400 percent. Thus, while the stock has only gone up 50 percent, the call option buyer has made 400 percent on his investment. However, if the stock falls below $20 by the time set for the expiration of the option, the call option buyer has lost his entire investment of $2 per share.

Experience has shown that most option traders lose money on balance. They shoot for large, highly leveraged profits, and in return run the risk of losing their entire capital. One trader, who ran an investment of $5,000 up to almost a million dollars over a period of two years was suddenly wiped out when the market turned against him. The experience was so traumatic that he lost his voice for three months. When the author met him some time later and asked him what had gone wrong, the trader sheepishly answered: "I got overconfident, overextended myself, and got cleaned out." The author does not recommend trading in stock options.

## Interest Rates

Although the Foundation for the Study of Cycles has postulated a 54-year cycle in English interest rates over the period 1729-1978, with an ideal high in 1978, they caution that there is a possibility that there is also a 60-year cycle at work, per *Cycles* of August 1980. In the October 1957 issue of *Cycles,* Edward R. Dewey of the Foundation correctly concluded: "As far as our knowledge of cycles goes, the indication is for generally upward interest rates for the next 20 years." See Figure 65.

The fluctuations in interest rates during the past decade has been so erratic that one prominent investment manager is quoted in the November 11, 1981 issue of *The Wall Street Journal,* as follows: "Pension managers think interest rates are attractive, but they're sick and tired of seeing volatility. Bonds are supposed to be nice, comfortable, high quality staid old ladies. Instead, they're wild young things that go all over the place." He therefore recommends a simple immunization strategy that was the subject of a classic paper in 1952. An immunization bond portfolio would consist of long-term bonds, which would rise in market value as interest rates fell and thus offset the decline in Treasury Note yields to lock in the original yield goal. The investment manager says, "An immunized bond portfolio is like a basket of apples and oranges—a precise mix of longer and shorter-term securities. If you aren't making it on the apples, you're making, it on the oranges. The sum of apples and oranges gives you what you need."

General Motors Corp. has directed its money managers to place about $2 billion of bond investments in contingent-immunization portfolios.

After having been "massacred" in October 1979, the bond market is currently enjoying a sharp rally under the influence of declining interest rates. Its future course will depend on whether or not inflation is brought under control. The author does not recommend trading in bonds.

## Interest Rate Futures

*The Wall Street Journal* on October 18, 1981, had a headline feature, "Uncertainty over Direction of Interest Rates Attracts Investors to Financial Futures Market." That market trades contracts for the future delivery of securities such as Treasury bills or notes. The allure of the financial-futures market largely reflects its dual ability to let speculators gamble to make fast profits, while letting cautious investors protect themselves from the turmoil in today's money markets.

For a speculator, there isn't any way to avoid high risk in interest rate futures. Initial margin, or cash, demands are small—as little as $2,000 can control a 90-day Treasury bill with a face value of $1 million—so an investor doesn't have to be rich to have enormous potential liability. And frantic price movements in today's volatile money markets can multiply—or erase—his margin in minutes. Because of the risks, brokers and traders recommend that investors open a financial-futures account with a minimum of $5,000 or $10,000—all of it risk capital—and have at least 10 times that in net liquid assets,

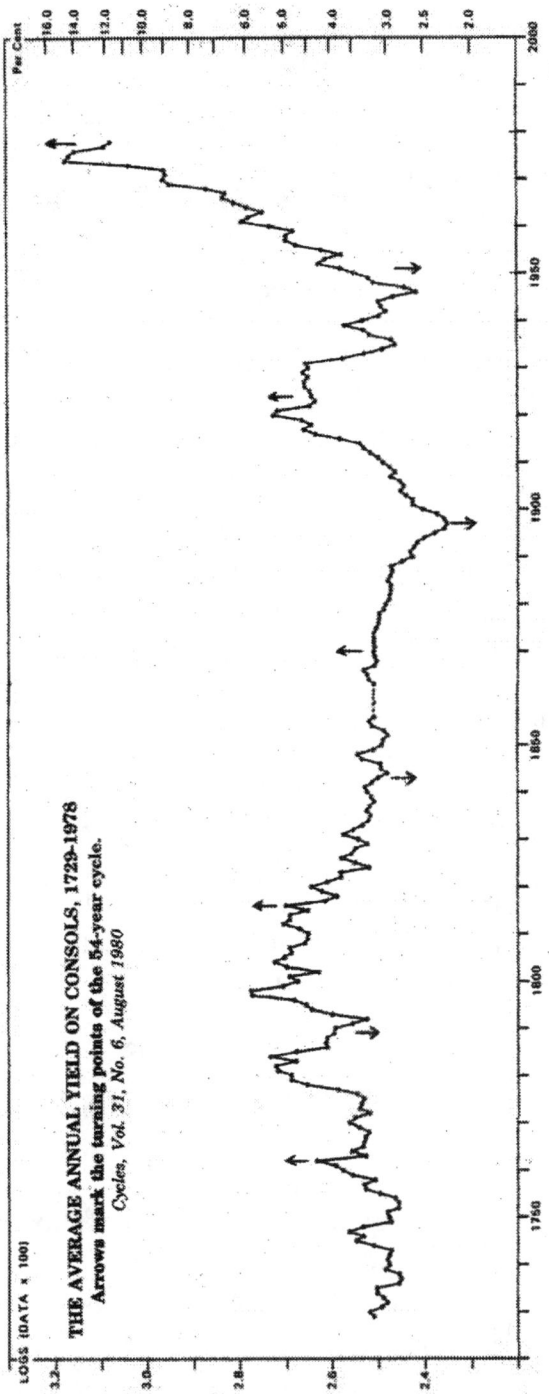

Figure 65. The Average Annual Yield on Consols 1729-1978.

backing their stake. "And if you lose that $6,000 you should quit, because you're no good and neither is your broker," says a financial-futures specialist.

*The Wall Street Journal* of November 12,

1981 had this headline: "Futures Pros Miss the Rally in Bonds, Bills." It went on to say that many professional traders, who make their living anticipating what the market will do, guessed wrong. The trading pits of the Chicago Board of Trade and the Chicago Mercantile Exchange are filled with traders who have survived by using tactics that work only as long as interest rates are rising. Now, many traders can't change their thinking or their strategies fast enough to exploit declining interest rates. Bond prices have risen 11 percent from the pre-rally levels of late October 1981 (see Figure 65).

Donald A. Bradley, in *Stock Market Prediction* (1948), stated: 'The first recorded mention of applying astrological dynamics to the problem of business forecasting in modern times appears to have been in 1543, during the Renaissance. Christopher Kurz of Antwerp, we are told, had devised an astronomical system for predicting the course of the money market. Ever since the attempts of Kurz, which were mildly successful, ambitious individuals have tried to contrive methods for predicting stock market movements through astrology." The author does not recommend gambling in the money markets.

### Kondratieff Wave Misconceptions

In Chapter 2, mention was made of a 47-60 year cycle in economic activity, known as the Kondratieff Wave, after its discoverer, the Russian economist N. D. Kondratieff. The following article by the author is reproduced from *Issue* of July 17, 1981, with the permission of Sinclair Securities Company, New York.

During the past ten years, increasing numbers of investment advisers have jumped aboard the Prophets of Doom bandwagon, using as their basis an erroneous interpretation of The Kindratieff Wave as enunciated in a book with that title published in 1972 by two American writers, J. B. Shuman and David Rosenau. The authors arbitrarily assumed a 50-year wave length and their uncritical followers contributed to the sharp but brief stock market declines that became known as 'The October 1978 Massacre', 'The October 1979 Massacre' and 'The April 1980 Massacre'. After each such 'massacre', the broad stock market averages recovered to make new all-time highs. The exception was the Dow Jones Industrial Average, which seems to be unable to stay very long above the psychological barrier of 1000.

"Just what is the Kondratieff Wave? It represents a theory advanced in 1919-1921 by the late Russian economist Nicholai D. Kondratieff to the effect that there is a long wave in economics. The wave was named for him. His first wave began in 1789, peaked in 1814, and ended in 1849, giving a cycle length of 60 years. The second wave began in 1849, peaked in 1864, and ended in 1896, giving a cycle length of 47 years. The third wave began in 1896, and peaked in 1920; it ended in 1932, giving a cycle length of only 36 years. Because Kondratieff's theory contradicted Marxist ideology, he was exiled to Siberia and was never heard from thereafter.

"Although neither Kondratieff nor his most eminent American supporter, Professor Joseph A. Shumpeter of Harvard University, ever gave a definite length to the Kondratieff Wave, Shuman and Rosenau arbitrarily assumed a wave length of 50 years, on the basis of which they constructed a theoretical model of business activity which reasonably fit the two and one-half waves peaking in 1814, 1864 and 1920. Shuman and Rosenau omitted any reference to the American Revolutionary War, World War II, the Korean War, and the Vietnam War; they arrived at the following erroneous conclusions:

"If we overlay our model on actual prices from the World War I peak to the present (1972), we find that it conforms well from the peak (which actually occurred in 1920, just after the War) to the late 1930s. However, after nearly two decades of a declining price trend, a combination of New Deal programs and huge armament expenditures that began just prior to World

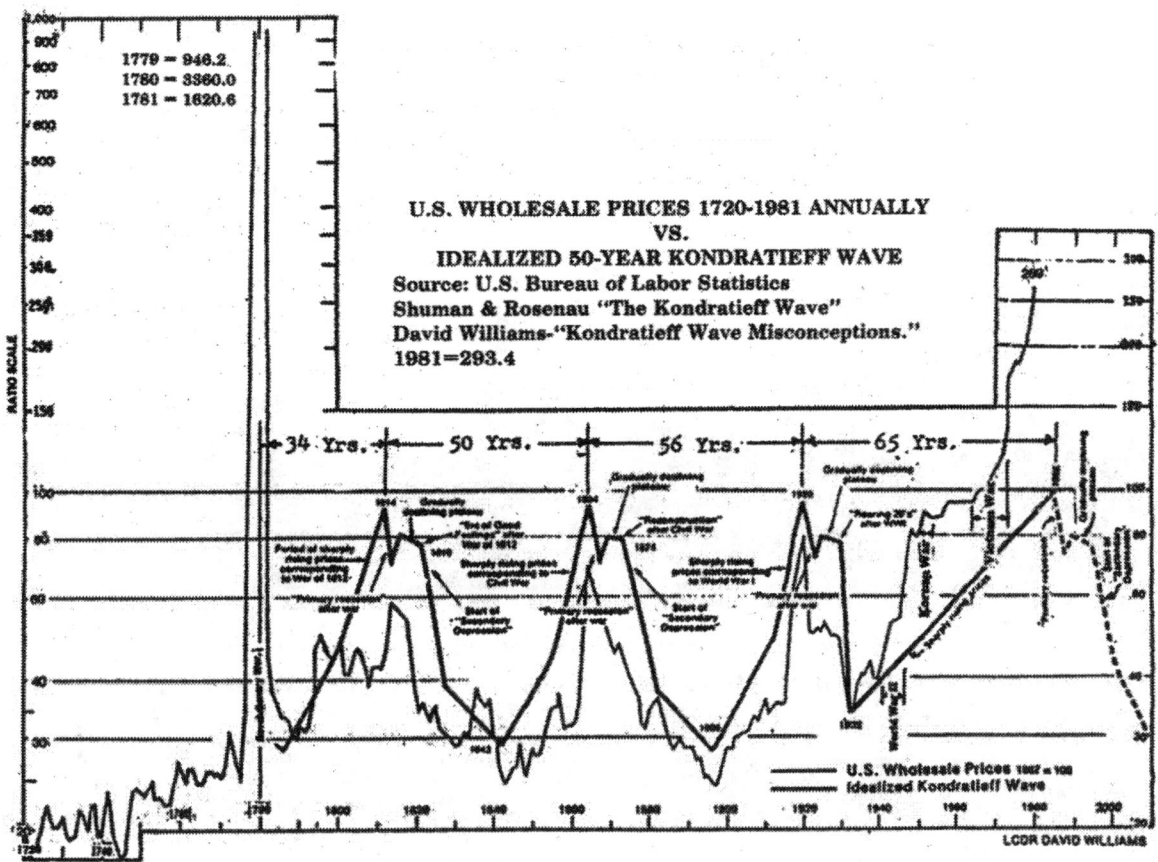

*Figure 66. U.S. Wholesale Prices vs. Idealized Kondratieff Wave.*

War II (probably chiefly the latter) the trend reversed about a decade early. The model indicates that the trend should have reversed in 1950. Actually it did so about ten years earlier. From 1950 on, however, the model resumes its accuracy. There are two decades of gradually rising prices, with another sharp peak (the fourth in a row) predicted for about 1970, following a period of sharply rising prices." But that is not what history records.

Where did Shuman and Rosenau go astray? Firstly, they ignored the inflation during the Revolutionary War, which forced U.S. Wholesale Prices up to 3360 (index 1967 = 100) in 1780, with a corresponding reduction in the purchasing power of the Continental dollar. Warren and Pearson, in *Prices*, record that in *May 1781 one dollar of hard money exchanged for $400 to $1,000 of paper currency.* In 1790 Congress redeemed the outstanding Continental currency at the rate of one cent on the dollar, from which rose the expression "not worth a continental."

Secondly, Shuman and Rosenau attempted to predict the future course of the economy on the basis of only 2½ cycles. But, as all students of cycles know, that is not a valid basis. As Figure 66 shows, the time spans between cycle peaks were: 34, 50, 56, and 65 years, which average out to 51¼ years. Students of the sunspot cycle know that you cannot predict the length of the next sunspot cycle from the average of 11 years throughout the past two centuries, when the actual cycle length has varied from a minimum of eight years to a maximum of 16 years. In Figure 66, the minimum was 34 years and the maximum is expected to be 65 years (to 1985).

By omitting any consideration of the Revolutionary War period, Shuman and Rosenau

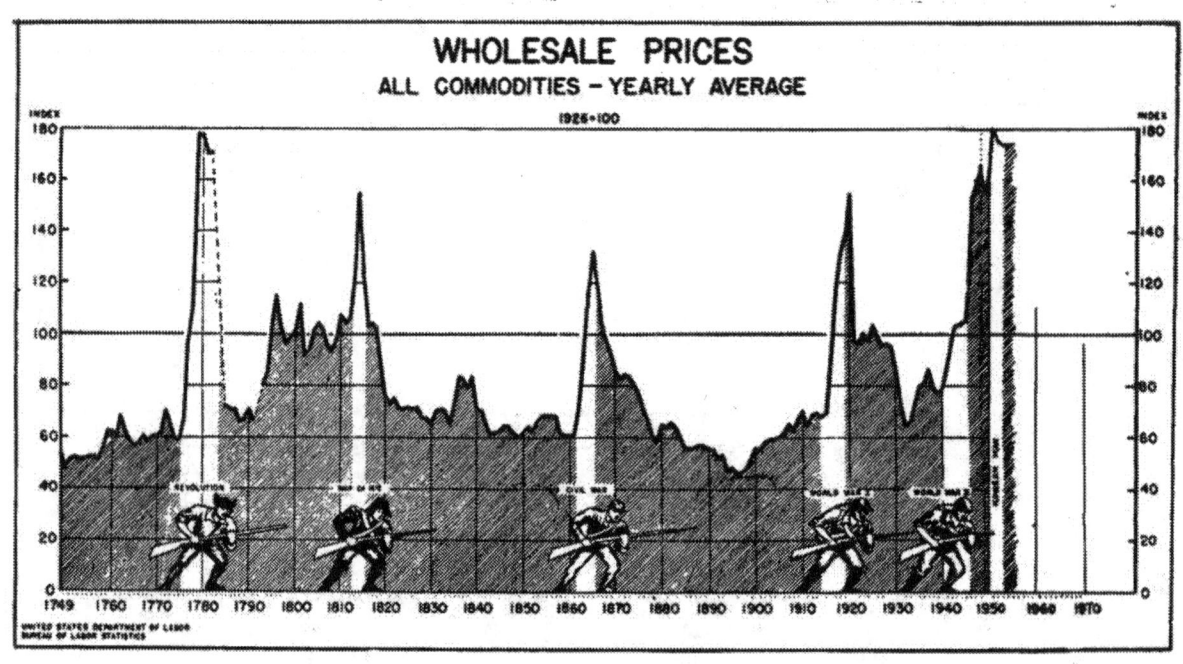

*Figure 67. Wholesale Pries, All Commodities, Yearly Average, 1926 = 100.*

(who are not economists) made the same mistake as the professional economists of Montgomery Ward did in 1948, when they advised Sewell Avery, then the Board Chairman, that prices were due to decline after World War II. Avery therefore let leases on older stores expire and did not open any new stores. The result was a loss in potential sales of more than one billion dollars.

Lest the reader say, "Oh, that is just Monday morning quarter-backing," the writer must inform the reader that he had prepared a chart in 1947 (Figure 67) per U.S. Bureau Labor Statistics to illustrate the effect of wars on wholesale prices in lectures given to the purchasing staff of Con-Edison. This chart was presented to the public in a paper by the writer, "Prices and Price Policies," at the 24th Annual Mid-Winter Conference of the Public Utility Buyers' Group, National Association of Purchasing Agents, February 15, 1955 in Houston, Texas. This was Chart 1 of the exhibits accompanying the lecture.

Furthermore, Shumah and Rosenau (and their followers) fell victim to the delusions that the eminent economist J.K. Galbraith described in *Money* (1975), as follows: "In the decade from the mid-1960s to the mid-1970s, economic policy was to be extensively guided *by prediction that was deeply subordinate to hope.*"

The only recent writer who seems to have doubts about the popular conception of the Kondratieff Wave is Dick A. Stoken, who made the following statement at a meeting of The Society for the Investigation of Recurring Events (SIRE): "Capitalistic economies have experienced an approximately 50-year cycle of boom and bust—Kondratieff cycles—since the beginning of industrialization in the late 18th century. . . . We live in a world where things are constantly changing, and because the economic structure has changed, it is to be expected that *the Kondratieff Cycle would unfold in a somewhat different manner than it did prior to the Keynesian Revolution."*

Finally, in a lecture delivered by the writer on April 16, 1947, at the Henry George School of Social Science in New York, the writer described a 56-year pattern in American business activity that began with the *Panic of 1761* (following the close of the French and Indian Wars). The second 56-year pattern began with the *Panic of 1817*, the third began with the *Panic of 1873*, the fourth began with *the Panic of 1929*, and the fifth will be ushered in by the *Panic of 1985!*

The following comments were made following publication of the article: "The preceding article by Commander Williams to my mind is a pragmatic analysis of the overall long cycle affecting economic behavior. The long cycle is like the tide which influences the direction of flow of a stream. In this case the flow is economic events and the message of the article is that the tide may well be in a process of alteration. Within five years the problem of focus could well be deflationary pressures rather than inflationary events. If this is to be an objective reality the precious metals markets will reflect it by containing their recoveries in the form of cyclical appreciation in prices rather than a leap into the stratosphere of inflationary panic.

"Commander Williams, as a tireless researcher, has pointed out certain adjustments to the common view of this long cycle. His comments do not alter the original considerations drawn from the previously published analysis. They will, however, serve to arm you intellectually to understand unfolding events in terms of time and amplitude. As such you will not be dealing economically against mystery but rather you will understand the nature of unfolding events.

"I strongly recommend that you keep this and the preceding articles on long cycle analysis in your personal files and review them at least once a year.

"The next recovery in precious metals might well set a trap for the complacent. The complacent are those theologians of any investment vehicle who feel that no circumstance whatsoever can alter their conclusions. Personally I feel this attitude which is prevalent in precious metals will be phenomenally asset-consuming in the next recovery exhaustion." (Reproduced by permission of James Sinclair, Partner, Sinclair Securities Company, 90 Broad Street, New York, N.Y. 10004.)

## History of Silver Prices

### Introduction

Gold and silver were used to facilitate trade as early as 3000 B.C., when merchants in the ancient Mesopotamian cities of Mari and Ebla established an exchange rate of 5 ounces of silver to one ounce of gold. For the more than 2,000 years, from 1670 B.C. to 422 A.D., the ratio varied from a low of 8.93 to 1 in 59-44 B.C. to a high of 18 to 1 in 422 A.D. During the following 1,000 years it fell to 15 to 1 for the years 527-1453. For the next three centuries the ratio fluctuated between a low of 10.75 to 1 in 1501-1520 to a high of 15.52 to 1 in 1702, dropping to 15.17 to in 1792, when the first coinage law of the U.S. was passed fixing the ratio at 15 to 1. In 1932, the ratio rose to 72 to 1 and on January 21, 1980, when both metals made their all-time highs, the ratio was 17.7 to 1. It is currently (July 10, 1981) 45.77 to 1.

### Silver Prices

The silver and gold used in commercial transactions were originally in the form of nuggets or bars, which were always weighed. Not until about 700 B.C. were these precious metals coined (by the Lydians in Asia Minor.) Up until the 6th Century B.C., silver was the money of everyday life in the Greek city states. On the other hand, the money of the Roman Empire consisted of crude copper bars or nuggets, which

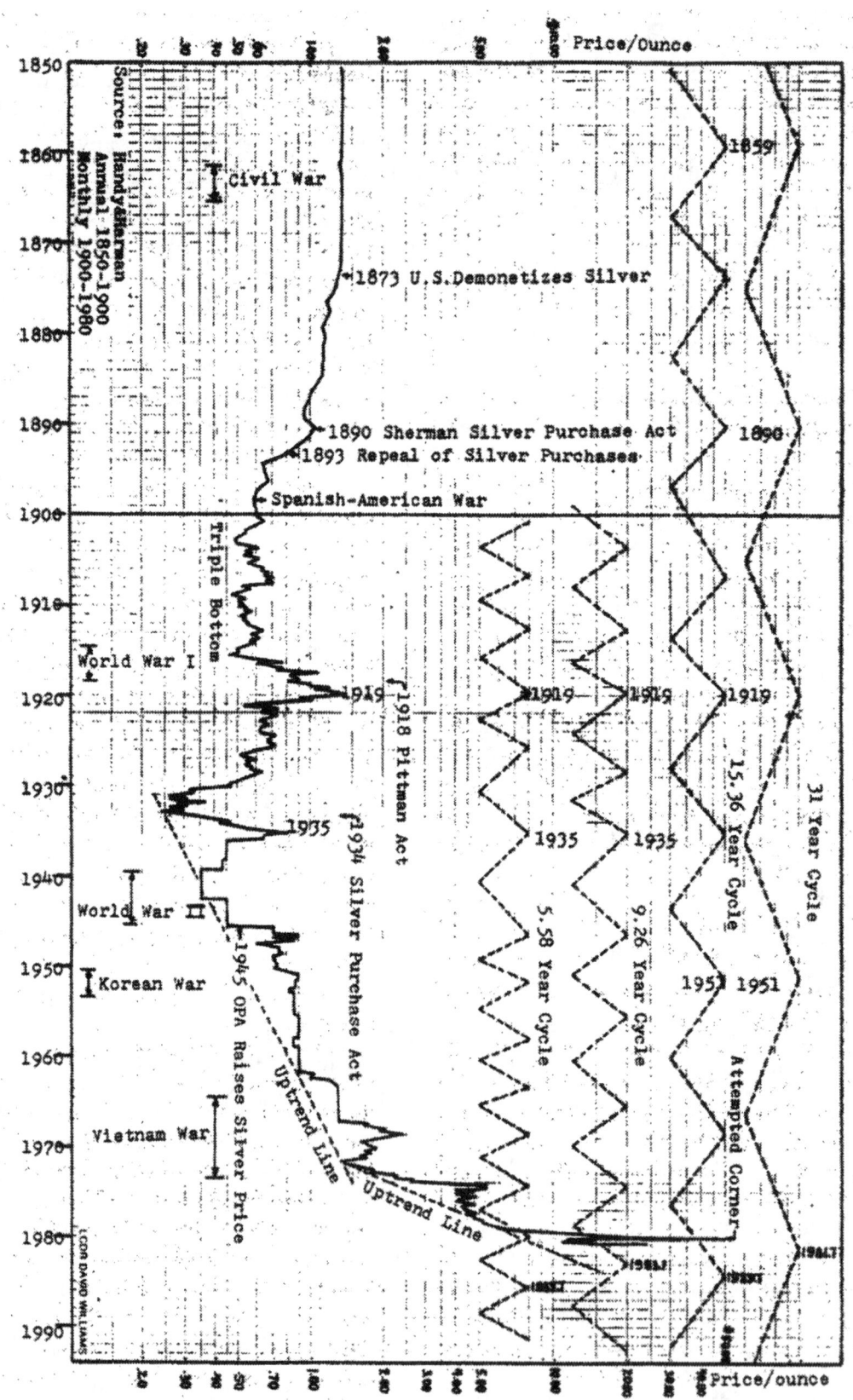

*Figure 68. Silver Prices 1850-1980.*

were weighed until the reign of King Servius Tullus (578-534 B.C.), who was the first ruler to stamp the weight on these bars or nuggets. Not until 269 B.C. was silver coined in Rome, at which time a Bimetallic Standard was established between copper and silver.

When the U.S. on April 2, 1792 established a 15 to 1 ratio, gold was undervalued and disappeared from circulation. To correct this situation, Congress, on June 18, 1834, changed the ratio to 16 to 1, at which ratio gold was slightly overvalued and silver undervalued; hence silver coins began to disappear. Thus, from 1792 to 1860, when payment in specie was stopped and paper "greenbacks" were used for currency, the U.S. was on a Bimetallic Standard. Since silver coins had practically disappeared from circulation by 1873, silver was dropped from the list of U.S. coins by the Act of February 12, 1873, the so-called "crime of 1873" and the U.S. was to all intents and purposes on the Gold Standard, which became official through the Gold Act of March 14, 1900.

England had a similar experience, for while silver had been the common measure of value prior to A.D. 1377, silver and gold coins were used in the ratio of 16 to 1 up to 1816. But France and most of the other European countries used a 15½ to 1 ratio. Silver therefore drifted to France and gold to England, until in 1816 England abandoned Bimetallism and adopted the Gold Standard. Most of the European countries began to demonetize silver in 1873, which threw large amounts of it on the market as metal and decreased its value. Hence, silver began a rapid decline until 1902, when the ratio of silver to gold rose to 39.15 to 1. Following the end of World War I, the price of silver rose and the ratio dropped to 15.20 to 1 in November 1919—the approximate level which had prevailed for some 300 years. From that level silver prices dropped and the ratio rose to 72.27 in 1932.

Figure 68 shows the dramatic change that has taken place in silver prices since silver was demonetized in 1873. While silver was used as money from 1850 through 1872, the price remained fairly constant at around $1.32 per ounce. But after the demonetization, silver became just another commodity, subject to Law of Supply and Demand. Prices declined as silver metal was dumped on the market, but after forming a Triple Bottom in November 1902, December 1908, and September 1915, at the 40-45 cent level, a meteoric rise occurred to $1.085 in September 1917. Prices then dropped to 83 cents in October 1917 in anticipation of the passage of the Pittman Act of April 25, 1918, which authorized the Secretary of the Treasury to melt and sell as bullion up to 350 million silver dollars and to later purchase an equal amount at $1.00 an ounce. Prices thereafter rose to a peak of $1.375 an ounce in November 1919, aided by a) the sale of 300 million ounces of silver to the British Government during 1918-1919 for use in India, whose people mistrusted British paper money, and by b) heavy buying of silver by the Chinese in 1919 following the lifting of war-time restrictions.

After the end of World War I, deflation, demonetization, and the debasement of foreign silver coins forced the price of silver down to 52.5 cents an ounce in March 1921. Prices rebounded to 73.5 cents in October 1921 and May 1922, as the U.S. Government bought 200 million ounces of silver during the years 1920-1923 under the provisions of the Pittman Act. The price then moved sideways until September 1925, before plunging to the all-time low of 24 cents in December 1932. This drastic decline was accelerated by the unfavorable 1926 Report of the Royal Commission on Indian Currency, which resulted in heavy sales from the Indian Government silver reserves, as India moved toward the demonitization of silver in 1929. A checkered rise to $2.464 in June 1968 reflects the effects of U.S. Government price-fixing during World War II, the Korean and Vietnam Wars. Following a profit-taking drop to $1.32 in November 1971, a meteoric rise to an all-time high of $48 on January 21, 1980 took place.

Beginning in June 1974, Gertrude Shirk, Editor of *Cycles* magazine, published by the prestigious Foundation for the Study of Cycles, began a series of cyclical studies of silver prices from 1850 to 1980, which revealed the existence of the following cycles: 31, 15.36, 9.26 and 5.58 years in length. The 5.58 year cycle was considered to be "the most dominant component in silver prices." It correctly indicated the peaks of 1919, 1935, 1968, 1974, and 1980. The next ideal peak in silver prices is estimated to occur during the summer of 1985, but in the meantime the price would decline to about the summer of 1982. All four cycles are shown in Figure 68, which was prepared by the author for his article, "Historical Survey: Silver Prices" in *Cycles* in January/February of 1981.

The decline from the January 21, 1980 peak is clearly shown in Figure 69, on which is plotted the daily New York Cash Price quoted by Handy and Harmon. Particular attention is directed to the Head and Shoulders Tops of January and September 1980 and the "50 percent Retracement Line," which connects the two "heads" shown in Figure 69. As Figure 69 indicates, the price of silver broke below the Double Bottom support of March-May 1980 to a low of 8.3 cents on July 8, 1981, and after a brief rally is still headed downward towards the next support level at $4-5 an ounce, when a sideways movement should take place, before a sustained rise occurs.

While cycle analysis does not indicate how high or how low prices may go, nor does it necessarily mean that the low point should come exactly midway between the two high points, experience shows that prices normally decline faster than they rise. Thus, silver should be accumulated at the $4-5 level and held to 1985, when a new all-time high should occur. However, attempts to "corner" the silver market will fail, as they have in the past. The following silver mining stocks should also be purchased: Asarco, Callahan, Hecla, and Sunshine Mining, but on a sliding scale. Though Asarco is primarily a copper producer, it is the largest producer of silver—a by-product—in the U.S.

Since the above was written, silver prices have not broken the $8 floor that has been in effect for six months since July 1981. Eight is a Fibonacci Number, as explained in Chapter 12. If the $8 level should be broken, the next support level would be at $5, since 5 is the preceding Fibonacci Number in the series.

## History of Gold Prices

### Introduction

Gold was the most important metal found in Ancient Egypt ca. 3000 B.C.), but its use was restricted to the rulers and the nobility for personal adornment and to the priesthood for temple ornaments and objects of worship. Barley was used by the common people as the medium of exchange. However, to facilitate trade with other countries, gold ornaments of known weight and convenient shape were used as early as 2000 B.C. When the rich, alluvial deposits of the Nile Delta were exhausted, gold was imported from Nubia in the form of dust tied in linen bags, or small fragments of metal fused into little nuggets or rings, about 1400 B.C. The use of gold coins for currency is believed to have originated with the Lydians of Asia Minor about 700 B.C.

When the Romans abandoned Britain at the beginning of the 5th Century A.D., they took the precious metals—gold and silver—with them, and as a result commodity prices fell very low. Since the time of the Norman Conquest of England in 1066, until the change to decimal coinage in 1971, English money had consisted of pounds, shillings and pence, with 20 shillings to the pound and 12 pence to the shilling. The pound sterling was an actual pound in weight of silver containing 5,400 grains (Troy) with a purity of 92.5 percent or 4995 grains of pure silver (Troy). But then came the debasement of the

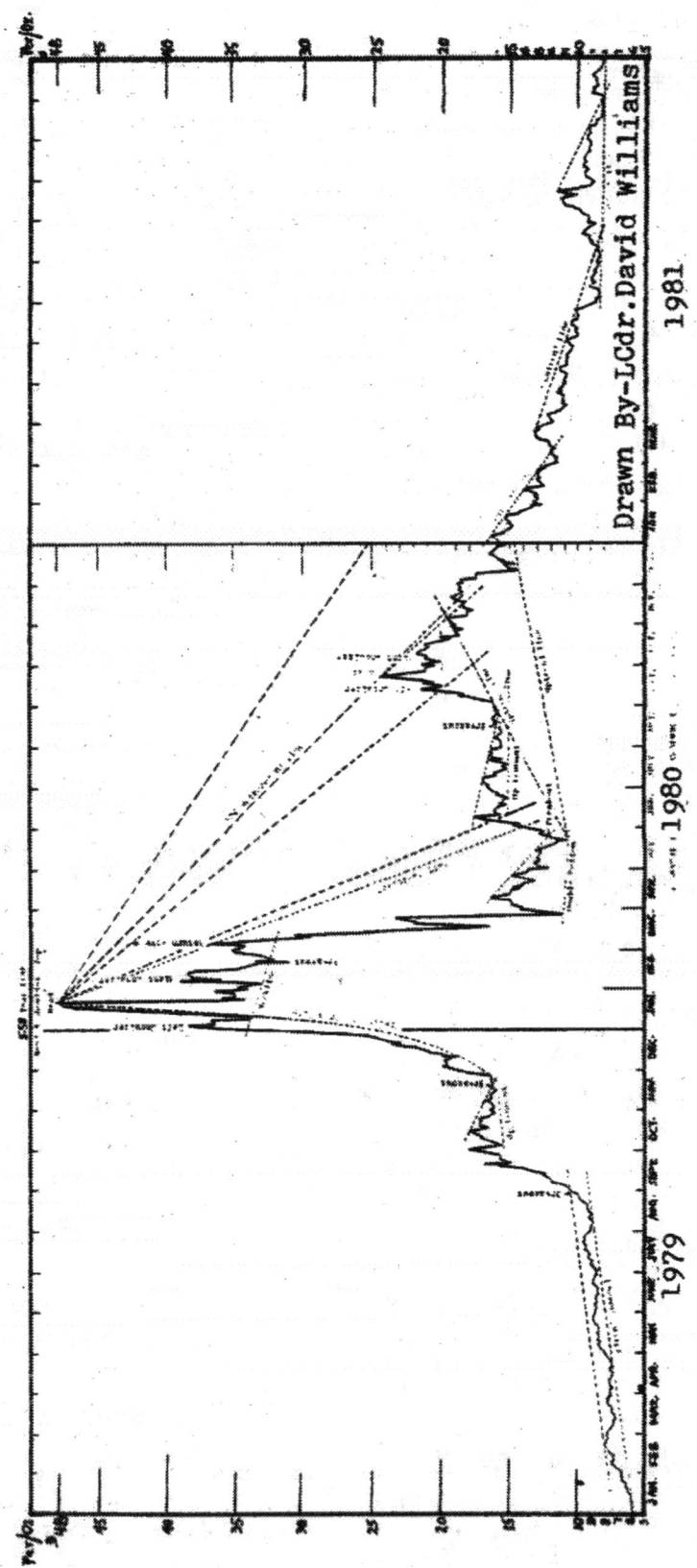

*Figure 69. Daily Cash Silver Prices 1979-1981.*

currency, so that by the time of Queen Elizabeth's great Recoinage Act of 1560, the weight of pure silver in the pound sterling had fallen to 1,761 grains (Troy). The greatest reductions came after a long period of declining commodity prices. Gold coins were similarly debased.

## Gold Prices

Figure 70, derived from *The Golden Constant* by R.W. Jastrow (1977), traces the price of gold in England from 1343 to 1980. It shows that in the 351 years (1345-1696) the price rose 550 percent or at the rate of 1.57 percent per year. The Bank of England was incorporated on July 27, 1694, and began to exert a steadying influence on the price of gold for the next 234 years, 1699-1930. England had been on a silver basis up to 1377, and on a Bimetallic basis for the next 340 years. But it went on the Gold Standard (de facto) when the Proclamation of December 22, 1717 established the guinea at 21 shillings gold, with the Royal Mint price of gold set at 3 pounds, 17 shillings, 10.5 pence (£3, 17s, 10.5d) per standard ounce. But it wasn't until a century later, that the gold standard became official (de jure) with the passage of Lord Peel's Act of 1819, which reaffirmed the Royal Mint price of £3, 17s, 10.5d. The price of gold remained substantially constant for more than two centuries (1717-1931), except during the Napoleonic and World War I periods. But, on September 21, 1931, the British Government suspended the Gold Standard. Then began a meteoric rise of 82 percent until the outbreak of World War II in 1939. Since a contributing factor was the action of the U.S. Government, which went off the Gold Standard in March 1933 and raised the price of gold to $35 an ounce, we will now briefly review the history of gold prices in the U.S. (see Figure 71).

As we have previously seen, Congress on April 2, 1792 adopted a Bimetallic Standard for its currency, with gold priced at $19.39 an ounce, which was maintained until the War of 1812. Specie payments were suspended in August 1814, and the price of gold rose to $21.72 in 1814, $23.07 in 1815, $19.78 in 1816 and then to par ($19.39) when specie payments were resumed on February 20, 1817. The price of gold was raised to $20.67 an ounce on June 28, 1834, at which level it remained for the next century until 1934, except for brief periods during the panics of 1837, 1857 and the Civil War. Specie payments were suspended between May 10, 1837 and May 10, 1838. On July 15, 1837, American gold coins at New York City commanded premiums of 9 to 10 percent, and the Spanish dollar rose 11 to 12 percent.

Twenty years after the *Panic of 1837* came the Panic *of 1857*. Specie payments were suspended on September 24, 1857, and were not resumed until December 12, 1857. In the meantime gold dollars commanded a premium. The Civil War was largely financed by the issuance of paper money, "Greenbacks", the first issue of which was authorized by the Act of July 17, 1861. Specie payments were suspended between December 31, 1861 and January 1, 1879. During that period the price of gold jumped from $20.67 to $59.12 an ounce (on July 1, 1864), at which price the "Greenback" dollar was only worth 35 cents. The decline from the Civil War high was briefly interrupted in September 1869, when Jay Gould and Jim Fisk attempted to "corner" the gold market. On Black Friday, September 24, 1869, the price of gold was $33.49 an ounce, but collapsed when the U.S. Treasury dumped $4 million ounces of gold on the market.

The *Panic of 1873* resulted in the longest depression in U.S. history, and the price of gold dropped from $23.56 in 1873 to $20.67 (par) on January 1, 1879. It may be recalled that the U.S. went on the Gold Standard (de facto) when Congress on February 12, 1873, omitted silver from the list of coins and stipulated that only gold would be granted the free coinage privilege. Although the price of gold remained steady during the *Panic of 1893* because of the tremendous increase in world gold production since 1890, the Prime Discount Rate for 60-90 day bills at New

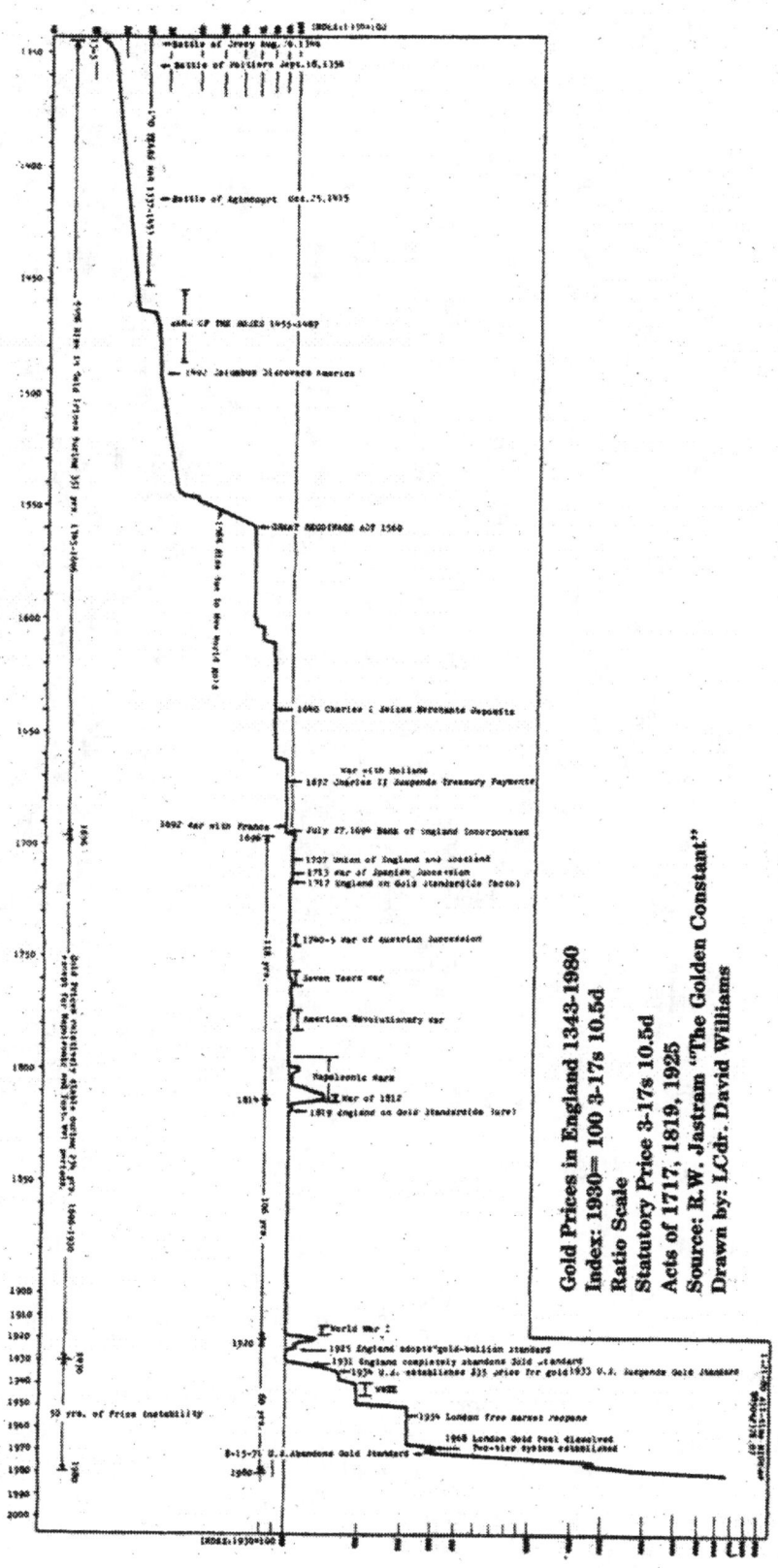

*Figure 70. Gold Prices in England 1343-1980.*

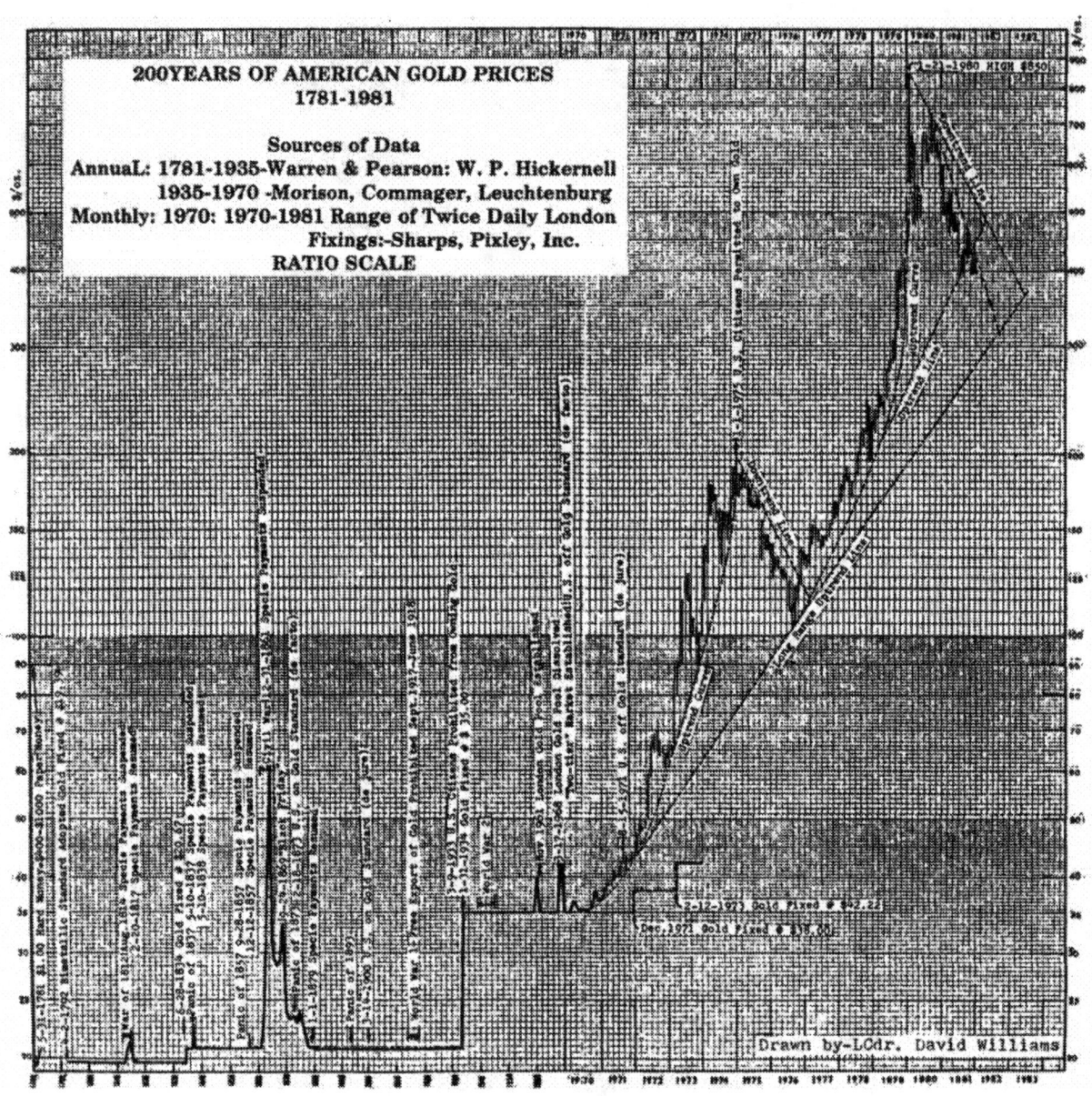

*Figure 71. 200 Years of American Gold Prices 1781-1981.*

York shot up to 36 percent!

World War I (1914-1915) changed the United States from the world's greatest debtor to the world's greatest creditor. Although President Wilson barred the free export of gold between September 1917 and June 1918, the price of gold remained unchanged at $20.67 an ounce, because the U.S. was acquiring Europe's gold. The war wrecked the monetary standards of every nation in the world; hence, in order to restore normal commercial practices, an international conference was held in Genoa, Italy on April 20, 1922. It proclaimed that all European currencies should be based on a common standard gold, and established a "gold exchange" standard, under which smaller nations, which had little gold, could substitute the currency of Britain in pounds sterling or that of the U.S. in dollars, instead of an actual gold reserve behind their currency.

Since, as we have seen, England went off the Gold Standard on September 21, 1931, and the

U.S. on March 9, 1933, and the price of gold was raised to $35 an ounce by the U.S. on January 31, 1934, an international conference was held in July 1944 at Bretton Woods, New Hampshire, to stabilize the post-war gold price level. The conference participants agreed to use U.S. dollars as their reserve currency, and the U.S. agreed to guarantee the stability of the dollar by exchanging dollar for gold at the rate of $35 an ounce. Thus, by the mid-1950s, the U.S. had 75 percent of the Free World's gold stock in its reserve. But, as Europe recovered from the devastation of World War II, it began to turn in its surplus paper dollars to the U.S. Treasury for gold at the fixed price of $35 an ounce.

The first free market for gold reopened in 1948 in Paris, in 1950 in Switzerland, and in London in 1954, where the price went up to $40 an ounce in October 1960. So, in 1961, the London Gold Pool was established by eight of the world's most powerful Central Banks to stabilize the free market price of gold at $35.0875 an ounce. The Pool succeeded in maintaining that price for the next four years. But, in 1967, Britain devalued the pound sterling by 15 percent and the price of gold soared on the private markets as bankers and investors converted sterling notes into gold. Then France withdrew from the London Gold Pool in June 1967 and on March 17, 1968, the Pool was dissolved and replaced by a "two-tier" market, under which monetary gold could only be used for official settlements between Central Banks at $35 an ounce. The other "tier" was used for private buyers, who could purchase gold freely on the open market at prices set by the Law of Supply and Demand. The price of gold rose 32 percent between 1967 and 1969, and then took off on an explosive rise unprecedented in monetary history, precipitated by the U.S. abandonment of the Gold Standard (de jure) on August 15, 1971. The ensuing wild gyrations in the price of gold are dramatically shown in Figure 72.

The tremendous rise from the $210 level in January 1979 to the all-time high of $850 an ounce on January 21, 1980, and the subsequent crash to $474 on March 18, 1980, the rise to $720.50 on September 23, 1980, followed by the decline through 1981, is graphically portrayed in Figure 72. Technicians will readily recognize the Head and Shoulders tops of $850 on January 21, 1980, and $720.50 on September 23, 1980. A Downtrend Line drawn through these two tops has remained unbroken since the latter date. It would, however, appear that gold prices are leveling off around the 391-400 level and will probably move sideways before starting up during the summer of 1982. (Gold dropped to $296 on June 21, 1982.)

*Cycles in English Gold Prices:* Jastrow stated: "The rise in gold prices in England by more than 60 percent from 1343 to 1492 was fundamentally due to an increase in the demand for gold to support rising levels of commercial activity in the face of essentially static stocks of the metal. Then came the flood of silver and gold from the New World. But demand continued to outstrip supply and the price of gold climbed to a level in 1717 below which it has never fallen since." As Figure 70 shows, the price of gold remained very nearly constant for more than two centuries (1717-1931), except for the Napoleonic and World War I periods. The time span between peaks was: 1968-1814 or 118 years, 1814-1920, or 106 years. A meteoric rise then occurred during the next 60 years.

*Cycles in American Gold Prices:* Figure 71 shows evidence of a 22.11 year cycle between Tops, as per Table 55.

An alternate count would be to omit the Panic of 1857 and substitute the Civil War, when gold shot up to $59.12 an ounce on July 1, 1864. The average cycle length remains unchanged at 22.11 years. This is the same length as the Sunspot Cycle, with alternate peaks reversed, as shown on Figure 13 of Chapter 5. No causal relationship is to be inferred. A comparison of the gold price peaks with the sunspot peaks is shown in Table 56.

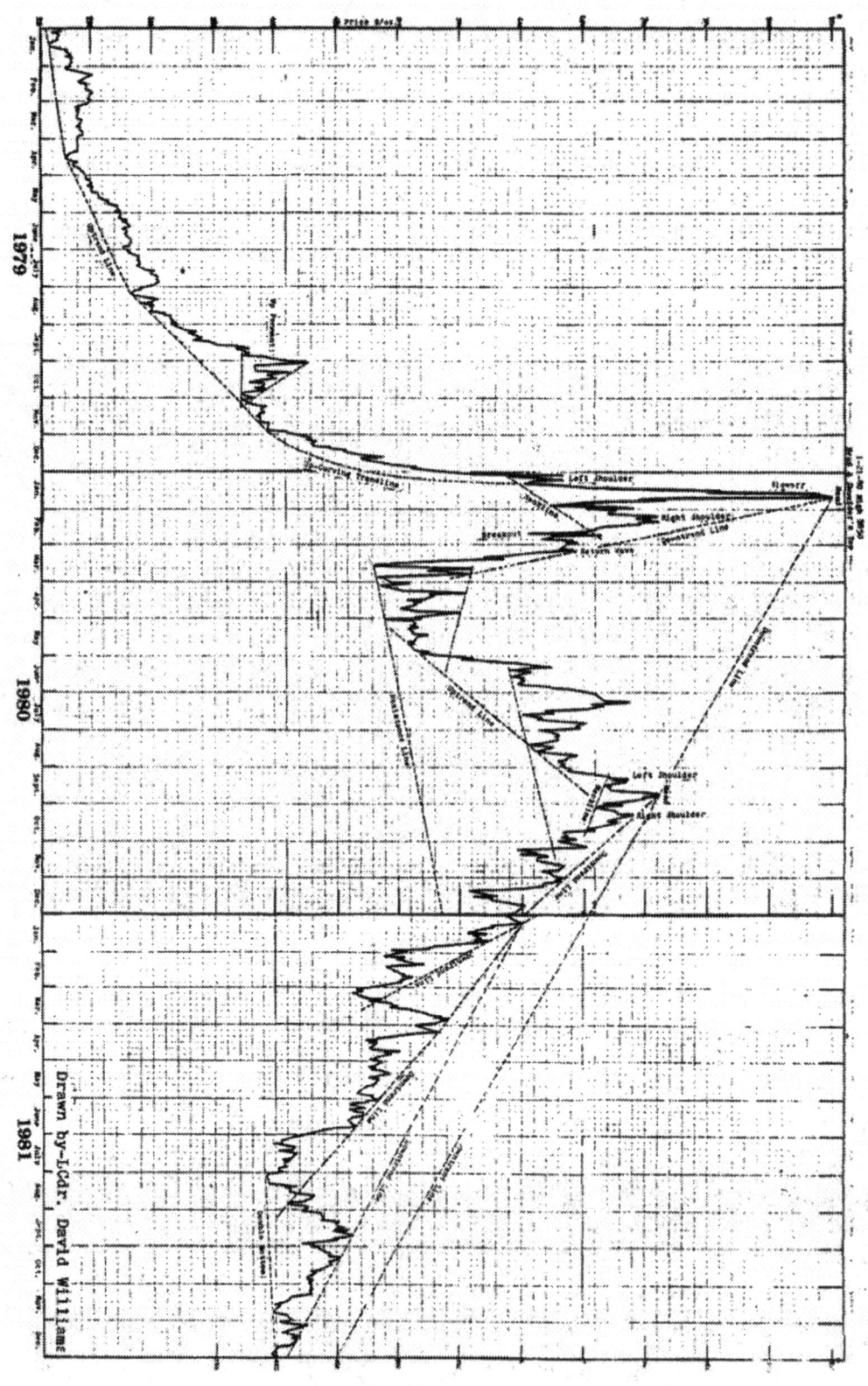

Figure 72. Daily Cash Gold Prices 1979-1981.

### Table 55. The 22.11-Year Cycle of Tops in U.S. Gold Prices.

| Date | Price | Years Between Tops | Note |
|---|---|---|---|
| 5/31/1781 | $19,390.00 | | $400-1,000 in paper for $1 hard currency (Revolutionary War) |
| 1815 | 23.07 | 34 | War of 1812 |
| June 1837 | 22.70 | 22 | Panic of 1837 |
| Sept. 1857 | Premium | 20 | Panic of 1857 |
| Sept. 1873 | 23.50 | 16 | Panic of 1873 |
| Oct. 1893 | 20.67 | 20 | Panic of 1893 Discount Rate 36 percent |
| Sept. 1917 | 20.67 | 24 | World War I, free export of gold barred |
| 1/31/1934 | 35.00 | 17 | U.S. off the Gold Standard |
| Oct. 1960 | 40.00 | 26 | Free Market |
| 1/21/1980 | 850.00 | -- | All-time High |
| | *Average* | 22.11 Years | |

### Table 56. Correlation Between Peaks in Gold Prices and Peaks in Sunspots.

| Date | Gold Price | Sunspot Date | Number | Gold Price |
|---|---|---|---|---|
| 5/31/1781 | $19,390 | May 1778 | 238.9 | *3 years late |
| 1815 | 23.07 | Mar. 1816 | 73.7 | 1 year early |
| June 1837 | 22.70 | Jan. 1837 | 188.0 | 5 months late |
| Sept. 1857 | Premium | July 1860 | 116.7 | 10 months early |
| Sept. 1873 | 23.30 | Sept. 1872 | 114.6 | 1 year late |
| Oct. 1893 | 20.67 | Aug. 1893 | 129.2 | 2 months late |
| Sept. 1917 | 20.67 | Aug. 1917 | 154.5 | 1 month late |
| 1/31/1934 | 35.00 | Aug. 1937 | 145.1 | 3 years early |
| Oct. 1960 | 40.00 | Oct. 1957 | 253.8 | 1 year late |
| 1/21/1980 | 850.00 | Sept. 1979 | 188.7 | *4 months late |

50 percent on target, 30 percent within 1 year, 20 percent within 3 years

*Remarks: The highest prices for gold in 200 years came a) 3 years after the sunspot peak of May 1778, during the American Revolution, and b) 4 months after the sunspot peak of September 1979!

A shorter cycle averaging 5 years, 5 months appears in the data from March 1969 as follows:

March 1969 to December 30, 1974—5 years, 9 months ($43.825 to $197.50), and December 30, 1974 to January 21, 1980—5 years, 1 month ($197.50 to $850, all-time High). The next theoretical low of the current 5 year, 5 months cycle would occur during the summer of 1982, to be followed by a new high during the summer of 1985. But there is no relationship between the movement of gold prices and sunspots during this period.

## Conclusion

As the charts clearly show, there has been a fundamental change in the nature of gold prices in England and America during the past decade. From a monetary reserve of the principal nations of the Western World at $35 an ounce, gold has first become a monetary commodity and then just another commodity. It has thus become the world's greatest speculative medium, through which international traders express their economic, political and social judgments. Gold rises and falls, but never changes hands. Prices explode or wilt for any reason or no reason. Traders on the floors of the commodity exchanges throughout the world have displaced the central banks in their influence on gold prices.

As gold approaches its cyclical low of $300-400 in the summer of 1982, scale purchases of the following stocks should be rewarding: ASA, Campbell Redlake, Dome Mines, Homestake and selected South African golds, such as Vaal Reefs, Western Holdings, Buffelsfontein and Hartbeestfontein.

Finally, a word of advice to those who are fearful of the "Prophets of Doom", who for the past 20 years have been predicting that the dollar would become worthless because of wild inflation of the currency. Warren & Pearson, in *Prices, (1935)*, flatly stated: *"There is no serious danger of wild inflation, except following revolution."* History bears them out, because we have seen what happened during the American Revolution, the French Revolution, the Russian Revolution and the German Revolution. To which might be added the American Civil War, which really was a revolt of the South against the North. Confederate paper money became worthless!

It is interesting to note that in 1781, when the Continental currency became worthless, Neptune, the planet of inflation, was in the fifth house of speculation of the U.S. Gemini rising natal chart, while Pluto, the planet of regeneration, was in the ninth house of foreign affairs. This *trine* configuration will not recur again until the year 2103. So stop worrying!!!

# Appendix I
# Zurich Relative Sunspot Numbers

Sources: 1749-1957, Chernosky, E.J. And M.P. Hagan, "The Zurich Sunspot Number and Its Variation for 1700-1957," *Journal of Geophysical Research*, Vol. 63, Number 4, December 1958.
1958-1972, World Data Center for Solar-Terrestrial Physics, NOAA, Boulder, Colorado.
1973-1981, *Sky & Telescope*.

|  | 1749 | 1750 | 1751 | 1752 | 1753 | 1754 | 1755 | 1756 | 1757 | 1758 | 1759 | 1760 | 1761 | 1762 | 1763 | 1764 |
|---|---|---|---|---|---|---|---|---|---|---|---|---|---|---|---|---|
| Jan | 58.0 | 73.3 | 70.0 | 35.0 | 44.0 | 0.0 | 10.2 | 12.5 | 14.1 | 37.6 | 48.3 | 67.3 | 70.0 | 43.8 | 56.5 | 59.7 |
| Feb | 62.6 | 75.9 | 43.5 | 50.0 | 32.0 | 3.0 | 11.2 | 7.1 | 21.2 | 52.0 | 44.0 | 59.5 | 91.0 | 72.8 | 31.9 | 59.7 |
| Mar | 70.0 | 89.2 | 45.3 | 71.0 | 45.7 | 1.7 | 6.8 | 5.4 | 26.7 | 49.0 | 46.8 | 74.7 | 80.7 | 45.7 | 34.2 | 40.2 |
| Apr | 55.7 | 88.3 | 56.4 | 59.3 | 38.0 | 13.7 | 6.5 | 9.4 | 30.0 | 72.3 | 47.0 | 58.3 | 71.7 | 60.2 | 32.9 | 34.4 |
| May | 85.0 | 90.0 | 60.7 | 59.7 | 36.0 | 20.7 | 0.0 | 12.5 | 38.1 | 46.4 | 49.0 | 72.0 | 107.2 | 39.9 | 32.7 | 44.3 |
| Jun | 83.5 | 100.0 | 50.7 | 39.6 | 31.7 | 26.7 | 0.0 | 12.9 | 12.8 | 45.0 | 50.0 | 48.3 | 99.3 | 77.1 | 35.8 | 30.0 |
| Jul | 94.8 | 85.4 | 66.3 | 78.4 | 22.0 | 18.8 | 8.6 | 3.6 | 25.0 | 44.0 | 51.0 | 66.0 | 94.1 | 33.8 | 54.2 | 30.0 |
| Aug | 66.3 | 103.0 | 59.8 | 29.3 | 39.0 | 12.3 | 3.2 | 6.4 | 51.3 | 38.7 | 71.3 | 75.6 | 91.1 | 67.7 | 26.5 | 30.0 |
| Sep | 75.9 | 91.2 | 23.5 | 27.1 | 28.0 | 8.2 | 17.8 | 11.8 | 39.7 | 62.5 | 77.2 | 61.3 | 100.7 | 68.5 | 68.1 | 28.2 |
| Oct | 75.5 | 85.7 | 23.2 | 46.6 | 25.0 | 24.1 | 23.7 | 14.3 | 32.5 | 37.7 | 59.7 | 50.6 | 88.7 | 69.3 | 46.3 | 28.0 |
| Nov | 158.6 | 63.3 | 28.5 | 37.6 | 20.0 | 13.2 | 6.8 | 17.0 | 64.7 | 43.0 | 46.3 | 59.7 | 89.7 | 77.8 | 60.9 | 26.0 |
| Dec | 85.2 | 75.4 | 44.0 | 40.0 | 6.7 | 4.2 | 20.0 | 9.4 | 33.5 | 43.0 | 57.0 | 61.0 | 46.0 | 77.2 | 61.4 | 25.7 |
| Mean | 80.9 | 83.4 | 47.7 | 47.8 | 30.7 | 12.2 | 9.6 | 10.2 | 32.4 | 47.6 | 54.0 | 62.9 | 85.9 | 61.2 | 45.1 | 36.4 |

|  | 1765 | 1766 | 1767 | 1768 | 1769 | 1770 | 1771 | 1772 | 1773 | 1774 | 1775 | 1776 | 1777 | 1778 | 1779 | 1780 |
|---|---|---|---|---|---|---|---|---|---|---|---|---|---|---|---|---|
| Jan | 24.0 | 12.0 | 27.4 | 53.5 | 73.9 | 104.0 | 36.0 | 100.9 | 54.6 | 46.5 | 4.4 | 21.7 | 45.0 | 177.3 | 114.7 | 70.0 |
| Feb | 26.0 | 11.0 | 30.0 | 66.1 | 64.2 | 142.5 | 46.2 | 90.8 | 29.0 | 65.4 | 0.0 | 11.6 | 36.5 | 109.3 | 165.7 | 98.0 |
| Mar | 25.0 | 36.6 | 43.0 | 46.3 | 64.3 | 80.1 | 46.7 | 31.1 | 51.2 | 55.7 | 11.6 | 6.3 | 39.0 | 134.0 | 118.0 | 98.0 |
| Apr | 22.0 | 6.0 | 32.9 | 42.7 | 96.7 | 51.0 | 64.9 | 92.2 | 32.9 | 43.8 | 11.2 | 21.8 | 95.5 | 145.0 | 145.0 | 95.0 |
| May | 20.2 | 26.8 | 29.8 | 77.7 | 73.6 | 70.1 | 152.7 | 38.0 | 41.1 | 51.3 | 3.9 | 11.2 | 80.3 | 238.9 | 140.0 | 107.2 |
| Jun | 20.0 | 3.0 | 33.3 | 77.4 | 94.4 | 83.3 | 119.5 | 57.0 | 28.4 | 28.5 | 12.3 | 19.0 | 80.7 | 171.6 | 113.7 | 88.0 |
| Jul | 27.0 | 3.3 | 21.9 | 52.6 | 118.6 | 109.8 | 67.7 | 77.3 | 27.7 | 17.5 | 1.0 | 1.0 | 95.0 | 153.0 | 143.0 | 86.0 |
| Aug | 29.7 | 4.0 | 40.8 | 66.8 | 120.3 | 126.3 | 58.5 | 56.2 | 12.7 | 6.6 | 7.9 | 24.2 | 112.0 | 140.0 | 112.0 | 86.0 |
| Sep | 16.0 | 4.3 | 42.7 | 74.8 | 148.8 | 104.4 | 101.4 | 50.5 | 29.3 | 7.9 | 3.2 | 16.0 | 116.2 | 171.7 | 111.0 | 93.7 |
| Oct | 14.0 | 5.0 | 44.1 | 77.8 | 158.2 | 103.6 | 90.0 | 78.6 | 26.3 | 14.0 | 5.6 | 30.0 | 106.5 | 156.3 | 124.0 | 77.0 |
| Nov | 14.0 | 5.7 | 54.7 | 90.6 | 148.1 | 132.2 | 99.7 | 61.3 | 40.9 | 17.5 | 15.1 | 35.0 | 146.0 | 150.3 | 114.0 | 60.0 |
| Dec | 13.0 | 19.2 | 53.3 | 111.8 | 112.0 | 102.3 | 95.7 | 64.0 | 43.2 | 12.2 | 7.9 | 40.0 | 157.3 | 105.0 | 110.0 | 58.7 |
| Mean | 20.9 | 11.4 | 37.8 | 69.8 | 106.1 | 100.8 | 81.6 | 66.5 | 34.8 | 30.6 | 7.0 | 19.8 | 92.5 | 154.4 | 125.9 | 84.8 |

|  | 1781 | 1782 | 1783 | 1784 | 1785 | 1786 | 1787 | 1788 | 1789 | 1790 | 1791 | 1792 | 1793 | 1794 | 1795 | 1796 |
|---|---|---|---|---|---|---|---|---|---|---|---|---|---|---|---|---|
| Jan | 98.7 | 54.0 | 28.0 | 13.0 | 6.5 | 37.2 | 134.7 | 138.0 | 114.0 | 103.0 | 72.7 | 58.0 | 56.0 | 45.0 | 21.4 | 22.0 |
| Feb | 74.7 | 37.5 | 38.7 | 8.0 | 8.0 | 47.6 | 106.0 | 129.2 | 125.3 | 127.5 | 62.0 | 64.0 | 55.0 | 44.0 | 39.9 | 23.8 |
| Mar | 53.0 | 37.0 | 26.7 | 11.0 | 9.0 | 47.7 | 87.4 | 143.3 | 120.0 | 96.3 | 74.0 | 63.0 | 55.5 | 38.0 | 12.6 | 15.7 |
| Apr | 68.3 | 41.0 | 28.3 | 10.0 | 15.7 | 85.4 | 127.2 | 108.5 | 123.3 | 94.0 | 77.2 | 75.7 | 53.0 | 28.4 | 18.6 | 31.7 |
| May | 104.7 | 54.3 | 23.0 | 6.0 | 20.7 | 92.3 | 134.8 | 113.0 | 123.5 | 93.0 | 73.7 | 62.0 | 52.3 | 55.7 | 31.0 | 21.0 |
| Jun | 97.7 | 38.0 | 25.2 | 9.0 | 26.3 | 59.0 | 99.2 | 154.2 | 120.0 | 91.0 | 64.2 | 61.0 | 51.0 | 41.5 | 17.1 | 6.7 |
| Jul | 73.5 | 37.0 | 32.2 | 6.0 | 36.3 | 83.0 | 128.0 | 141.5 | 117.0 | 69.3 | 71.0 | 45.8 | 50.0 | 41.0 | 12.9 | 26.9 |
| Aug | 66.0 | 44.0 | 20.0 | 10.0 | 20.0 | 89.7 | 137.2 | 136.0 | 103.0 | 87.0 | 43.0 | 60.0 | 29.3 | 40.0 | 25.7 | 1.5 |
| Sep | 51.0 | 34.0 | 18.0 | 10.0 | 32.0 | 111.5 | 157.3 | 141.0 | 112.0 | 77.3 | 66.5 | 59.0 | 24.0 | 11.1 | 13.5 | 18.4 |
| Oct | 27.3 | 23.2 | 8.0 | 8.0 | 47.2 | 112.3 | 157.0 | 142.0 | 89.7 | 84.3 | 61.7 | 59.0 | 47.0 | 28.5 | 19.5 | 11.0 |
| Nov | 67.0 | 31.5 | 15.0 | 17.0 | 40.2 | 116.0 | 141.5 | 94.7 | 134.0 | 82.0 | 67.0 | 57.0 | 44.0 | 67.4 | 25.0 | 8.4 |
| Dec | 35.2 | 30.0 | 10.5 | 14.0 | 27.3 | 112.7 | 174.0 | 129.5 | 135.5 | 74.0 | 66.0 | 56.0 | 45.7 | 51.4 | 18.0 | 5.1 |
| Mean | 68.1 | 38.5 | 22.8 | 10.2 | 24.1 | 82.9 | 130.0 | 130.9 | 118.1 | 89.9 | 66.6 | 60.0 | 46.9 | 41.0 | 21.3 | 16.0 |

|  | 1797 | 1798 | 1799 | 1800 | 1801 | 1802 | 1803 | 1804 | 1805 | 1806 | 1807 | 1808 | 1809 | 1810 | 1811 | 1812 |
|---|---|---|---|---|---|---|---|---|---|---|---|---|---|---|---|---|
| Jan | 14.4 | 2.0 | 4.3 | 6.9 | 27.0 | 47.8 | 50.0 | 45.3 | 61.0 | 39.0 | 12.0 | 0.0 | 7.2 | 0.0 | 0.0 | 11.3 |
| Feb | 4.2 | 4.0 | 12.6 | 9.3 | 29.0 | 47.0 | 50.8 | 48.3 | 44.1 | 29.6 | 12.2 | 4.5 | 9.2 | 0.0 | 0.0 | 1.9 |
| Mar | 4.0 | 12.4 | 21.7 | 13.9 | 30.0 | 40.8 | 29.5 | 48.0 | 51.4 | 32.7 | 9.6 | 0.0 | 0.9 | 0.0 | 0.0 | 0.7 |
| Apr | 4.0 | 1.1 | 8.4 | 0.0 | 31.0 | 42.0 | 25.0 | 50.6 | 37.5 | 27.7 | 23.8 | 12.3 | 2.5 | 0.0 | 0.0 | 0.0 |
| May | 7.3 | 0.0 | 8.2 | 5.0 | 32.0 | 44.0 | 44.3 | 33.4 | 39.0 | 26.4 | 10.0 | 13.5 | 2.0 | 0.0 | 0.0 | 1.0 |
| Jun | 11.1 | 0.0 | 10.8 | 23.7 | 31.2 | 46.0 | 36.0 | 34.8 | 40.5 | 25.6 | 12.0 | 13.5 | 7.7 | 0.0 | 0.0 | 1.3 |
| Jul | 4.3 | 0.0 | 2.1 | 21.0 | 35.0 | 48.0 | 48.3 | 47.3 | 37.6 | 30.0 | 12.7 | 6.7 | 0.3 | 0.0 | 6.6 | 0.5 |
| Aug | 6.0 | 3.0 | 0.0 | 19.5 | 38.7 | 50.0 | 34.1 | 43.1 | 42.7 | 26.3 | 12.0 | 8.0 | 0.2 | 0.0 | 0.0 | 15.6 |
| Sep | 5.7 | 2.4 | 0.0 | 11.5 | 33.5 | 51.8 | 45.3 | 53.0 | 44.4 | 24.0 | 5.7 | 11.7 | 0.4 | 0.0 | 2.4 | 5.2 |
| Oct | 6.9 | 1.5 | 4.6 | 12.3 | 32.8 | 38.5 | 54.3 | 62.3 | 29.4 | 27.0 | 8.0 | 4.7 | 0.0 | 0.0 | 6.1 | 3.9 |
| Nov | 5.8 | 12.5 | 2.7 | 10.5 | 39.8 | 34.5 | 51.0 | 61.0 | 41.0 | 25.0 | 2.6 | 10.5 | 0.0 | 0.0 | 0.8 | 7.9 |
| Dec | 3.0 | 9.9 | 8.6 | 40.1 | 48.2 | 50.0 | 48.0 | 60.0 | 38.3 | 24.0 | 0.0 | 12.3 | 0.0 | 0.0 | 1.1 | 10.1 |
| Mean | 6.4 | 4.1 | 6.8 | 14.5 | 34.0 | 45.0 | 43.1 | 47.5 | 42.2 | 28.1 | 10.1 | 8.1 | 2.5 | 0.0 | 1.4 | 5.0 |

|      | 1813 | 1814 | 1815 | 1816 | 1817 | 1818 | 1819 | 1820 | 1821 | 1822 | 1823 | 1824 | 1825 | 1826 | 1827 | 1828 |
|------|------|------|------|------|------|------|------|------|------|------|------|------|------|------|------|------|
| Jan  | 0.0  | 22.2 | 19.2 | 26.3 | 36.4 | 34.9 | 32.5 | 19.2 | 21.5 | 0.0  | 0.0  | 21.6 | 5.0  | 17.7 | 34.6 | 52.8 |
| Feb  | 10.3 | 12.0 | 32.2 | 68.8 | 57.9 | 22.4 | 20.7 | 26.6 | 4.3  | 0.9  | 0.0  | 10.8 | 15.5 | 15.2 | 47.4 | 64.4 |
| Mar  | 1.9  | 5.7  | 26.2 | 73.7 | 96.2 | 29.7 | 3.7  | 4.5  | 5.7  | 16.1 | 0.6  | 0.0  | 22.4 | 36.7 | 57.8 | 65.0 |
| Apr  | 16.6 | 23.8 | 31.6 | 58.8 | 26.4 | 34.5 | 20.2 | 19.4 | 9.2  | 13.5 | 0.0  | 19.4 | 3.8  | 24.0 | 46.0 | 61.1 |
| May  | 5.5  | 5.8  | 9.8  | 44.3 | 21.2 | 53.1 | 19.6 | 29.3 | 1.7  | 1.6  | 0.0  | 2.8  | 15.4 | 32.4 | 66.3 | 89.1 |
| Jun  | 11.2 | 14.9 | 55.9 | 43.6 | 40.0 | 36.4 | 35.0 | 10.8 | 1.8  | 5.6  | 0.0  | 0.0  | 15.4 | 37.1 | 56.7 | 98.0 |
| Jul  | 18.3 | 18.5 | 35.5 | 38.8 | 50.0 | 28.0 | 31.4 | 20.6 | 2.5  | 7.9  | 0.5  | 0.0  | 30.9 | 52.5 | 42.9 | 54.3 |
| Aug  | 8.4  | 2.3  | 47.2 | 23.2 | 45.0 | 31.5 | 26.1 | 25.9 | 4.8  | 2.1  | 0.0  | 1.4  | 25.4 | 39.6 | 53.7 | 76.4 |
| Sep  | 15.3 | 8.1  | 31.5 | 47.8 | 36.7 | 26.1 | 14.9 | 5.2  | 4.4  | 0.0  | 0.0  | 20.5 | 15.7 | 18.9 | 49.6 | 50.4 |
| Oct  | 27.8 | 19.3 | 33.5 | 56.4 | 25.6 | 31.7 | 27.5 | 9.0  | 16.8 | 0.4  | 0.0  | 25.2 | 15.6 | 50.6 | 57.2 | 34.7 |
| Nov  | 16.7 | 14.5 | 37.2 | 38.1 | 28.9 | 10.9 | 25.1 | 7.9  | 4.4  | 0.0  | 0.0  | 0.0  | 11.7 | 39.5 | 48.2 | 57.0 |
| Dec  | 14.3 | 20.1 | 65.0 | 29.9 | 28.4 | 25.8 | 30.6 | 9.7  | 0.0  | 0.0  | 20.4 | 0.8  | 22.0 | 68.1 | 46.1 | 46.9 |
| Mean | 12.2 | 13.9 | 35.4 | 45.8 | 41.1 | 30.4 | 23.9 | 15.7 | 6.6  | 4.0  | 1.8  | 8.5  | 16.6 | 36.3 | 49.7 | 62.5 |

|      | 1829 | 1830 | 1831 | 1832 | 1833 | 1834 | 1835 | 1836 | 1837 | 1838 | 1839 | 1840 | 1841 | 1842 | 1843 | 1844 |
|------|------|------|------|------|------|------|------|------|------|------|------|------|------|------|------|------|
| Jan  | 43.0 | 52.2 | 47.5 | 30.9 | 11.3 | 4.9  | 7.5  | 88.6 | 188.0| 144.9| 107.6| 81.2 | 24.0 | 20.4 | 13.3 | 9.4  |
| Feb  | 49.4 | 72.1 | 60.1 | 55.5 | 14.9 | 18.1 | 24.5 | 107.6| 175.6| 84.8 | 102.5| 87.7 | 29.9 | 22.1 | 3.5  | 14.7 |
| Mar  | 72.3 | 84.6 | 93.4 | 55.1 | 11.8 | 3.9  | 19.7 | 98.1 | 134.6| 140.8| 77.7 | 65.5 | 29.7 | 21.7 | 8.3  | 13.6 |
| Apr  | 95.0 | 107.1| 54.6 | 26.9 | 2.8  | 1.4  | 61.5 | 142.9| 138.2| 126.6| 61.8 | 65.9 | 42.6 | 26.9 | 8.8  | 20.8 |
| May  | 67.5 | 66.3 | 38.1 | 41.3 | 12.9 | 8.8  | 43.6 | 111.4| 111.3| 137.6| 53.8 | 69.2 | 67.4 | 24.9 | 21.1 | 12.0 |
| Jun  | 73.9 | 65.1 | 33.4 | 26.7 | 1.0  | 7.8  | 33.2 | 124.7| 158.0| 94.5 | 54.6 | 48.5 | 55.7 | 20.5 | 10.5 | 3.7  |
| Jul  | 90.8 | 43.9 | 45.2 | 13.9 | 7.0  | 8.7  | 59.8 | 116.7| 162.8| 108.2| 84.7 | 60.7 | 30.8 | 12.6 | 9.5  | 21.2 |
| Aug  | 78.3 | 50.7 | 54.9 | 8.9  | 5.7  | 4.9  | 59.0 | 107.8| 134.0| 78.8 | 131.1| 57.8 | 39.3 | 26.5 | 11.8 | 23.9 |
| Sep  | 52.8 | 62.1 | 37.9 | 8.2  | 11.6 | 11.5 | 100.8| 95.1 | 96.3 | 73.6 | 132.7| 74.0 | 35.1 | 18.5 | 4.2  | 6.9  |
| Oct  | 57.2 | 84.4 | 46.2 | 21.1 | 7.5  | 24.8 | 95.2 | 137.4| 123.7| 90.8 | 90.8 | 49.8 | 28.5 | 38.1 | 5.3  | 21.5 |
| Nov  | 67.6 | 81.2 | 43.5 | 14.3 | 5.9  | 30.5 | 100.0| 120.9| 107.0| 77.4 | 68.8 | 54.3 | 19.8 | 40.5 | 19.1 | 10.7 |
| Dec  | 56.5 | 82.1 | 28.9 | 27.5 | 9.9  | 34.5 | 77.5 | 206.2| 129.8| 79.8 | 63.6 | 53.7 | 38.8 | 17.6 | 12.7 | 21.6 |
| Mean | 67.0 | 71.0 | 47.8 | 27.5 | 8.5  | 13.2 | 56.9 | 121.5| 138.3| 103.2| 85.8 | 63.2 | 36.8 | 24.2 | 10.7 | 15.0 |

|      | 1845 | 1846 | 1847 | 1848 | 1849 | 1850 | 1851 | 1852 | 1853 | 1854 | 1855 | 1856 | 1857 | 1858 | 1859 | 1860 |
|------|------|------|------|------|------|------|------|------|------|------|------|------|------|------|------|------|
| Jan  | 25.7 | 38.7 | 62.6 | 159.1| 156.7| 78.0 | 75.5 | 68.4 | 41.1 | 15.4 | 12.3 | 0.5  | 13.7 | 39.0 | 83.7 | 81.5 |
| Feb  | 43.6 | 51.0 | 44.9 | 111.8| 131.7| 89.4 | 105.4| 67.5 | 42.9 | 20.0 | 11.4 | 4.9  | 7.4  | 34.9 | 87.6 | 88.0 |
| Mar  | 43.3 | 63.9 | 85.7 | 108.9| 96.5 | 82.6 | 64.6 | 61.2 | 37.7 | 20.7 | 17.4 | 0.4  | 5.2  | 57.5 | 90.3 | 98.9 |
| Apr  | 56.9 | 69.2 | 44.7 | 107.1| 102.5| 44.1 | 56.5 | 65.4 | 47.6 | 26.4 | 4.4  | 6.5  | 11.1 | 38.3 | 85.7 | 71.4 |
| May  | 47.8 | 59.9 | 75.4 | 102.2| 80.6 | 61.6 | 62.6 | 54.9 | 34.7 | 24.0 | 9.1  | 0.0  | 29.2 | 41.4 | 91.0 | 107.1|
| Jun  | 31.1 | 65.1 | 85.3 | 123.8| 81.2 | 70.0 | 63.2 | 46.9 | 40.0 | 21.1 | 5.3  | 5.0  | 16.0 | 44.5 | 87.1 | 108.6|
| Jul  | 30.6 | 46.5 | 52.2 | 139.2| 78.0 | 39.1 | 36.1 | 42.0 | 45.9 | 18.7 | 0.4  | 4.6  | 22.2 | 56.7 | 96.2 | 116.7|
| Aug  | 32.3 | 54.8 | 140.6| 132.5| 61.3 | 61.6 | 57.4 | 39.7 | 50.4 | 15.8 | 3.1  | 5.9  | 16.9 | 55.3 | 106.8| 100.3|
| Sep  | 29.6 | 107.1| 161.2| 100.3| 93.7 | 86.2 | 67.9 | 37.5 | 33.6 | 22.4 | 0.0  | 4.4  | 42.4 | 80.1 | 105.8| 92.2 |
| Oct  | 40.7 | 55.9 | 180.4| 132.4| 71.5 | 71.0 | 62.5 | 67.3 | 42.3 | 12.7 | 9.7  | 4.5  | 40.6 | 91.2 | 114.6| 90.1 |
| Nov  | 39.4 | 60.4 | 138.9| 114.6| 99.7 | 54.8 | 50.9 | 54.3 | 28.8 | 28.2 | 4.2  | 7.7  | 31.4 | 51.9 | 97.2 | 97.9 |
| Dec  | 59.7 | 65.5 | 109.6| 159.9| 97.0 | 60.0 | 71.4 | 45.4 | 23.4 | 21.4 | 3.1  | 7.2  | 37.2 | 66.8 | 81.0 | 95.6 |
| Mean | 40.1 | 61.5 | 98.5 | 124.3| 95.9 | 66.5 | 64.5 | 54.2 | 39.0 | 20.6 | 6.7  | 4.3  | 22.8 | 54.8 | 93.8 | 95.7 |

|      | 1861 | 1862 | 1863 | 1864 | 1865 | 1866 | 1867 | 1868 | 1869 | 1870 | 1871 | 1872 | 1873 | 1874 | 1875 | 1876 |
|------|------|------|------|------|------|------|------|------|------|------|------|------|------|------|------|------|
| Jan  | 62.3 | 63.1 | 48.3 | 57.7 | 48.7 | 31.6 | 0.0  | 15.6 | 60.9 | 77.3 | 88.3 | 79.5 | 88.7 | 60.8 | 14.6 | 14.3 |
| Feb  | 77.8 | 64.5 | 56.7 | 47.1 | 39.3 | 38.4 | 0.7  | 15.8 | 59.3 | 114.9| 125.3| 120.1| 107.0| 64.2 | 22.2 | 15.0 |
| Mar  | 101.0| 43.6 | 66.4 | 66.3 | 39.5 | 24.6 | 9.2  | 26.5 | 52.7 | 159.4| 143.2| 88.4 | 98.3 | 46.4 | 33.8 | 31.2 |
| Apr  | 98.5 | 53.7 | 40.6 | 35.8 | 29.4 | 17.6 | 5.1  | 36.6 | 41.0 | 160.0| 162.4| 102.1| 76.2 | 32.0 | 29.1 | 2.3  |
| May  | 56.8 | 64.4 | 53.8 | 40.6 | 34.5 | 12.9 | 2.9  | 26.7 | 104.0| 176.0| 145.5| 107.6| 47.9 | 44.6 | 11.5 | 5.1  |
| Jun  | 87.8 | 84.0 | 40.8 | 57.8 | 33.6 | 16.5 | 1.5  | 31.1 | 108.4| 135.6| 91.7 | 109.9| 44.8 | 38.2 | 23.9 | 1.6  |
| Jul  | 78.0 | 73.4 | 32.7 | 54.7 | 26.8 | 9.3  | 5.0  | 28.6 | 59.2 | 132.4| 103.0| 105.5| 66.9 | 67.8 | 12.5 | 15.2 |
| Aug  | 82.5 | 62.5 | 48.1 | 54.8 | 37.8 | 12.7 | 4.9  | 34.4 | 79.6 | 153.8| 110.0| 92.9 | 68.2 | 61.3 | 14.6 | 8.8  |
| Sep  | 79.9 | 66.6 | 22.0 | 28.5 | 21.6 | 7.3  | 9.8  | 43.8 | 80.6 | 136.0| 80.3 | 114.6| 47.5 | 28.0 | 2.4  | 9.9  |
| Oct  | 67.2 | 42.0 | 39.9 | 33.9 | 17.1 | 14.1 | 13.5 | 61.7 | 69.4 | 146.4| 89.0 | 103.5| 47.4 | 34.3 | 12.7 | 14.3 |
| Nov  | 53.7 | 50.6 | 37.7 | 57.6 | 24.6 | 9.0  | 9.3  | 59.1 | 77.4 | 147.5| 105.4| 112.0| 55.4 | 28.9 | 17.7 | 9.9  |
| Dec  | 80.5 | 40.9 | 41.2 | 28.6 | 12.8 | 1.5  | 25.2 | 67.6 | 104.3| 130.0| 90.3 | 83.9 | 49.2 | 29.3 | 9.9  | 8.2  |
| Mean | 77.2 | 59.1 | 44.0 | 47.0 | 30.5 | 16.3 | 7.3  | 37.3 | 73.9 | 139.1| 111.2| 101.7| 66.3 | 44.7 | 17.1 | 11.3 |

|      | 1877 | 1878 | 1879 | 1880 | 1881 | 1882 | 1883 | 1884 | 1885 | 1886 | 1887 | 1888 | 1889 | 1890 | 1891 | 1892 |
|------|------|------|------|------|------|------|------|------|------|------|------|------|------|------|------|------|
| Jan  | 24.4 | 3.3  | 0.8  | 24.0 | 36.3 | 45.0 | 60.6 | 91.5 | 42.8 | 29.9 | 10.3 | 12.7 | 0.8  | 5.3  | 13.5 | 69.1 |
| Feb  | 8.7  | 6.0  | 0.6  | 27.5 | 53.2 | 69.3 | 46.1 | 86.9 | 71.8 | 25.9 | 13.2 | 7.1  | 8.5  | 0.6  | 22.2 | 75.6 |
| Mar  | 11.7 | 7.8  | 0.0  | 19.5 | 51.5 | 67.5 | 42.8 | 86.8 | 49.8 | 57.3 | 4.2  | 7.8  | 7.0  | 5.1  | 10.4 | 49.9 |
| Apr  | 15.8 | 0.1  | 6.2  | 19.3 | 51.7 | 95.8 | 82.1 | 76.1 | 55.0 | 43.7 | 6.9  | 5.1  | 4.3  | 1.6  | 20.5 | 69.6 |
| May  | 21.2 | 5.8  | 2.4  | 23.5 | 43.5 | 64.1 | 32.1 | 86.5 | 73.0 | 30.7 | 20.0 | 7.0  | 2.4  | 4.8  | 41.1 | 79.6 |
| Jun  | 13.4 | 6.4  | 4.8  | 34.1 | 60.5 | 45.2 | 76.5 | 51.2 | 83.7 | 27.1 | 15.7 | 7.1  | 6.4  | 1.3  | 48.3 | 76.3 |
| Jul  | 5.9  | 0.1  | 7.5  | 21.9 | 76.9 | 45.4 | 80.6 | 53.1 | 66.5 | 30.3 | 23.3 | 3.1  | 9.7  | 11.6 | 58.8 | 76.8 |
| Aug  | 6.3  | 0.0  | 10.7 | 46.1 | 58.0 | 40.4 | 46.0 | 55.8 | 50.0 | 16.9 | 21.4 | 2.8  | 20.6 | 8.5  | 33.2 | 101.4|
| Sep  | 16.4 | 5.3  | 6.1  | 66.0 | 53.2 | 57.7 | 61.9 | 39.5 | 21.4 | 7.4  | 8.8  | 6.5  | 17.2 | 53.8 | 62.8 |      |
| Oct  | 6.7  | 1.1  | 12.3 | 43.0 | 64.0 | 59.2 | 83.6 | 47.8 | 38.7 | 8.6  | 6.6  | 2.1  | 2.1  | 11.2 | 51.5 | 70.5 |
| Nov  | 14.5 | 4.1  | 12.9 | 30.7 | 54.8 | 84.4 | 84.5 | 38.6 | 33.3 | 0.3  | 6.9  | 10.7 | 0.2  | 9.6  | 41.9 | 65.4 |
| Dec  | 2.3  | 0.5  | 7.2  | 29.6 | 47.3 | 41.8 | 75.9 | 47.2 | 21.7 | 12.4 | 20.7 | 6.7  | 6.7  | 7.8  | 32.2 | 78.6 |
| Mean | 12.3 | 3.4  | 6.0  | 32.3 | 54.3 | 59.7 | 63.7 | 63.5 | 52.2 | 25.4 | 13.1 | 6.8  | 6.3  | 7.1  | 35.6 | 73.0 |

|      | 1893  | 1894  | 1895  | 1896 | 1897 | 1898 | 1899 | 1900 | 1901  | 1902  | 1903 | 1904 | 1905 | 1906  | 1907  | 1908 |
|------|-------|-------|-------|------|------|------|------|------|-------|-------|------|------|------|-------|-------|------|
| Jan  | 75.0  | 83.2  | 63.3  | 29.0 | 40.6 | 30.2 | 19.5 | 9.4  | 0.2   | 5.2   | 8.3  | 31.6 | 54.8 | 46.5  | 76.4  | 39.2 |
| Feb  | 73.0  | 84.6  | 67.2  | 57.4 | 29.4 | 36.4 | 9.2  | 13.6 | 2.4   | 0.0   | 17.0 | 24.5 | 85.8 | 31.3  | 108.2 | 33.9 |
| Mar  | 65.7  | 52.3  | 61.0  | 52.0 | 29.1 | 38.3 | 18.1 | 8.6  | 4.5   | 12.4  | 13.5 | 37.2 | 66.5 | 64.5  | 60.7  | 28.7 |
| Apr  | 88.1  | 81.6  | 76.9  | 43.8 | 31.0 | 14.5 | 14.2 | 16.0 | 0.0   | 0.0   | 26.1 | 43.0 | 39.3 | 55.3  | 52.6  | 57.6 |
| May  | 84.7  | 101.2 | 67.5  | 27.7 | 20.0 | 25.8 | 7.7  | 15.2 | 10.2  | 2.8   | 14.6 | 39.5 | 48.0 | 57.7  | 43.0  | 40.8 |
| Jun  | 88.2  | 98.9  | 71.5  | 49.0 | 11.3 | 22.3 | 20.5 | 12.1 | 5.8   | 1.4   | 16.3 | 41.9 | 49.0 | 63.2  | 40.4  | 48.1 |
| Jul  | 88.8  | 106.0 | 47.8  | 45.0 | 27.8 | 9.0  | 13.5 | 8.3  | 0.7   | 0.9   | 27.9 | 50.6 | 73.0 | 103.3 | 49.7  | 39.5 |
| Aug  | 129.2 | 70.3  | 68.9  | 27.2 | 21.8 | 31.4 | 2.9  | 4.3  | 1.0   | 2.3   | 28.8 | 58.2 | 58.8 | 47.7  | 54.3  | 90.5 |
| Sep  | 77.9  | 65.9  | 57.7  | 61.3 | 48.1 | 34.8 | 8.4  | 8.3  | 0.6   | 7.6   | 11.1 | 30.1 | 55.0 | 56.1  | 85.0  | 86.9 |
| Oct  | 79.7  | 75.5  | 67.9  | 28.4 | 14.3 | 34.4 | 13.0 | 12.9 | 3.7   | 16.3  | 38.9 | 54.2 | 78.7 | 17.8  | 66.4  | 32.3 |
| Nov  | 75.1  | 66.6  | 47.2  | 38.0 | 8.4  | 30.9 | 7.8  | 4.5  | 3.8   | 10.3  | 44.5 | 38.0 | 107.2| 38.9  | 61.5  | 45.5 |
| Dec  | 93.8  | 60.0  | 70.7  | 42.6 | 33.3 | 12.6 | 10.5 | 0.3  | 0.0   | 1.1   | 45.6 | 54.6 | 55.5 | 64.7  | 47.3  | 39.5 |
| Mean | 84.9  | 78.0  | 64.0  | 41.8 | 26.2 | 26.7 | 12.1 | 9.5  | 2.7   | 5.0   | 24.4 | 42.0 | 63.5 | 53.8  | 62.0  | 48.5 |

|      | 1909 | 1910 | 1911 | 1912 | 1913 | 1914 | 1915 | 1916  | 1917  | 1918  | 1919  | 1920 | 1921 | 1922 | 1923 | 1924 |
|------|------|------|------|------|------|------|------|-------|-------|-------|-------|------|------|------|------|------|
| Jan  | 56.7 | 26.4 | 3.4  | 0.3  | 2.3  | 2.8  | 23.0 | 45.3  | 74.7  | 96.0  | 48.1  | 51.1 | 31.5 | 11.8 | 4.5  | 0.5  |
| Feb  | 46.6 | 31.5 | 9.0  | 0.0  | 2.9  | 2.6  | 42.3 | 55.4  | 71.9  | 65.3  | 79.5  | 53.9 | 28.3 | 26.4 | 1.5  | 5.1  |
| Mar  | 66.3 | 21.4 | 7.8  | 4.9  | 0.5  | 3.1  | 38.8 | 67.0  | 94.8  | 72.2  | 66.5  | 70.2 | 26.7 | 54.7 | 3.3  | 1.8  |
| Apr  | 32.3 | 8.4  | 16.5 | 4.5  | 0.9  | 17.3 | 41.3 | 71.8  | 74.7  | 80.5  | 51.8  | 14.8 | 32.4 | 11.0 | 6.1  | 11.3 |
| May  | 36.0 | 22.2 | 9.0  | 4.4  | 0.0  | 5.2  | 33.0 | 74.5  | 114.1 | 76.7  | 88.1  | 33.3 | 22.2 | 8.0  | 3.2  | 20.8 |
| Jun  | 22.6 | 12.3 | 2.2  | 4.1  | 0.0  | 11.4 | 68.8 | 87.7  | 114.9 | 59.4  | 111.2 | 38.7 | 33.7 | 5.8  | 9.1  | 24.0 |
| Jul  | 35.8 | 14.1 | 3.5  | 3.0  | 1.7  | 5.4  | 71.6 | 53.5  | 119.8 | 107.6 | 64.7  | 27.5 | 41.9 | 10.9 | 3.5  | 26.1 |
| Aug  | 23.1 | 11.5 | 4.0  | 0.3  | 0.2  | 7.7  | 69.6 | 35.2  | 154.5 | 101.7 | 69.0  | 19.2 | 22.8 | 6.5  | 0.5  | 19.3 |
| Sep  | 38.8 | 26.2 | 4.0  | 9.5  | 1.2  | 12.7 | 49.5 | 45.1  | 129.4 | 79.9  | 54.7  | 36.3 | 17.8 | 4.7  | 13.2 | 25.1 |
| Oct  | 58.4 | 38.3 | 2.6  | 4.6  | 3.1  | 8.2  | 53.5 | 50.7  | 72.2  | 85.0  | 52.8  | 49.6 | 18.2 | 6.2  | 11.6 | 25.6 |
| Nov  | 55.8 | 4.9  | 4.2  | 1.1  | 0.7  | 16.4 | 42.5 | 65.6  | 96.4  | 83.4  | 42.0  | 27.2 | 17.8 | 7.4  | 10.0 | 22.5 |
| Dec  | 54.2 | 5.8  | 2.2  | 6.4  | 3.8  | 22.3 | 34.5 | 53.0  | 129.3 | 59.2  | 34.9  | 29.9 | 20.3 | 17.5 | 2.8  | 16.5 |
| Mean | 43.9 | 18.6 | 5.7  | 3.6  | 1.4  | 9.6  | 47.4 | 57.1  | 103.9 | 80.6  | 63.6  | 37.6 | 26.1 | 14.2 | 5.8  | 16.7 |

|      | 1925 | 1926 | 1927 | 1928 | 1929 | 1930 | 1931 | 1932 | 1933 | 1934 | 1935 | 1936  | 1937  | 1938  | 1939  | 1940  |
|------|------|------|------|------|------|------|------|------|------|------|------|-------|-------|-------|-------|-------|
| Jan  | 5.5  | 71.8 | 81.6 | 83.5 | 68.9 | 65.3 | 14.6 | 12.1 | 12.3 | 3.4  | 18.9 | 62.8  | 132.5 | 98.4  | 80.3  | 50.5  |
| Feb  | 23.2 | 70.0 | 93.0 | 73.5 | 64.1 | 49.2 | 43.1 | 10.6 | 22.2 | 7.8  | 20.5 | 74.3  | 128.5 | 119.2 | 77.4  | 59.4  |
| Mar  | 18.0 | 62.5 | 69.6 | 85.4 | 60.2 | 35.0 | 30.0 | 11.2 | 10.1 | 4.3  | 23.1 | 77.1  | 83.9  | 86.5  | 64.6  | 83.3  |
| Apr  | 31.7 | 38.5 | 93.5 | 80.6 | 52.8 | 38.2 | 31.2 | 11.2 | 2.9  | 11.3 | 12.2 | 74.9  | 109.3 | 101.0 | 109.1 | 60.7  |
| May  | 42.8 | 64.3 | 79.1 | 76.9 | 58.2 | 36.8 | 24.6 | 17.9 | 3.2  | 19.7 | 27.3 | 54.6  | 116.7 | 127.4 | 118.3 | 54.4  |
| Jun  | 47.5 | 73.5 | 59.1 | 91.4 | 71.9 | 28.8 | 15.3 | 22.2 | 5.2  | 6.7  | 45.7 | 70.0  | 130.0 | 97.5  | 101.0 | 83.9  |
| Jul  | 38.5 | 52.3 | 54.9 | 96.0 | 70.2 | 21.9 | 17.4 | 9.6  | 2.8  | 9.3  | 33.9 | 52.3  | 145.1 | 165.3 | 97.6  | 67.5  |
| Aug  | 37.9 | 61.6 | 53.8 | 83.8 | 66.5 | 24.9 | 13.0 | 6.8  | 0.2  | 8.3  | 30.1 | 87.0  | 137.7 | 115.7 | 105.8 | 105.5 |
| Sep  | 60.2 | 60.8 | 68.4 | 89.7 | 34.4 | 32.1 | 19.0 | 4.0  | 5.1  | 4.0  | 42.1 | 76.0  | 100.7 | 89.6  | 112.8 | 66.5  |
| Oct  | 69.2 | 71.5 | 63.1 | 61.4 | 54.0 | 34.4 | 10.0 | 8.9  | 3.0  | 5.7  | 53.2 | 89.0  | 124.9 | 99.1  | 88.1  | 55.0  |
| Nov  | 58.6 | 60.5 | 67.2 | 50.3 | 81.1 | 35.6 | 18.7 | 8.2  | 0.6  | 8.7  | 64.2 | 115.4 | 74.4  | 122.2 | 68.1  | 58.4  |
| Dec  | 98.6 | 79.4 | 45.2 | 59.0 | 108.0| 25.8 | 17.8 | 11.0 | 0.3  | 15.4 | 61.5 | 123.4 | 88.8  | 92.7  | 42.1  | 68.3  |
| Mean | 44.3 | 63.9 | 69.0 | 77.8 | 65.0 | 35.7 | 21.2 | 11.1 | 5.7  | 8.7  | 36.1 | 79.7  | 114.4 | 109.6 | 88.8  | 67.8  |

|      | 1941 | 1942 | 1943 | 1944 | 1945 | 1946  | 1947  | 1948  | 1949  | 1950  | 1951  | 1952 | 1953 | 1954 | 1955 | 1956  |
|------|------|------|------|------|------|-------|-------|-------|-------|-------|-------|------|------|------|------|-------|
| Jan  | 45.6 | 35.6 | 12.4 | 3.7  | 18.5 | 47.6  | 115.7 | 108.5 | 119.1 | 101.6 | 59.9  | 40.7 | 26.5 | 0.2  | 23.1 | 73.6  |
| Feb  | 44.5 | 52.8 | 28.9 | 0.5  | 12.7 | 86.2  | 133.4 | 86.1  | 182.3 | 94.8  | 59.9  | 22.2 | 3.9  | 0.5  | 20.8 | 124.0 |
| Mar  | 46.4 | 54.2 | 27.4 | 11.0 | 21.5 | 76.6  | 129.8 | 94.8  | 157.5 | 109.7 | 55.9  | 22.0 | 10.0 | 10.9 | 4.9  | 118.4 |
| Apr  | 32.8 | 60.7 | 26.1 | 0.3  | 32.0 | 75.7  | 149.8 | 189.7 | 147.0 | 113.4 | 92.9  | 29.1 | 27.8 | 1.8  | 11.3 | 110.7 |
| May  | 29.5 | 25.0 | 14.1 | 2.5  | 30.6 | 84.9  | 201.3 | 174.0 | 106.2 | 106.2 | 108.5 | 23.4 | 12.5 | 0.8  | 28.9 | 136.6 |
| Jun  | 59.8 | 11.4 | 7.6  | 5.0  | 36.2 | 73.5  | 163.9 | 167.8 | 121.7 | 83.6  | 100.6 | 36.4 | 21.8 | 0.2  | 31.7 | 116.6 |
| Jul  | 66.9 | 17.7 | 13.2 | 5.0  | 42.6 | 116.2 | 157.9 | 142.2 | 125.8 | 91.0  | 61.5  | 39.3 | 8.6  | 4.8  | 26.7 | 129.1 |
| Aug  | 60.0 | 20.2 | 19.4 | 16.7 | 25.9 | 107.2 | 188.8 | 157.9 | 123.8 | 85.2  | 61.0  | 54.9 | 23.5 | 8.4  | 40.7 | 169.6 |
| Sep  | 65.9 | 17.2 | 10.0 | 14.3 | 34.9 | 94.4  | 169.4 | 143.3 | 145.3 | 51.3  | 83.1  | 28.2 | 19.3 | 1.5  | 42.7 | 173.2 |
| Oct  | 46.3 | 19.2 | 7.8  | 16.9 | 68.8 | 102.3 | 163.6 | 136.3 | 131.6 | 61.4  | 51.6  | 23.8 | 8.2  | 7.0  | 58.5 | 155.3 |
| Nov  | 38.3 | 30.7 | 10.2 | 10.8 | 46.0 | 123.8 | 128.0 | 95.8  | 143.5 | 54.8  | 52.4  | 22.1 | 1.6  | 9.2  | 89.2 | 201.3 |
| Dec  | 33.7 | 22.5 | 18.8 | 28.4 | 27.4 | 121.7 | 116.5 | 138.0 | 117.6 | 54.1  | 45.8  | 34.3 | 2.5  | 7.6  | 76.9 | 192.1 |
| Mean | 47.5 | 30.6 | 16.3 | 9.6  | 33.2 | 92.6  | 151.6 | 136.2 | 135.1 | 83.9  | 69.4  | 31.4 | 13.9 | 4.4  | 38.0 | 141.7 |

|      | 1957  | 1958  | 1959  | 1960  | 1961 | 1962 | 1963 | 1964 | 1965 | 1966 | 1967  | 1968  | 1969  | 1970  | 1971 | 1972 |
|------|-------|-------|-------|-------|------|------|------|------|------|------|-------|-------|-------|-------|------|------|
| Jan  | 165.0 | 202.5 | 217.4 | 146.3 | 57.9 | 38.7 | 19.8 | 15.3 | 17.5 | 28.2 | 110.9 | 121.8 | 104.4 | 111.5 | 91.3 | 61.5 |
| Feb  | 130.2 | 164.9 | 143.1 | 106.0 | 46.1 | 50.3 | 24.4 | 17.7 | 14.2 | 24.4 | 93.6  | 111.9 | 120.5 | 127.8 | 79.0 | 88.4 |
| Mar  | 157.4 | 190.7 | 185.7 | 102.2 | 53.0 | 45.6 | 17.1 | 16.5 | 11.7 | 25.3 | 111.8 | 92.2  | 135.8 | 102.9 | 60.7 | 80.1 |
| Apr  | 175.2 | 196.0 | 163.3 | 122.0 | 61.4 | 46.4 | 29.3 | 8.6  | 6.8  | 48.7 | 69.5  | 81.2  | 106.8 | 109.5 | 71.8 | 63.2 |
| May  | 164.6 | 175.3 | 172.0 | 119.6 | 51.0 | 43.7 | 43.0 | 9.5  | 24.1 | 46.3 | 86.5  | 127.2 | 120.0 | 127.5 | 67.5 | 80.5 |
| Jun  | 200.7 | 171.5 | 168.7 | 110.2 | 77.4 | 42.0 | 35.9 | 9.1  | 15.9 | 47.7 | 67.3  | 110.3 | 106.0 | 106.8 | 49.8 | 88.0 |
| Jul  | 187.2 | 191.4 | 149.6 | 121.7 | 70.2 | 21.8 | 19.5 | 3.1  | 11.9 | 56.7 | 91.5  | 96.1  | 96.8  | 112.5 | 81.0 | 76.5 |
| Aug  | 158.0 | 200.2 | 199.6 | 134.1 | 55.8 | 21.8 | 33.2 | 9.3  | 8.9  | 51.2 | 107.2 | 109.3 | 96.0  | 93.0  | 61.4 | 76.8 |
| Sep  | 235.8 | 201.2 | 145.2 | 127.2 | 63.6 | 51.3 | 38.8 | 4.7  | 16.8 | 50.2 | 76.8  | 117.2 | 91.3  | 99.5  | 50.2 | 64.0 |
| Oct  | 253.8 | 181.5 | 111.4 | 82.8  | 37.7 | 39.5 | 35.3 | 6.1  | 20.1 | 57.2 | 88.2  | 107.7 | 95.7  | 86.6  | 51.7 | 61.3 |
| Nov  | 210.9 | 152.3 | 124.0 | 89.6  | 32.6 | 26.9 | 23.4 | 7.4  | 15.8 | 57.2 | 94.3  | 86.0  | 93.5  | 95.2  | 63.2 | 41.6 |
| Dec  | 239.4 | 187.6 | 125.0 | 85.6  | 39.9 | 23.2 | 14.9 | 15.1 | 17.0 | 70.4 | 126.4 | 109.8 | 97.9  | 83.5  | 82.2 | 45.3 |
| Mean | 189.9 | 184.7 | 158.8 | 112.3 | 53.9 | 37.5 | 27.9 | 10.2 | 15.1 | 47.0 | 93.8  | 105.9 | 105.5 | 104.5 | 66.6 | 68.9 |

|      | 1973 | 1974 | 1975 | 1976 | 1977 | 1978 | 1979 | 1980 | 1981 | 1982 | 1983 |
|------|------|------|------|------|------|------|------|------|------|------|------|
| Jan  | 43.4 | 27.6 | 18.9 | 8.5  | 15.7 | 49.3 | 165.8| 159.6| 114.4| 110.7| 85.8 |
| Feb  | 42.9 | 26.0 | 11.5 | 4.6  | 22.6 | 89.8 | 138.0| 155.0| 143.5| 162.6| 50.1 |
| Mar  | 46.0 | 21.3 | 11.5 | 23.0 | 8.0  | 93.8 | 137.0| 126.2| 133.8| 153.7| 66.5 |
| Apr  | 57.7 | 40.3 | 5.1  | 19.5 | 13.2 | 94.7 | 102.8| 164.1| 156.2| 122.5| 79.7 |
| May  | 42.4 | 39.5 | 9.0  | 12.7 | 18.3 | 79.3 | 134.6| 179.9| 126.0| 81.4 | 100.2|
| Jun  | 39.5 | 36.0 | 11.4 | 12.4 | 38.4 | 94.1 | 150.5| 157.3| 89.8 | 110.4|      |
| Jul  | 23.1 | 55.8 | 28.2 | 12.1 | 21.2 | 68.4 | 159.6| 136.3| 144.2| 102.6|      |
| Aug  | 25.6 | 33.6 | 39.7 | 16.9 | 29.9 | 56.7 | 143.5| 135.4| 158.2| 105.9|      |
| Sep  | 59.6 | 40.2 | 18.9 | 13.4 | 44.1 | 137.3| 188.7| 155.0| 169.3| 119.2|      |
| Oct  | 30.9 | 47.1 | 9.1  | 21.8 | 41.3 | 122.8| 188.2| 164.7| 161.2| 94.3 |      |
| Nov  | 23.9 | 25.0 | 19.4 | 5.5  | 26.6 | 96.6 | 185.0| 147.9| 135.6| 98.5 |      |
| Dec  | 23.3 | 20.5 | 7.8  | 15.0 | 41.3 | 119.1| 182.2| 174.4| 147.1| 126.4|      |
| Mean | 38.0 | 34.5 | 15.5 | 13.8 | 26.7 | 92.5 | 155.4| 154.6| 139.9| 115.7|      |

**Courtesy: The Foundation for the Study of Cycles
124 South Highland Avenue, Pittsburgh, PA 15206**

# Appendix 2

Systematic Period Reconnaissances of Sunspot Numbers, 1700-1965
(Alternate Cycles Reversed, Adjusted for the 22.22-Year Cycle, and with
Excessive Peaks and Troughs Minimized)
Compared to Synodic Periods of the Five Outer Planets   *Cycles*, October 1968

| | *Sunspots* | | | *Planets* | *Difference* |
|---|---|---|---|---|---|
| *1* | *2* | *3* | *4* | *5* | *6* |
| Fraction of 266 years | Period (in years) | Amplitude | Names of Planets | Synodic Period (in yrs.) | Synodic Periods vs. Sunspot Periods (in yrs.) |
| - | - | - | Pluto & Neptune | 492. | - |
| 1.30 | 204.62 | 3.42 | | | |
| - | - | - | Neptune & Uranus | 171.4 | - |
| 2.15 | 123.72 | 1.41 | Uranus & Pluto | 126.94 | +3.23 |
| 3.30 | 80.61 | 1.35 | | | |
| 4.40 | 60.45 | 2.72 | | | |
| 5.10 | 52.16 | 2.27 | | | |
| 5.85 | 45.47 | 2.24 | Saturn & Uranus | 45.36 | -0.11 |
| 7.05 | 37.73 | 5.92 | | | |
| - | - | - | Saturn & Neptune | 35.87 | - |
| - | - | - | Saturn & Pluto | 33.42 | - |
| 8.30 | 32.05 | 2.72 | | | |
| 9.70 | 27.42 | 5.71 | | | |
| 10.50 | 25.33 | 7.15 | | | |
| 12.40 | 21.45 | 6.35 | | | |
| 13.45 | 19.78 | 10.56 | Jupiter & Saturn | 19.86 | +0.08 |
| 14.80 | 17.97 | 19.74 | | | |
| 17.00 | 15.65 | 9.29 | | | |
| 18.15 | 14.66 | 3.72 | | | |
| 19.30 | 13.78 | 6.97 | Jupiter & Uranus | 13.81 | +0.03 |
| - | - | - | Jupiter & Neptune | 12.78 | - |
| 21.45 | 12.40 | 5.15 | Jupiter & Pluto | 12.46 | +0.06 |

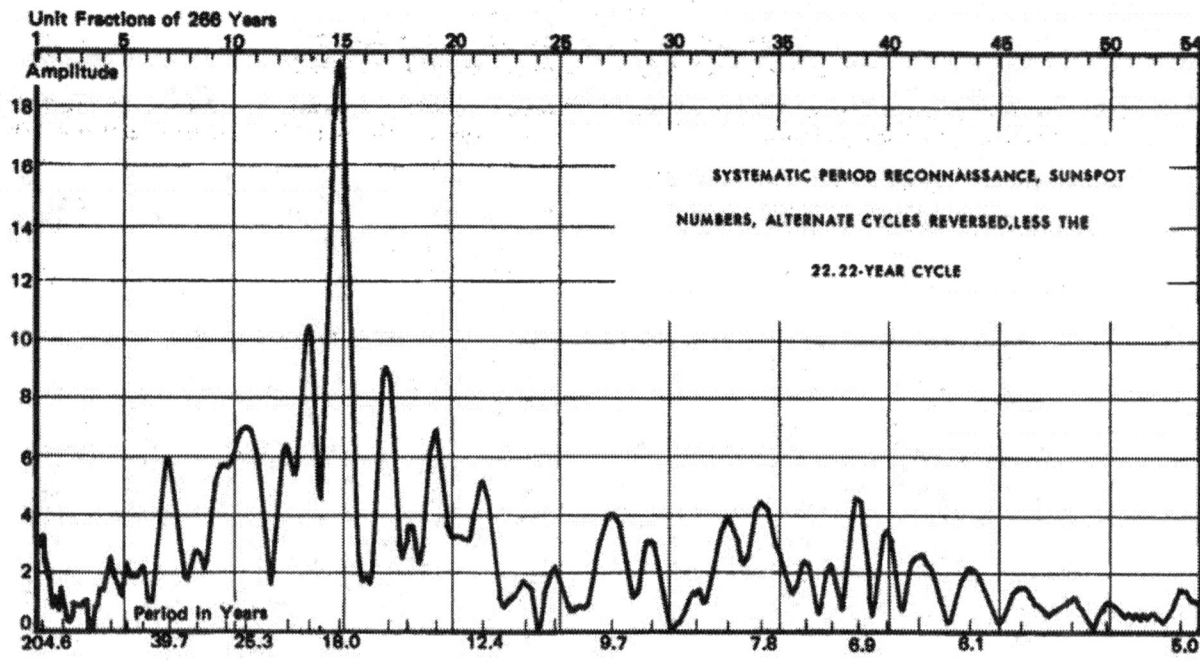

*Figure 4. Systematic Period Reconnaissance of the Double Sunspot Cycle. Sunspot Numbers Less the 22.22-Year Cycle and with Excessive Values Minimized.*

The peak of a periodogram will reveal the *exact* period of a real cycle except a) as the trial periods are too far apart to do so, and b) as the situation is distorted by randoms (or other cycles), and c) as the situation is distorted by "echoes" from other cycles concurrently present in the series.

Figure 5 shows a periodogram made from an analysis of 100 years of controlled data consisting entirely of consecutive 6-year zigzag waves. The cycle is shown by the peak at the 16⅔ fraction of 100. By the 15⅔ and 17⅔ fractions of 100, it is completely washed out. All peaks cycles should normally be removed before a cycle analysis is attempted. Such removal is standard procedure, especially in economic and sociological series (war) and in medical series (pandemics). Experiments with controlled data have shown the usefulness and desirability of this procedure.

The peaks, 12 years and up, from the periodogram of sunspot numbers with alternate cycles reversed are noted as possible cycles in the listing made in Table 1. These suggested minor cycles on the sun give us the periods which are compared to the synodic periods of the outer planets.

# Appendix 3
# Data for Wood's Planet-Sunspot Correlations

Source: *Nature*, Vol. 240, November 10, 1972

### Table 1. Comparison of Sunspot Cycle Peak Dates with Dates of Peak Planetary Tidal Fluctuation.

| Sunspot cycle No. | Sunspot peak date | Tidal peak date | $E_{pp}$ | $\dot{N}_{Ss}$ at peak |
|---|---|---|---|---|
| -13 | 1604.5 | 1605.4 | -0.9 | |
| -12 | 1615.5 | 1617.5 | -2.0 | |
| -11 | 1626.0 | 1628.3 | -2.3 | no data |
| -10 | 1639.7 | 1639.5 | +0.2 | |
| -9 | 1649.0 | 1650.5 | -1.5 | |
| | | Uranus-Neptune period 1 | | |
| -8 | 1660.0 | 1661.5 | -1.5 | |
| -7 | 1675.0 | 1672.1 | +2.9 | |
| -6 | 1685.0 | 1683.3 | +1.7 | |
| -5 | 1693.0 | 1693.7 | -0.7 | |
| -4 | 1705.5 | 1705.1 | +0.4 | no data |
| -3 | 1718.2 | 1716.2 | +2.0 | |
| -2 | 1727.5 | 1727.0 | +0.5 | |
| -1 | 1738.7 | 1738.4 | +0.3 | |
| 0 | 1750.1 | 1749.8 | +0.3 | 92 |
| 1 | 1761.5 | 1760.6 | +0.9 | 86 |
| 2 | 1769.8 | 1772.2 | -2.4 | 116 |
| 3 | 1778.5 | 1782.8 | -4.3 | 158 |
| 4 | 1788.2 | 1794.1 | -5.9 | 141 |
| 5 | 1804.8 | 1805.6 | -0.8 | 49 |
| 6 | 1816.4 | 1816.6 | -0.2 | 49 |
| | | Uranus-Neptune period 2 | | |
| 7 | 1830.0 | 1827.0 | +3.0 | 72 |
| 8 | 1837.2 | 1838.2 | -1.0 | 147 |
| 9 | 1848.3 | 1848.7 | -0.4 | 132 |
| 10 | 1860.2 | 1859.5 | +0.7 | 98 |
| 11 | 1870.7 | 1871.0 | -0.3 | 140 |
| 12 | 1884.0 | 1881.0 | -3.0 | 75 |
| 13 | 1893.9 | 1893.1 | +0.8 | 88 |
| 14 | 1906.3 | 1904.5 | +1.8 | 63 |
| 15 | 1917.7 | 1915.9 | +1.8 | 105 |
| 16 | 1928.4 | 1927.1 | +1.3 | 78 |
| 17 | 1937.6 | 1937.9 | -0.3 | 119 |
| 18 | 1947.5 | 1949.5 | -2.0 | 152 |
| 19 | 1958.2 | 1960.7 | -2.5 | 201 |
| 20 | 1969.3 | 1971.3 | -2.0 | 110 |

|  |  | Forecast* |  |  |
|---|---|---|---|---|
| 21 | 1982.0 | 1982.0 | 0 | 60 |
| 22 | 1993.4 | 1992.9 | +0.5 | 60 |
|  |  | Uranus-Neptune period 3 |  |  |
| 23 | 2002.1 | 2004.1 | -2.0 | 80 |
| 24 | 2014.0 | 2014.5 | -0.5 | 130 |
| 25 | 2025.6 | 2026.1 | -0.5 | 130 |
| 26 | 2036.1 | 2037.6 | -1.5 | 90 |
| 27 | 2048.3 | 2048.3 | 0 | 120 |
| 28 | 2056.6 | 2059.1 | -2.5 | 70 |
| 29 | 2071.4 | 2070.9 | +0.5 | 90 |
| 30 | 2079.5 | 2081.5 | -2.0 | 70 |
| 31 | 2093.6 | 2092.6 | +1.0 | 100 |
| 32 | 2104.4 | 2103.9 | +0.5 | 90 |

*Assuming $E_{pp}$ and $N_{SsPk}$ repeat about every 170 to 180 years in the future as in the past. Data above are grouped by Uranus-Neptune synodic periods, but other physical factors may be more significant. Average cycle lengths are: sunspots, 11.05 years, and planet tides, 11.08 years.—K.D. Wood, Aerospace Engineering Sciences, University of Colorado, Boulder, Colorado

### Table 2. Comparison of Sunspot Cycle Valley Dates with Dates of Maximum Relative Angle Q and Values of Q at N as min.

| Cycle No. | $N_{Ss}$ min Date | $\varphi_r$ max date | $E_{pp}$ | $\varphi_r$ at $N_{Ss}$ min |
|---|---|---|---|---|
| -13, -12 | 1610.8 | 1610.3 | +0.5 | 36° |
| -12, -11 | 1619.0 | 1621.7 | -2.7 | 12°b |
| -11, -10 | 1634.0 | 1633.1 | +0.9 | 38° |
| -10, -9 | 1645.0 | 1644.3 | +0.7 | 34° |
| -9, -8 | 1655.0 | 1655.7 | -0.7 | 36°b |
|  | Uranus-Neptune period 1 |  |  |  |
| -8, -7 | 1666.0 | 1666.7 | -0.7 | 33°b |
| -7, -6 | 1679.5 | 1678.1 | +1.4 | 30° |
| -6, -5 | 1689.5 | 1688.9 | +0.6 | 42° |
| -5, -4 | 1698.0 | 1700.3 | -2.3 | 24° |
| -4, -3 | 1712.0 | 1710.9 | +1.1 | 39° |
| -3, -2 | 1723.5 | 1722.5 | +1.0 | 37° |
| -2, -1 | 1734.0 | 1733.0 | +1.0 | 43° |
| -1, 0 | 1745.0 | 1744.0 | +1.0 | 37° |
| 0, 1 | 1755.2 | 1755.0 | +0.2 | 40° |
| 1, 2 | 1766.5 | 1765.6 | +0.9 | 40° |
| 2, 3 | 1775.4 | 1771.1 | -1.6 | 36° |
| 3, 4 | 1784.4 | 1787.8 | -3.1 | 15°b |
| 4, 5 | 1798.4 | 1798.9 | -0.5 | 36°b |
| 5, 6 | 1811.0 | 1810.2 | +0.8 | 40° |

|  |  | Uranus-Neptune period 2 |  |  |
|---|---|---|---|---|
| 6, 7 | 1823.2 | 1821.4 | +1.8 | 23° |
| 7, 8 | 1833.9 | 1833.0 | +0.9 | 35° |
| 8, 9 | 1843.7 | 1844.0 | −0.3 | 41°b |
| 9, 10 | 1856.0 | 1855.2 | +0.8 | 35° |
| 10, 11 | 1867.2 | 1866.1 | +1.1 | 36° |
| 11, 12 | 1878.9 | 1877.5 | +1.4 | 29° |
| 12, 13 | 1890.1 | 1888.5 | +0.6 | 35° |
| 13, 14 | 1901.5 | 1899.1 | +2.4 | 35° |
| 14, 15 | 1913.3 | 1910.1 | +3.2 | 27° |
| 15, 16 | 1923.5 | 1920.9 | +2.6 | 25° |
| 16, 17 | 1933.8 | 1931.7 | +2.1 | 36° |
| 17, 18 | 1944.2 | 1942.9 | +1.3 | 33° |
| 18, 19 | 1954.4 | 1953.9 | +0.5 | 40° |
| 19, 20 | 1964.8 | 1965.3 | −0.5 | 41°b |
|  |  | Forecast* |  |  |
| 20, 21 | 1977.0 | 1976.2 | +0.2 | 35° |
| 21, 22 | 1988.8 | 1987.6 | +1.4 | 35° |
| 22, 23 | 1997.7 | 1999.0 | +1.0 | 35° |

*Assuming mean $E_{pp}$ follows pattern about every 170 to 180 years, and $\varphi_r = 35°$ at minimum $N_{Ss}$.

All angles $\varphi_r$ are after $\varphi_r$ max except those labeled b (= before).

The forecast values of peak sunspot number $N_{SsPk}$ shown in Table 1 also assume that the 170 to 180 year cycle pattern of the past repeats in the future. Because the past mismatch averages about 15 smoothed monthly sunspots, I estimate that the probably error of the $N_{SsPk}$ forecast is about 15.

Table 1 includes a forecast of peak dates and sunspot numbers for the next 130 years (12 sunspot cycles). The tidal peak dates are as certain as the future positions of the planets. For future sunspot peak date estimates, I assumed that $E_{pp}$ varies with time with the same 170 year to 180 year cycle in the future as it has in the past. Because of the past data in Table 1, I believe that the estimated future sunspot peak dates have a probable error of substantially less than one year (but of course, in view of the errors of cycles 3 and 4, possible errors of several years).

Table 2 includes forecast dates for the next three tidal valleys, using a procedure similar to that described for peaks.

# Appendix 4
# Crawford 9-year Cycle vs. Cleveland Trust Business Index

| Crawford | *Highs* Index | Result | Crawford | *Lows* Index | Result |
|---|---|---|---|---|---|
| July 1836 | Feb. 1837 | 7 mos too soon | July 1831 | July 1834 | 3 yrs too soon |
| July 1845 | June 1847 | 2 yrs too soon | July 1840 | Jan. 1843 | 18 mos too soon |
| July 1854 | Mar. 1854 | OK | July 1849 | Feb. 1849 | OK |
| July 1863 | Apr. 1864 | 9 mos too soon | July 1858 | Jan. 1858 | OK |
| July 1872 | Jan. 1873 | 6 mos too soon | July 1867 | Dec. 1865 | 20 mos too late |
| July 1881 | Jan. 1881 | 6 mos too soon | July 1876 | Dec. 1876 | OK |
| July 1890 | May 1890 | OK | July 1885 | Feb. 1885 | OK |
| July 1899 | Jan. 1900 | 6 mos too soon | July 1894 | June 1894 | OK |
| July 1908 | Jan. 1906 | 2½ yrs too late | July 1903 | Dec. 1903 | OK |
| July 1917 | Oct. 1916 | 9 mos too late | July 1912 | July 1911 | 1 yr too late |
| July 1926 | July 1929 | 3 yrs too soon | July 1921 | Apr. 1921 | OK |
| July 1935 | Mar. 1937 | 22 mos too soon | July 1930 | July 1932 | 2 yrs too soon |
| July 1944 | Nov. 1943 | 8 mos too late | July 1939 | June 1938 | 13 mos too late |
| July 1953 | May 1953 | OK | July 1948 | Oct. 1949 | 15 mos too soon |
| July 1962 | July 1969 | 7 yrs too soon | July 1957 | Mar. 1958 | 8 mos too soon |
| July 1971 | May 1973 | 22 mos too soon | July 1966 | Mar. 1967 | 8 mos too soon |
| July 1980 | July 1979 | 1 yr too soon | July 1975 | Apr. 1975 | OK |

# Appendix 5
# Hutner Composite Cycle vs. Cleveland Trust Company Index

| | *Highs* | | | *Lows* | |
|---|---|---|---|---|---|
| *Hutner* | *Index* | *Result* | *Hutner* | *Index* | *Result* |
| Jan. 1860 | Sept. 1860 | 9 mos early | Oct. 1854 | Dec. 1854 | OK |
| Jan. 1863 | Mar. 1864 | 15 mos early | Jan. 1865 | Aug. 1865 | OK |
| Jan. 1870 | June 1870 | OK | Oct. 1877 | Feb. 1878 | OK |
| Jan. 1873 | Jan. 1873 | OK | Dec. 1887 | Apr. 1888 | OK |
| Jan. 1880 | Mar. 1880 | OK | Mar. 1898 | Sep. 1896 | 18 mos late |
| Jan. 1883 | Dec. 1882 | OK | Mar. 1911 | July 1911 | OK |
| Jan. 1890 | May 1890 | OK | June 1921 | July 1921 | OK |
| Jan. 1893 | Mar. 1893 | OK | Sept. 1931 | July 1932 | 10 mos early |
| June 1896 | Sept. 1895 | OK | Dec. 1933 | Feb. 1946 | 14 mos early |
| Mar. 1903 | Apr. 1903 | OK | Sept. 1954 | Sept. 1954 | OK |
| Mar. 1905 | Jan. 1906 | 10 mos early | July 1965 | Mar. 1967 | 18 mos early |
| July 1913 | Feb. 1913 | OK | July 1975 | Apr. 1975 | OK |
| June 1916 | Sept. 1916 | OK | | | |
| June 1923 | June 1923 | OK | | | |
| Oct. 1926 | Oct. 1926 | OK | | | |
| June 1929 | July 1929 | OK | | | |
| Dec. 1936 | Mar. 1937 | OK | | | |
| Nov. 1940 | Feb. 1944 | 15 mos early | | | |
| Jan. 1947 | Jan. 1947 | OK | | | |
| Feb. 1950 | Aug. 1951 | OK | | | |
| Jan. 1957 | Feb. 1957 | OK | | | |
| Mar. 1960 | Mar. 1960 | OK | | | |
| Sept. 1966 | Oct. 1966 | OK | | | |
| Mar. 1970 | Aug. 1969 | OK | | | |
| Mar. 1973 | Apr. 1973 | OK | | | |
| Mar. 1980 | July 1979 | 8 mos late | | | |

# Appendix 6
# The 30 Stocks Used in the Dow Jones Industrial Average

| *Stock* | *Closing Prices* | |
|---|---|---|
| | *8/14/81* | *8/17/81* |
| Allied Corp. | 53.500 | 53.500 |
| Aluminum Co. | 27.375 | 27.375 |
| American Brands | 41.000 | 41.000 |
| American Can | 36.625 | 36.375 |
| American Tel & Tel | 58.750 | 58.000 |
| Bethlehem Steel | 23.000 | 22.750 |
| Du Pont | 43.125 | 42.750 |
| Eastman Kodak | 72.000 | 71.375 |
| Exxon | 35.125 | 34.750 |
| General Electric | 58.125 | 58.000 |
| General Foods | 32.125 | 32.000 |
| General Motors | 48.000 | 47.500 |
| Good Year | 19.875 | 19.750 |
| Inco | 18.500 | 18.250 |
| IBM | 58.000 | 56.750 |
| International Harvester | 12.750 | 11.625 |
| International Paper | 47.500 | 46.125 |
| Johns-Manville | 19.625 | 19.125 |
| Merck | 86.000 | 82.500 |
| Minnesota M & M | 52.625 | 51.875 |
| Owens-Illinois | 28.750 | 29.250 |
| Proctor & Gamble | 70.125 | 70.000 |
| Sears Roebuck | 17.500 | 17.125 |
| Standard Oil of California | 45.500 | 45.500 |
| Texaco | 39.125 | 38.625 |
| Union Carbide | 56.000 | 55.500 |
| United Technologies | 52.000 | 51.125 |
| U.S. Steel | 28.875 | 28.875 |
| Westinghouse Electric | 28.000 | 28.000 |
| Woolworth | 22.000 | 22.000 |
| *Totals* | $1,231.500 | $1,217.375 |
| *Arithmetical Avg. = ÷ 30* | $41.050 | $40.579 |
| *DJI Average = ÷ 1.314* | 937.210 | 926.460 |
| *Quoted in The Wall Street Journal* | 936.930 | 936.750 |

Compiled by Lcdr. David Williams

# Glossary

**Amplitude:** The extent of the swing on each side of the average, or the total move between low and high.

**Angle:** The distance measured in degrees that two planets are apart. *Hard* angles are: 0°, 45°, 90°, 135°, 180°, 225°, 270°, 315°; *Soft* angles are: 30°, 60°, 120°, 150°, 210°, 240°, 300°, 330°. Hard angles are said to be inharmonious, while soft angles are said to be harmonious in their effects.

**Animism:** The belief that events are brought about through the agency of the innumerable spirits of the earth, air, water, or fire, which could be controlled by the spells, exorcisms or incantations of the Shamau, sorcerer, or witch-doctor.

**Anthropology:** The science of man's development and history. The part in a planet's orbit which is furthest from the sun.

**Apocalyptic:** Any remarkable revelation, such as the revelation made to the Apostle John.

**Arbitrage:** The simultaneous buying and selling of the same thing, such as bonds, currencies, commodities, or stocks in different markets, in order to profit by the difference in prices quoted in such markets.

**Archaeology:** The science or study of history from relics and remains of antiquity.

**Aspect:** The angular separation of planets, viz: 0° conjunction, 60° sextile, 90° square, 120° trine, 180° opposition.

**Aspectarian:** A table showing the angular separation between planets each day.

**Astral Energy:** Energy emanating from the stars.

**Astral Light:** Light emanating from the stars.

**Astro Economics:** The study of the correlation between planetary cycles and business, commodity, or stock cycles.

**Astrology:** The study of the influence of planetary movements and positions on man. Natal astrology deals with the influence on individuals; mundane astrology deals with the influence on nations; financial astrology deals with the influence on business, stocks and commodities.

**Astrometeorology:** The study of the influence of the heavenly bodies on the weather.

**Astronomy:** The science of the heavenly bodies, their motions, magnitudes, distances, and physical constitution.

**Astrophysics:** That branch of physics that treats of the appearance and constitution of heavenly bodies.

**Atmospheric Pressure:** The unit of pressure per unit of air of the air surrounding the earth or any heavenly body. For the earth it is 15 pounds per square inch at the equator.

**Atom:** One of the hypothetical indivisible parts of which all matter is supposed to be formed.

**Augur:** To prognosticate from signs or omens.

**Aurora Borealis:** A brilliant nocturnal radiance often seen in the sky of northern latitudes, during magnetic storms.

**Automatic Writing:** Writing of a supernatural agency, such as the handwriting on the Wall during Belshazzars feast, as related in the Bible; books written through dictation from a supernatural agency, such as *The Secret Doctrine* by Madame Blavatsky.

**Average:** 1. Arithmetic, obtained by adding the values of each item and then dividing the total by the number of items. 2. Geometric, obtained by taking the product of the items and then extracting the corresponding root of this product.

**Averages or Stock Indexes:** 1. The Dow-Jones Industrial Average is the oldest continuous average of stock prices in the U.S. It began in 1884 as a simple average of 10 railroad stocks and one industrial stock, which were eventually increased to 20 stocks. With the growth of industry, it became necessary to add more stocks of industrial companies, so on June 5, 1896, *The Wall Street Journal* printed two lists of stocks—20 railroad and 12 industrial. The average of each list was still obtained by calculating a simple average of the closing daily prices.

Between January 1897 and June 1926, 28 substitutions were made in the railroad list. 18 substitutions were made in the industrial list between January 1897 and September 1916, when the number of such stocks was increased from 12 to 20, of which, only 8 of the original stocks were retained—the other 12 being new additions. A further change had been made on October 13, 1915, when the computation of the averages was changed from a percentage to a dollar basis. Between 1915 and 1925 there have been about 15 changes in the original list of 20 stocks. The list was then expanded to 30 stocks on October 1, 1928.

While these 30 stocks comprise only 1½ percent of the total 2,000 stocks listed on the New York Stock Exchange, they account for about one-third of the total market value. As a result of stock splits, recapitalizations, substitutions, etc., the divisor, which originally was 30, has dropped to 1.314 as of August 13, 1981, whereas the arithmetical average was $41.05 versus the Dow-Jones Industrial Average of 936.93 quoted in *The Wall Street Journal* of August 14, 1981.

2. The Standard & Poor's 500 Stock Price Average is a broader index consisting of 400 industrial, 20 transportation, 40 utility and 40 financial stocks, beginning on March 1, 1957. It is a capitalization weighted index, which measures the total market value of the stocks included in the index. The market value of a stock is calculated by multiplying the number of common shares outstanding by the current price per share. The values for the individual stocks are then added to determine the total value of all the stocks in the index. This index is based on the total market value of the 500 stocks for the years 1941-1943, and the Base Number is 10.

Since this index is based on the number of shares of the individual stocks outstanding, the stock of a company having, say 300 million shares outstanding, has 300 times the influence on this Average as does the issue of a company with only one million shares outstanding. Thus, while the Standard & Poor's Average is superior to the Dow-Jones Industrial Average as a measure of the fluctuations in the total value of the stocks listed on the New York Stock Exchange, there are times when an unusual degree of popularity of the 15 or 20 stocks with the largest capitalizations can give a misleading picture of what is going on in the market as a whole.

3. The N.Y.S.E. Composite Average: The New York Stock Exchange began the publication in 1966 of a stock index covering every stock listed on the Exchange, with a Base of 50 as of December 31, 1965. It is a capitalization-weighted index of some 2,000 stocks, whereas the Standard & Poor's comprises only 500 stocks.

4. The Value Line Average was established in January 1962 for some 1,600 stocks on the basis of geometrically averaging the daily percent change in the monitored stocks. For ex-

ample, if the geometric average percent change of the 1600 stocks on a given day is plus two percent, and the previous day's reading of the Value Line Average was 100, then the average was increased by two points (2 percent x 100), resulting in a new reading of 102. The Value Line Average thus assigns each of the stocks contained therein equivalent percentage weights. Thus, IBM, which may be quoted at a price in hundreds of dollars and has a market value in the tens of billions of dollars, is treated the same as a stock quoted at $2.00 a share and with a total market value of $20 million.

But there is a serious flaw in the way that the Average is computed because the percent changes are averaged geometrically, i.e., by averaging the logarithms of each item and then finding the anti-logarithm of the average, which produces a result that is lower than the true answer. The cumulative consequence is that the Value Line Average has a *downward* bias, which makes its current level deceptively low.

5. Other unweighted averages are: 1) The Indicator Digest Average of Indicator Digest, Inc.; 2) The N.Y.U.A. of the Professional Tape Reader; 3) The Zupi Index of Dr. Martin Zweig.

All three averages are derived from the data base of Quotron Systems, Inc. The average is computed as follows: The percent change of each stock is added up and an average obtained. If this average for a given day is 1 percent, the new index value is 1.01 times the Base. If the Base were $50, the new value would be 50 x 1.01 = $50.50.

But these three unweighted averages also have a *downward* bias. For example, a stock which has increased in price from $10 to $20 has gained 100 percent. However, the computer calculates the percent change by dividing the $10 increase by the $20 ending price, which gives a percent change of only 50 percent whereas the $10 increase should have been divided by the $10 starting price, which correctly gives a 100 percent increase. This peculiarity of the computer seems incredible, but it is a fact according to *Market Logic* (1976) by Norman G. Fosback. While the extent of the downward bias may be relatively insignificant on a day to day basis, it becomes considerable over a span of years. For example, the Quotron based index of New York Stock Exchange stocks should have been twice their December 31, 1975 level to properly reflect the price, including dividends, of the component stocks during the previous 10-year period.

6. The Total Return Index of Market Logic was developed in 1975 by the Institute for Econometric Research, Inc., Ft. Lauderdale, Florida. It has the following two advantages: 1) it gives equal weight on an arithmetic basis to the correctly calculated daily percent change of every common stock, regardless of whether it is priced at $1 or $100, or whether the company is large or small, and 2) it includes dividend return as well as price changes (over one-half the total return of all common stocks throughout history has been from dividends).

**Biology:** The science of life or living organisms in all its forms and phenomena.

**Biophysics:** The physics of biological processes or phenomena.

**Boom:** Sudden business activity or prosperity. The peak of the business cycle.

**Business Cycles:** A type of fluctuation found in the aggregate economic activity of nations that organize their work mainly in business enterprises. A cycle consists of expansions occurring about the same time in many economic activities, followed by similarly general recessions, contractions and revivals which merge into the expansion phase of the next cycle. This series of changes is recurrent, but not periodic; in duration, business cycles vary from more than one year to 10 or 12 years.

**Canonical:** Regular, lawful, accepted, or approved, i.e., canonical law.
**Celestial:** Of or pertaining to the sky or heaven.
**Celestial Equator:** The great circle of the celestial sphere, lying in the same plane as the earth's equator.
**Charts:** A graph showing changes and variations in prices.
**Chromosphere:** A layer of red gas surrounding the sun or a star.
**Clairaudience:** The ability to perceive sounds that cannot be heard normally.
**Clairvoyant:** One who has intuitive perception or preternatural knowledge when in a trance.
**Climatology:** The science of climate.
**Configuration:** Arrangement of planets.
**Conjunction:** When two or more planets have the same degree of longitude.
**Cosine:** The sine of the complement of a given angle.
**Cosmic:** Pertaining to the universe at large. Cosmic rays from outside the solar system.
**Cosmology:** A theory of the universe, including astronomy, geography and geology.
**Credit:** Transfer of property on promise of future payment, such as bonds, stocks, real estate.
**Crisis:** A sudden and decisive change in business.
**Currency:** The current medium of exchange, either coin or bank notes.
**Current:** Electricity passing through a conductor.
**Cycle:** A period of time, at the end of which certain aspects or motions of the heavenly bodies repeat themselves; a series that repeats itself. Cycles comes from the Greek word for circle. Actually, the word cycle means coming around again to the place of beginning. When there is a fairly regular period of time, the correct word to use is *Rhythm,* from another Greek word meaning "measured time." Rhythmic cycles are almost universal in nature.
**Cyclone:** A violent and destructive wind storm with winds blowing inward and spirally.
**Decennial Pattern:** An average of statistical data taken at 10-year intervals.
**Depression:** The low point of the business cycle, characterized by poor business.
**Divination:** The art of foretelling the future by assumed supernatural aid.
**Dynamo-electric:** Electricity produced through the movement of a conductor across a magnetic field, as in a dynamo. The earth is a dynamo, for the moisture of the ocean which is evaporated by the sun at the equator is carried by the wind across the earth's magnetic field and creates a ring of electric current that encircles the earth.
**Eccentricity:** Planetary orbits do not form a perfect circle, but are elliptical in shape.
**Economics:** The science that treats of the production and distribution of wealth.
**Electricity:** A fundamental physical agency caused by the pressure and motions of electrons, protons, and other charged particles.
**Electron:** A particle of negative electricity.
**Electrodynamics:** The branch of physics that deals with the interactions of electric, magnetic and mechanical phenomena.
**Electromagnetism:** The phenomena associated with the relations between electricity and magnetism.
**Electrostatic:** Pertaining to static electricity.

**Ephemeris:** A table showing the positions of heavenly bodies on a number of dates in a regular sequence.

**Equator:** The great circle on a sphere or heavenly body whose plane is perpendicular to the axis, viz: the great circle of the earth, equidistant from the North Pole and the South Pole.

**Equinox:** The time when the sun crosses the plane of the earth's equator, making night and day of equal length all over the earth and occurring about March 21 (Vernal Equinox) and September 22 (Autumnal Equinox).

**Ethics:** A system of moral principles.

**Force Field:** A charged particle changes the properties of the space around it by creating a field in that space. Thus, another charged particle placed near the first is not affected directly by the first particle, but rather by the field created by the first particle.

**Foresight:** Knowledge or insight gained by looking forward to the future.

**Futures:** A contract to take delivery at a given price at a future time, of a stock, bond, commodity, or currency.

**Fourier Series:** An infinite series that involves linear combinations of sines and cosines.

**Galactic Center:** The gravitational center around which the sun revolves. Astrology has hypothetically placed this at 0° Capricorn (270° celestial longitude) which is confirmed by recently published results of thousands of calculations of spectroscopic radial velocity measurements and other thousands by the parallax method of determining proper motion. In consequence the astronomers have arrived at a position of the center of the Milky Way Galaxy at R.A. 270°, declination + 29.7°. Therefore, at the time of the Winter Solstice, the galactic center is a few degrees south of the sun. The plane of the sun's orbit is presumed to be approximately that of the galactic center, which is inclined to the earth's orbit by about 50°. More recent authorities place the galactic center at 266°.

**Galactic Equator:** The great circle on the celestial sphere that is equidistant from the galactic poles, being inclined approximately 62° to the celestial equator and lying about one degree north of the center line of the Milky Way.

**Galaxy:** A large system of stars held together by mutual gravitation and isolated from similar systems by vast regions of space. Our solar system is immersed in the Milky Way Galaxy.

**Geiger Counter:** An instrument for detecting ionizing radiations; used chiefly to measure radioactivity.

**Geocentric:** As viewed or measured from the center of the earth.

**Geology:** The science dealing with the physical history of the earth.

**Geomagnetism:** Pertaining to terrestrial magnetism. The earth is a magnet.

**Gravity:** The force of attraction by which terrestrial bodies tend to fall toward the center of the earth.

**Harmonic Analysis:** A method of discovering the constituent periodicities which enter into the construction of a given series of data arranged in a time series.

**Helicoid:** Coiled or curving like a spiral.

**Heliocentric:** As seen or measured from the center of the sun.

**Humanities:** The study of classical languages and literature.

**Index Number:** A quantity whose variation over a period of time measures the change in some phenomenon, as prices, stocks, geomagnetism.

**Inflation:** Undue expansion or increase of the currency of a country, especially by the issuance of paper money that is not redeemable in specie. This causes a substantial rise in prices.

**Interest:** A sum paid or charged for the use of money or for borrowing money.

**Ion:** An electrically charged particle of an atom.

**Ionization:** To change into ions.

**Ionosphere:** The region of the earth's atmosphere consisting of several ionized layers extending from about 50 to 250 miles above the surface of the earth.

**Karma:** Action which brings upon oneself inevitable results, good or bad, either in this life or in a reincarnation.

**Kilowatt (KW):** 1,000 watts of electrical energy. A long wave in economics running from 40 to 60 years long.

**Law of:** 1. Action and reaction. Action and reaction are equal but opposite in direction.

2. Averages. A statistical principle to show a more or less predictable ratio between the number of random trials of an event and its occurrence.

3. Causality. Everything that happens, and everything that exists, necessarily happens or exists as the consequence of a previous state of things.

4. Cause and Effect. A cause may be said to be that which immediately precedes any change, and which, existing at any future time in similar circumstances, has been always, and will be always, immediately followed by a similar change.

5. Conservation of Energy. The principle that in a system that does not undergo any force from outside the system, the amount of energy is constant.

6. Gravitation. The force acting between two bodies is directly proportioned to the masses of the two bodies and inversely proportioned to the square of the distance between them.

7. Motion. A body at rest tends to remain at rest, while a body in motion continues in motion unless acted on by an external force.

8. Supply and Demand. The price of any commodity or service is determined by the ratio of supply to demand; the greater the demand, the higher the price, and vice versa.

**Liquidation:** The process of realizing on assets and of discharging liabilities in connection with closing an estate or going out of business.

**Logic:** The science which investigates the principles of correct or reliable inferences.

**Lunation:** A conjunction of the sun and moon every 29½ days, approximately.

**Magnet:** A metal such as iron or steel that possesses the property of attracting other pieces.

**Magnetism:** The properties of attraction possessed by magnets.

**Magnetic Field:** The condition of space in the vicinity of a magnetic or current-carrying substance manifesting itself as a force on a moving charge within that space.

**Magnetic Storm:** A temporary disturbance of the earth's magnetic field, induced by radiation and streams of charged particles from the sun.

**Magnetic Tail:** A conical section of charged particles from the sun that form behind a planet.

**Magnetometer:** An instrument for measuring the intensity of the earth's magnetic field.

**Margin Borrowing:** Borrowing money to buy stocks or bonds from a broker.

**Mechanistic:** Pertaining to a mechanical view of the world rather than a humanistic concept.

**Medium:** A person said to possess supernatural powers.

**Meteorology:** The science of the atmosphere, weather and climate.

**Moving Average:** A mathematical method of smoothing data. The smoothed data is often used as a trend.

**Mystic:** A person said to have occult or supernatural power.

**Nodes:** The points in space where the planets in their heliocentric orbits cross the ecliptic, which is the path of the earth around the sun. When passing from below the ecliptic to above, it is called the Ascending or North Node, and vice versa for the Descending or South Node. The moon's nodes are the points where the moon's orbit crosses the earth's orbit (the ecliptic). These points regress or move backward through the twelve signs of the zodiac in 18.6 years, which is known as the regression of the moon's nodes.

**Occult:** Beyond the range of ordinary knowledge.

**Omen:** Anything perceived or happening that is believed to portend a good or evil event in the future.

**Opposition:** Planets that are 180° apart in longitude.

**Options:** Contracts to buy or sell commodities or stocks at a fixed price payable at a future date.

**Oracle:** An utterance, often ambiguous or obscure, given by a priest or priestess at a temple as the response of a god or goddess to an inquiry, vide the Delphic Oracle.

**Orb:** The space within which the influence of a planet is supposed to act.

**Oscillation:** A single swing in one direction of a swinging body.

**Panic:** A sudden, widespread fear concerning financial affairs leading to credit contraction and widespread sale of securities at depressed prices in an effort to acquire cash.

**Perigee:** The point in a heavenly body's orbit where it is nearest to the earth.

**Perihelion:** The point in a heavenly body's orbit where it is nearest to the sun.

**Periodicity:** The tendency to recur at regular intervals.

**Periodogram:** A mathematical technique for deriving cycles from statistical data.

**Philosophy:** The science dealing with the principles and truths of being, knowledge, or conduct.

**Photon:** A quantum of electromagnetic radiation or light.

**Photosynthesis:** The synthesis of complex organic materials using sunlight as the source of energy.

**Planetary Rulership:** Certain planets are said to have an affinity for certain products, viz: Venus for copper, Mars for iron and steel, Neptune for gas and oil, Saturn for real estate, Uranus for electric utilities, Pluto for underground minerals, the Sun for gold, the Moon for silver, but there is disagreement among astrologers.

**Precipitation:** Falling rain, snow, or hail.

**Prediction:** The art of foretelling the future.

**Probability:** The relative frequency with which an event occurs or is likely to occur.

**Prophecy:** The foretelling or prediction of what is to come.

**Prophet:** A person who speaks for God or a deity, or by divine inspiration.

**Prosperity:** A successful, flourishing, or thriving condition of the economy.

**Proton:** An elementary particle that is a constituent of all atomic nuclei, having a positive charge equal in magnitude to the electron.

**Psychic:** A person who is specially sensitive to supernatural influences or forces.

**Psychology:** The science of the mind or of human nature.

**Radiation:** The process by which energy is emitted as particles or waves, vide, solar radiation.

**Radiant Energy:** Energy transmitted by electromagnetic waves.

**Rhythm:** The regular recurrence of an act or function.

**Secular:** Of or pertaining to worldly things; also the trend over a long period of time.

**Sextile:** Planets separated by 60° of longitude.

**Short Selling:** Selling something you do not own in the hope of buying it back at a lower price.

**Sidereal:** Determined by or from the stars, vide, sidereal time, or sidereal radiation.

**Sine:** The ratio of the side opposite a given angle in a right triangle to the hypotenuse.

**Sine Curve:** A curve described by the equation $Y = \sin Y$. One of the characteristics of a sine curve is that it repeats the same pattern over and over again indefinitely. Any curve which does this is said to be periodic. Planetary orbits, which are elliptical in shape, are predictable, but because the time elapsing between successive aspects of a pair of planets is not uniform, the aspects cannot be represented by a sine curve.

**Solar:** Of or pertaining to the sun.

**Solar Constant:** The rate at which solar radiation is received outside the earth's atmosphere.

**Solar Flares:** Complex patterns of white-hot gaseous filaments in the sun's atmosphere that suddenly blaze up to 10 times normal brilliancy in hydrogen light. They reach their maximum intensity five or ten minutes after their first appearance and then slowly decay in the next hour or two. They may cover an area of up to 1,000 million square miles of the sun's atmosphere. Their importance derives not only from their significance in solar physics, but also from the effects which they produce on earth, such as slowing down the rate of the earth's rotation.

**Solar Ingress:** The sun's entry into Aries, Cancer, Libra, Capricorn, marking the beginning of the seasons.

**Solar Radiation:** The radiation from the sun covers a wide range of wavelengths, infrared to ultraviolet.

**Solar Wind:** An ionized gas or plasma composed of highly charged particles that travel outward from the sun, with a velocity of about 400 kilometers per second near the earth.

**Soothsayer:** A person who professes to foretell future events.

**Spectrum:** The broad range of the physical properties of light.

**Speculate:** Engage in any business enterprise involving considerable risk or the chance of big profits.

**Speculum:** A tabulation showing the angular separation between planets.

**Spiritualist:** An adherent of spiritualism; a person who concerns himself with the spiritual side of things.

**Square:** Planets that are 90° apart in longitude. A market where stocks and bonds are traded.

**Sunspots:** Relative dark spots which appear periodically on the Sun's surface and affect terrestrial magnetism and other phenomena.

**Sunspot Cycle:** The cycle, averaging about 11 years, in which the frequency of sunspots varies from a maximum to a minimum and back again to a maximum.

**Sybil:** A priestess said to be able to predict the future; vide the Sybilline Oracle of Rome.

**Synchroton:** An electrical device for the electrostatic acceleration of particles of matter or energy.

**Synodical:** Pertaining to successive conjunctions of two planets.

**Technical Analysis:** An attempt to measure and evaluate on a mathematical basis the psychological condition of the stock market.

**Terrestrial:** Pertaining to the earth.

**Theories of:** 1. *The Business Cycle.* a) *The Theory of Free Oscillations* depends upon the internal structure of the system, viz; the Corn-Hog Cycle, during which the high price of hogs and the low price of corn lead to over production in the first case, and under prediction in the second. This in turn reverses the price structure and cyclical fluctuations ensue.

b) *The Theory of Forced Oscillation* depends upon forces external to the system, forces whose origins are non-economic, vide: sunspots, the 8-year Venus cycle, planetary cycles.

c) *The Theory of Erratic Shock.* The source of energy which maintains the system is erratic shock, viz: new innovations, exploitations, discoveries.

d) *The Theory of Historic Analogy* is based on the assumption that history tends to repeat itself in cyclical fluctuation. It is assumed that there are certain uniformities in the economy which can be discovered by an analysis of past experience. By means of statistics, observation, or theory, it is discovered that a certain situation "A" in the past has always been followed by another situation "B". Assuming that this results from a relationship in the economy which will not change, it can be predicted that the next time "A" occurs, "B" will follow.

e) *The Sunspot Theory of the Business Cycle.* Sir William Herschel found in 1801 that when there were few or no sunspots, farm crops in England were low and hence prices were high; conversely, when the number of sunspots was high, crops were abundant and prices were low.

2. Einstein: a) *Theory of Relativity* states that mass and energy are interchangeable; there can be no motion at a speed greater than that of light in a vacuum, viz: 186,000 miles per second.

b) *Photoelectric Theory.* When light strikes certain metals, an emission of electrons from the surface occurs. The ejected electron absorbs the entire energy of the photon of light, independent of distance. Thus, science validates astrological theory that the effects of the planets are not diminished by distance. This has also been corraborated by John Nelson's observations that Pluto, farthest from the sun, has the same effect as planets closer to the sun.

**Thorium:** A radioactive metallic element used as a source of nuclear energy.

**Transformer:** An electrical device that changes electrical energy from one voltage to another.

**Tree Rings:** Annual layers formed in a tree by which the age of the tree may be determined.

**Trine:** Planets separated by $120°$ in longitude.

**Ultraviolet Light:** Beyond the violet in the spectrum of light having wavelengths shorter than 4000 angstroms.

**Uranium:** A radioactive metallic element used as a source of nuclear energy.

**Vector:** A graphical representation of the magnitude and direction of a force.

**Witchcraft:** The art or practices of a witch, vide: The Witch of Endor.

# Bibliography

Abetti, G. *The Sun*. D. Van Nostrand Company, New York, 1938.
    *The Sun*. The Macmillan Company, New York, 1957.

Abbot, C.G. "The Sun Makes the Weather," *The Scientific Monthly*, March & April, 1946.
    "Sixty Years of Weather Forecasts," *Smithsonian Misc. Coll.*, Washington, D.C., April 28, 1955.
    "Periods Related to 273 Mos. or 22¾ yrs," *Smithsonian Misc. Coll.*, Washington, D.C., September 13, 1956.

Anderson, C.N. "A Reproduction of the Sunspot Cycle," *Bell System Technical Journal*, New York, 1939.

Arhenius, S. "Cosmic Influences of Physiological Phenomena," *Amer. Jour. Obstetrics & Gynecology*, April 1959.

Ayres, L.P. "The Nature & Status of Business Research," *Jour. Amer. Stat. Assn.*, March 1922.
    *Turning Points in Business Cycles*. The Macmillan Company, New York, 1939.

Barnes, L. *Handbook of Business Forecasting*. Prentice-Hall, Inc., New York, 1949.

Bean, L.H. *How to Predict the Stock Market*. Greenwood Press, Westport, CN, 1962.

Benjamine, E. *Beginner's Horoscope Reader*. Llewellyn Publications, Ltd., St. Paul, MN, 1943.

Benner, S. *Benner's Prophecies of Future Ups & Downs in Prices*. Robert Clark Co., Cincinnati, OH, 1875.

Beveridge, W.H. "Wheat Prices & Rainfall in Western Europe," *Journal of Royal Statistical Society 85 (3)*, London, 1922.

Birkeland, K. *Archives des Sciences Physiques et Naturales, Vol. 4*, Geneva, 1896.

Bleiberg, R. "The Financial Markets & Business," Vista International Hotel, New York, 1981.

Blizzard, J.B. "Correlation Between Planetary Conjunctions & Proton Events," Joint Mtg-Amer. Astr. Soc. & Oper. Res. Soc., 1969.

Bollinger, C.J. *Atlas of Planetary & Solar Climate*. Battenberg Press, Norman, OK, 1960.

Bradley, D.A. *Stock Market Prediction*. Llewellyn Publications, Ltd., St. Paul, MN, 1948.

Bratt, E.C. *Business Cycles & Forecasting*. Business Publications, Inc., Chicago, IL, 1940.

Brown, T. *The Relation of Cause and Effect*. Henry G. Bohn, London, 1833.

Brown, E.W. "A Possible Explanation of the Sunspot Period," *Mo. Not. Roy. Astr. Soc. Vol. 60.*, London, 1900.

Burns, A.F. & Mitchell, W.C. *Measuring Business Cycles*. Nat. Bur. of Econ. Res., New York, 1947.

Burr, H.S. & Northrop, F.S.C. "The Electrodynamic Theory of Life," *Quarterly Revue of Biology, Vol. 10*, 1935.

Carrington, R.C., *Observations of the Spots on the Sun*. Williams & Norgate, London, 1863.

Chapman, S. & Bartels, J. *Geomagnetism*. Clarendon Press, Oxford, 1940.

Chase, S. *Power of Words*. Harcourt, Brace & Co., New York, 1953.

Clayton, H.H. *World Weather*. The Macmillan Company, New York, 1923.

"Planets and Sunspots," *Popular Astronomy*, November 1941.

*Solar Relations to Weather & Life*, The Clayton Weather Service, Canton, MA, 1943.

Clements, H. *The Solution of the Sunspot Mystery*. Privately Published, December 1900.

Clough, H.W. "The 11-Year Sunspot Period," *Monthly Weather Review*, April 1933.

Coe, J. *Combination of 3½ and 9-Year Cycles*. Privately Published, 1943.

Collin, R. *The Theory of Celestial Influence*. Vincent Stuart, London, 1954.

Cowell, P.H. "Eclipses," *Royal Observatory of England,* London, 1905.

Crawford, P.O. "The Crawford 9-Year Cycle of Business Activity," *Business & Systems Management,* 1934.

Dampier, W. *A History of Science*. Cambridge University Press, New York, 1940.

Davidson, F., Stibbs, A.M. and Kevan, E.F. *The New Bible Commentary,* Wm. B. Eerdman's Pub. Co., Grand Rapids, MI, 1953.

Davidson, W.F. "The Magnetic Storm of March 24, 1940," *EEI Bulletin,* July 1940.

"Sunspot Disturbances of Terrestrial Magnetism," *Electrical Engineering,* February 1941.

Davis, H.T. *The Analysis of Economic Time Series*. The Principia Press, Bloomington, IN, 1941.

de la Rue, Stewart and Loewy. "Researches in Solar Physics," *Proceedings of the Royal Society of London,* 1869-70.

"Investigations of Planetary Influences," Proceedings of the Royal Society of London, Vol. 20, 1872.

de Vore. *Encyclopedia of Astrology*. Philosophical Library, New York, 1947.

Dewey, E.R. and Dakin, E.F. *Cycles—The Science of Prediction*. Henry Holt & Co., New York, 1947.

Dewey, E.R. and Maudino, O. "Cycles—The Mysterious Forces that Trigger Events," Foundation for the Study of Cycles, Pittsburgh, PA, 1971.

Dewey, E.R. Articles in *Cycles* magazine. Foundation for the Study of Cycles, Pittsburgh, PA, 1944-1949.

Digby, W. *Natural Law in Terrestrial Phenomena*. Wm. Hutchinson & Co., London, 1902.

Douglas, A.E. *Climatic Cycles & Tree Growth*. Carnegie Institution, Washington, DC, 1928.

Drew, G.A. *New Methods for Profit in the Stock Market*. The Metcalf Press, Boston, 1948.

Dull, T. and B. *Deutshe Medizinische Wochenschift*. G1,95, Berlin, 1935.

Ellison, M.A. *The Sun & Its Influence*. The Macmillan Company, New York, 1985.

Erlewine, M. *The Sun is Shining—Heliocentric Ephemeris,* Heart Center, Ann Arbor, MI, 1975.

*Encyclopedia, Cambridge*. "The Galactic Center," 1977.

*Encyclopedia, Larousse*. "The Galactic Center," 1967.

*Encyclopedia, Van Nostrand*. "The Galactic Center," 1968.

Fisher, A. *The Mathematical Theory of Probabilities*. The Macmillan Co., New York, 1915.

Fosback, N.G. "Stock Market Logic," The Institute for Econometric Research, Ft. Lauderdale, FL, 1976.

Friedman, H., Becker, R.O. and Bachman, C.H. "Geomagnetic Parameters & Hospital Admissions," *Nature 200,* 1963.

Funk, J.M. *The 56-Year Cycle in American Business Activity*. Privately Published, Ottowa, IL,

1932.

Galbraith, K. *Money*. Houghton Mifflin Co., Boston, 1975.

Garcia-Mata C. and Shaffner, F.I. "Solar & Economic Relationships," *Quarterly Journal of Economics,* November, 1934.

Garriott, E.B. *The New York American & Journal*, Sunday Edition, August 17, 1912.

Gaubis, A. "The Deceanial Pattern," Foundation for the Study of Cycles, New York, December 14, 1960.

Gauquelin, M. *The Cosmic Clock*. Harry Regnery, Chicago, IL, 1967.

*Astrology & Science*. Peter Davies, London, 1970.

Gosh, M. "Comparative Increase of Ionizatiori," *Journal of Geophysical Research,* March, 1953.

Gribbin, J.R. and Plagemann, S.H. *The Jupiter Effect*. The Macmillan Press Ltd., London, 1974.

*The Jupiter Effect Reconsidered*. Random House, New York, 1982.

Hale, G.E. "Signals from the Stars," *The Astrophysical Journal,* 1924.

Head, R. "Position of Planets Linked to Solar Flares," *Technology Week,* May 15, 1968.

Herschel, N.S. "Observations of the Sun," *Phil. Trans. Royal Society of London,* April 16, 1801.

Herschel, J.F.W. *Outlines of Astronomy*. Longmans Green, London, 1867.

Hickernell, W.F. *Financial & Business Forecasting*. Alexander Hamilton Institute, New York, 1928.

Hodgson, R. "A Curious Appearance Seen in the Sun," *Mo. Not. Royal Astr. Soc. 20, 15,*1859.

Hoppe, D.J. *The Dow Theory Sell Signal July 20*. Privately Published, 1981.

Huntington, E. *Earth and Sun*. Yale University Press, New Haven, 1923.

"The Frontier," Armour Research Foundation, Armour Institute, Chicago, IL, 1944.

*The Mainsprings of Civilization*. John Wiley & Sons, New York, 1945.

Jastram, R.W. *The Golden Constant*. John Wiley & Sons, Inc., New York, 1977.

*Silver—The Restless Metal*. John Wiley & Sons, Inc., New York, 1981.

Jastrow, R.W. *The Religion of Babylonia & Assyria*. Grinn & Co., New York, 1898.

Jeans, J.H. *The Mysterious Universe*. Ridgway Books, Philadelphia, PA, 1931.

Jevons, W.S. "A Serious Fall in the Value of Gold," Brit. Assoc. for the Advancement of Science, 1863.

"The Solar Period and the Price of Corn," Bristol Meeting, British Association, 1875.

"The Periodicity of Commercial Crises," Dublin Meeting, British Association, August 11, 1878.

"Commercial Crises & Sunspots," *Nature,* November 14, 1898.

*Investigations in Currency & Finance*. Macmillan & Co., New York, 1884.

Jevons, H.S. "The Sun's Heat and Trade Activity," *Contemporary Review*, August, 1909.

"The Causes of Fluctuations in Industrial Activity," The Royal Statistical Society, London, August 16, 1933.

Jiler, W.L. *How Charts Can Help You in the Stock Market*. Commodity Res. Pub. Corp., New York, 1962.

Johnson, M.O. *Correlation of Cycles*. Phillips & Van Orden Co., Inc., San Francisco, 1946.

Jordan, D.F. *Business Forecasting*. Prentice Hall, Inc., New York, 1923.

Katona, G. "Economic Psychology," *Scientific American,* October, 1964.

King, H.P. "Hutner's Chart," *Cycles,* March, 1975.

King, W.L. "Sine Curve Fitting," *The Annalist,* May 1, 1931.

    *The Causes of Economic Fluctuations.* The Ronald Press, New York, 1938.

    "Hutner's Chart," *Cycles,* March, 1953.

Kitchin, J. *Review of Economic Statistics.* January 1923.

Kondratieff, N.D. "The Long Wave in Economic Life," *Cycles Magazine,* December 1973.

Langley, N. *Edgar Cayce on Reincarnation.* Hawthorne Books, New York, 1968.

Lawrence, W.L. *The New York Times,* May 15, 1960.

Lenart, F.L. "Biometeorological Influences on Life and Death," *LeConcourse Medical,* Paris, April 28, 1962.

Lewisohn, R. *Science, Prophecy & Prediction.* Harper & Bros., New York, 1961.

Lockyer, N. "Evidence on Sunspots & Rainfall," *Famine Series of Bluebooks*, Appendix 1, 1878.

Luby, W.A. "Planets & Sunspots," *Popular Astronomy,* December, 1940.

Macaulay, F.R. "The Movement of Interest Rates," Nat. Bur. of Econ. Research, New York, 1938.

MacCraig, H. *The 200 Year Ephemeris.* Macoy Publishing Co., New York, 1949.

Maisel, S.J. *Fluctuations, Growth & Forecasting.* John Wiley & Sons, Inc., New York, 1951.

Maunder, A.S.D. "An Apparent Influence on the Earth," *Mo. Nat. Roy. Astro. Soc.,* May 1907.

McNish, A.G. "Magnetic Storm," *EEI Bulletin,* July 1940.

McWhirter, L. *McWhirter Theory of Stock Market Forecasting.* Astro-Book Co., New York, 1938.

Meldahl, K.G. *Tidal Forces in the Sun's Corona.* Berlingske Forlag, Copenhagen, 1938.

Menaker, W. and A. "Birth Data," *Amer. Journal of Obstetrics & Gynecology,* April 1959.

Michelsen, N.F. *The American Ephemerisi 1931-1990.* Astro Computing Services, San Diego, CA, 1976.

    *The American Heliocentric Ephemeris 1901-2000.* Astro Computing Services, San Diego, CA, 1982.

Mills, J. "Credit Cycles & the Origin of Commercial Panics," *Transactions of Manchester Statistical Society,* December 1867.

Mitchell, W.C. *Business Cycles & Their Causes.* University of California Press, Berkeley, CA, 1960.

Moore, H.L. *Economic Cycles—Their Law & Cause.* The Macmillan Co., New York, 1914.

    "The Origin of the 8-Year Generating Cycle," *Quarterly Journal of Economics,* November 1921.

    *Generating Economic Cycles.* The Macmillan Co., New York, 1923.

Mortimer, C.G. *The New York World-Telegram & Sun.* June 15, 1958.

Nelson, J.H. "Short Wave Radio Propagation Correlation with Planetary Positions," *RCA Review,* March 1951.

    *Cosmic Patterns.* AFA, Tempe, AZ, 1974.

    *The Propagation Wizard's Handbook.* 73 Inc., Peterboro, NH, 1978.

Neugebauer, O. *The Exact Sciences in Antiquity.* Princeton University Press, Princeton, NJ, 1952.

Norton, W.A. *A Treatise on Astronomy,* John Wiley & Sons, Inc., New York, 1867.

O'Neill, J.J. Letter to Sydney Omarr, July 8, 1951.

Persons, W.M. *Forecasting Business Cycles*. John Wiley & Sons, Inc., New York, 1931.

Peterson, W.F. *Man, Weather and Sun*. Charles G. Thomas, Springfield, IL, 1947.

Piccardi, G. *Astrophysical Phenomenon & Terrestrial Events*. Palaise de la Decouverte, Paris, 1957.

*The Chemical Basis of Medical Climatology*. Charles G. Thomas, Springfield, IL, 1962.

Pogson, N.R. "East Indian Famine," *Report of Famine Commission, Appendix 5*, 1858.

*Miscellaneous Papers: Blue Book 32, 22*, 1881.

Portig, W.H. "Position of Planets Linked to Solar Flair Prediction," *Technology Week,* May 15, 1967.

Poumailloux, M. and Viart. "Correlation Possible Entre l'Incidence des Infarctus," *Bul-de l'Acadamie Nat. de Med. 143,* Paris, 1959.

Purucker, G. de. *The 'Esoteric Tradition*. Theosophical University Press, Pasadena, CA, 1973.

Ravitz, L.J. "Periodic Changes in the Electromagnetic Field," *Annals N.Y. Acad: Science,* October 30, 1962.

Rawlinson, G. *The Five Great Monarchies*. Dodd, Mead & Co., New York, 1862.

Sanford, F. "The Frequency of Planetary Configurations," *Smith. Misc. Coll.,* Washington, DC, 1937.

Sayce, A.H. *The Religion of Ancient Babylpnia*. Williams & Norgate, London, 1887.

Schabacker, R.W. *Stock Market Theory & Practice*. B.C. Forbes Publishing Co., New York, 1930.

Schove, D.J. "The Sunspot Cycle A.D. 301-1950," *Journal of Cycle Research, Vol. 2 No. 4,* 1953.

"The Sunspot Cycle 649 B.C.-A.D. 2000," *Journal of Geophysical Research,* June 1955.

Schuster, A. "The Influence of Planets on the Formation of Sunspots," Proc. Roy. Soc., London, 1910-11.

Schwabe. H. "Periodicitat der Sonnenflecken," *Astronomische Nachrichtew, XXI, 234,* 1844.

Shirk, G. "The Hutner Chart," *Cycles,* March 1960.

"The 40.68 Month Cycle," *Cycles,* 1964-74.

"The 9.2-Year Cycle," *Cycles,* April/May 1977.

"The 10.36-Year Cycle," *Cycles,* July 1978.

"The History of Silver Prices," *Cycles,* 1974-80.

Silberling, N.J. *The Dynamics of Business*. McGraw-Hill Book Co., Inc., New York, 1943.

Singer, F.S., Maple, E. and Bowen, W.A. "Evidence for Ionospheric Currents," *Journal of Geophysical Res.*, Vol. 56, 1957.

Stetson, H.T. *Earth, Radio & Stars*. McGraw-Hill Book Co., Inc., New York, 1934.

*Sunspots in Action*. Ronald Press, New York, 1948.

Smith, E.L. *Tides in the Affairs of Men*. The Macmillan Co., New York, 1939.

Smith, J.G. and Duncan, A.J. *Elementary Statistics & Applications*. McGraw-Hill Book Co., Inc., New York, 1944.

Stahlman, W.B. and Gingerich, O. *Solar & Planetary Longitudes*. University of Wisconsin Press, Madison, WI, 1963.

Stearn, J. *Edgar Cayce—The Sleeping Prophet*. Doubleday & Co., Garden City, NY, 1966.

Takata, M. *Archiv fur Meteorologie, Geophysik und Bioklimatologie Serie B.ll,* 1951.

Tchijevsky, A.L. "Epidemic Catastrophies & Periodic Solar Activity," Amer. Met. Soc. Mtg., Philadelphia, PA, December 30, 1926.

Tice, J.W. *Elements of Meteorology.* Met. Res. & Pub. Co., St. Louis, MO, 1875.

Tucker, W.J. *The Principles, Theory & Practice of Scientific Prediction.* Science & Humanity, Ltd. London, 1930.

*The Principles of Scientific Astrology.* J.B. Lippincott Co., Philadelphia, PA, 1938.

Tuckerman, B. *Planetary, Lunar & Solar Positions.* American Philosophical Society, Philadelphia, PA, 1962.

Vaux, J.E. "The 9.2-Year Cycle," *Cycles,* May/June 1976.

Warren, G.F. and Pearson, F.A. *Prices.* John Wiley & Sons, Inc., New York, 1933.

Williams, D. "Rhythmic Cycles in American Business," Henry George School of Social Science, New York, April 16, 1947.

"Prices & Price Policies," NAPA Meeting, Houston, TX, February 15, 1955.

*Astro-Economics.* Llewellyn Publications, Ltd., St. Paul, MN, 1959.

"Business Cycle Forecasting," *Journal of Cycle Research, Vol. 8 No. 2,* April, 1959.

"Cycles-Real and Synthetic," Foundation for the Study of Cycles, New York, January 13, 1960.

"Magnetic Storm & Elec. Pwr. Line Disturbances," *Journal of Cycle Research, Vol. 10 No. 3,* July 1961.

"Stock Market & Business Forecasts," Dell *Horoscope,* 1964-1981.

"Stock Market Outlook," Sec. Inv. Rec. Events (SIRE), New York, September 12, 1974.

"Historical Survey-Silver Prices," *Cycles Magazine,* January/February 1981.

"The Long Wave in American Economic History," *Cycles,* July 1981.

"Historical Survey—Gold Prices," *Cycles*, September/October 1981.

Wolf, R. *Transactions of Society of Natural Philosophy,* Berne, Switzerland, 1852.

Wood, K.D. "Sunspots & Planets," *Nature, Vol. 240,* November 10, 1972.

Wood, S.W. "Long Term Weather Cycles & Their Causes," *Illinois Engineer,* September 1949.

"Lake Ontario as a Business Index," *Changing Times,* September 1949.

"Current Economic Trends," *American Institute of Economic Research,* Great Barrington, MA, June 1958.

"The Embattled Economists," *Forbes Magazine,* June 15, 1958.

Wright, W.G. *Quarterly Journal of Economics,* November 1921.

Young, C.A. *A Textbook of General Astronomy,* Gimn & Co., Boston, MA, 1899.

# Index

Abbetti, G., 43, 46, 110
Abbott, C. G., 43, 44
Adams, A. B., 8
Adrian, E. D., 17
Anderson, C. N., 46
Aristotle, 5
Astro-Economics, 101, 102, 165
Ayres, L. P., 2, 18, 70, 81
Barnes, L., 4
Baruch, B. M., 4
Bean, L.H., 138
Benner, S., 1, 63, 64-65
Beveridge, Sir W. H., 40, 89
Birkeland, K., 33, 51
Bleiberg, R., 151, 153
Blizard, J. B., 35
Bollinger, C. J., 34
Bradley, D. A., 196
Bratt, E.C., 8
Bray, C.W., 17
Brown, E.W., 29
Brown, T., 119
Burns, A. F., 4
Burr, H. S. & Northrop, F. S. C., 61
Business Cycle Theories, 3, 63, 89
   Erratic Shock, 7
   Forced Oscillations, 7
   Free Oscillations, 7
   Historic Analysis, 8
   Unknown Causes, 8, 89
     a) Harmonic Analysis, 89
     b) Empirical Curve Fitting, 90
       King's Sine Curve, 90, 91, 93
       Crawford's 9 yr. Cycle, 90, 92
       Hutner's Cycles, 93, 94, 95
   Sunspots, 23
   Benner's Price Cycles, 63-65
   Moore's 8 year Venus Cycle, 65-67
   McWhirter's North Node, 67-69
   Funk's 56 year Pattern, 70-71
   Kondratieff Long Wave, 6, 90, 196
Buying on Margin, 193
Carrington, R. C., 27, 43
Cayce, E., 109, 119
Chapman, S. and Bartels, J., 43
Chase, S., 4, 9, 98, 116
Clarke, H. 5, 12
Clayton, H. H., 30, 31, 33, 40, 89
Clough, M.W., 40
Clements, H., 29
Coe, J., 124
Collin, R., 118
Conversion of Signs, 159
Cooper, P., 5
Cowell, P.H., 99
Crawford, P. O., 90, 92, 220
Cycles: definitions of, 123
   Agricultural, 40
   Business 3, 63, 84
   Climate and Weather, 40, 41
   Forecasting, ix, 4
   Length of:
     3½-year Kitchin, 90
     3½-year Jevons, 90
     4-4½-year Mars-Jupiter, 138
     5.58-year Silver, 202
     8-year Venus, 6, 7, 65-67
     9-year Juglar, 6, 8, 16
     9.2-year, 122, 135
     9.93-year Jupiter-Saturn Cycle, 28
     10-year Business, 5, 12
     10.466-year Business, 15
     11-year Business, 5, 12
     11.11-year Sunspot, 11
     11.19-year Jupiter-Venus-Earth Cycle, 34
     11.19-year Sunspot Cycle, 34
     11.86-year Jupiter Cycle, 27
     18.6-year Nodal Cycle, 135

22-year Alternate Sunspot Cycle, 27, 41
22.11-year Gold Price Cycle, 207
40-month Business, 16
56-year Pattern of U. S. Business, 70, 92

*Cycle Research, Journal of*, 1, 9
Dampier, Sir W., 98
Danson, J.T., 5
Darwin, G.H., 103
Davidson, W. P., 50
Davis, A.J., 8, 11
Davis, H. T., 20, 89
Dawes, W. R., 24
Dewey, E. R., 2, 34, 64, 121, 122, 123, 124, 130, 141-144
Dietz, D., 116
Digby, W., 29
Dolotov, V.A., 42
Douglas, A. E., 40
Drew, G. A., 116
Dull, T. and B., 60
Dun's Review, 65
Duncan, A. J., 8
Ellison, M.A., 43
Faraday, M., 25
Fibonacci, L., 140
Fisher, A., 5, 118
*Forbes Magazine*, 97
Fosback, N. G., 134, 148
Franklin, C. W., 43
Friedman, H., Becker, R.O. & Bachman, C.H., 61
Fullmer, C. J., 40
Funk, J. M., 1, 72
Galactic Center, 144
Galbraith, J. K., 9
Gallilei, V., 113
Garcia-Mata, C., 16, 17
Garriott, E. B., 40
Gaubis, A., 109, 126
Gauquelin, M., 60
Gillette, H.P., 41
George, Henry (School), 1, 71, 199
Germaine, L. W., 50

Gosh, M., 114
Granville, J., 151
Gribbin, J.R. and Plagemann, S.H., 50
Hale, G.E., 24, 41
Hamilton, W. P., 148
Harbord, J. G., 97
Head,R., 44, 45
Herschel, Sir J. F. W., 19
Herschel, Sir W., 1, 11, 20, 39
Hickernell, W. F., 1, 6
Hodgson, R., 43
Hoppe, D.J., 149
Hotelling, H., 7
Huntington, E., 28, 29, 40, 118
Hutner, S., 1, 93, 94, 95, 221
Interest Rate Futures, 195
Jastrow, M., Jr., 108, 204
Jeans, Sir J. H., 117
Jevons, H. S., 16, 17
Jevons, W. S., 1, 12-16, 24, 39, 63
Jiler, W. L., 108
Johnson, M. O., 32, 41
Jordan, D. F., 4, 7, 118
Juglar, C., 6, 7, 16
Jung,C.G., 2
Katonah, G., 4
King, H. P., 93
King, W.I., 90, 91, 93
Keynes, Lord J. M., 5
Kitchin, J., 6, 16
Kondratieff, N. D., 6, 196
Lamont, T.W., 4, 42
Langley, N., 119
Langton, W., 6
Lawes, C.G., 121
Laws of: Cause & Effect, 8, 119
Causality, 8, 118, 120
Lenart, F.L, 118
Lockyer, Sir N., 40
Loeb, J., 3
Luby, W. A., 31
Macaulay, F. R., 1, 97, 119

McNish, A.G., 51, 52
McWhirter, L., 67-69
Maisel, S. J., 8, 119
Magnetism, Terrestrial, 18
Magnetic Storms, 43
Mass Psychology, 17
Meldahl, K. G., 31
Menaker, W. & A., 113
Menzel, D.H., 46
Mills, J., 1, 6, 12
Mitchell, W. C., 4
Moore, H. L., 7, 8, 65-67
Mortimer, C. G., 1, 7
Nelson, J. H., 1, 44, 46, 47, 75, 117
Neugebauer, O., 110
Newton, Sir I., 33, 34
New York Academy of Sciences, 56
Omarr, S., 115
O'Neill, J. J., 99, 115
Panics: 1761, 71; 1781, 71; 1801, 71; 1817, 75; 1837, 75; 1857, 77; 1873, 79; 1893, 79; 1913-1914, 79; 1929, 81; 1949, 81; 1969, 83; 1985, 199
Pay, R., 43
Personal Investing:
    Who should invest or speculate, 170
    What stock to buy, 170
    Corporate horoscope analysis, 172
    Fairchild Camera, 173
    Con Edison, 178
    Asarco, 181
    Homestake, 187
Persons, W. M., 7, 17, 119
Peterson, W. F., 41, 115
Piccardi, G., 60, 61, 109
Pogson, N.R., 39
Polarity of Aspects, 160
Poumailloux, J. and Viart. R., 61
Predictive Methods:
    Through dream interpretation, 106
    From omens, 109
    From astrology, 110

Prices:
    Silver, 199
    Gold, 202
    Wholesale, 197
Purucker, G. de, 117
Ravitz, L. J., 61, 118
Rawlinson, G., 111
Roberts, W.O. 46
Rogers, J. E. T., 12
Russell, R., 148
Samuelson, P. A., 20
Sanford, F., 31
Sayce, A.H., 108
Schabacher, R. W., 107
Schove, D.J., 12, 24
Schumpeter, J. A., 196
Schuster, Sir A., 30, 39, 52, 91
Schwabe, S. H., 12, 24
Sepharial, 73
Shaffner, F. I., 17
Shirk, G., 122-123, 124
Short Selling, 193
Shuman, J.B. and Rosenau, D., 196
Silberling, M. J., 18, 71
Singer, K. B., et al, 51
SIRE (Soc. for Investigation of Recurring Events), 198
Sismondi, J. C. L. de., 5
Smith, E.L., 127
Smith, J. G. and Duncan, A. J., 8, 98, 118
Solar Activity: Effects on:
    Agriculture & Climate, 39
    Science, 42
    Telegraph, Submarine & Telephone Lines, 43
    Radio Transmission, 46
    Electric Power Systems:
        Overhead transmission lines, 50
        High voltage underground cable, 53
    Other fields of technology, 59
    Health, 60
Solar System, 144, 127
Sonnet, C. P., 44

Stahlman, W. B. and Gingerich, D., 102
Stetson, H. T., 41, 42
Stewart, B., 14, 29
Stock Market Averages:
   Dow-Jones Industrial, 131
   Standard & Poor's, 131, 132
   New York Stock Exchange, 132
   Indicator Digest, 134
   Total Return, 134
   Value Line, 132
Stock Market Cycles:
   9.2-year, 122
   38-41-month, 123
   Coe's Combined Cycle, 125
   Decennial Pattern, 126-129
   Real and Synthetic Cycles, 128
Stock Market Planetary Cycles:
   Planetary Cause of 9.225-year Cycle, 135
   Moore's 8-year Venus Cycle, 29, 137
   Planetary Cause of 4-4½-year Cycle, 138
   Stock Prices & Planets in Tenth House, 142
Stock Market Forecasting Systems:
   The Dow Theory, 147
   Chartist Indicators, 149
   The McWhirter Theory, 153
   Williams Solar Ingress, 158

Williams Running Total, 162
Sunspots, Planetary Cause of:
   Sunspot theory, 11, 33
   Planetary Correlations, 217
Sunspot Numbers, 18, 19, 211
Sunspot Period Reconnaissance, 215
Takata, M., 60
Tchichevsky, A. L., 30, 60
Thales, 5
Tice, J., 29
Tucker, W.J., 113, 114
Tuckerman, B., 99
Twain, M., 121
Valliere, J. T., 100
Vaux, J.E., 123
Voight, H., 30
Wait, O.K., 114
Warren, G. F. and Pearson, F. A., 3, 210
Weaver, E.G., 17
Wicksell, K., 7
Wolf, R., 12, 24, 39
Wood, K. D., 37, 42
Wood, S.W., 41
Wright. P.G., 67
Young, C. A., 30